The Art of Prolog

MIT Press Series in Logic Programming
Ehud Shapiro, editor

The Art of Prolog: Advanced Programming Techniques, by Leon Sterling and
Ehud Shapiro

The Art of Prolog

Advanced Programming Techniques

Leon Sterling

Ehud Shapiro

The MIT Press
Cambridge, Massachusetts
London, England

PUBLISHER'S NOTE

This format is intended to reduce the cost of publishing certain works in book form
and to shorten the gap between editorial preparation and final publication. Detailed
editing and composition have been avoided by photographing the text of this book
directly from the authors' prepared copy.

This book was set in TEX by Sarah Fliegelmann
at the Weizmann Institute of Science
and printed and bound by The MIT Press
in the United States of America

Library of Congress Cataloging-in-Publication Data

Sterling, Leon.
    The art of Prolog.

    (MIT Press series in logic programming)
    Includes index.
    1. Prolog (Computer program language) I. Shapiro, Ehud Y. II. Title. III. Series.
QA76.73.P76S74   1986   005.13'3   86-10529
ISBN 0-262-19250-0 (hard)
        0-262-69105-1 (paper)

To Ruth, Miriam, Michal, and Danya

Contents

Preface

The origins of this book lie in graduate student courses aimed at teaching advanced Prolog programming. There is a wealth of techniques that has emerged in the fifteen years since the inception of Prolog as a programming language. Our intention in this book has been to make accessible the programming techniques that kindled our own excitement, imagination and involvement in this area.

The book fills a general need. Prolog, and more generally logic programming, have received wide publicity in recent years. Currently available books and accounts, however, typically describe only the basics. All but the simplest examples of the use of Prolog have remained essentially inaccessible to people outside the Prolog community.

We emphasize throughout the book the distinction between logic programming and Prolog programming. Logic programs can be understood and studied, using two abstract, machine independent concepts: truth and logical deduction. One can ask whether an axiom in a program is true, under some interpretation of the program symbols; or whether a logical statement is a consequence of the program. These questions can be answered independently of any concrete execution mechanism.

On the contrary, Prolog is a programming language, borrowing its basic constructs from logic. Prolog programs have precise operational meaning: they are instructions for execution on a computer -- a Prolog machine. Prolog programs in good style can almost always be read as logical statements, thus inheriting some of the abstract properties of logic programs. Most important, the result of a computation of such a Prolog program is a logical consequence of the axioms in it. Effective Prolog programming requires an understanding of the theory of logic programming.

The book consists of four parts: logic programming, the Prolog language, advanced techniques, and applications. The first part is a self-contained introduction to logic programming. It consists of five chapters. The first chapter introduces the basic constructs of logic programs. Our account differs from other introductions to logic programming by explaining the basics in terms of logical deduction. Other accounts explain the basics from the background of resolution from which logic programming originated. We have found the former to be a more effective means of teaching the material, which students find intuitive, and easy to understand.

The second and third chapters of Part I introduce the two basic styles of logic programming: database programming and recursive programming. The fourth chapter discusses the computational model of logic programming, introducing unification, while the fifth chapter presents some theoretical results without proofs. In developing this part to enable the clear explanation of advanced techniques, we have introduced new concepts, and reorganized others. In particular in the discussion of types and termination. Other issues such as complexity and correctness are concepts whose consequences have not yet been fully developed in the logic programming research community.

The second part is an introduction to Prolog. It consists of Chapters 6 through 13. Chapter 6 discusses the computational model of Prolog as opposed to logic programming, and gives a comparison between Prolog and conventional programming languages such as Pascal. Chapter 7 discusses the differences between composing Prolog programs and logic programs. Examples are given of basic programming techniques.

The next five chapters introduce system-provided predicates that are essential to make Prolog a practical programming language. We classify Prolog system predicates into four categories: those concerned with efficient arithmetic, structure inspection, meta-logical predicates that discuss the state of the computation, and extra-logical predicates that achieve side-effects outside the computational model of logic programming. One chapter is devoted to the most notorious of Prolog extra-logical predicates, the cut. Basic techniques using these system predicates are explained. The final chapter of the section gives assorted pragmatic programming tips.

The main part of the book is Part III. We describe advanced Prolog programming techniques that have evolved in the Prolog programming community, illustrating each with small yet powerful example programs. The examples typify the applications for which the technique is useful. The six chapters cover nondeterministic programming, incomplete data structures, parsing with DCGs, second-order programming, search techniques, and the use of meta-interpreters.

The final part consists of four chapters that show how the material in the rest of the book can be combined to build application programs. A common request of Prolog newcomers is to see larger applications. They understand how to write elegant short programs but have difficulty in building a major program. The applications covered are game-playing programs, a prototype expert system for evaluating requests for credit, a symbolic equation solver and a compiler.

During the development of the book, it has been necessary to reorganize the foundations and basic examples existing in the folklore of the logic programming community. Our structure constitutes a novel framework for the teaching of Prolog.

Material from this book has been used successfully for several courses on logic programming and Prolog: in Israel, the United States and Scotland. The material more than suffices for a one semester course to first-year graduate students or advanced undergraduates. There is considerable scope for instructors to particularize a course to suit a special area of interest.

A recommended division of the book for a 13-week course to senior undergraduates or first-year graduates is as follows: 4 weeks on logic programming, encouraging students to develop a declarative style of writing programs, 4 weeks on basic Prolog programming, 3 weeks on advanced techniques, and 2 weeks spent on applications. The advanced techniques should include some discussion of nondeterminism, incomplete data structures, basic second-order predicates, and basic meta-interpreters. Other sections can be covered instead of applications. Application areas that can be stressed are search techniques in artificial intelligence, building expert systems, writing compilers and parsers, symbol manipulation, and natural language processing.

There is considerable flexibility in the order of presentation. The material from Part I should be covered first. The material in Part III and IV can be interspersed with the material in Part II to show the student how larger Prolog programs using more advanced techniques are composed in the same style as smaller examples.

Our assessment of students has usually been 50% by homework assignments throughout the course, and 50% by project. Our experience has been that students are capable of a significant programming task for their project. Examples of projects are prototype expert systems, assemblers, game-playing programs, partial evaluators, and implementations of graph theory algorithms.

For the student who is studying the material on her own, we strongly advise reading through the more abstract material in Part I. A good Prolog programming style develops from thinking declaratively about the logic of a situation. The theory in Chapter 5, however, can be skipped until a later reading.

The exercises in the book range from very easy and well-defined to difficult and open-ended. Most of them are suitable for homework exercises. Some of the more open-ended exercises were submitted as course projects.

The code in this book is essentially in Edinburgh Prolog. The course has been given where students used several different variants of Edinburgh Prolog, and no problems were encountered. All the examples run on Wisdom Prolog, which is discussed in the appendixes.

We acknowledge and thank the people who contributed directly to the book. We also thank, collectively and anonymously, all those who indirectly contributed by influencing our programming styles in Prolog. Improvements were suggested by Lawrence Byrd, Oded Maler, Jack Minker, Richard O'Keefe, Fernando Pereira, and several anonymous referees.

We appreciate the contribution of the students who sat through courses as material from the book was being debugged. The first author acknowledges students at the University of Edinburgh, the Weizmann Institute of Science, Tel Aviv University, and Case Western Reserve University. The second author taught courses at the Weizmann Institute, Hebrew University of Jerusalem and other short courses to industry.

We are grateful to many people for assisting in the technical aspects of producing a book. We especially thank Sarah Fliegelmann who produced the various drafts and camera-ready copy, above and beyond the call of duty. This book may not have appeared without her tremendous efforts. Arvind Bansal prepared the index and helped with the references. Yehuda Barbut drew most of the figures. Max Goldberg and Shmuel Safra prepared the appendix. The publishers, MIT Press, were helpful and supportive.

Finally, we acknowledge the support of family and friends without which nothing would get done.

Introduction

The inception of logic is tied with that of scientific thinking. Logic provides a precise language for the explicit expression of one's goals, knowledge, and assumptions. Logic provides the foundation for deducing consequences from premises; for studying the truth or falsity of statements given the truth or falsity of other statements; for establishing the consistency of one's claims; and for verifying the validity of one's arguments.

Computers are relatively new in our intellectual history. Similar to logic, they are both the object of scientific study, and a powerful tool for the advancement of scientific endeavor in general. Like logic, computers require a precise and explicit statement of one's goals and assumptions. Unlike logic, which has developed with the power of the human thinking as the only external consideration, the development of computers has been governed from the start by severe technological and engineering constraints. Although computers were intended for use by humans, the difficulties in constructing them were so dominant, that the language for expressing problems to the computer and instructing it how to solve them was designed from the perspective of the engineering of the computer alone.

Almost all modern computers are based on the early concepts of von Neumann and his colleagues, which emerged during the 1940's. The von Neumann machine is characterized by a large uniform store of memory cells, and a processing unit with some local cells, called registers. The processing unit can load data from memory to registers, perform arithmetic or logical operations on registers, and store values of registers back into memory. A program for a von Neumann machine consists of a sequence of instructions to perform such operations, and an additional set of control instructions, which can affect the next instruction to be executed, possibly depending on the content of some register.

As the problems of building computers were gradually understood and solved, the problems of using them mounted. The bottleneck ceased to be the inability of the computer to perform the human's instructions, but rather the inability of the human to instruct, or program, the computer. A search for programming languages convenient for humans to program in has begun. Starting from the language understood directly by the computer, the machine language, better notations and formalisms were developed. The main outcome of these efforts was languages that were easier for humans to express themselves in, but still mapped rather directly to the underlying machine language. Although increasingly abstract, the languages in the mainstream of development, starting from assembly language, through Fortran, Algol, Pascal, and Ada, all carried the mark of the underlying machine — the von Neumann architecture.

To the uninitiated intelligent person, who is not familiar with the engineering constraints that lead to its design, the von Neumann machine seems an arbitrary, even bizzare, device. Thinking in terms of its constrained set of operations is a non-trivial problem, which sometimes stretches the adaptiveness of the human mind to its limits.

These characteristic aspects of programming von Neumann computers have lead to a separation of work: there were those who thought how to solve the problem, and designed the methods for its solution, and there were the coders, who performed the mundane and tedious task of translating the instructions of the designers to instructions a computer can digest.

Both logic and programming require the explicit expression of one's knowledge and methods in an acceptable formalism. The task of making one's knowledge explicit is tedious. However, formalizing one's knowledge in logic is often an intellectually rewarding activity, and usually reflects back on or adds insight to the problem under consideration. In contrast, formalizing one's problem and method of solution using the von Neumann instruction set rarely has these beneficial effects.

We believe that programming can be, and should be, an intellectually rewarding activity; that a good programming language is a powerful conceptual tool — a tool for organizing, expressing, experimenting with, and even communicating one's thoughts; that treating programming as "coding," the last, mundane, intellectually trivial, but time-consuming and tedious phase of solving a problem using a computer system, is perhaps at the very roots of what has been known as the "software crisis."

Rather, we think that programming can be, and should be, part of the problem solving process itself; that thoughts should be organized as programs, so that consequences of a complex set of assumptions can be investigated by "running" the assumptions; that a conceptual solution to a problem should be developed hand-in-hand with a working program that demonstrates it and exposes its different aspects. Suggestions in this direction have been made under the title "rapid prototyping."

To achieve this goal in its fullest — to become true mates of the human thinking process — computers have still a long way to go. However, we find it both appropriate and gratifying from a historical perspective that logic, a companion to the human thinking process since the early days of human intellectual history, has been discovered as a suitable stepping-stone in this long journey.

Although logic has been used as a tool for designing computers, and for reasoning about computers and computer programs since almost their beginning, the use of logic directly as a programming language, termed *logic programming*, is quite recent.

Logic programming, as well as its sister approach, functional programming, departs radically from the mainstream of computer languages. Rather then being derived, by a series of abstractions and reorganizations, from the von Neumann machine model and instruction set, it is derived from an abstract model, which has no direct relationship or dependency to one machine model or another. It is based on the belief that instead of the human learning to think in terms of the operations of a computer, which some scientists and engineers at some point in history happened to find easy and cost-effective to build, the computer should perform instructions that are easy for humans to provide. In its ultimate and purest form, logic programming suggests that even explicit instructions for operation not be given but, rather, the knowledge about the problem and assumptions that are sufficient to solve it be stated explicitly, as logical axioms. Such a set of axioms constitutes an alternative to the conventional program. The program can be executed by providing it with a problem, formalized as a logical statement to be proved, called a goal statement. The execution is an attempt to solve the problem, that is, to prove the goal statement, given the assumptions in the logic program.

A distinguishing aspect of the logic used in logic programming is that a goal statement typically is existentially quantified: it states that there exist some individuals with some property. An example of a goal statement is that there exists a list X such that sorting the list $[3,1,2]$ gives X. The mechanism used to prove the goal statement is constructive: if successful, it provides the identity of the unknown individuals mentioned in the goal statement, which constitutes the output of the computation. In the example above, assuming that the logic program contains appropriate axioms defining the *sort* relation, the output of the computation would be $X=[1,2,3]$.

These ideas can be summarized in the following two metaphorical equations:

program = set of axioms

computation = constructive proof of a goal statement from the program

The ideas behind these equations can be traced back as far as intuitionistic mathematics and proof theory of the early century. They are related to Hilbert's program, to base the the entire body of mathematical knowledge on logical foundations, to provide mechanical proofs for its theories, starting from the axioms of logic and set theory alone. It is interesting to note that the fall of this program, which ensued the incompleteness and undecidability results of Gödel and Turing, also marks the beginning of the modern age of computers.

The first use of this approach in practical computing is a sequel to Robinson's unification algorithm and resolution principle, published in 1965. Several hesitant attempts were made to use this principle as a basis of for a computational mechanism, but they did not gain any momentum. The beginning of logic programming can be attributed to Kowalski and Colmerauer. Kowalski formulated the procedural interpretation of Horn clause logic. He showed that an axiom

$$A \text{ if } B_1 \text{ and } B_2 \text{ and } \dots \text{ and } B_n$$

can be read, and executed, as a procedure of a recursive programming language, where A is the procedure head and the B_i's are its body. In addition to the declarative reading of the clause, A is true if the B_i's are true, it can be read as follows: to solve (execute) A, solve (execute) B_1 and B_2 and $\dots$ and B_n. In this reading, the proof procedure of Horn clause logic is the interpreter of the language, and the unification algorithm, which is at the heart of the resolution proof procedure, performs the basic data manipulation operations of variable assignment, parameter passing, data selection, and data construction.

At the same time, early 1970's, Colmerauer and his group at the University of Marseille-Aix developed a specialized theorem prover, written in Fortran, which they used to implement natural language processing systems. The theorem prover, called Prolog (for Programation et Logique), embodied Kowalski's procedural interpretation. Later, van Emden and Kowalski developed a formal semantics for the language of logic programs, showing that its operational, model-theoretic, and fixpoint semantics are the same.

In spite of all the theoretical work and the exciting ideas, the logic programming approach seemed unrealistic. At the time of its inception, researchers in the U.S. began to recognize the failure of the "next-generation AI languages," such as Micro-Planner and Conniver, which developed as a substitute for Lisp. The main claim against these languages was that they were hopelessly inefficient, and very difficult to control. Given their bitter experience with logic-based high-level languages, it is no great surprise that U.S. AI scientists, when hearing about Prolog, thought that the Europeans are over-excited over what we, Americans, have already suggested, tried, and discovered not to work.

In that atmosphere the Prolog-10 compiler was almost an imaginary being. Developed in the mid to late 1970's by David H.D. Warren and his colleagues, this efficient implementation of Prolog dispelled all the myths about the impracticality of logic programming. That compiler, which is still one of the finest implementations of Prolog around, delivered on pure list-processing programs performance comparable to the best Lisp systems available at the time. Furthermore, the compiler itself was written almost entirely in Prolog, suggesting that fairly classical programming tasks, not just sophisticated AI applications, can benefit from the power of logic programming.

The impact of this implementation cannot be over-exaggerated. Without it, the accumulated experience that has lead to this book would not have existed.

In spite of the promise of the ideas, and the practicality of their implementation, most of the Western computer science and AI research community was ignorant, outwardly hostile, or, at best, indifferent to logic programming. By 1980, the number of researchers actively engaged in logic programming were only a few dozens in the U.S., and about one hundred around the world.

No doubt logic programming would have remained a fringe activity in computer science for quite a little longer were it not for the announcement of the Japanese Fifth Generation Project, which took place in October 1981. Although the research program the Japanese have presented was rather baggy, faithful to their tradition of achieving consensus at almost all cost, the important role of logic programming in the next generation of computer systems was presented loud and clear.

Since that time the Prolog language has undergone a rapid transit from adolescence to maturity. There are numerous commercially available Prolog implementations on most widespread computers. There is a large number of Prolog programming books, directed to different audiences and emphasizing different aspects of the language. And the language itself has more-or-less stabilized, having a *de facto* standard, the Edinburgh Prolog family.

The maturity of the language means that it is no longer a concept for scientists yet to shape and define, but rather a given object, with all its vices and virtues. It is time to recognize that, on the one hand, Prolog is falling short of the high goals of logic programming, but that, on the other hand, it is a powerful, productive, and practical programming formalism. Given the standard life cycle of computer programming languages, the next few coming years will witness whether these properties will show their merit only in the classroom or will also be proven useful in the field, where people pay money to solve problems they care about.

So what are the current active subjects of research in logic programming and Prolog? The answer to this question can be found in the regular scientific journals and conferences of the field. The *Logic Programming Journal*, the *Journal of New Generation Computing*, the *International Conference on Logic Programming*, and the *IEEE Symposium on Logic Programming*, as well as in the general computer science journals and conferences.

Clearly, one of the dominant areas of interest is the relationship between logic programming, Prolog, and parallelism. The promise of parallel computers, combined with the parallelism that seems to be available in the logic programming model, have lead to numerous attempts, which are still ongoing, to execute Prolog in parallel, and to devise novel concurrent programming languages based on the logic programming computation model. This, however, is a subject for another book.

Part I
Logic Programs

A logic program is a set of axioms, or rules, defining relationships between objects. A computation of a logic program is a deduction of consequences of the program. A program defines a set of consequences, which is its meaning. The art of logic programming is constructing concise and elegant programs that have the desired meaning.

Chapter 1

Basic Constructs

The basic constructs of logic programming, terms and statements, are inherited from logic. There are three basic statements: facts, rules and queries. There is a single data structure: the logical term.

1.1 Facts

The simplest kind of statement is called a *fact*. Facts are a means of stating that a relationship holds between objects. An example is

father(abraham,isaac).

This fact says that Abraham is the father of Isaac, or that the relation *father* holds between the individuals named *abraham* and *isaac*. Another name for a relationship is a *predicate*. Names of individuals are known as *atoms*. Similarly *plus(2,3,5)* expresses the relationship that 2 plus 3 is 5. The familiar *plus* relationship can be realized via a set of facts that defines the addition table. An initial segment of the table is

plus(0,0,0).	plus(0,1,1).	plus(0,2,2).	plus(0,3,3).
plus(1,0,1).	plus(1,1,2).	plus(1,2,3).	plus(1,3,4).

A sufficiently large segment of this table, which happens to be also a legal logic program, will be assumed as the definition of the *plus* relation throughout this chapter.

The syntactic conventions used throughout the book are introduced as needed. The first is the case convention. It is significant that the names of

father(terach,abraham).   male(terach).
father(terach,nachor).   male(abraham).
father(terach,haran).   male(nachor).
father(abraham,isaac).   male(haran).
father(haran,lot).   male(isaac).
father(haran,milcah).   male(lot).
father(haran,yiscah).

                                    female(sarah).
mother(sarah,isaac).   female(milcah).
                                    female(yiscah).

Program 1.1: A Biblical family database

both predicates and atoms in facts begin with a lowercase letter, as opposed to an uppercase letter. These names are italicized when they appear in running text.

A finite set of facts constitutes a *program*. This is the simplest form of logic program. A set of facts is also a description of a situation. This insight is the basis of database programming, to be discussed in the next chapter. An example database of family relationships from the Bible is given as Program 1.1. The predicates *father, mother, male,* and *female* express the obvious relationships.

1.2   Queries

The second form of statement in a logic program is a *query*. Queries are a means of retrieving information from a logic program. A query asks whether a certain relation holds between objects. For example, the query *father(abraham,isaac)?* asks whether the *father* relation holds between *abraham* and *isaac*. Given the facts of Program 1.1, the answer to this query is *yes*.

Syntactically, queries and facts look the same, but can be distinguished by the context. When there is a possibility of confusion, a terminating period will indicate a fact, while a terminating question mark will indicate a query. We call the entity without the period or question mark a *goal*. A fact *P*. states that the goal *P* is true. A query *P?* asks whether the goal *P* is true. A *simple query* consists of a single goal.

Answering a query with respect to a program is determining whether the query is a logical consequence of the program. We define logical consequence incrementally through this section. Logical consequences are obtained by applying deduction rules. The simplest rule of deduction is *identity*: from *P* deduce *P*. A query is a logical consequence of an identical fact.

Operationally, answering simple queries using a program containing facts like Program 1.1 is straightforward. Search for a fact in the program which implies the query. If a fact identical to the query is found, the answer is *yes*.

The answer *no* is given if a fact identical to the query is not found, because the fact is not a logical consequence of the program. This answer does not reflect on the truth of the query; it merely says that we failed to prove the query from the program. Both the queries *female(abraham)?* and *plus(1,1,2)?* will be answered *no* with respect to Program 1.1.

1.3   The logical variable, substitutions and instances

A logical variable stands for an unspecified individual, and is used accordingly. Consider its use in queries. Suppose we wanted to know of whom *abraham* was the father. One way is to ask a series of queries, *father(abraham,lot)?*, *father(abraham,milcah)?*, ..., *father(abraham,isaac)?*, ... until an answer *yes* is given. A variable allows a better way of expressing the query as *father(abraham,X)?*, to which the answer is *X=isaac*. Used in this way, *variables are a means of summarizing many queries*. A query containing a variable asks whether there is a value for the variable that makes the query a logical consequence of the program, as explained further below.

Variables in logic programs behave differently from variables in conventional programming languages. They stand for an unspecified but single entity, rather than for a store location in memory.

Having introduced variables, we can define *terms*, the single data structure in logic programs. The definition is inductive. Constants and variables are terms. Also compound terms, or structures, are terms. A *compound term* comprises a functor (called the principal functor of the term) and a sequence of one or more arguments, which are terms. A *functor* is characterized by its *name*, which is an atom, and its *arity*, or number of arguments. Syntactically compound terms have the form $f(t_1,t_2,\ldots,t_n)$ where the functor has name f and is of arity n, and the t_i's are the arguments. Examples of compound terms include *s(0)*, *hot(milk)*, *name(john,doe)*, *list(a,list(b,nil))*, *foo(X)*, and *tree(tree(nil,3,nil),5,R)*.

Queries, goals, and more generally terms where variables do not occur are called *ground*. Where variables do occur, they are called *nonground*. For example, *foo(a,b)* is ground, whereas *bar(X)* is not.

Definition: A *substitution* is a finite set (possibly empty) of pairs of the form $X_i = t_i$, where X_i is a variable and t_i is a term, and $X_i \neq X_j$ for every $i \neq j$, and X_i does not occur in t_j, for any i and j. ∎

An example of a substitution consisting of a single pair is $\{X = isaac\}$. Substitutions can be applied to terms. The result of applying a substitution θ to a term A, denoted by $A\theta$, is the term obtained by replacing every occurrence of X by t in A, for every pair $X = t$ in θ.

The result of applying $\{X = isaac\}$ to the term *father(abraham,X)* is the term *father(abraham,isaac)*.

Definition: A is an *instance* of B if there is a substitution θ such that $A = B\theta$. ∎

The goal *father(abraham,isaac)* is an instance of *father(abraham,X)* by this definition. Similarly *mother(sarah,isaac)* is an instance of *mother(X,Y)* under the substitution $\{X = sarah, Y = isaac\}$.

1.4   Existential queries

Logically speaking, variables in queries are existentially quantified, which means, intuitively, that the query *father(abraham,X)?* reads: "Does there exist an X such that *abraham* is the father of X?" More generally, a query $p(T_1, T_2, \ldots, T_n)?$, which contains the variables $X_1, X_2, \ldots, X_k$ reads: "Are there $X_1, X_2, \ldots, X_k$ such that $p(T_1, T_2, \ldots, T_n)?$" For convenience, existential quantification is usually omitted.

The next deduction rule we introduce is *generalization*: an existential query P is a logical consequence of an instance of it, $P\theta$, for any substitution θ. The fact *father(abraham,isaac)* implies that there exists an X such that *father(abraham,X)* is true, namely $X = isaac$.

Operationally, to answer an existential, nonground, query using a program of facts, find a fact that is an instance of the query. The answer, or *solution*, is that instance. The answer is *no* if there is no suitable fact in the program.

Answering nonground queries is performing a computation whose output is an instance of the query. We sometimes represent this instance by a substitution that, if applied to the query, results in the solution instance.

In general, an existential query may have several solutions. Program 1.1 shows that Haran is the father of three children. Thus the query *father(haran,X)?* has the solutions $\{X = lot\}$, $\{X = milcah\}$, $\{X = yiscah\}$. Another query with multiple solutions is $plus(X,Y,4)$? for finding numbers that add up to 4. Solutions are, for example, $\{X=0,\ Y=4\}$ and $\{X=1,\ Y=3\}$. Note that the different variables X and Y correspond to (possibly) different objects.

An interesting variant of the last query is $plus(X,X,4)$? which insists that the two numbers that add up to 4 be the same. It has a unique answer $\{X=2\}$.

1.5   Universal facts

Variables are also useful in facts. Suppose that all the Biblical characters like pomegranates. Instead of including in the program an appropriate fact for every individual:

> $likes(abraham,pomegranates)$.
> $likes(sarah,pomegranates)$.
> $\vdots$

a fact $likes(X,pomegranates)$ can say it all. Used in this way, *variables are a means of summarizing many facts.* The fact $times(0,X,0)$ summarizes all the facts stating that 0 times some number is 0.

Variables in facts are implicitly universally quantified, which means, intuitively, that the fact $likes(X,pomegranates)$ states that for all X, X likes pomegranates. In general a fact $p(T_1,\ldots,T_n)$ reads that for all $X_1,\ldots,X_k$, where the X_i's are variables occuring in the fact, $p(T_1,\ldots,T_n)$ is true. Logically, from a universally quantified fact one can deduce any instance of it. For example, from $likes(X,pomegranates)$ deduce $likes(abraham,pomegranates)$.

This is the third deduction rule, called *instantiation*: From a universally quantified statement P deduce an instance of it $P\theta$, for any substitution θ.

As for queries, two unspecified objects, denoted by variables, can be constrained to be the same by using the same variable name. The fact $plus(0,X,X)$ expresses that 0 is a left identity for addition. It reads that for all values of X, 0 plus X is X. A similar use occurs when translating the English statement, "everybody likes himself" to $likes(X,X)$.

Answering a ground query with a universally quantified fact is straightforward. Search for a fact for which the query is an instance. For example, the answer to $plus(0,2,2)$? is *yes*, based on the fact $plus(0,X,X)$. Answering a nonground query using a nonground fact involves a new definition: a common instance of two terms.

Definition: C is a *common instance* of A and B if it is an instance of A and an instance of B. In other words, if there are substitutions θ_1 and θ_2 such that $C = A\theta_1$ is syntactically identical to $B\theta_2$.   ■

For example, the goals $plus(0,3,Y)$ and $plus(0,X,X)$ have a common instance $plus(0,3,3)$. Applying the substitution $\{Y=3\}$ to $plus(0,3,Y)$ and the substitution $\{X=3\}$ to $plus(0,X,X)$ both yield $plus(0,3,3)$.

In general, to answer a query using a fact, search for a common instance of the query and fact. The answer is the common instance, if one exists. Otherwise the answer is *no*.

Answering an existential query with a universal fact using a common instance involves two logical deductions. The fact is deduced from the instance by the rule of instantiation, and the instance is deduced from the query by the rule of generalization.

1.6   Conjunctive queries and shared variables

An important extension to the queries discussed so far is *conjunctive queries*. Conjunctive queries are a conjunction of goals posed as a query, for example, $father(terach,X),father(X,Y)$? or in general, $Q_1,\ldots,Q_n$? Simple queries are a special case of conjunctive queries when there is a single goal. Logically it asks whether a conjunction is deducible from the program. We use ',' throughout to denote logical 'and.' Do not confuse the comma that separates the arguments in a goal with commas used to separate goals, denoting conjunction.

In the simplest conjunctive queries all the goals are ground, for example, $father(abraham,isaac), male(lot)$? The answer to this query using Program 1.1 is clearly *yes* as both goals in the query are facts in the program. In general, the query $Q_1,\ldots,Q_n$? where each Q_i is a ground goal is answered yes with respect to a program P if each Q_i is implied by P. Hence ground conjunctive queries are not very interesting.

Conjunctive queries are interesting when there are one or more *shared variables*, variables that occur in two different goals of the query. An example is the query $father(haran,X),male(X)$?. The scope of a variable in a conjunctive query is the whole conjunction. Thus the query $p(X),q(X)$? reads: "Is there an X such that *both* $p(X)$ and $q(X)$?" Like in simple queries, variables in conjunctive queries are implicitly existentially quantified.

Shared variables are used as a means of constraining a simple query by restricting the range of a variable. We have already seen an example with the query *plus(X,X,4)?* where the solution of numbers adding up to 4 was restricted to the numbers being the same. Consider the query *father(haran,X),male(X)?* Here solutions to the query *father(haran,X)?* are restricted to children that are male. Program 1.1 shows there is only one solution, *{X=lot}*. Alternatively this query can be viewed as restricting solutions to the query *male(X)?* to individuals who have Haran for a father.

A slightly different use of a shared variable can be seen in the query *father(terach,X),father(X,Y)?* On the one hand it restricts the sons of *terach* to those who are themselves fathers. On the other hand it considers individuals *Y*, whose fathers are sons of *terach*. There are several solutions, for example, *{X=abraham, Y=isaac}*, and *{X=haran, Y=lot}*.

A conjunctive query is a logical consequence of a program *P* if all the goals in the conjunction are consequences of *P*, where shared variables are instantiated to the same values in different goals. A sufficient condition is that there is a ground instance of the query that is a consequence of *P*. This instance then deduces the conjuncts in the query via generalization.

The restriction to ground instances is unnecessary, and will be lifted in Chapter 4 when we discuss the computation model of logic programs. We employ this restriction in the meantime to simplify the discussion in the coming sections.

Operationally, to solve the conjunctive query $A_1, A_2, \ldots, A_n$? using a program *P*, find a substitution θ such that $A_1\theta$ and ... and $A_n\theta$ are ground instances of facts in *P*. The same substitution applied to all the goals ensures that instances of variables are common throughout the query. For example, consider the query *father(haran,X), male(X)?* with respect to Program 1.1. Applying the substitution *{X=lot}* to the query gives the ground instance *father(haran,lot), male(lot)?* which is a consequence of the program.

1.7   Rules

Interesting conjunctive queries are defining relationships in their own right. The query *father(haran,X),male(X)?* is asking for a son of Haran. The query *father(terach,X),father(X,Y)?* is asking about grandchildren of Terach. This brings us to the third and most important statement in logic programming, a rule, which enables us to define new relationships in terms of existing relationships.

Rules are statements of the form:

$$A \leftarrow B_1, B_2, \ldots, B_n.$$

where $n \geq 0$. A is the *head* of the rule, and the B_i's are its *body*. Both A and the B_i's are goals. Rules, facts and queries are also called *Horn clauses*, or *clauses* for short. Note that a fact is just a special case of a rule when $n=0$. Facts are also called *unit clauses*. We also have a special name for clauses with one goal in the body, namely when $n=1$. Such a clause is called an *iterative clause*. As for facts, variables appearing in rules are universally quantified, and their scope is the whole rule.

A rule expressing the son relationship is

son(X,Y) ← father(Y,X), male(X).

Similarly one can define a rule for the daughter relationship:

daughter(X,Y) ← father(Y,X), female(X).

A rule for the grandfather relationship is

grandfather(X,Z) ← father(X,Y), father(Y,Z).

Rules can be viewed in two ways. First, they are a means of expressing new or complex queries in terms of simple queries. A query *son(X,haran)?* to the program that contains the above rule for *son* is translated to the query *father(haran,X), male(X)?* according to the rule, and solved as before. A new query about the *son* relationship has been built from simple queries involving *father* and *male* relationships. Interpreting rules in this way is their *procedural* reading. The procedural reading for the grandfather rule is: "To answer a query *is X the grandfather of Y*, answer the conjunctive query *is X the father of Z and Z the father of Y*."

The second view of rules comes from interpreting the rule as a logical axiom. The backward arrow ← is used to denote logical implication. The *son* rule reads: "*X* is a son of *Y* if *Y* is the father of *X* and *X* is male." In this view rules are a means of defining new or complex relations using other, simpler, relationships. The predicate *son* has been defined in terms of the predicates *father* and *male*. The associated reading of the rule is known as the *declarative* reading. The declarative reading of the grandfather rule is: "For all *X*, *Y*, and *Z*, *X* is the grandfather of *Y* if *X* is the father of *Z* and *Z* is the father of *Y*."

Although formally all variables in a clause are universally quantified, we will sometimes refer to variables that occur in the body of the clause, but not in its head, as if they are existentially quantified inside the body. For example, the *grandfather* rule can be read: "For all *X* and *Y*, *X* is the grandfather of *Y* if there exists a *Z* such that *X* is the father of *Z* and *Z* is the father of *Y*." The formal justification of this verbal transformation will not be given, and we treat it just as convenience. Whenever it is a source of confusion, the reader can resort back to the formal reading of a clause, in which all variables are universally quantified from the outside.

To incorporate rules into our framework of logical deduction, we need the law of modus ponens. Modus ponens states that from B and $A \leftarrow B$ we can deduce A.

Definition: The law of *universal modus ponens* says that from the rule

$$R = (A \leftarrow B_1, B_2, \ldots, B_n)$$

and the facts

$$B_1'.$$
$$B_2'.$$
$$\vdots$$
$$B_n'.$$

A' can be deduced, if

$$A' \leftarrow B_1', B_2', \ldots, B_n'$$

is an instance of R.   ∎

Universal modus ponens includes identity and instantiation as special cases.

We are now in a position to give a complete definition of the concept of a logic program and of its associated concept of logical consequence.

Definition: A *logic program* is a finite set of rules.   ∎

Definition: An existentially quantified goal G is a logical consequence of a program P if there is a clause in P with a ground instance $A \leftarrow B_1, \ldots, B_n$, $n \geq 0$, such that $B_1, \ldots, B_n$ are logical consequences of P and A is an instance of G.   ∎

Note that the goal G is a logical consequence of a program P if and only if G can be deduced from P by a finite number of applications of the rule of universal modus ponens.

Consider the query *son(S,haran)?* with respect to Program 1.1 augmented by the rule for *son*. The substitution $\{X=lot, Y=haran\}$ applied to the rule gives the instance *son(lot,haran)* ← *father(haran,lot)*, *male(lot)*. Both the goals in the body of this rule are facts in Program 1.1. Thus universal modus ponens implies the query with answer *S=lot*.

Operationally, answering queries reflects the definition of logical consequence. Guess a ground instance of a goal, and a ground instance of a rule, and recursively answer the conjunctive query corresponding to the body of that rule. To prove a goal A, with program P, choose a rule $A_1 \leftarrow B_1,B_2,\ldots,B_n$ in P, and guess substitution θ such that $A=A_1\theta$, and $B_i\theta$ is ground for $1 \leq i \leq n$. Then recursively prove each $B_i\theta$. This procedure can involve arbitrarily long chains of reasoning. It is difficult in general to guess the correct ground instance and choose the right rule. We show in Chapter 4 how the guessing of an instance can be removed.

The rule given for *son* is correct, but is an incomplete specification of the relationship. For example, we cannot conclude that Isaac is the son of Sarah. What is missing is that a child can be the son of a mother as well as the son of a father. A new rule expressing this relationship can be added, namely

    son(X,Y) ← mother(Y,X), male(X).

Similarly, to define the relation *grandparent* would take four rules to include both cases of *father* and *mother*:

    grandparent(X,Y) ← father(X,Y), father(Y,Z).
    grandparent(X,Y) ← father(X,Y), mother(Y,Z).
    grandparent(X,Y) ← mother(X,Y), father(Y,Z).
    grandparent(X,Y) ← mother(X,Y), mother(Y,Z).

There is a better, more compact, way of expressing these rules. We need to define the auxiliary relationship, *parent*, as being a father or a mother. Part of the art of logic programming is deciding on what intermediate predicates to define to achieve a complete, elegant axiomatization of a relationship. The rules defining *parent* are straightforward, capturing the definition of a parent being a father or a mother. Logic programs can incorporate alternative definitions, or more technically disjunction, by having alternative rules, as for *parent*:

    parent(X,Y) ← father(X,Y).
    parent(X,Y) ← mother(X,Y).

Rules for *son* and *grandparent* are now, respectively:

    son(X,Y) ← parent(Y,X), male(X).
    grandparent(X,Y) ← parent(X,Z), parent(Z,Y).

A collection of rules with the same predicate in the head, such as the pair of parent rules, is called a *procedure*. We shall see later that under the operational interpretation of these rules by Prolog, such a collection of rules is indeed the analogue of procedures or subroutines in conventional programming languages.

Input: A ground query Q and a program P

Output: *yes* if a proof of Q from P was found,
             no otherwise

Algorithm:
             Initialize the resolvent to Q
             while the resolvent $A_1,\ldots,A_n$ is not empty
             begin
             choose a goal A_i, $1 \leq i \leq n$, and
             a ground instance of a clause
                   $A \leftarrow B_1, B_2, \ldots, B_k$, $k \geq 0$ in P, such that $A = A_i$
                   (if no such clause exists, exit the while loop);
                   determine the new resolvent
                   $A_1, \ldots, A_{i-1}, B_1, \ldots, B_k, A_{i+1}, \ldots, A_n$
             end
             If the resolvent is empty, output *yes*; otherwise output *no*.

Figure 1.1: An abstract interpreter for logic programs

1.8   A simple abstract interpreter

An operational procedure for answering queries has been informally described and progressively developed in the previous sections. We flesh out the details here to give an abstract interpreter for logic programs. In keeping with the restriction of universal modus ponens to ground goals, the interpreter only answers ground queries.

The abstract interpreter performs yes/no computations. It takes a program P and a ground query Q and gives as output *yes* if Q is deducible from P and *no* otherwise. The interpreter may also fail to terminate if the goal is not deducible from the program, and in such a case it produces no answer at all. The steps of the interpreter are given in Figure 1.1.

The current goal at any stage of the computation is called the *resolvent*. A *trace* of the interpreter is the sequence of resolvents produced during the computation, together with the choices made. Consider the query *son(lot,haran)?* with respect to Program 1.2, a subset of the facts of Program 1.1 together with rules defining *son* and *daughter*. Figure 1.2 is a trace of answering the query.

The trace implicitly contains a proof of the ground query from the program. A more convenient representation of the proof is with a proof tree. We define the necessary concepts.

```
father(abraham,isaac).      male(isaac).
father(haran,lot).          male(lot).
father(haran,milcah).       female(milcah).
father(haran,yiscah).       female(yiscah).

son(X,Y) ← father(Y,X), male(X).
daughter(X,Y) ← father(Y,X), female(X).
```

Program 1.2: Biblical family relationships

Definition: A *ground reduction* of a goal G by a program P is the replacement of G by the body of a ground instance of a rule in P, whose head is identical to the chosen goal. ∎

Later the definition is relaxed to general (nonground) reductions. A reduction is the basic computational step in logic programming. It corresponds to an application of universal modus ponens. It also corresponds to one iteration of the while loop of the interpreter in Figure 1.1. The goal replaced in a reduction is *reduced*, and the new goals are *derived*.

We relate these concepts to our example trace in Figure 1.2. There are three reductions in the trace. The first reduces the goal *son(lot,haran)* and produces two derived goals, *father(haran,lot)* and *male(lot)*. The second reduction is of *father(haran,lot)* producing no derived goals. The third reduction also produces no derived goals in reducing *male(lot)*.

A *proof tree* consists of nodes and edges which represent the goals reduced during the computation. The root of the proof tree for a simple query is the query itself. The nodes of the tree are the goals which are reduced during the computation. There is a directed edge from a node to each node corresponding to a derived goal of the reduced goal. The proof tree for a conjunctive query is just the collection of proof trees for the individual goals in the conjunction. Figure 1.3 gives a proof tree for the program trace in Figure 1.2.

There are two unspecified choices in the interpreter. The goal to reduce from the resolvent must be chosen, as well as the clause (and an appropriate ground instance) to reduce it. The two choices have very different natures.

The selection of the goal to be reduced is arbitrary. In any given resolvent all the goals must be reduced. It can be shown that the order of reductions is immaterial for finding a proof. That is, if there is a proof for a goal, then there is a proof no matter in which order the reductions are made. In terms of the proof tree, this means that the order of branches is irrelevant.

Input: son(lot,haran)? and Program 1.2
          Resolvent is not empty
              Choose son(lot,haran)   (the only choice)
              Choose son(lot,haran) ← father(haran,lot), male(lot).
              New resolvent is father(haran,lot), male(lot)?
          Resolvent is not empty
              Choose father(haran,lot)
              Choose father(haran,lot).
              New resolvent is male(lot)?
          Resolvent is not empty
              Choose male(lot)
              Choose male(lot).
              New resolvent is empty

Output: *yes*

Figure 1.2: Tracing the interpreter

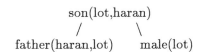

Figure 1.3: A simple proof tree

In contrast, the choice of the clause and a suitable ground instance is critical. In general, there are several choices of a clause, and infinitely many ground instances. The choice is made nondeterministically. The concept of nondeterministic choice is used in the definition of many computation models, e.g. finite automata and Turing machines, and proves to be a powerful theoretical concept. A nondeterministic choice is an unspecified choice from a number of alternatives, which is supposed to be made in a "clairvoyant" way: if only some of the alternatives lead to a successful computation (in our case, to finding a proof), then one of them is chosen. Formally, the concept is defined as follows: a computation that contains nondeterministic choices is *defined* to succeed if there is a sequence of nondeterministic choices that lead to success. Of course, no real machine can implement directly this definition. However, it can be approximated in a useful way, as done in Prolog, and explained in Chapter 6.

The interpreter given in Figure 1.1 can be extended to answer nonground existential queries by an initial additional step: guess a ground instance of the query. This is identical to the step in the interpreter of guessing ground instances of the rules. It is difficult in general to guess the correct ground instance, since that means knowing the result of the computation before performing it.

A new concept is needed to lift the restriction to ground instances and remove the burden of guessing them. We show in Chapter 4 how the guess of ground instances can be eliminated, and introduce the computation model of logic programs more fully. Until then it is assumed that the correct choices can be made.

An important measure provided by proof trees is the number of nodes in the tree. It indicates how many reduction steps are performed in a computation. We use the measure as a basis of comparison between different programs in Chapter 3.

1.9 The meaning of a logic program

How can we know if a logic program says what we wanted it to say? If it is correct, or incorrect? In order to answer such questions, we have to define what is the meaning of a logic program. Once defined, we can now examine if the program means what we have intended it to mean.

Definition. The *meaning* of a logic program P, $M(P)$, is the set of ground unit goals deducible from P. ∎

From this definition it follows that the meaning of a logic program composing just of ground facts, such as Program 1.1, is the program itself. In other words, for simple programs, the program "means just what it says." Consider Program 1.1 augmented with the two rules defining the *parent* relation. What is its meaning? It contains, in addition to the facts on fathers and mothers, mentioned explicitly in the program, also all facts of the form $parent(X, Y)$, for every pair X and Y such that $father(X, Y)$ or $mother(X, Y)$ is in the program. This example shows that the meaning of a program contains explicitly whatever the program states implicitly.

Assuming that we define the intended meaning of a program also to be a set of ground unit goals, we can ask what is the relationship between the actual and the intended meanings of a program. We can check whether everything the program says is correct, or whether the program says everything we wanted it to say.

Informally, we say that a program is *correct* with respect to some intended meaning M if the meaning of P, $M(P)$, is a subset of M. That is, a correct program does not say things that were not intended. A program is *complete* with respect to M if M is a subset of $M(P)$. That is, a complete program says everything that is intended. It follows that a program P is correct and complete with respect to an intended meaning M if $M=M(P)$.

Throughout the book, when meaningful predicate and constant names are used, the intended meaning of the program is assumed to be the one intuitively implied by the choice of names.

For example, the program for the *son* relation containing only the first axiom that uses *father* is incomplete with respected to the intuitively understood intended meaning of *son*, since it cannot deduce *son(isaac,sarah)*. If we add to it the rule

son(X,Y) ← mother(Y,X), male(X).

it would make the program incorrect with respect to the intended meaning, since it deduces *son(sarah,isaac)*.

The notions of correctness and completeness of a logic program are studied further in Chapter 5.

Although the notion of truth is not defined fully here, we will say that a ground goal is *true* with respect to an intended meaning if it is a member of it, and *false* otherwise. We will say it is simply *true* if it is a member of the intended meaning implied the names of the predicate and constant symbols appearing in the program.

1.10   Summary

We conclude this section with a summary of the constructs and concepts introduced, filling in the remaining necessary definitions.

The basic structure in logic programs is a term. A *term* is a constant, a variable or a compound term. Constants denote particular individuals such as integers and atoms, while variables denote a single but unspecified individual. The symbol for an atom can be any sequence of characters, which is quoted if there is possibility of confusion with other symbols (such as variables or integers). Symbols for variables are distinguished by beginning with an uppercase letter.

A *compound term* comprises a functor (called the principal functor of the term) and a sequence of one or more terms called *arguments*. A *functor* is characterized by its *name*, which is an atom, and its *arity* or number of arguments. Constants are considered functors of arity 0. Syntactically, compound terms have the form $f(t_1,t_2,\ldots,t_n)$ where the functor has name f and is of arity n, and the t_i's are the arguments. A functor f of arity n is denoted f/n. Functors with the same name but different arities are distinct. Terms are *ground* if they contain no variables; otherwise they are *nonground*. *Goals* are atoms or compound terms, and are generally nonground.

A *substitution* is a finite set (possibly empty) of pairs of the form $X=t$, where X is a variable and t is a term, with no two pairs having the same variable as left-hand side. For any substitution $\theta=\{X_1=t_1,X_2=t_2,\ldots,X_n=t_n\}$ and term s, the term $s\theta$ denotes the result of simultaneously replacing in s each occurrence of the variable X_i by t_i, $1 \leq i \leq n$; the term $s\theta$ is called an *instance* of s.

A *logic program* is a finite set of clauses. A *clause* or *rule* is a universally quantified logical sentence of the form

$$A \leftarrow B_1,B_2,\ldots,B_k. \qquad k \geq 0,$$

where A and the B_i's are goals. Such a sentence is read declaratively "A is implied by the conjunction of the B_i's," and is interpreted procedurally "to answer query A, answer the conjunctive query $B_1,B_2,\ldots,B_k$." A is called the clause's *head* and the B's the clause's *body*. If $k=0$, the clause is known as a *fact* or *unit clause* and written $A.$, meaning A is true under the declarative reading, and goal A is satisfied under the procedural interpretation. If $k=1$, the clause is known as an *iterative clause*.

A *query* is a conjunction of the form

$$A_1,\ldots,A_n? \qquad n > 0,$$

where the A_i's are goals. Variables in a query are understood to be existentially quantified.

A *computation* of a logic program P finds an instance of a given query logically deducible from P. A goal G is deducible from a program P if there is an instance A of G where $A \leftarrow B_1,\ldots,B_n$, $n \geq 0$, is a ground instance of a clause in P, and the B_i's are deducible from P. Deduction of a goal from an identical fact is a special case.

The *meaning* of a program P is inductively defined using logical deduction. The set of ground instances of facts in P are in the meaning. A ground goal G is in the meaning if there is a ground instance $G \leftarrow B_1,\ldots,B_n$ of a rule in P such that $B_1,\ldots,B_n$ are in the meaning. The meaning consists of the ground instances that are deducible from the program.

An intended meaning M of a program is also a set of ground unit goals. A program P is *correct* with respect to an intended meaning M if $M(P)$ is a subset of M. It is *complete* with respect to M if M is a subset of $M(P)$. Clearly, it is correct and complete with respect to its intended meaning, which is the desired situation, if $M=M(P)$.

A ground goal is *true* with respect to an intended meaning if it is a member of it, and *false* otherwise.

Logical deduction is defined syntactically here, and hence also the meaning of logic programs. In Chapter 5 alternative ways of describing the meaning of logic programs are presented, and their equivalence with the current definition is discussed.

Chapter 2
Database Programming

There are two basic styles of using logic programs: defining a logical database, and manipulating data structures. This chapter discusses database programming. A logic database is comprised of a set of facts and rules. We show how a set of facts can define relations, as in relational databases. We show how rules can define complex relational queries, as in relational algebra. Together, a logic program composed of a set of facts and rules of a rather restricted format can express the functionalities associated with relational databases.

2.1 Simple databases

We begin by revising Program 1.1, the biblical database, and its augmentation with rules expressing family relationships. The database itself had four basic predicates, *father/2*, *mother/2*, *male/1*, and *female/1*. We adopt a convention from database theory and give for each relation a *relation scheme* that specifies the role that each position in the relation (or argument in the goal) is intended to represent. Relation schemes for the four predicates here are, respectively, *father(Father,Child)*, *mother(Mother,Child)*, *male(Person)*, and *female(Person)*. The mnemonic names are intended to speak for themselves.

We adopt the typographic convention that relation schemes are given in italics. Variables are given mnemonic names in rules, but usually X or Y when discussing queries. Multi-word names are handled differently for variables and predicates. Each new word in a variable is started with a capital letter, for example, *NieceOrNephew*, while words are delimited by underscores for predicate and function name, for example, *schedule_conflict*.

New relations are built from these basic relationships by defining suitable rules. Appropriate relation schemes for the relations introduced in the previous

abraham≠isaac.   abraham≠haran.   abraham≠lot.
abraham≠milcah.   abraham≠yiscah.   isaac≠haran.
isaac≠lot.   isaac≠milcah.   isaac≠yiscah.
haran≠lot.   haran≠milcah.   haran≠yiscah.
lot≠milcah.   lot≠yiscah.   milcah≠yiscah.

Figure 2.1: Defining inequality

chapter are *son(Son,Parent)*, *daughter(Daughter,Parent)*, *parent(Parent,Child)*, and *grandparent(Grandparent,Grandchild)*. From the logical viewpoint, it is unimportant which relationships are defined by facts and which by rules. For example, if the available database consisted of *parent*, *male* and *female* facts, the rules defining *son* and *grandparent* are still correct. New rules must be written for the relationships no longer defined by facts, namely *father* and *mother*. Suitable rules are:

father(Dad,Child) ← parent(Dad,Child), male(Dad).
mother(Mum,Child) ← parent(Mum,Child), female(Mum).

Interesting rules can be obtained by making relationships explicit that are present in the database only implicitly. For example, since we know the father and mother of a child, we know which couples produced offspring, or to use a Biblical term, procreated. This is not given explicitly in the database but a simple rule can be written recovering the information. The relation scheme is *procreated(Man,Woman)*.

procreated(Man,Woman) ← father(Man,Child), mother(Woman,Child).

This reads: "*Man* and *Woman* procreated if there is a *Child* such that *Man* is the father of *Child* and *Woman* is the mother of *Child*."

Another example of information that can be recovered from the simple information present is sibling relationships — brothers and sisters. We give a rule for *brother(Brother,Sibling)*.

brother(Brother,Sib) ←
        parent(Parent,Brother), parent(Parent,Sib), male(Brother).

This reads: "*Brother* is the brother of *Sib* if *Parent* is a parent of both *Brother* and *Sib*, and *Brother* is male."

There is a problem with the definition of brother given above. The query *brother(X,X)?* is satisfied for any male child *X*, which is not our understanding of the brother relationship.

    uncle(Uncle,Person) ←
        brother(Uncle,Parent), parent(Parent,Person).
    sibling(Sib1,Sib2) ←
        parent(Parent,Sib1), parent(Parent,Sib2), Sib1 ≠ Sib2.
    cousin(Cousin1,Cousin2) ←
        parent(Parent1,Cousin1),
        parent(Parent2,Cousin2),
        sibling(Parent1,Parent2).

Program 2.1: Defining family relationships

In order to preclude such cases from the meaning of the program we introduce a predicate $\neq$(*Term1,Term2*). It is convenient to write this predicate as an infix operator. Thus *Term1* $\neq$ *Term2* is true if *Term1* and *Term2* are different. For the present it is restricted to constant terms. It can be defined, in principle, by a table $X \neq Y$ for every two different individuals X and Y in the domain of interest. Figure 2.1 gives the appropriate table for Program 1.1.

The new brother rule is

    brother(Brother,Sib) ←
        parent(Parent,Brother),
        parent(Parent,Sib),
        male(Brother),
        Brother ≠ Sib.

The more relationships that are present, the easier it is to define complicated relationships. Program 2.1 defines the relations *uncle(Uncle,NieceOrNephew)*, *sibling(Sib1,Sib2)*, and *cousin(Cousin1,Cousin2)*. More examples are posed as exercises at the end of the section.

Another relationship implicit in the family database is whether a woman is a mother. This is determined by using the *mother/2* relationships. The new relationship scheme is *mother(Woman)*, and is defined by the rule:

    mother(Woman)← mother(Woman,Child).

This reads: A *Woman* is a mother if she is the mother of some *Child*. Note that we have used the same predicate name, *mother*, to describe two different *mother* relationships. The *mother* predicate takes a different number of arguments, i.e., has a different arity, in the two cases. In general the same predicate name denotes a different relationship when it has a different arity.

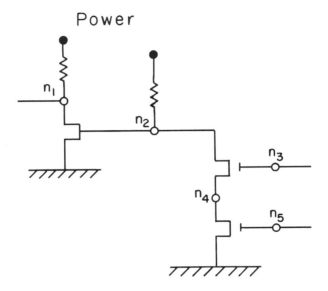

Figure 2.2: A logical circuit

We change examples, lest the example of family relationships become inces-
tuous, and consider describing simple logical circuits. A circuit can be viewed
from two perspectives. The first is the topological layout of the physical components usually described in the circuit diagram. The second is the interaction of
functional units. Both views are easily accommodated in a logic program. The
circuit diagram is represented by a collection of facts, while rules describe the
functional components.

Program 2.2 is a database giving a simplified view of the logical and-gate
drawn in Figure 2.2. The facts are the connections of the particular resistors
and transistors comprising the circuit. The relation scheme for resistors is *resis-
tor(End1,End2)* and for transistors *transistor(Gate,Source,Drain)*.

The program demonstrates the style of commenting of logic programs we will
follow throughout the book. Each interesting procedure is preceded by a relation
scheme for the procedure, and English text defining the relation. We recommend

```
resistor(power,n1).
resistor(power,n2).

transistor(n2,ground,n1).
transistor(n3,n4,n2).
transistor(n5,ground,n4).
```

inverter(Input, Output) ←
    Output is the inversion of *Input.*

```
inverter(Input,Output) ←
    transistor(Input,ground,Output),
    resistor(power,Output).
```

nand_gate(Input1,Input2,Output) ←
    Output is the logical nand of *Input1* and *Input2.*

```
nand_gate(Input1,Input2,Output) ←
    transistor(Input1,X,Output),
    transistor(Input2,ground,X),
    resistor(power,Output).
```

and_gate(Input1,Input2,Output) ←
    Output is the logical and of *Input1* and *Input2.*

```
and_gate(Input1,Input2,Output) ←
    nand_gate(Input1,Input2,X),
    inverter(X,Output).
```

Program 2.2: A circuit for a logical and_gate

this style of commenting, which emphasizes the declarative reading of programs, for Prolog programs as well.

Particular configurations of resistors and transistors fulfill roles captured via rules defining the functional components of the circuit. The circuit describes an and-gate, which takes two input signals and produces as output the logical *and* of these signals. One way of building an and-gate, and how this circuit is composed, is to connect a nand-gate with an inverter. Relation schemes for these three components are *and_gate(Input1,Input2,Output)*, *nand_gate(Input1,Input2,Output)*, and *inverter(Input,Output)*.

To appreciate Program 2.2, let us read the inverter rule. This states that an inverter is built up from a transistor with the source connected to the ground, and a resistor with one end connected to the power source. The gate of the transistor

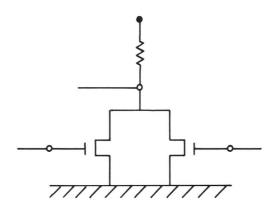

Figure 2.3: An or-gate

is the input to the inverter, while the free end of the resistor must be connected to the drain of the transistor, which forms the output of the inverter. Sharing of variables is used to insist on the common connection.

Consider the query *and_gate(In1,In2,Out)?* to Program 2.2. It has the solution {*In1=n3,In2=n5,Out=n1*}. This solution confirms that the circuit described by the facts is an and-gate, and indicates the inputs and output.

Exercises for Section 2.1

(i)   Modify the rule for *brother* to give a rule for *sister*, the rule for *uncle* to give a rule for *niece*, and the rule for *sibling* so that it only recognizes full siblings, i.e., those that have the same mother and father.

(ii) Using a predicate *married_couple(Wife,Husband)*, define the relationships: *mother_in_law*, *brother_in_law*, and *son_in_law*.

(iii) Describe the logical circuit for an or-gate depicted in Figure 2.3 using a logic program like Program 2.2. Extend the program to a nor-gate using an inverter.

2.2   Structured data and data abstraction

A limitation of Program 2.2 for describing the and-gate is the treatment of the circuit as a black box. There is no indication of the structure of the circuit in the answer to the *and_gate* query, even though the structure has been implicitly used in finding the answer. The rules tell us that the circuit represents an and-gate, but the structure of the and-gate is present only implicitly. We remedy this by adding an extra argument to each of the goals in the database. For uniformity, the extra argument becomes the first argument. The base facts simply acquire an identifier. Proceeding from left to right in the diagram of Figure 2.2, we label the resistors *r1* and *r2*, and the transistors *t1*, *t2* and *t3*.

Names of the functional components should reflect their structure. An inverter is composed of a transistor and a resistor. To represent this, we need structured data. The technique is to use a compound term, $inv(T,R)$, where T and R are the respective names of the inverter's component transistor and resistor. Analogously, the name of a nand-gate will be $nand(T1,T2,R)$, where $T1$, $T2$ and R name the two transistors and resistor that comprise a nand-gate. Finally, an and-gate can be named in terms of an inverter and a nand-gate. The modified code containing the names appears in Program 2.3.

The query *and_gate*$(G,In1,In2,Out)$? has solution { $G=and(nand(t2,t3,r2)$, $inv(t1,r1)),In1=n3,In2=n5,Out=n1$}. $In1$, $In2$, and Out have their previous values. The complicated structure for G reflects accurately the functional composition of the and-gate.

Structuring data is important in programming in general and in logic programming in particular. It is used to organize data in a meaningful way. Rules can be written more abstractly, ignoring irrelevant details. More modular programs can be achieved this way, as a change of data representation need not mean a change in all the program, as shown by the following example.

Consider the following two ways of representing a fact about a lecture course on complexity given on Monday from 9 to 11 by David Harel in the Feinberg building, room A:

    course(complexity,monday,9,11,david,harel,feinberg,a).

and

    course(complexity,time(monday,9,11),lecturer(david,harel),
        location(feinberg,a)).

The first fact represents *course* as a relationship between eight items — a course name, a day, a starting hour, a finishing hour, a lecturer's first name, a lecturer's

resistor(R,Node1,Node2) ←
    R is a resistor between *Node1* and *Node2*.

resistor(r1,power,n1).
resistor(r2,power,n2).

transistor(T,Gate,Source,Drain) ←
    T is a transistor whose gate is *Gate*,
    source is *Source*, and drain is *Drain*.

transistor(t1,n2,ground,n1).
transistor(t2,n3,n4,n2).
transistor(t3,n5,ground,n4).

inverter(I,Input,Output) ←
    I is an inverter which inverts *Input* to *Output*.

inverter(inv(T,R),Input,Output) ←
    transistor(T,Input,ground,Output),
    resistor(R,power,Output).

nand_gate(Nand,Input1,Input2,Output) ←
    Nand is a gate forming the logical nand, *Output*,
    of *Input1* and *Input2*.

nand_gate(nand(T1,T2,R),Input1,Input2,Output) ←
    transistor(T1,Input1,X,Output),
    transistor(T2,Input2,ground,X),
    resistor(R,power,Output).

and_gate(And,Input1,Input2,Output) ←
    And is a gate forming the logical and, *Output*,
    of *Input1* and *Input2*.

and_gate(and(N,I),Input1,Input2,Output) ←
    nand_gate(N,Input1,Input2,X),
    inverter(I,X,Output).

Program 2.3: The circuit database with names

surname, a building, and a room. The second fact makes *course* a relationship between four items — a name, a time, a lecturer, and a location with further qualification. The time is composed of a day, a starting time and a finishing time, lecturers have a first name and a surname, and locations are specified by a building and a room. The second fact reflects more elegantly the relationships

lecturer(Lecturer,Course) ←
    course(Course,Time,Lecturer,Location).

duration(Course,Length) ←
    course(Course,time(Day,Start,Finish),Lecturer,Location),
    plus(Start,Length,Finish).

teaches(Lecturer,Day) ←
    course(Course,time(Day,Start,Finish),Lecturer,Location).

occupied(Room,Day,Time) ←
    course(Course,time(Day,Start,Finish),Lecturer,Room),
    Start ≤ Time, Time ≤ Finish.

Program 2.4: Course rules

that hold.

The four argument version of *course* enables more concise rules to be written by abstracting the details which are irrelevant to the query. Program 2.4 is comprised of some examples. The *occupied* rule assumes a predicate less than or equal, represented as a binary infix operator ≤.

Rules not concerning with the particular values of a structured argument need not "know" how the argument is structured. For example, the rules for *duration* and *teaches* represent time explicitly as *time(Day,Start,Finish)* because the *Day* or *Start* or *Finish* times of the course are desired. In contrast, the rule for *lecturer* does not. This leads to greater modularity, as the representation of time can be changed without affecting the rules that do not inspect it.

We do not have definite rules to decide whether to use structured data or not. Not using structured data allows a uniform representation where all the data are simple. The advantages of structured data are compactness of representation which more accurately reflects our perspective of a situation, and modularity. We can relate the discussion to conventional programming languages. Facts are the counterpart of tables, while structured data correspond to records with aggregate fields.

We believe that the appearance of a program is important, particularly when attempting difficult problems. A good structuring of data can make a difference when programming complex problems.

Some of the rules in Program 2.4 are recovering relationships between two individuals, *binary* relationships, from the single, more complicated one. All the course information could have been written in terms of binary relationships as follows:

>   day(complexity,monday).
>   start_time(complexity,9).
>   finish_time(complexity,11).
>   lecturer(complexity,harel).
>   building(complexity,feinberg).
>   room(complexity,a).

Rules would then be expressed differently, reverting to the previous style of making implicit connections explicit. For example,

>   teaches(Lecturer,Day) ←
>   lecturer(Course,Lecturer), day(Course,Day).

Exercises for Section 2.2

(i)   Add rules defining the relationships *location(Course,Building),busy(Lecturer, Time)* and *cannot_meet(Lecturer1,Lecturer2)*. Assume course facts as above.

(ii) Possibly using relationships from Exercise (i), define the relationship *schedule_conflict(Time,Place,Course1,Course2)*.

(iii) Add an extra argument to the family relationship rules to represent the relationship, e.g., *father(X,Y,pa(X,Y))*.
      (Hint: Follow the example of the circuit database.)

(iv) Design a small database for an application of your own choice. Use a single predicate to express the information, and invent suitable rules.

2.3   Recursive rules

The rules described so far define new relationships in terms of existing ones. An interesting extension is recursive definitions of relationships which define relationships in terms of themselves. One way of viewing recursive rules is as generalization of a set of nonrecursive rules.

Consider a series of rules defining ancestors — grandparents, greatgrandparents, etc:

>   grandparent(Ancestor,Descendant) ←
>   parent(Ancestor,Person), parent(Person,Descendant).
>   greatgrandparent(Ancestor,Descendant) ←

parent(Ancestor,Person), grandparent(Person,Descendant).
greatgreatgrandparent(Ancestor,Descendant) ←
    parent(Ancestor,Person), greatgrandparent(Person,Descendant).

A clear pattern can be seen, which can be expressed in a rule defining the relationship of *ancestor(Ancestor,Descendant)*:

ancestor(Ancestor,Descendant) ←
    parent(Ancestor,Person), ancestor(Person,Descendant).

This rule is a generalization of the rules above.

A logic program for *ancestor* also requires a nonrecursive rule, the choice of which affects the meaning of the program. If the fact *ancestor(X,X)* is used, defining the *ancestor* relationship to be reflexive, people will be considered to be their own ancestors. This is not the intuitive meaning of ancestor. Program 2.5 is a logic program defining the ancestor relationship, where parents are considered ancestors.

The *ancestor* relationship is the transitive closure of the *parent* relationship. In general finding the transitive closure of a relationship is easily captured in a logic program, by using a recursive rule.

Consider the problem of testing connectivity in a directed graph. A directed graph can be represented as a logic program by a collection of facts. A fact *edge(Node1,Node2)* is present in the program if there is an edge from *Node1* to *Node2* in the graph. Figure 2.4 gives a graph, while Program 2.6 is its description as a logic program.

Two nodes are connected if there is a series of edges that can be traversed to get from the first node to the second. That is, the relationship *connected(Node1,Node2)*, which is true if *Node1* and *Node2* are connected, is the transitive closure of the *edge* relationship. For example, *a* and *e* are connected in the graph in Figure 2.4, but *b* and *f* are not. Program 2.7 defines the relationship. The meaning of the program is the set of goals *connected(X,Y)*, where *X* and *Y* are connected. Note that *connected* is a transitive reflexive relationship, due to the choice of base fact.

Exercises for Section 2.3

(i)   A stack of blocks can be described by a collection of facts *on(Block1, Block2)*, which is true if *Block1* is on *Block2*. Define a predicate *above(Block1, Block2)* that is true if *Block1* is above *Block2* in the stack. (Hint: *Above* is the transitive closure of *on*.)

ancestor(Ancestor,Descendant) ←
    Ancestor is an ancestor of *Descendant*.

ancestor(Ancestor,Descendant) ←
    parent(Ancestor,Descendant).
ancestor(Ancestor,Descendant) ←
    parent(Ancestor,Person), ancestor(Person,Descendant).

Program 2.5: The ancestor relationship

edge(a,b).   edge(a,c).   edge(b,d).
edge(c,d).   edge(d,e).   edge(f,g).

Program 2.6: A directed graph

connected(Node1,Node2) ←
    Node1 is connected to *Node2* in the
    graph defined by the *edge/2* relation.

connected(Node,Node).
connected(Node1,Node2) ← edge(Node1,Link), connected(Link,Node2).

Program 2.7: The transitive closure of the edge relationship

```
a  →  b           f
↓     ↓           ↓
c  →  d  →  e     g
```

Figure 2.4: A simple graph

2.4   Logic programs and the relational database model

Logic programs can be viewed as a powerful extension to the relational database model, the extra power coming from the ability to specify rules. Many of the concepts introduced have meaningful analogues in terms of databases. The converse is also true. The basic operations of the relational algebra are easily expressed within logic programming.

Procedures composed solely of facts correspond to relations, the arity of the relation being the arity of the procedure. Five basic operations define the relational algebra: union, set difference, Cartesian product, projection and selection. We show how each is translated into a logic program.

The union operation creates a relation of arity n from two relations r and s, both of arity n. The new relation, denoted here r_union_s, is the union of r and s. It is defined directly as a logic program by two rules:

$$r\_union\_s(X_1,\ldots,X_n) \leftarrow r(X_1,\ldots,X_n).$$
$$r\_union\_s(X_1,\ldots,X_n) \leftarrow s(X_1,\ldots,X_n).$$

Set difference involves negation. We assume a predicate *not*. Intuitively, a goal *not* G is true with respect to a program P if G is not a logical consequence of P. Negation in logic programs is discussed in Chapter 5, where limitations of the intuitive definition are indicated. The definition is correct, however, if we only deal with ground facts, as is the case with relational databases.

The definition of r_diff_s of arity n where r and s are of arity n is

$$r\_diff\_s(X_1,\ldots,X_n) \leftarrow r(X_1,\ldots,X_n), not\ s(X_1,\ldots,X_n).$$
$$r\_diff\_s(X_1,\ldots,X_n) \leftarrow s(X_1,\ldots,X_n), not\ r(X_1,\ldots,X_n).$$

Cartesian product can be defined in a single rule. If r is a relation of arity m, and s is a relation of arity n, then r_x_s is a relation of arity $m+n$ defined by

$$r\_x\_s(X_1,\ldots,X_m,X_{m+1},\ldots,X_{m+n}) \leftarrow r(X_1,\ldots,X_m), s(X_{m+1},\ldots,X_{m+n}).$$

Projection involves forming a new relation comprising only some of the attributes of an existing relation. This is straightforward for any particular case. For example, the projection $r13$ selecting the first and third arguments of a relation of arity 3 is

$$r13(X_1,X_3) \leftarrow r(X_1,X_2,X_3).$$

Selection is similarly straightforward for any particular case. Consider a relation consisting of tuples whose third components are greater than their second, and a relation where the first component is Smith or Jones. In both cases a relation r of arity 3 is used to illustrate. The first example creates a relation $r1$:

$$r1(X_1,X_2,X_3) \leftarrow r(X_1,X_2,X_3), X_2 > X_3.$$

The second example creates a relation $r2$, which requires a disjunctive relationship, $smith\_or\_jones$:

$$r2(X_1,X_2,X_3) \leftarrow r(X_1,X_2,X_3), smith\_or\_jones(X_1).$$

$smith\_or\_jones(smith).$
$smith\_or\_jones(jones).$

Some of the derived operations of the relational algebra are more closely related to the constructs of logic programming. We mention two, intersection and the natural join. If r and s are relations of arity n, the intersection, r_meet_s is also of arity n and is defined in a single rule.

$$r\_meet\_s(X_1,\ldots,X_n) \leftarrow r(X_1,\ldots,X_n),\ s(X_1,\ldots,X_n).$$

A natural join is precisely a conjunctive query with shared variables.

2.5   Background

Readers interested in pursuing the connection between logic programming and database theory are referred to the many papers that have been written on the subject. A good starting place is the review paper by Minker et al. (1984). There are earlier papers on logic and databases in Gallaire and Minker (1978). Another interesting book is about the implementation of a database query language in Prolog (Li, 1983). Our discussion of relational databases follows Ullman (1982). Another good account of relational databases can be found in Maier (1983).

In general, an n-ary relation can be replaced by $n+1$ binary relations, as shown by Kowalski (1979). If one of the arguments forms a key for the relation, as does the course name in the above example in Section 2.2, n binary relations suffice.

Chapter 3

Recursive Programming

The programs of the previous section essentially retrieve information from, and manipulate, finite data structures. In general mathematical power is gained by considering infinite or potentially infinite structures. Finite instances then follow as special cases. Logic programs harness this power by using recursive data types.

Logical terms can be classified into types. A *type* is a (possibly infinite) set of terms. Some types are conveniently defined by unary relations. A relation *p/1* defines the type *p* to be the set of X's such that $p(X)$.

For example, the *male/1* and *female/1* predicates used previously define the *male* and *female* types.

More complex types can be defined by recursive logic programs. Such types are called *recursive types*. Types defined by unary recursive programs are called *simple recursive types*. A program defining a type is called a *type definition*.

In this chapter we show logic programs defining relations over simple recursive types, such as integers, lists and binary trees, and also programs over more complex types, such as polynomials.

3.1 Arithmetic

The simplest recursive data type, natural numbers, arises from the foundations of mathematics. Arithmetic is based on the natural numbers. This section gives logic programs for performing arithmetic.

In fact, Prolog programs for performing arithmetic differ considerably from their logical counterparts, as we will see in later chapters. However, it is useful to

$natural\_number(X) \leftarrow$
    X is a natural number.

natural_number(0).
natural_number(s(X)) $\leftarrow$ natural_number(X).

Program 3.1: Defining the natural numbers

spend time discussing the logic programs. There are two main reasons. Firstly, the operations of arithmetic are usually thought of functionally rather than relationally. Presenting examples for such a familiar area emphasizes the change in thinking necessary for composing logic programs. Second, it is more natural to discuss the underlying mathematical issues, such as correctness and completeness of programs.

The natural numbers are built from two constructs, the constant symbol 0 and the successor function s of arity 1. All the natural numbers are then recursively given as 0, $s(0)$, $s(s(0))$, $s(s(s(0)))$, ... We adopt the convention that $s^n(0)$ denotes the integer n, that is, n applications of the successor function to 0.

As in the previous chapter, we give a relation scheme for each predicate, together with the intended meaning of the predicate. Recall that a program P is *correct* with respect to an intended meaning M if the meaning of P is a subset of M. It is *complete* if M is a subset of the meaning of P. It is correct and complete if its meaning is identical to M. Proving correctness establishes that everything deducible from the program is intended. Proving completeness establishes that everything intended is deducible from the program. Two typical correctness and completeness proofs are given in this section.

The simple type definition of natural numbers is neatly encapsulated in the logic program, Program 3.1. The relation scheme used is $natural\_number(X)$, with intended meaning that X is a natural number. The program consists of one unit clause and one iterative clause (a clause with a single goal in the body). Such a program is called *minimal recursive*.

Proposition: Program 3.1 is correct and complete with respect to the set of goals $natural\_number(s^i(0))$, for $i \geq 0$.

Proof: (1) Completeness. Let N be a natural number. We show that the goal $natural\_number(N)$ is deducible from the program by giving an explicit proof tree. Either N is 0 or of the form $s^N(0)$. The proof tree for the goal $natural\_number(0)$ is trivial. The proof tree for the goal $natural\_number(s(\ldots s(0) \ldots))$ contains N reductions, using the rule in Program 3.1, to reach the fact $natural\_number(0)$, as is shown in the left half of Figure 3.1.

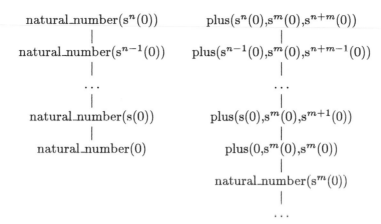

Figure 3.1: Proof trees establishing completeness of programs

(2) Correctness. Suppose that *natural_number*(X) is deducible from Program 3.1, in n deductions. We prove that *natural_number*(X) is in the intended meaning of the program by induction on n. If $n=0$, then the goal must have been proved using a unit clause, which implies that $X=0$. If $n > 0$, then the goal must be of the form *natural_number*($s(X1)$), since it is deducible from the program, and further *natural_number*($X1$) is deducible in $n-1$ deductions. By the induction hypothesis, $X1$ is in the intended meaning of the program, i.e. $X1 = s^k(0)$ for some $k > 0$. ∎

The natural numbers have a natural order. Program 3.2 is a logic program defining the relationship less than or equal to according to the order. We denote the relationship with a binary infix symbol, or *operator*, $\leq$ according to mathematical usage. The expression $0 \leq X$ is nonetheless a term with functor $\leq/2$, and arguments 0 and X, and is syntactically equivalent to '$\leq$'$(0,X)$.

The relation scheme is $N_1 \leq N_2$. The intended meaning of Program 3.2 is all ground facts $X \leq Y$ where X and Y are natural numbers and X is less than or equal to Y. Exercise (ii) at the end of the section is to prove the correctness and completeness of Program 3.2.

The recursive definition of $\leq$ is not "computationally efficient." The proof tree establishing that a particular N is less than a particular M has $M+2$ nodes. We usually think of testing whether one number is less than another as a unit operation, independent of the size of the numbers. Indeed Prolog does not define arithmetic according to the axioms presented in this section, but uses the underlying arithmetic capabilities of the computer directly.

$X \leq Y \leftarrow$
    X and Y are natural numbers,
    such that X is less than or equal to Y.

$0 \leq X \leftarrow$ natural_number(X).
$s(X) \leq s(Y) \leftarrow X \leq Y$.

natural_number(X) $\leftarrow$ See Program 3.1

Program 3.2: The less than or equal relation

$plus(X, Y, Z) \leftarrow$
    X, Y and Z are natural numbers,
    such that Z is the sum of X and Y.

plus(0,X,X) $\leftarrow$ natural_number(X).
plus(s(X),Y,s(Z)) $\leftarrow$ plus(X,Y,Z).

natural_number(X) $\leftarrow$ See Program 3.1

Program 3.3: Addition

Addition is a basic operation defining a relationship between two natural numbers and their sum. In Section 1.1 a table of the *plus* relationship was assumed for all relevant natural numbers. A recursive program captures the relationship elegantly and more compactly, and is given as Program 3.3. The intended meaning of Program 3.3 is the set of facts *plus(X,Y,Z)* where X, Y and Z are natural numbers and $X+Y=Z$.

Proposition: Programs 3.1 and 3.3 constitute a correct and complete axiomatization of addition, with respect to the standard intended meaning of *plus/3*.

Proof: (1) Completeness. Let X, Y, and Z be natural numbers such that $X+Y=Z$. We give a proof tree for the goal *plus(X,Y,Z)*. If X equals 0, then Y equals Z. Since Program 3.1 is a complete axiomatization of the natural numbers, there is a proof tree for *natural_number(Y)*, which is easily extended to a proof tree for *plus(0,Y,Y)*. Otherwise, X equals $s^n(0)$ for some n. If Y equals $s^m(0)$, then Z equals $s^{n+m}(0)$. The proof tree in the right half of Figure 3.1 establishes completeness.

(2) Correctness. Let *plus(X,Y,Z)* be in the meaning. A simple inductive argument on the size of X, similar to the one used in the previous proposition, establishes that $X+Y=Z$.   ∎

Addition is usually considered to be a function of two arguments rather than a three place relation. Generally logic programs corresponding to functions of

n arguments define $n+1$ place relations. Computing the value of a function is achieved by posing a query with n arguments instantiated and the argument place corresponding to the value of the function uninstantiated. The solution to the query is the value of the function with the given arguments. To make the analogy clearer, we give a functional definition of addition corresponding to the logic program.

$$0+X = X.$$
$$s(X)+Y = s(X+Y).$$

One advantage that relational programs have over functional programs is the multiple uses that can be made of the program. For example, the query $plus(s(0),s(0),s(s(0)))$? means checking whether $1+1=2$. (We feel free to use the more readable decimal notation when mentioning numbers.) As for $\leq$, the program for $plus$ is not efficient. The proof tree confirming that the sum of N and M is $N+M$ has $N+M+2$ nodes.

Posing the query $plus(s(0),s(0),X)$?, an example of the standard use, calculates the sum of 1 and 1. However, the program can just as easily be used for subtraction by posing a query such as $plus(s(0),X,s(s(s(0))))$? The computed value of X is the difference between 3 and 1, namely 2. Similarly asking a query with the first argument uninstantiated, and the second and third instantiated, also performs subtraction.

A more novel use exploits the possibility of a query having *multiple solutions*. Consider the query $plus(X,Y,s(s(s(0))))$? It reads: "Do there exist numbers X and Y that add up to 3." In other words, find a partition of the number 3 into the sum of two numbers, X and Y. There are several solutions.

A query with multiple solutions becomes more interesting when the properties of the variables in the query are restricted. There are two forms of restriction. using extra conjuncts in the query, and instantiating variables in the query. We saw examples of this when querying a database. Exercise (ii) at the end of this section requires to define a predicate $even(X)$, which is true if X is an even number. Assuming such a predicate, the query $plus(X,Y,N),even(X),even(Y)$? gives a partition of N into two even numbers. The second type of restriction is exemplified by the query $plus(s(s(X)),s(s(Y)),N)$? which insists that each of the numbers adding up to N is strictly greater than one.

Almost all logic programs have multiple uses. Consider Program 3.2 for $\leq$, for example. The query $s(0) \leq s(s(0))$? checks whether 1 is less than or equal to 2. The query $X \leq s(s(0))$? finds numbers X less than or equal to 2. It even computes pairs of numbers less than or equal to each other with the query $X \leq Y$?

Program 3.3 defining addition is not unique. For example, the logic program

plus(X,0,X) ← natural_number(X).
plus(X,s(Y),s(Z)) ← plus(X,Y,Z).

has precisely the same meaning as Program 3.3 for *plus*. Two programs are to be expected due to the symmetry between the first two arguments. A proof of correctness and completeness given for Program 3.3 applies to this program by reversing the roles of the symmetric arguments.

The meaning of the program for *plus* would not change even if it consisted of the two programs combined. This composite program is undesirable, however. There are several different proof trees for the same goal. It is important both for runtime efficiency and for textual conciseness that axiomatizations of logic programs be minimal.

We define a *type condition* to be a call to the predicate defining the type. For natural numbers, a type condition is any goal of the form *natural_number(X)*.

In practice, both Programs 3.2 and 3.3 are simplified by omitting the body of the base rule, *natural_number(X)*. Without this test, facts such as $0 \leq a$ and *plus(0,a,a)*, where a is an arbitrary constant, will be in the programs' meanings. Type conditions are necessary for correct programs. However, type conditions distract from the simplicity of the programs and affect the size of the proof trees. Hence in the following we might omit explicit type conditions from the example programs.

The basic programs shown are the building blocks for more complicated relationships. A typical example is defining multiplication as repeated addition. Program 3.4 reflects this relationship. The relation scheme is *times(X,Y,Z)* meaning X times Y equals Z.

Exponentiation is defined as repeated multiplication. Program 3.5 for *exp(N,X,Y)* expresses the relationship that $X^N = Y$. It is analogous to Program 3.4 for *times(X,Y,Z)*, with *exp* and *times* replacing *times* and *plus*, respectively. The base cases for exponentiation are $X^0 = 1$ for all positive values of X, and $0^N = 0$ for positive values of N.

A definition of the factorial function uses the definition of multiplication. Recall that $N! = N \cdot (N-1) \cdot \ldots \cdot 2 \cdot 1$. The predicate *factorial(N,F)* relates a number N to its factorial F. Program 3.6 is its axiomatization.

Not all relationships concerning natural numbers are defined recursively. Relations can also be defined in the style of programs in Chapter 2. An example is Program 3.7 determining the minimum of two numbers via the relation *minimum(N1,N2,Min)*.

times(*X*,*Y*,*Z*) ←
     X, *Y* and *Z* are natural numbers,
     such that *Z* is the product of *X* and *Y*.

times(0,X,0).
times(s(X),Y,Z) ← times(X,Y,W), plus(W,Y,Z).

plus(X,Y,Z) ← See Program 3.3

Program 3.4: Multiplication as repeated addition

exp(*N*,*X*,*Y*) ←
     N, *X*, and *Y* are natural numbers,
     such that *Y* equals *X* raised to the power *N*.

exp(s(10),0,0).
exp(0,s(X),s(0)).
exp(s(N),X,Y) ← exp(N,X,Z), times(Z,X,Y).

times(X,Y,Z) ← See Program 3.4

Program 3.5: Exponentiation as repeated multiplication

factorial(*N*,*F*) ←
     F equals *N* factorial.

factorial(0,s(0)).
factorial(s(N),F) ← factorial(N,F1), times(s(N),F1,F).

times(X,Y,Z) ← See Program 3.4

Program 3.6: Computing factorials

minimum(*N1*,*N2*,*Min*) ←
     The minimum of the natural numbers *N1* and *N2* is *Min*.

minimum(N1,N2,N1) ← N1 ≤ N2.
minimum(N1,N2,N2) ← N2 ≤ N1.

N1 ≤ N2 ← See Program 3.2

Program 3.7: The minimum of two numbers

$mod(X, Y, Z) \leftarrow$
    Z is the remainder of the integer division of X by Y.

mod(X,Y,Z) ← Z < Y, times(Y,Q,W), plus(W,Z,X).

Program 3.8a: A non-recursive definition of modulus

$mod(X, Y, Z) \leftarrow$
    Z is the remainder of the integer division of X by Y.

mod(X,Y,X) ← X < Y.
mod(X,Y,Z) ← plus(X1,Y,X), mod(X1,Y,Z).

Program 3.8b: A recursive definition of modulus

Composing a program to determine the remainder after integer division reveals an interesting phenomenon — different mathematical definitions of the same concept are translated into different logic programs. Programs 3.8a and 3.8b give two definitions of the relation $mod(X, Y, Z)$, which is true if Z is the value of X modulo Y, or in other words Z is the remainder of X divided by Y. The programs assume a relation < as specified in exercise (i) at the end of the section.

Program 3.8a illustrates the direct translation of a mathematical definition, which is a logical statement, into a logic program. The program corresponds to an existential definition of the integer remainder: "Z is the value of X mod Y if Z is strictly less than Y, and there exists a number Q such that $X = Q \cdot Y + Z$. In general mathematical definitions are easily translated to logic programs.

We can relate Program 3.8a to constructive mathematics. Although seemingly an existential definition, it is also constructive, due to the constructive nature of <, *plus* and *times*. The number Q, for example, proposed in the definition will be explicitly computed by *times* in any use of *mod*.

In contrast to Program 3.8a, Program 3.8b is defined recursively. It constitutes an algorithm for finding the integer remainder based on repeated subtraction. The first rule says that X mod Y is X if X is strictly less than Y. The second rule says that the value of X mod Y is the same as $X-Y$ mod Y. The effect of any computation to determine the modulus is to repeatedly subtract Y from X until it becomes less than Y and hence is the correct value.

The mathematical function X *mod* Y is not defined when Y is zero. Neither Program 3.8a nor Program 3.8b have goals $mod(X, 0, Z)$ in their meaning for any values of X or Z. The test of "<" guarantees that.

The computational model gives a way of distinguishing between the two

$ackermann(X,Y,A) \leftarrow$
    A is the value of Ackermann's
    function for the natural numbers X and Y.

ackermann(0,N,s(N)).
ackermann(s(M),0,Val) ← ackermann(M,s(0),Val).
ackermann(s(M),s(N),Val) ←
    ackermann(s(M),N,Val1), ackermann(M,Val1,Val).

Program 3.9: Ackermann's function

programs for *mod*. Given a particular X, Y and Z satisfying *mod*, we can compare the size of their proof trees. In general proof trees produced with Program 3.8b will be smaller than those produced with Program 3.8a. In that sense Program 3.8b is more "efficient." We defer more rigorous discussions of efficiency till the discussions on lists, where the insights gained will carry over to Prolog programs.

Another example of translating a mathematical definition directly into a logic program is writing a program that defines Ackermann's function. Ackermann's function is the simplest example of a recursive function which is not primitive recursive. It is a function of two arguments, defined by three cases:

ackermann(0,N) = N+1.
ackermann(M,0) = ackermann(M−1,1).
ackermann(M,N) = ackermann(M 1,ackermann(M,N−1)).

Program 3.9 is a translation of the functional definition into a logic program. The predicate *ackermann(M,N,A)* denotes that $A=ackermann(M,N)$. The third rule involves two calls to Ackermann's function, one to compute the value of the second argument.

This is more cleanly expressed in the functional definition. In general functional notation is more readable for pure functional definitions such as Ackermann's function. Another example is seen in Program 3.8a. Expressing that $X=Q \cdot Y+Z$, a statement about functions, is a little awkward with relational logic programs.

The final example in this section is the Euclidean algorithm for finding the greatest common divisor of two natural numbers, recast as a logic program. Like Program 3.8b, it is a recursive program not based on the recursive structure of numbers. The relation scheme is $gcd(X,Y,Z)$, with intended meaning that Z is the greatest common divisor (or gcd) of two natural numbers X and Y. It uses either of the two programs, 3.8a or 3.8b, for *mod*.

$gcd(X,Y,Z) \leftarrow$
    Z is the greatest common divisor of
    the natural numbers X and Y.

gcd(X,Y,Gcd) ← mod(X,Y,Z), gcd(Y,Z,Gcd).
gcd(X,0,X)← X > 0.

Program 3.10: The Euclidean algorithm

The first rule in Program 3.10 is the logical essence of the Euclidean algorithm. The gcd of X and Y is the same as the gcd of Y and X *mod* Y. A proof that Program 3.10 is correct depends on the correctness of the above mathematical statement about greatest common divisors. The proof that the Euclidean algorithm is correct similarly rests on this result.

The second fact in Program 3.10 is the base fact. It must be specified that X is greater than 0 to preclude *gcd(0,0,0)* from being in the meaning. The gcd of 0 and 0 is not well defined.

Exercises for Section 3.1

(i) Modify Program 3.2 for $\leq$ to axiomatize the relations $<$, $>$, and $\geq$. Discuss multiple uses of these programs.

(ii) Prove that Program 3.2 is a correct and complete axiomatization of $\leq$.

(iii) Prove that a proof tree for the query $s^n(0) \leq s^m(0)$ using Program 3.2 has $M+2$ nodes.

(iv) Define predicates *even(X)* and *odd(X)* for determining if a natural number is even or odd.
(Hint: Modify Program 3.1 for *natural_number*.)

(v) Write a logic program defining the relationship *fib(N,F)* to determine the Nth Fibonacci number F.

(vi) The predicate *times* can be used for computing exact quotients with queries such as $times(s(s(0)),X,s(s(s(s(0)))))$? to find the result of 4 divided by 2. The query $times(s(s(0)),X,s(s(s(0))))$? to find $3/2$ has no solution. Many applications require the use of integer division that would calculate $3/2$ to be 1. Write a program to compute integer quotients.
(Hint: Use repeated subtraction.)

(vii) Modify Program 3.10 for finding the gcd of two integers so that it performs repeated subtraction directly, rather than use the *mod* function.

(Hint: The program repeatedly subtracts the smaller number from the larger number until the two numbers are equal.)

3.2   Lists

The basic structure for arithmetic is the unary successor functor. Although complicated recursive functions such as Ackermann's function can be defined, the use of a unary recursive structure is limited. This section discusses the binary structure, the *list*.

The first argument of a list holds an *element*, and the second argument is recursively the rest of the list. Lists are sufficient for most computations — attested to by the success of the programming language LISP, which has lists as its basic compound data structure. Arbitrarily complex structures can be represented with lists, though it is more convenient to use different structures when appropriate.

For lists, as for numbers, a constant symbol is necessary to terminate recursion. This "empty list," referred to as nil, will be denoted here by the symbol [ ]. We also need a functor of arity two. Historically the usual functor for lists is "." (pronounced dot), which overloads the use of the period. It is convenient to define a separate, special syntax. The term .(X, Y) is denoted $[X|Y]$. Its components have special names: X is called the *head* and Y is called the *tail*.

The term $[X|Y]$ corresponds to a cons pair in LISP. The corresponding jargon for head and tail is respectively *car* and *cdr*.

Figure 3.2 illustrates the relationship between lists written with different syntax. The first column writes lists with the dot functor, and is the way lists are considered as terms in logic programs. The second column gives the square bracket equivalent of the dot syntax. The third column is an improvement upon the syntax of the second column, essentially hiding the recursive structure of lists. In this syntax, lists are written as a sequence of elements enclosed in square brackets and separated by commas. The empty list used to terminate the recursive structure is suppressed. Note the use of "cons pair notation" within the third column, when the list has a variable tail.

Terms built with the dot functor are more general than lists. Program 3.11 defines a list precisely. Declaratively it reads: "A list is either the empty list or a cons pair whose tail is a list." The program is analogous to Program 3.1 defining natural numbers, and is the simple type definition of lists.

Figure 3.3 gives a proof tree for the goal *list*$([a,b,c])$. Implicit in the proof

list(*Xs*) ←
    Xs is a list.

list([ ]).
list([X|Xs]) ← list(Xs).

Program 3.11: Defining a list

Formal object	Cons pair syntax	Element syntax
.(a,[ ])	[a|[ ]]	[a]
.(a,.(b,[ ]))	[a|[b|[ ]]]	[a,b]
.(a,.(b,.(c,[ ])))	[a|[b|[c |[ ]]]]	[a,b,c]
.(a,X)	[a|X]	[a|X]
.(a,.(b,X))	[a|[b|X]]	[a,b|X]

Figure 3.2: Equivalent forms of lists

list([a,b,c])
|
list([b,c])
|
list([c])
|
list([ ])

Figure 3.3: Proof tree verifying a list

tree are ground instances of rules in Program 3.11, for example, *list*([*a,b,c*]) ←
list([*b,c*]). We specify the particular instance here explicitly, as instances of lists
in cons pair notation can be confusing. [*a,b,c*] is an instance of [*X|Xs*] under the
substitution {*X=a,Xs=*[*b,c*]}.

Because lists are richer data structures than numbers there is a great variety
of interesting relationships that can be specified with them. Perhaps the most
basic operation with lists is determining whether a particular element is in a list.
The predicate expressing this relationship is *member*(*Element,List*). Program 3.12
is a recursive definition of *member/2*.

Declaratively, the reading of Program 3.12 is straightforward. *X* is an element
of a list if it is the head of the list by the first clause, or if it is a member of the
tail of the list by the second clause. The meaning of the program is the set of all

$member(Element, List) \leftarrow$
    $Element$ is an element of the list $List$.

member(X,[X|Xs]).
member(X,[Y|Ys]) $\leftarrow$ member(X,Ys).

Program 3.12: Membership of a list

$prefix(Prefix, List) \leftarrow$
    $Prefix$ is a prefix of $List$.

prefix([ ],Ys).
prefix([X|Xs],[X|Ys]) $\leftarrow$ prefix(Xs,Ys).

$suffix(Suffix, List) \leftarrow$
    $Suffix$ is a suffix of $List$.

suffix(Xs,Xs).
suffix(Xs,[Y|Ys]) $\leftarrow$ suffix(Xs,Ys).

Program 3.13: Prefixes and suffixes of a list

ground instances $member(X,Xs)$ where X is an element of Xs. We omit the type condition in the first clause. Alternatively it would be written

    $member(X,[X|Xs]) \leftarrow list(Xs)$.

This program has many interesting applications to be revealed throughout the book. Its basic uses are checking whether an element is in a list with a query such as $member(b,[a,b,c])$?, finding an element of a list with a query such as $member(X,[a,b,c])$?, and finding a list containing an element with a query such as $member(b,X)$? This last query may seem strange, but there are programs that are based on this use of $member$.

We use the following conventions wherever possible when naming variables in programs involving lists. If X is used to denote the head of a list, then Xs will denote its tail. More generally, plural variable names will denote lists of elements while singular names will denote individual elements. Numerical suffixes will denote variants of lists. Relation schemes will still contain mnemonic names.

Our next example is a predicate $sublist(Sub,List)$ for determining whether Sub is a sublist of $List$. A sublist needs the elements to be consecutive: $[b,c]$ is a sublist of $[a,b,c,d]$, whereas $[a,c]$ is not.

It is convenient to define two special cases of sublists to make the definition of $sublist$ easier. It is good style when composing logic programs to define meaningful

$sublist(Sub, List)$ ←
  Sub is a sublist of $List$.

a: Suffix of a prefix

  sublist(Xs,Ys) ← prefix(Ps,Ys), suffix(Xs,Ps)

b: Prefix of a suffix

  sublist(Xs,Ys) ← prefix(Xs,Ss), suffix(Ss,Ys).

c: Recursive definition of sublist

  sublist(Xs,Ys) ← prefix(Xs,Ys).
  sublist(Xs,[Y|Ys]) ← sublist(Xs,Ys).

d: Suffix of a prefix, using append

  sublist(Xs,AsXsBs) ←
      append(As,XsBs,AsXsBs), append(Xs,Bs,XsBs).

e: Prefix of a suffix, using append

  sublist(Xs,AsXsBs) ←
      append(AsXs,Bs,AsXsBs), append(As,Xs,AsXs).

Program 3.14: Determining sublists of lists

relationships as auxiliary predicates. The two cases considered are initial sublists, or prefixes, of a list, and terminal sublists, or suffixes, of a list. The programs are interesting in their own right.

The predicate *prefix(Prefix,List)* is true if *Prefix* is an initial sublist of *List*, for example, *prefix([a,b],[a,b,c])* is true. The companion predicate to *prefix* is *suffix(Suffix,List)* determining if *Suffix* is a terminal sublist of *List*. For example, *suffix([b,c],[a,b,c])* is true. Both predicates are defined in Program 3.13. The type condition *list(Xs)* should be added to the base fact in each predicate to give the correct meaning.

An arbitrary sublist can be specified in terms of prefixes and suffixes: namely as a suffix of a prefix, or as a prefix of a suffix. Program 3.14a expresses the logical rule that *Xs* is a sublist of *Ys* if there exists *Ps* such that *Ps* is a prefix of *Ys* and *Xs* is a suffix of *Ps*. Program 3.14b is the dual definition of a sublist as a prefix of a suffix.

The predicate *prefix* can also be used as the basis of a recursive definition of

$append(Xs, Ys, XsYs) \leftarrow$
    $XsYs$ is the result of concatenating
    the lists Xs and Ys.

append([ ],Ys,Ys).
append([X|Xs],Ys,[X|Zs]) $\leftarrow$ append(Xs,Ys,Zs).

Program 3.15: Appending two lists

append([a,b],[c,d],[a,b,c,d])
    |
append([b],[c,d],[b,c,d])
    |
append([ ],[c,d],[c,d])

Figure 3.4: A proof tree for appending two lists

sublist. This is given as Program 3.14c. The base rule reads that a prefix of a list is a sublist of a list. The recursive rule reads that the sublist of a tail of a list is a sublist of the list itself.

The predicate *member* can be viewed as a special case of *sublist* defined by the rule

    member(X,Xs) $\leftarrow$ sublist([X],Xs).

The basic operation with lists is concatenating two lists to give a third list. This defines a relationship, $append(Xs, Ys, Zs)$, between two lists Xs, Ys and the result Zs of joining them together. The code for *append*, Program 3.15, is identical in structure to the basic program for combining two numbers together, Program 3.3 for *plus*.

Figure 3.4 gives a proof tree for the goal $append([a,b],[c,d],[a,b,c,d])$. The tree structure suggests that its size is linear in the size of the first list. In general, if Xs is a list of n elements, the proof tree for $append(Xs, Ys, Zs)$ has $n+1$ nodes.

There are multiple uses for *append* similar to the multiple uses for *plus*. The basic use is to concatenate two lists by posing a query such as $append([a,b,c],[d,e],Xs)$? with answer $Xs=[a,b,c,d,e]$. A query such as $append(Xs,[c,d],[a,b,c,d])$? finds the difference $Xs=[a,b]$ between the lists $[c,d]$ and $[a,b,c,d]$. Unlike *plus*, *append* is not symmetric in its first two arguments, and thus there are two distinct versions of finding the difference between two lists.

The analogous process to partitioning a number is splitting a list. The query

$reverse(List, Tsil) \leftarrow$
   $Tsil$ is the result of reversing the list $List$.

a: Naive reverse

   reverse([ ],[ ]).
   reverse([X|Xs],Zs) $\leftarrow$ reverse(Xs,Ys), append(Ys,[X],Zs).

b: Reverse-accumulate

   reverse(Xs,Ys) $\leftarrow$ reverse(Xs,[ ],Ys).

   reverse([X|Xs],Acc,Ys) $\leftarrow$ reverse(Xs,[X|Acc],Ys).
   reverse([ ],Ys,Ys).

Program 3.16: Reversing a list

$append(As,Bs,[a,b,c,d])$?, for example, asks for lists As and Bs such that appending Bs to As gives the list $[a,b,c,d]$. Queries about splitting lists are made more interesting by partially specifying the nature of the split lists. The predicates *member, sublist, prefix* and *suffix* introduced previously can all be defined in terms of append by viewing the process as splitting a list.

The most straightforward definitions are for *prefix* and *suffix*, which just specify which of the two split pieces are of interest:

   prefix(Xs,Ys) $\leftarrow$ append(Xs,As,Ys).
   suffix(Xs,Ys) $\leftarrow$ append(As,Xs,Ys).

Sublist can be written using two *append* goals. There are two distinct variants, given as Programs 3.14d and 3.14e. These two programs are obtained from Programs 3.14a and 3.14b, respectively, where *prefix* and *suffix* are replaced by *append* goals.

Member can be defined using *append*, as follows:

   member(X,Ys) $\leftarrow$ append(As,[X|Xs],Ys).

This says that X is a member of Ys if Ys can be split into two lists where X is the head of the second list.

A similar rule can be written to express the relation $adjacent(X,Y,Zs)$ that two elements X and Y are adjacent in a list Zs:

   adjacent(X,Y,Zs) $\leftarrow$ append(As,[X,Y|Ys],Zs).

Another relationship easily expressed through *append* is determining the last

$length(Xs,N) \leftarrow$
    The list Xs has N elements.

length([ ],0).
length([X|Xs],s(N)) $\leftarrow$ length(Xs,N).

Program 3.17: Determining the length of a list

element of a list. The desired pattern of the second argument to *append*, a list with one element, is built into the rule:

last(X,Xs) $\leftarrow$ append(As,[X],Xs).

Repeated applications of append can be used to define a predicate *reverse(List, Tsil)*. The intended meaning of *reverse* is that *Tsil* is a list containing the elements in the list *List* in reverse order to how they appear in *List*. An example of a goal in the meaning of the program is *reverse([a,b,c],[c,b,a])*. The naive version, given as Program 3.16a, is the logical equivalent of the recursive formulation in any language: recursively reverse the tail of the list, and then add the first element at the back of the reversed tail.

There is an alternative way of defining *reverse* without calling *append* directly. We define an auxiliary predicate *reverse(Xs, Ys, Zs)* which is true if *Zs* is the result of appending *Ys* to the elements of *Xs* reversed. It is defined in Program 3.16b. The predicate *reverse/3* is related to *reverse/2* by the first clause in Program 3.16b.

Program 3.16b is more efficient than Program 3.16a. Consider Figure 3.5 with proof trees for the goal *reverse([a,b,c,d],[d,c,b,a])* using both programs. In general the size of the proof tree of Program 3.16a is quadratic in the number of elements in the list to be reversed, while that of Program 3.16b is linear.

The insight in Program 3.16b is the use of a better data structure for representing the sequence of elements, which we discuss in more detail in Chapters 7 and 15.

The final program in this section, Program 3.17, expresses a relationship between numbers and lists, using the recursive structure of each. The predicate *length(Xs,N)* is true if *Xs* is a list of length *N*, that is, contains *N* elements, where *N* is a natural number. For example, *length([a,b],s(s(0)))* indicating [a,b] has two elements is in the program's meaning.

Let us consider the multiple uses of Program 3.17. The query *length([a,b],X)?* computes the length, *2*, of a list [a,b]. In this way *length* is regarded as a function of a list, with the functional definition

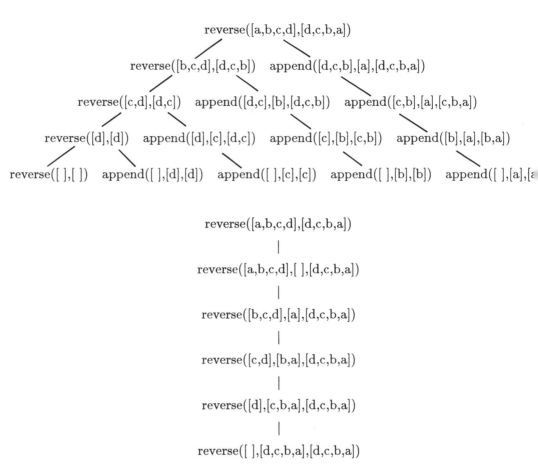

Figure 3.5: Proof trees for reversing a list

$$\text{length}([\,]) = 0$$
$$\text{length}([X|Xs]) = s(\text{length}(Xs)).$$

The query *length([a,b],s(s(0)))?* checks whether the list *[a,b]* has length *2*. The query *length(Xs,s(s(0)))?* generates a list of length *2* with variables for elements.

Exercises for Section 3.2

(i)　A variant of Program 3.14 for *sublist* is defined by the following three rules.

　　　subsequence([X|Xs],[X|Ys]) ← subsequence(Xs,Ys).
　　　subsequence(Xs,[Y|Ys]) ← subsequence(Xs,Ys).
　　　subsequence([ ],Ys).

　　Explain why this program has a different meaning from Program 3.14.

(ii)　Write recursive programs for *adjacent* and *last* which have the same meaning as the predicates defined in the text in terms of *append*.

(iii)　Write a program for *double(List,ListList)* where every element in *List* appears twice in *ListList*, e.g. *double([1,2,3],[1,1,2,2,3,3])* is true.

(iv)　Compute the size of the proof tree as a function of the size of the input list, for Programs 3.16a and 3.16b defining *reverse*.

(v)　Define the relation *sum(ListOfIntegers,Sum)*, which holds if Sum is the sum of the *ListOfIntegers*.
　　　(a) Using *plus/3*.
　　　(b) Without using any auxiliary predicate.
(Hint: Three axioms are enough.)

3.3　　Composing recursive programs

　　No explanation has been given so far about how the example logic programs have been composed. To some extent we claim that the composition of logic programs is a skill learned by apprenticeship or osmosis, and most definitely by practice. For simple relationships, the best axiomatizations have an aesthetic elegance which look obviously correct when written down. Through solving the exercises, the reader may find, however, that there is a difference between recognizing and constructing elegant logic programs.

　　This section gives more example programs involving lists. Their presentation, however, places more emphasis on how the programs might be composed. Two principles are illustrated: how to blend procedural and declarative thinking, and how to develop a program top-down.

　　We have shown the dual reading of clauses: declarative and procedural. How do they interrelate when composing logic programs? Pragmatically, one thinks procedurally when programming. However, one thinks declaratively when considering issues of truth and meaning. One way to blend them in logic programming is to compose procedurally and then interpret the result as a declarative statement. Construct a program with a given use in mind; then consider if the alternative uses make declarative sense. We apply this to a program for deleting elements from a list.

The first, and most important, step is to specify the intended meaning of the relationship. There are clearly three arguments involved when deleting elements from a list: an element X to be deleted, a list $L1$ which might have occurrences of X, and a list $L2$ with all occurrences of X deleted. An appropriate relation scheme is $delete(L1,X,L2)$. The natural meaning is all ground instances where $L2$ is the list $L1$ with all occurrences of X removed.

When composing the program, it is easiest to think of one specific use. Consider the query $delete([a,b,c,b],b,X)$?, a typical example of finding the result of deleting an element from a list. The answer here is $X=[a,c]$. The program will be recursive on the first argument. Let's don our procedural thinking caps.

We begin with the recursive part. The usual form of the recursive argument for lists is $[X|Xs]$. There are two possibilities to consider, one where X is the element to be deleted, and one where it is not. In the first case the result of recursively deleting X from Xs is the desired answer to the query. The appropriate rule is

delete([X|Xs],X,Ys) ← delete(Xs,X,Ys).

Switching hats, the declarative reading of this rule is: "The deletion of X from $[X|Xs]$ is Ys if the deletion of X from Xs is Ys." The condition that the head of the list and the element to be deleted are the same is specified by the shared variable in the head of the rule.

The second case where the element to be deleted is different from X, the head of the list, is similar. The result required is a list whose head is X and whose tail is the result of recursively deleting the element. The rule is

delete([X|Xs],Z,[X|Ys]) ← X≠Z, delete(Xs,Z,Ys).

The rule's declarative reading is: "The deletion of Z from $[X|Xs]$ is $[X|Ys]$ if Z is different from X and the deletion of Z from Xs is Ys." In contrast to the previous rule, the condition that the head of the list and the element to be deleted are different is made explicit in the body of the rule.

The base case is straightforward. No elements can be deleted from the empty list, and the required result is also the empty list. This gives the fact $delete([\ ],X,[\ ])$. The complete program is collected together as Program 3.18.

delete(List,X,HasNoXs) ←
> The list *HasNoXs* is the result of removing all
> occurrences of X from the list *List*.

delete([X|Xs],X,Ys) ← delete(Xs,X,Ys).
delete([X|Xs],Z,[X|Ys]) ← X≠Z, delete(Xs,Z,Ys).
delete([ ],X,[ ]).

Program 3.18: Deleting all occurrences of an element from a list

select(HasXs,X,OneLessXs) ←
> The list *OneLessXs* is the result of removing
> one occurrence of X from the list *HasXs*.

select(X,[X|Xs],Xs).
select(X,[Y|Ys],[Y|Zs]) ← select(X,Ys,Zs).

Program 3.19: Selecting an element from a list

Let us review the program we have written, and consider alternative formulations. Omitting the condition $X \neq Z$ from the second rule in Program 3.18 gives a variant of *delete*. This variant has a less natural meaning since any number of occurrences of an element may be deleted. For example, *delete([a,b,c,b],b,[a,c])*, *delete([a,b,c],b,[a,c,b])*, *delete([a,b,c,b],b,[a,b,c])* and *delete([a,b,c,b],b[a,b,c,b])* are all in the meaning of the variant.

Both Program 3.18 and the variant above include in their meaning instances where the element to be deleted does not appear in either list, for example, *delete([a],b,[a])* is true. There are applications where this is not desired. Program 3.19 defines *select(X,L1,L2)*, a relationship that has a different approach to elements not appearing in the list. The meaning of *select(X,L1,L2)* is all ground instances where *L2* is the list *L1* where exactly one occurrence of X has been removed.

The program is a hybrid of Program 3.12 for *member* and Program 3.18 for *delete*. Its declarative reading is: "X is selected from $[X|Xs]$ to give Xs; or X is selected from $[Y|Ys]$ to give $[Y|Zs]$ if X is selected from Ys to give Zs." We use *select* to aid the construction of a naive program for sorting lists, presented below.

A major thrust in programming has been the emphasis on a top-down design methodology, together with stepwise refinement. Loosely, the methodology is to state the general problem, break it down into subproblems, and then solve the pieces. A top-down programming style is one natural way for composing logic programs. Our description of programs throughout the book will be mostly top-down. The rest of this section describes the composition of two programs for sorting a list: permutation sort and quicksort. Their top-down development is stressed.

A logical specification of sorting a list is finding an ordered permutation of a list. This can be written down immediately as a logic program. The basic relation scheme is *sort(Xs, Ys)*, where *Ys* is a list containing the elements in *Xs* sorted in ascending order:

$$\text{sort(Xs,Ys)} \leftarrow \text{permutation(Xs,Ys), ordered(Ys).}$$

The top-level goal of sorting has been decomposed. We must now define *permutation* and *ordered*.

Testing whether a list is ordered ascendingly can be expressed in the two clauses given below. The fact says that a list with a single element is necessarily ordered. The rule says that a list is ordered if the first element is less than or equal to the second, and if the rest of the list, beginning from the second element, is ordered:

$$\text{ordered([X]).}$$
$$\text{ordered([X,Y|Ys])} \leftarrow \text{X} \leq \text{Y, ordered([Y|Ys]).}$$

A program for *permutation* is more delicate. One view of the process of permuting a list is selecting an element nondeterministically to be the first element of the permuted list, then recursively permuting the rest of the list. We translate this view into a logic program for *permutation*, using Program 3.19 for *select*. The base fact says that the empty list is its own unique permutation:

$$\text{permutation(Xs,[Z|Zs])} \leftarrow \text{select(Z,Xs,Ys), permutation(Ys,Zs).}$$
$$\text{permutation([ ],[ ]).}$$

Another procedural view of generating permutations of lists is recursively permuting the tail of the list and inserting the head in an arbitrary position. This view also can be encoded immediately. The base part is identical to the previous version:

$$\text{permutation([X|Xs],Zs)} \leftarrow \text{permutation(Xs,Ys), insert(X,Ys,Zs).}$$
$$\text{permutation([ ],[ ]).}$$

The predicate *insert* can be defined in terms of Program 3.19 for *select*.

$$\text{insert(X,Ys,Zs)} \leftarrow \text{select(X,Zs,Ys).}$$

Both procedural versions of *permutation* have clear declarative readings.

$sort(Xs, Ys) \leftarrow$
   The list Ys is an ordered permutation of the list Xs.

sort(Xs,Ys) $\leftarrow$ permutation(Xs,Ys), ordered(Ys).

permutation(Xs,[Z|Zs]) $\leftarrow$ select(Z,Xs,Ys), permutation(Ys,Zs).
permutation([ ],[ ]).

ordered([X]).
ordered([X,Y|Ys]) $\leftarrow$ X $\leq$ Y, ordered([Y|Ys]).

Program 3.20: Permutation sort

$sort(Xs, Ys) \leftarrow$
   The list Ys is an ordered permutation of the list Xs.

sort([X|Xs],Ys) $\leftarrow$ sort(Xs,Zs),insert(X,Ys,Zs).
sort([ ],[ ]).

insert(X,[ ],[X]).
insert(X,[Y|Ys],[Y|Zs]) $\leftarrow$ X > Y, insert(X,Ys,Zs).
insert(X[Y|Ys],[X,Y|Ys]) $\leftarrow$ X $\leq$ Y.

Program 3.21: Insertion sort

The "naive" sorting program, which we call permutation sort, is collected together as Program 3.20. It is an example of the generate-and-test paradigm to be discussed fully in Chapter 14.

The problem of sorting lists is well studied. Permutation sort is not a good method for sorting lists in practice. Much better algorithms come from applying a "divide and conquer" strategy to the task of sorting. The insight is to sort a list by dividing it into two pieces, recursively sorting the pieces, and then joining the two pieces together to give the sorted list. The methods for dividing and joining the lists must be specified. There are two extreme positions. The first is to make the dividing hard, and the joining easy. This approach is taken by the quicksort algorithm. We give a logic program for quicksort below. The second position is making the joining hard, but the dividing easy. This is the approach of merge sort, which is posed as exercise (iv) at the end of the section, and insertion sort, shown in Program 3.21.

In insertion sort, one element (typically the first) is removed from the list. The rest of the list is sorted recursively; then the element is inserted, preserving the orderedness of the list.

$sort(Xs, Ys) \leftarrow$
  The list Ys is an ordered permutation of the list Xs.

quicksort([X|Xs],Ys) ←
    partition(Xs,X,Littles,Bigs),
    quicksort(Littles,Ls),
    quicksort(Bigs,Bs),
    append(Ls,[X|Bs],Ys).
quicksort([ ],[ ]).

partition([X|Xs],Y,[X|Ls],Bs) ← X ≤ Y, partition(Xs,Y,Ls,Bs).
partition([X|Xs],Y,Ls,[X|Bs]) ← X > Y, partition(Xs,Y,Ls,Bs).
partition([ ],Y,[ ],[ ]).

Program 3.22: Quicksort

The insight in quicksort is to divide the list by choosing an arbitrary element in it, and then to split the list into the elements smaller than the chosen element and the elements larger than the chosen element. The sorted list is composed of the smaller elements, followed by the chosen element, and then the larger elements. The program we describe chooses the first element of the list as the basis of partition.

Program 3.22 defines *sort* using the quicksort algorithm. The recursive rule for *sort* reads: "Ys is a sorted version of $[X|Xs]$ if *Littles* and *Bigs* are a result of partitioning Xs according to X, Ls and Bs are the result of sorting *Littles* and *Bigs* recursively, and Ys is the result of appending $[X|Bs]$ to Ls.

Partitioning a list is straightforward, and is similar to the program for deleting elements. There are two cases to consider: when the current head of the list is smaller than the element being used for the partitioning, and when the head is larger than the partitioning element. The declarative reading of the first *partition* clause is: "Partitioning a list whose head is X and whose tail is Xs according to an element Y gives the lists $[X|Littles]$ and *Bigs*, if X is less than or equal to Y and partitioning Xs according to Y gives the lists *Littles* and *Bigs*." The second clause for *partition* has a similar reading. The base case is that the empty list is partitioned into two empty lists.

Exercises for Section 3.3

(i) Write a program for *substitute*$(X,Y,L1,L2)$ where $L2$ is the result of substituting Y for all occurrences of X in $L1$, e.g. *substitute*$(a,x,[a,b,a,c],[x,b,x,c])$

is true, whereas *substitute*($a,x,[a,b,a,c],[a,b,x,c]$) is false.

(ii) What is the meaning of the variant of *select*

> select(X,[X|Xs],Xs).
> select(X,[Y|Ys],[Y|Zs]) ← X≠Y, select(X,Ys,Zs).

(iii) Write a program for *no_doubles*($L1,L2$) where $L2$ is the result of removing all duplicate elements from $L1$, e.g. *no_doubles*($[a,b,c,b],[a,c,b]$) is true. (Hint: Use *member*.)

(iv) Write programs for *even_permutation*(Xs,Ys) and *odd_permutation*(Xs,Ys) which find Ys, the even and odd permutations respectively, of a list Xs. For example, *even_permutation*($[1,2,3],[2,3,1]$) and *odd_permutation*($[1,2,3]$, $[2,1,3]$) are true.

(v) Write a program for merge sort.

3.4   Binary trees

The next recursive data type we consider is binary trees. These structures have an important place in many algorithms.

Binary trees are represented by the ternary functor *tree(Element,Left,Right)*, where *Element* is the element at the node, and *Left* and *Right* are the left and right subtrees respectively. The empty tree is represented by the atom *void*. For example, the tree

would be represented as

> *tree(a,tree(b,void,void),tree(c,void,void))*.

Logic programs manipulating binary trees are similar to those manipulating lists. As with natural numbers and lists, we start with the type definition of binary trees. It is given as Program 3.23. Note that the program is *doubly recursive*; that is, there are two goals in the body of the recursive rule with the same predicate as the head of the rule. This is due to the doubly recursive nature of binary trees, and will be seen also in the rest of the programs of this section.

Let us write some tree processing programs. Our first example tests whether an element appears in a tree. The relation scheme is *tree_member(Element,Tree)*.

binary_tree(Tree) ←
  Tree is a binary tree.

binary_tree(void).
binary_tree(tree(Element,Left,Right)) ←
  binary_tree(Left), binary_tree(Right).

Program 3.23: Defining binary trees

tree_member(Element, Tree) ←
  Element is an element of the binary tree *Tree*.

tree_member(X,tree(X,Left,Right)).
tree_member(X,tree(Y,Left,Right)) ← tree_member(X,Left).
tree_member(X,tree(Y,Left,Right)) ← tree_member(X,Right).

Program 3.24: Testing tree membership

isotree(Tree1, Tree2) ←
  Tree1 and *Tree2* are isomorphic binary trees.

isotree(void,void).
isotree(tree(X,Left1,Right1),tree(X,Left2,Right2) ←
  isotree(Left1,Left2), isotree(Right1,Right2).
isotree(tree(X,Left1,Right1),tree(X,Left2,Right2) ←
  isotree(Left1,Right2), isotree(Right1,Left2).

Program 3.25: Determining when trees are isomorphic

The relation is true if *Element* is one of the nodes in the tree. Program 3.24 contains the definition. The declarative reading of the program is "*X* is a member of a tree if it is the element at the node (by the fact) or if it is a member of the left or right subtree (by the two recursive rules)."

The two branches of a binary tree are distinguishable, but for many applications the distinction is not relevant. Consequently a useful concept is isomorphism, which defines when unordered trees are essentially the same. Two binary trees *T1* and *T2* are *isomorphic* if *T2* can be obtained by reordering the branches of the subtrees of *T1*. Figure 3.6 shows three simple binary trees. The first two are isomorphic; the third is not.

Isomorphism is an equivalence relation, with a simple recursive definition. Two empty trees are isomorphic. Otherwise, two trees are isomorphic if they have identical elements at the node, and, either both the left subtrees and the

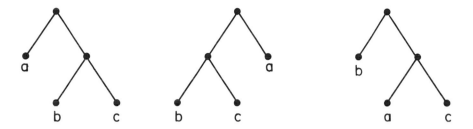

Figure 3.6: Comparing trees for isomorphism

right subtrees are isomorphic, or the left subtree of one is isomorphic with the right subtree of the other, and the two other subtrees are isomorphic.

Program 3.25 defines a predicate *isotree(Tree1, Tree2)* which is true if *Tree1* and *Tree2* are isomorphic. The predicate is symmetric in its arguments.

Programs related to binary trees involve double recursion, one for each branch of the tree. The double recursion can be manifest in two ways. Programs can have two separate cases to consider, as in Program 3.24 for *tree_member*. In contrast, Program 3.12 testing membership of a list has only one recursive case. Alternatively the body of the recursive clause has two recursive calls, as in each of the recursive rules for *isotree* in Program 3.25.

The task in Exercise 3.3(i) is to write a program for substituting for elements in lists. An analogous program can be written for substituting elements in binary trees. The predicate *substitute(X, Y, OldTree, NewTree)* is true if *NewTree* is the result of replacing all occurrences of *X* by *Y* in *OldTree*. An axiomatization of *substitute/4* is given as Program 3.26.

Many applications involving trees require access to the elements appearing as nodes. Central is the idea of a tree *traversal* which is a sequence of the nodes of the tree in some predefined order. There are three possibilities for the linear order of traversal: *preorder*, where the value of the node is first, then the nodes in the left subtree, followed by the nodes in the right subtree, *inorder*, where the left nodes come first followed by the node itself, and the right nodes, and *postorder* where the node comes after the left and right subtrees.

A definition of each of the three traversals is given in Program 3.27. The recursive structure is identical; the only difference between the programs is the order the elements are composed by the various *append* goals.

$substitute(X, Y, TreeX, TreeY)$ ←
> The binary tree *TreeY* is the result of replacing all
> occurrences of *X* in the binary tree *TreeX* by *Y*.

substitute(X,Y,void,void).
substitute(X,Y,tree(X,Left,Right),tree(Y,Left1,Right1)) ←
    substitute(X,Y,Left,Left1), substitute(X,Y,Right,Right1).
substitute(X,Y,tree(Z,Left,Right),tree(Z,Left1,Right1)) ←
    X≠Z, substitute(X,Y,Left,Left1), substitute(X,Y,Right,Right1).

Program 3.26: Substituting for a term in a tree

$pre\_order(Tree,Pre)$ ←
> *Pre* is a pre-order traversal of the binary tree *Tree*.

pre_order(tree(X,L,R),Xs) ←
    pre_order(L,Ls), pre_order(R,Rs), append([X|Ls],Rs,Xs).
pre_order(void,[ ]).

$in\_order(Tree,In)$ ←
> *In* is an in-order traversal of the binary tree *Tree*.

in_order(tree(X,L,R),Xs) ←
    in_order(L,Ls), in_order(R,Rs), append(Ls,[X|Rs],Xs).
in_order(void,[ ]).

$post\_order(Tree,Post)$ ←
> *Post* is a post-order traversal of the binary tree *Tree*.

post_order(tree(X,L,R),Xs) ←
    post_order(L,Ls),
    post_order(R,Rs),
    append(Rs,[X],Rs1),
    append(Ls,Rs1,Xs).
post_order(void,[ ]).

Program 3.27: Traversals of a binary tree

Exercises for Section 3.4

(i)   Define a program for *subtree(S, T)* where *S* is a subtree of *T*.

(ii)   Define the relation *sum_tree(TreeOfIntegers,Sum)*, which holds if *Sum* is the
      sum of the integer elements in *TreeOfIntegers*.

(iii) Define the relation *ordered(TreeOfIntegers)*, which holds if *Tree* is an ordered tree of integers, that is, for each node in the tree the elements in the left subtree are smaller then the element in the node, and the elements in the right subtree are larger then the element in the node.
(Hint: Define two auxiliary relations, *ordered_left(X, Tree)*, and *ordered_right(X, Tree)*, which hold if both *X* is smaller (larger) than the root of *Tree*, and *Tree* is ordered.)

(iv) Define the relation *tree_insert(X, Tree, Tree1)*, which holds if *Tree1* is an ordered tree resulting from inserting *X* into the ordered tree *Tree*. If *X* already occurs in *Tree*, then *Tree* and *Tree1* are identical.
(Hint: Four axioms suffice.)

3.5   Manipulating symbolic expressions

The logic programs illustrated so far in this chapter have manipulated natural numbers, lists, and binary trees. The programming style is applicable more generally. This section gives four examples of recursive programming — a program for defining polynomials, a program for symbolic differentiation, a program for solving the Towers of Hanoi problem, and a program for testing the satisfiability of Boolean formulae.

The first example is a program for recognizing polynomials in some term *X*. Polynomials are defined inductively. *X* itself is a polynomial in *X*, as is any constant. Sums, differences and products of polynomials in *X* are polynomials in *X*. So too are polynomials raised to the power of a natural number, and the quotient of a polynomial by a constant.

An example of a polynomial in the term x is $x^2 - 3x + 2$. This follows from it being the sum of the polynomials, $x^2 - 3x$ and 2, where $x^2 - 3x$ is recognized recursively.

A logic program for recognizing polynomials is obtained by expressing the rules given informally above in the correct form. Program 3.28 defines the relation *polynomial(Expression, X)* which is true if *Expression* is a polynomial in *X*. We give a declarative reading of two rules from the program.

The fact *polynomial(X, X)* says that a term *X* is a polynomial in itself. The rule

        polynomial(Term1+Term2,X) ←
            polynomial(Term1,X), polynomial(Term2,X)

polynomial(Expression,X) ←
    Expression is a polynomial in *X*.

polynomial(X,X).
polynomial(Term,X) ←
    constant(Term).
polynomial(Term1+Term2,X) ←
    polynomial(Term1,X), polynomial(Term2,X).
polynomial(Term1−Term2,X) ←
    polynomial(Term1,X), polynomial(Term2,X).
polynomial(Term1*Term2,X) ←
    polynomial(Term1,X), polynomial(Term2,X).
polynomial(Term1/Term2,X) ←
    polynomial(Term1,X), constant(Term2).
polynomial(Term↑N,X) ←
    natural_number(N), polynomial(X,Term).

Program 3.28: Recognizing polynomials

says that the sum *Term1+Term2* is a polynomial in *X* if both *Term1* and *Term2* are polynomials in *X*.

Other conventions used in Program 3.28 are the use of the unary predicate *constant* for recognizing constants, and the binary functor ↑ to denote exponentiation. The term *X↑Y* denotes X^Y.

The next example is a program for taking derivatives. The relation scheme is *derivative(Expression,X,DifferentiatedExpression)*. The intended meaning of *derivative* is that *DifferentiatedExpression* is the derivative of *Expression* with respect to *X*.

As for Program 3.28 for recognizing polynomials, a logic program for differentiation is just a collection of the relevant differentiation rules, written in the correct syntax. For example, the fact

derivative(X,X,s(0)).

expresses that the derivative of *X* with respect to itself is *1*. The fact

derivative(sin(X),X,cos(X)).

reads: "The derivative of *sin(X)* with respect to *X* is *cos(X)*." Natural mathematical notation can be used. A representative sample of functions and their derivatives is given in Program 3.29.

derivative(Expression,X,DifferentiatedExpression) ←
DifferentiatedExpression is the derivative of
Expression with respect to *X*.

derivative(X,X,s(0)).
derivative(X↑s(N),X,s(N)∗X↑N).
derivative(sin(X),X,cos(X)).
derivative(cos(X),X,−sin(X)).
derivative(c↑X,X,c↑X).
derivative(log(X),X,1/X).

derivative(F+G,X,DF+DG) ←
    derivative(F,X,DF),   derivative(G,X,DG).
derivative(F−G,X,DF−DG) ←
    derivative(F,X,DF), derivative(G,X,DG).
derivative(F∗G,X,F∗DG+DF∗G) ←
    derivative(F,X,DF), derivative(G,X,DG).
derivative(1/F,X,−DF/(F∗F)) ←
    derivative(F,X,DF).
derivative(F/G,X,(G∗DF−F∗DG)/(G∗G)) ←
    derivative(F,X,DF), derivative(G,X,DG).

Program 3.29: Derivative rules

Sums and products of terms are differentiated using the sum rule and product rule, respectively. The sum rule states that the derivative of a sum is the sum of derivatives. The appropriate clause is:

derivative(F+G,X,DF+DG) ←
    derivative(F,X,DF), derivative(G,X,DG).

The product rule is a little more complicated, but the logical clause is just the mathematical definition:

derivative(F∗G,X,F∗DG+DF∗G) ←
    derivative(F,X,DF), derivative(G,X,DG).

Program 3.29 also contains the reciprocal and quotient rules.

The chain rule is a little more delicate. It states that the derivative of $f(g(x))$ with respect to x is the derivative of $f(g(x))$ with respect to $g(x)$ times the derivative of $g(x)$ with respect to x. As stated, it involves quantification over functions, and is outside the scope of the logic programs we have presented.

> *hanoi(N,A,B,C,Moves)* ←
> *Moves* is a sequence of moves for solving the towers of
> Hanoi puzzle with *N* disks and three pegs, *A*, *B* and *C*.

hanoi(s(0),A,B,C,[A to B]).
hanoi(s(N),A,B,C,Moves)←
    hanoi(N,A,C,B,Ms1),
    hanoi(N,C,B,A,Ms2),
    append(Ms1,[A to B|Ms2],Moves).

Program 3.30: Towers of Hanoi

Nonetheless, a version of the chain rule is possible for each particular function. For example, we give the rule for differentiating X^N and $sin(X)$:

derivative(U↑s(N),X,s(N)*U↑N*DU) ← derivative(U,X,DU).
derivative(sin(U),X,cos(U)*DU) ← derivative(U,X,DU).

The difficulty of expressing the chain rule for differentiation arises from our choice of representation of terms. Both Programs 3.28 and 3.29 use the "natural" representation from mathematics where terms represent themselves. A term such as $sin(X)$ is represented using a unary structure *sin*. If a different representation were used, for example, *unary_term(sin,X)* where the name of the structure is made accessible, then the problem with the chain rule disappears. The chain rule can then be formulated as

derivative(unary_term(F,U),X,DF*DU) ←
    derivative(unary_term(F,U),U,DF), derivative(U,X,DU).

Note that all the rules in Program 3.29 would have to be reformulated in terms of this new representation, and would appear less natural.

People take for granted the automatic simplification of expressions when differentiating expressions. Simplification is missing from Program 3.29. The answer to the query *derivative(3*x+2,x,D)?* is *D=(3*1+0*x)+0*. We would immediately simplify *D* to *3*, but it is not specified in the logic program.

The next example is a solution to the "Towers of Hanoi" problem, a standard introductory example in the use of recursion. The problem is to move a tower of *n* disks from one peg to another, with the help of an auxiliary peg. There are two rules. Only one disk can be moved at a time, and a larger disk can never be placed on top of a smaller disk.

There is a legend associated with the game. Somewhere hidden in the surroundings of Hanoi, an obscure eastern village when the legend was first told,

is a monastery. The monks there are performing a task assigned to them by
God when the world was created — solving the above mentioned problem with 3
golden pegs and 64 golden disks. At the moment they complete their task, the
world will collapse into dust. Since the optimal solution to the problem with n
disks taken $2^n - 1$ moves, we need not lose any sleep over this possibility. The
number 2^{64} is comfortingly big.

The relation scheme for solving the problem is *hanoi(N,A,B,C,Moves)*. It is
true if *Moves* is the sequence of moves for moving a tower of N disks from peg A
to peg B using peg C as the auxiliary peg. This is an extension to usual solutions
which do not calculate the sequence of moves, but rather perform them. The
representation of the moves uses a binary functor *to*, written as an infix operator.
The term X *to* Y denotes that the top disk on peg X is moved to peg Y. The
program for solving the problem is given in Program 3.30.

The declarative reading of the heart of the solution, the recursive rule in
Program 3.30, is: "*Moves* is the sequence of moves of $s(N)$ disks from peg A to
peg B using peg C as an auxiliary, if *Ms1* is the solution for moving N pegs from
A to C using B, *Ms2* is the solution for moving N pegs from C to B using A, and
Moves is the result of appending $[A$ *to* $B|Ms2]$ to *Ms1*.

The recursion terminates with moving one peg. A slightly neater, but less
intuitive, base for the recursion is moving no disks. The appropriate fact is

   hanoi(0,A,B,C,[ ]).

The final example concerns Boolean formulae.

A *Boolean formula* is a term defined as follows: the constants *true* and *false*
are Boolean formulae; if X and Y are Boolean formulae, so are $X \lor Y$, $X \land Y$, and
$\sim X$, where $\lor$ and $\land$ are binary infix operators for disjunction and conjunction,
respectively, and $\sim$ is a unary prefix operator for negation.

A Boolean formula F is *true* if:

   F = 'true'
   F = X$\land$Y, and both X and Y are true
   F = X$\lor$Y, and either X or Y (or both) are true
   F = $\sim$X, and X is false.

A Boolean formula F is *false* if:

   F = 'false'
   F = X$\land$Y, and either X or Y (or both) are false
   F = X$\lor$Y, and both X and Y are false
   F = $\sim$X, and X is true.

satisfiable(Formula) ←
> There is a true instance of the Boolean formula *Formula*.

satisfiable(true).
satisfiable(X∧Y) ← satisfiable(X), satisfiable(Y).
satisfiable(X∨Y) ← satisfiable(X).
satisfiable(X∨Y) ← satisfiable(Y).
satisfiable(∼X) ← invalid(X).

invalid(Formula) ←
> There is a false instance of the Boolean formula *Formula*.

invalid(false).
invalid(X∨Y) ← invalid(X), invalid(Y).
invalid(X∧Y) ← invalid(X).
invalid(X∧Y) ← invalid(Y).
invalid(∼Y) ← satisfiable(Y).

Program 3.31: Satisfiability of Boolean formulae

Program 3.31 is a logic program for determining the truth or falsity of a Boolean formula. Since it can be applied to Boolean formulae with variables, it is actually more powerful than what seems on the surface. A Boolean formula with variables is *satisfiable* if it has a true instance. It is *invalid* if it has a false instance. These are the relations computed by the program.

Exercises for Section 3.5

(i)   Write a program to recognize if an arithmetic sum is normalized, that is, has the form $A+B$ where A is a constant and B is a normalized sum.

(ii) Write a type definition for Boolean formulae.

(iii) Write a program for recognizing whether a logical formula is in conjunctive normal form, namely is a conjunction of disjunctions of literals, where a literal is an atomic formula or its negation.

(iv) Write a program for the relation *negation_inwards(F1,F2)* which is true if *F2* is the logical formula resulting from moving all negation operators occurring in the formula *F1* inside conjunctions and disjunctions.

(v)   Write a program for converting a logical formula into conjunctive normal form, that is, a conjunction of disjunctions.

3.6   Background

Many of the programs in this chapter have been floating around the logic programming community, and their origins have become obscure. For example, several appear in Clocksin and Mellish (1984) and the uneven collection of short Prolog programs, "How to solve it in Prolog" by Coelho et al. (1980).

The classic reference for binary trees is Knuth (1968) and for sorting Knuth (1975).

Many of the basic programs for arithmetic and list processing have a simple structure which allows many correctness theorems to be proved automatically, see, for example, Boyer and Moore (1979) and Sterling and Bundy (1982).

Ackerman's function is discussed by Peter (1967).

Chapter 4

The Computation Model of Logic Programs

The computation model used in the first three chapters of the book has a severe restriction. All goals appearing in the proof trees are ground. All rule instances used to derive the goals in the proof trees are also ground. The abstract interpreter described assumes that the substitutions giving the desired ground instances can be guessed correctly. In fact the correct substitutions can be computed rather than guessed.

This chapter presents the full computation model of logic programs. The first section presents the unification algorithm which removes the guesswork in determining instances of terms. The second section presents an appropriately modified abstract interpreter, and gives example computations of logic programs.

4.1   Unification

The heart of the computation model of logic programs is the unification algorithm. Unification is the basis of most work in automated deduction, and the uses of logical inference in artificial intelligence.

Necessary terminology for describing the algorithm is repeated from Chapter 1, and new definitions are introduced as needed.

Recall that a term t is a common instance of two terms, t_1 and t_2, if there exist substitutions θ_1 and θ_2 such that t equals $t_1\theta_1$ and $t_2\theta_2$. A term s is *more general* than a term t if t is an instance of s, but s is not an instance of t. A term s is an *alphabetic variant* of a term t if both s is an instance of t, and t is an instance of s. Alphabetic variants are related by the renaming of variables which occur in the terms. For example, *member(X,tree(Left,X,Right))* and *member(Y,tree(Left,Y,Z))* are alphabetic variants.

A *unifier* of two terms is a substitution making the terms identical. If two terms have a unifier, we say they *unify*. There is a close relationship between unifiers and common instances. Any unifier determines a common instance, and conversely any common instance determines a unifier.

For example, *append([1,2,3],[3,4],List)* and *append([X|Xs],Ys,[X|Zs])* unify. A unifying substitution is {*X=1, Xs=[2,3], Ys=[3,4], List=[1|Zs]*}. Their common instance, determined by this unifying substitution, is *append([1,2,3],[3,4],[1|Zs])*.

A *most general unifier* or *mgu* of two terms is a unifier such that the associated common instance is most general. If two terms unify, then there is a unique most general unifier. The uniqueness is up to renaming of variables. Equivalently, two terms have a unique most general common instance, up to alphabetic variants.

A unification algorithm computes the most general unifier of two terms, if it exists, and reports *failure* otherwise.

The algorithm for unification presented here is based on solving equations. The input for the algorithm is two terms T_1 and T_2. The output of the algorithm is the mgu of the two terms if they unify, or *failure* if the terms do not unify. The algorithm uses a pushdown stack for storing the equations that need to be solved, and a location, θ, for collecting the substitution comprising the output.

The location θ is initially empty, and the stack is initialized to contain the equation $T_1 = T_2$. The algorithm consists of a loop of popping an equation from the stack and processing it. The loop terminates if failure occurs in processing an invalid equation, or when the stack becomes empty.

We consider the possible actions for dealing with the popped equation $S=T$. The simplest case is if S and T are identical constants or variables. This equation is correct, and nothing further needs to be done. The computation continues by popping the next equation from the stack.

If S is a variable, and T is a term not containing S, the following happens. The stack is searched for all occurrences of S, which are replaced by T. Similarly all occurrences of S in θ are replaced by T. Then the substitution $S=T$ is added to θ. It is significant that S does not occur in T. The test embodied by the phrase "not containing" is known as the *occurs check*.

If T is a variable, and S is a term not containing T, i.e., T satisfies the occurs check with respect to S, the symmetric sequence of actions happens.

Equations are added to the stack if S and T are compound terms with the same principal functor and arity, $f(S_1,\ldots,S_n)$ and $f(T_1,\ldots,T_n)$ say. For the terms to unify, each of the argument pairs must simultaneously unify. This is achieved by pushing the n equations, $S_i = T_i$, onto the stack.

In any other case, *failure* is reported, and the algorithm terminates. If the stack is emptied, the terms unify, and the unifier can be found in θ. The complete algorithm is given as Figure 4.1. The occurs check is embodied in the phrase "that does not occur in."

We do not prove the correctness of this algorithm, nor analyze its complexity. The interested reader is referred to the literature in the background section at the end of the chapter.

Consider attempting to unify the terms $append([a,b],[c,d],Ls)$ and $append([X|Xs],Ys,[X|\ Zs])$. The stack is initialized to the equation

$$append([a,b],[c,d],Ls)=append([X|Xs]\ Ys,[X|Zs]).$$

These two terms have the same functor, *append*, and arity, *3*, and so we add the three equations relating the subterms of the two terms. These are $[a,b]=[X|Xs]$, $[c,d]=Ys$, and $Ls=[X|Zs]$.

The next equation, $[a,b] =[X|Xs]$, is popped from the stack. These two compound terms have the same functor, ".", and arity, 2, and so two equations, $a=X$ and $[b]=Xs$ are added to the stack. Continuing, the equation $a=X$ is popped. This is covered by the second case in Figure 4.1. X is a variable not occurring in the constant, a. All occurrences of X in the stack are replaced by a. One equation is affected, namely $Ls=[X|Zs]$, which becomes $Ls=[a|Zs]$. The equation $X=a$ is added to the initially empty substitution, and the algorithm continues.

The next equation to be popped is $[b]=Xs$. Again this is covered by the second case. $Xs=[b]$ is added to the set of substitutions, and the stack is checked for occurrences of Xs. There are none, and the next equation is popped.

The second case also covers $[c,d]=Ys$. Another substitution, $Ys=[c,d]$, is added to the collection, and the final equation, $Ls=[a|Zs]$, is popped. This is handled by the symmetric first case. Ls does not occur in $[a|Zs]$, so the equation is added as is to the unifier, and the algorithm terminates successfully. The unifier is $X=a$, $Xs=[b]$, $Ys=[c,d]$, $Ls=[a|Zs]$. The common instance produced by the unifier is $append([a,b],[c,d],[a|Zs]$. Note that in this unification, the substitutions were not updated.

The occurs check is necessary to prevent the unification of terms such as $s(X)$ and X. There is no finite common instance of these terms.

Most Prolog implementations omit the occurs check from the unification algorithm, for pragmatic reasons. This issue is discussed further in Section 6.1

Input: Two terms T_1 and T_2 to be unified

Output: θ, the mgu of T_1 and T_2, or *failure*

Algorithm:

Initialize the substitution θ to be empty,
the stack to contain the equation $T_1 = T_2$,
and failure to *false.*

while stack not empty and no failure do

pop $X = Y$ from the stack

case

X is a variable that does not occur in Y:
substitute Y for X in the stack and in θ
add $X = Y$ to θ

Y is a variable that does not occur in X:
substitute X for Y in the stack and in θ
add $Y = X$ to θ

X and Y are identical constants or variables:
continue

X is $f(X_1, \ldots, X_n)$ and Y is $f(Y_1, \ldots, Y_n)$
for some functor f and $n > 1$:
push $X_i = Y_i$, $i = 1, \ldots n$, on the stack

otherwise:
failure := *true*

if failure, then output *failure*;
else output θ

Figure 4.1: A unification algorithm

When implementing the unification algorithm for a particular logic programming language, the explicit substitution in both the equations on the stack and
the unifier is avoided. Instead, logical variables and other terms are represented
by memory cells with different values, and variable binding is implemented by
assigning the memory cell representing a logical variable a reference to the cell
containing the representation of the term the variable is bound to. Therefore

substitute Y for X in stack and in θ
add $X = Y$ to substitutions

is replaced by

make X a reference to Y.

Exercises for Section 4.1

(i)   What is the mgu of $append([b],[c,d],L)$ and $append([X|Xs],Ys,[X|Zs])$?

(ii) What is the mgu of $hanoi(s(N),A,B,C,Ms)$ and $hanoi(s(s(0)),a,b,c,Xs)$?

4.2   An abstract interpreter for logic programs

We revise the abstract interpreter of Section 1.8 in the light of the unification algorithm. The result is the full computation model of logic programs. All the concepts introduced previously, such as goal reductions and computation traces, have their analogue in the full model.

A computation of a logic program can be described informally as follows. It starts from some initial (possibly conjunctive) query G and, if it terminates, has one of two results: success or failure. If a computation succeeds, the instance of G proved is conceived of as the output of the computation. A given query can have several successful computations, each resulting in a different output. In addition, it may have nonterminating computations, to which we associate no result.

The computation progresses via *goal reduction*. At each stage there is some resolvent, a conjunction of goals to be proved. A goal in the resolvent and clause in the logic program are chosen such that the clause's head unifies with the goal. The computation proceeds with a new resolvent, obtained by replacing the chosen goal by the body of the chosen clause in the resolvent, and then applying the most general unifier of the head of the clause and the goal. The computation terminates when the resolvent is empty. In this case, we say the goal is solved by the program.

To describe computations more formally we introduce some useful concepts. A *computation* of a goal $Q=Q_0$ by a program P is a (possibly infinite) sequence of triples $\langle Q_i, G_i, C_i \rangle$. Q_i is a (conjunctive) goal, G_i is a goal occurring in Q_i, and C_i is a clause $A \leftarrow B_1,\ldots,B_k$ in P renamed so that it contains new variable symbols not occurring in Q_j, $0 \le j \le i$. For all $i > 0$, Q_{i+1} is the result of replacing G_i by the body of C_i in Q_i, and applying the substitution θ_i, the most general unifier of G_i and A_i, the head of C_i; or the constant *true* if G_i is the only goal in Q_i and the body of C_i is empty; or the constant *fail*, if G_i and the head of C_i do not unify.

Input: A logic program P

                      A goal G

Output: $G\theta$, if this was the instance of G

                      decuded from P,

                      or *failure* if failure has occured.

Algorithm:

                Initialize the resolvent to be G, the input goal.

                While the resolvent is not empty do

                      Choose a goal A from the resolvent

                      and a (renamed) clause $A' \leftarrow B_1, B_2, \ldots, B_n$, $n \geq 0$, from P

                      such that A and A' unify with mgu θ

                      (exit if no such goal and clause exist).

                      Remove A from and add $B_1, B_2, \ldots$, and B_n to the resolvent.

                      Apply θ to the resolvent and to G.

                If the resolvent is empty output G, else output *failure*.

Figure 4.2: An abstract interpreter for logic programs

The goals $B_i\theta_i$ are said to be *derived* from G_j and C_j. A goal $G_j = B_{ik}\theta$, where B_{ik} occurs in the body of clause C_i, is said to be *invoked* by G_i and C_i. G_i is the *parent* of any goal it invokes. Two goals with the same parent goal are *sibling goals*.

A *trace* of a computation of a logic program $\langle Q_i, G_i, C_i \rangle$ is the sequence of pairs $\langle G_i, \theta_i' \rangle$, where θ_i' is the subset of the mgu θ_i computed at the ith reduction, restricted to variables in G_i.

We present an abstract interpreter for logic programs. It is an adaptation of the interpreter for ground goals (Figure 1.1). The restriction to using ground instances of clauses to effect reductions is lifted. Instead, the unification algorithm is applied to the chosen goal and head of the chosen clause to find the correct substitution to apply to the new resolvent.

Care needs to be taken with the variables in rules to avoid name clashes. Variables are local to a clause. Hence variables in different clauses that have the same name are, in fact, different. This is ensured by renaming the variables appearing in a clause each time the clause is chosen to effect a reduction. The new names must not include any of the variable names used previously in the computation.

The revised version of the interpreter is given as Figure 4.2. It solves a query

G with respect to a program *P*. The output of the interpreter is an instance of *G*, if a proof of such an instance if found, or *failure*, if a failure has occured during the computation. Note that the interpreter may also fail to terminate.

An instance of a query for which a proof is found is called a *solution* to the query.

The policy for adding and removing goals from the resolvent is called the *scheduling policy* of the interpreter. The abstract interpreter leaves the scheduling policy unspecified.

Consider solving the query $append([a,b],[c,d],Ls)$? by Program 3.15 for *append* using the abstract interpreter of Figure 4.2. The resolvent is initialized to be $append([a,b],[c,d],Ls)$. It is chosen as the goal to reduce, being the only one. The rule chosen from the program is

$$append([X|Xs], Ys, [X|Zs]) \leftarrow append(Xs, Ys, Zs).$$

The unifier of the goal and the head of the rule is $\{X=a,\ Xs=[b],\ Ys=[c,d],\ Ls=[a|Zs]\}$. A detailed calculation of this unifier appeared in the previous section. The new resolvent is the instance of $append(Xs, Ys, Zs)$ under the unifier, namely $append([b],[c,d],Zs)$. This goal is chosen in the next iteration of the loop. The same clause for *append* is chosen, but variables must be renamed to avoid a clash of variable names. The version chosen is

$$append([X1|Xs1], Ys1, [X1|Zs1]) \leftarrow append(Xs1, Ys1, Zs1).$$

The unifier of the head and goal is $\{X1=b,\ Xs1=[\ ],\ Ys1=[c,d],\ Zs=[b|Zs1]\}$. The new resolvent is $append([\ ],[c,d],Zs1)$. This time the fact, $append([\ ],Zs2,Zs2)$, is chosen; we again rename variables as necessary. The unifier this time is $\{Zs2=[c,d],\ Zs1=[c,d]\}$. The new resolvent is empty and the computation terminates.

To compute the result of the computation, we apply the relevant part of the mgu's calculated during the computation. The first unification instantiated *Ls* to $[a|Zs]$. *Zs* was instantiated to $[b|Zs1]$ in the second unification, and *Zs1* further became $[c,d]$. Putting it together, *Ls* has the value $[a|[b|[c,d]]]$, or more simply, $[a,b,c,d]$.

The computation can be represented by a trace. The trace of the *append* computation described above is presented in Figure 4.3. To make the traces clearer, goals are indented according to the indentation of their parent. A goal has an indentation depth of *d+1* if its parent has indentation depth *d*.

As another example, consider solving the query $son(S,haran)$ by Program 1.2. It is reduced using the clause $son(X,Y) \leftarrow father(Y,X),\ male(X)$. A most general

```
append([a,b],[c,d],Zs)          Zs=[a|Zs1]
   append([b],[c,d],Zs1)        Zs1=[b|Zs2]
      append([],[c,d],Zs2)      Zs2=[c,d]
         true
      Output: Zs=[a,b,c,d]
```

Figure 4.3: Tracing the appending of two lists

```
son(S,haran)                    son(S,haran)
   father(haran,S)    S=lot        male(S)            S=lot
   male(lot)                       father(haran,lot)
      true                            true
```

Figure 4.4: Different traces of the same solution

unifier is $\{X=S,\ Y=haran\}$. Applying the substitution gives the new resolvent *father(haran,S)*, *male(S)*. This is a conjunctive goal. There are two choices for the next goal to reduce. Choosing the goal *father(haran,S)* leads to the following computation. The goal unifies with the fact *father(haran,lot)* in the program, and the computation continues with S instantiated to *lot*. The new resolvent is *male(lot)*, which is reduced by a fact in the program, and the computation terminates. This is illustrated in the left trace in Figure 4.4.

The other possibility for computing $S=haran$ is choosing to reduce the goal *male(S)* before *father(haran,S)*. This goal is reduced by the fact *male(lot)* with S instantiated to *lot*. The new resolvent is *father(haran,lot)* which is reduced to the empty goal by the corresponding fact. This is the right trace in Figure 4.4.

Solutions to a query, obtained using the abstract interpreter, may contain variables. Consider the query *member(a,Xs)* with respect to Program 3.12 for *member*. This can be interpreted as asking what list Xs has the element a as a member. One solution, computed by the abstract interpreter, is $Xs=[a|Ys]$, namely a list with a as its head, and an unspecified tail. Solutions that contain variables denote an infinity of solutions — all their ground instances.

There are two choices in the interpreter of Figure 4.2: choosing the goal to reduce and choosing the clause to effect the reduction. These must be resolved in any realization of the computation model. The nature of the choices is fundamentally different.

The choice of goal to reduce is arbitrary; it does not matter which is chosen for the computation to succeed. If there is a successful computation by choosing a given goal, then there is a successful computation by choosing any other goal.

The two traces in Figure 4.4 illustrate two successful computations, where the choice of goal to reduce at the second step of the computation differs.

The choice of the clause to effect the reduction is nondeterministic. Not every choice will lead to a successful computation. For example, in both of the traces in Figure 4.4, we could have gone wrong. If we had chosen to reduce the goal *father(haran,S)* with the fact *father(haran,yiscah)*, we would not have been able to reduce the invoked goal *male(yiscah)*. For the second computation, had we chosen to reduce *male(S)* with *male(isaac)*, the invoked goal *father(haran,isaac)* could not have been reduced.

For some computations, for example, the computation illustrated in Figure 4.3, there is only one clause from the program which can reduce each goal. Such a computation is called *deterministic*. Deterministic computations mean that we do not have to exercise our nondeterministic imagination.

The alternative choices that can be made by the abstract interpreter, when trying to prove a goal, implicitly define a search tree, as described more fully in Section 5.3. The interpreter "guesses" a successful path in this search tree, corresponding to a proof of the goal, if one exists. However, dumber interpreters, without guessing abilities, can also be built, with the same power as our abstract interpreter. One possibility is to search this tree breadth first, that is, to explore all possible choices in parallel. This will guarantee that if there is a finite proof of the goal (i.e., a finite successful path in the search tree), it will be found.

Another possibility would be to explore the abstract search tree depth first. In contrast to the breadth first search strategy, the depth-first one does not guarantee finding a proof even if one exists, since the search tree may have infinite paths, corresponding to potentially infinite computations of the nondeterministic interpreter. A depth-first search of the tree might get lost in an infinite path, never finding a finite successful path, even if one exists.

In technical terms, the breadth-first search strategy defines a *complete* proof procedure for logic programs, whereas the depth-first one is *incomplete*. In spite of its incompleteness, depth-first search is the one incorporated in Prolog, for practical reasons, as explained in Chapter 6.

Let us give a trace of a longer computation, solving the Towers of Hanoi problem with 3 disks, using Program 3.30. It is a deterministic computation, and is given as Figure 4.5. The final *append* goal is given without unifications. It is straightforward to fill them in.

Computations such as that in Figure 4.5 can be compared to computations in more conventional languages. Unification can be seen to subsume many of the mechanisms of conventional languages: record allocation, assignment of and

```
hanoi(s(s(s(0))),a,b,c,Ms)
    hanoi(s(s(0)),a,c,b,Ms1)
        hanoi(s(0),a,b,c,Ms11)
            hanoi(0,a,c,b,Ms111)              Ms111=[ ]
            hanoi(0,c,b,a,Ms112)              Ms112=[ ]
            append([ ],[a to b],Ms11)         Ms11=[a to b]
        hanoi(s(0),b,c,a,Ms12)
            hanoi(0,b,a,c,Ms121)              Ms121=[ ]
            hanoi(0,a,c,b,Ms122)              Ms122=[ ]
            append([ ],[b to c],Ms12)         Ms12=[b to c]
        append([a to b],[a to c,b to c],Ms1)  Ms1=[a to b|Xs]
            append([ ],[a to c,b to c],Xs)    Xs=[a to c,b to c]
    hanoi(s(s(0)),c,b,a,Ms2)
        hanoi(s(0),c,a,b,Ms21)
            hanoi(0,c,b,a,Ms211)              Ms211=[ ]
            hanoi(0,b,a,c,Ms212)              Ms212=[ ]
            append([ ],[c to a],Ms21)         Ms21=[c to a]
        hanoi(s(0),a,b,c,Ms22)
            hanoi(0,a,c,b,Ms221)              Ms221=[ ]
            hanoi(0,c,b,a,Ms222)              Ms222=[ ]
            append([ ],[a to b],Ms22)         Ms22=[a to b]
        append([c to a],[c to b,a to b],Ms2)  Ms2=[c to a|Ys]
            append([ ],[c to b,a to b],Ys)    Ys=[c to b,a to b]
    append([a to b,a to c,b to c],[a to b,c to a,c to b,a to b],Ms)
        append([a to c,b to c],[a to b,c to a,c to b,a to b],Xs2)
            append([b to c],[a to b,c to a,c to b,a to b],Xs3)
                append([ ],[a to b,c to a,c to b,a to b],Xs4)
                    true
Output: Ms=[a to b,a to c,b to c,a to b,c to a,c to b,a to b]
```

Figure 4.5: Solving the Towers of Hanoi

access to fields in records, parameter passing, and more. We defer the subject till the computation model for Prolog is introduced in Chapter 6.

A computation of G by P *terminates* if $Gn=true$ or *fail* for some $n \geq 0$. Such a computation is finite and of *length n*. Successful computations correspond to terminating computations which end in *true*. Failing computations end in *fail*. All the traces given so far have been of successful computations.

Recursive programs admit the possibility of nonterminating computations. The query *append(Xs,[c,d],Ys)* with respect to *append* can be reduced arbitrarily

$$\begin{array}{ll}
\text{append}(Xs,[c,d],Ys) & Xs=[X|Xs1],\ Ys=[X|Ys1] \\
\quad \text{append}(Xs1,[c,d],Ys1) & Xs1=[X1|Xs2],\ Ys1=[X1|Ys2] \\
\qquad \text{append}(Xs2,[c,d],Ys2) & Xs2=[X2|Xs3],\ Ys2=[X2|Ys3] \\
\qquad\quad \text{append}(Xs3,[c,d],Ys3) & Xs3=[X3|Xs4],\ Ys3=[X3|Ys4] \\
\qquad\qquad \cdots & \cdots
\end{array}$$

Figure 4.6: A nonterminating computation

many times using the rule for *append*. In the process Xs becomes a list of arbitrary length. This corresponds to solutions of the query appending $[c,d]$ to an arbitrarily long list. It is illustrated in Figure 4.6.

All the traces presented so far have an important feature in common. If two goals G_i and G_j are invoked from the same parent, and G_i appears before G_j in the trace, then all goals invoked by G_i will appear before G_j in the trace. This scheduling policy makes traces easier to follow, by solving queries depth first.

The scheduling policy has another important effect: instantiating variables before their values are needed for other parts of the computation. A good ordering can mean the difference between a computation being deterministic or not.

Consider the computation traced in Figure 4.5. The goal

$$hanoi(s(s(s(0))),a,b,c,Ms)$$

is reduced to the following conjunction

$$hanoi(s(s(0)),a,b,c,Ms1),hanoi(s(s(0)),c,b,a,Ms2),app\,end(Ms1,Ms2,Ms).$$

If the *append* goal is now chosen, the *append* fact could be used (incorrectly) to reduce the goal. By reducing the two *hanoi* goals first, and all the goals they invoke, the *append* goal has the correct values for *Ms1* and *Ms2*.

We conclude this section with an observation. Computations have been described as a sequence of reductions. However, there is nothing inherently sequential about most of the computation. Parallel languages, for example, Concurrent Prolog, Parlog, and GHC, have been designed in order to exploit this potential parallelism.

Exercises for Section 4.2

(i) Trace the goal $sort([3,1,2],Xs)$? using the permutation sort (3.20), insertion sort (3.21), and quicksort (3.22) programs in turn.

(ii) Give a trace for the goal *derivative(3*sin(x)–4*cos(x),x,D)* using Program 3.29 for *derivative*.

(iii) Practice tracing your favorite computations.

4.3   Background

Unification plays a central role in automated deduction and the use of logical inference in artificial intelligence. It was first described in the landmark paper of Robinson (1965). Algorithms for unification have been the subject of much investigation: see, for example, Martelli and Montanari (1982), Paterson and Wegman (1978) and Dwork et al. (1984). Typical textbook descriptions appear in Bundy (1983) and Nilsson (1980).

A proof that the choice of goal to reduce from the resolvent is arbitrary can be found in Apt and van Emden (1982) or in the text of Lloyd (1984).

A method for replacing the runtime occurs check with compile-time analysis was suggested by Plaisted (1984).

Attempts have been made to make unification without the occurs check more than a necessary expedient for practical implementations of Prolog. In particular, Colmerauer (1982b) proposes a theoretical model for such unifications that incorporates computing with infinite terms.

A novel use of unification without the occurs check appears in Eggert and Chow (1983) where Escher-like drawings which gracefully tend to infinity are constructed.

Chapter 5

Theory of Logic Programs

There is a growing body of theory on logic programming. In this chapter we present results without proofs on five issues: semantics, correctness, complexity, search trees, and negation.

5.1   Semantics

Semantics assigns meanings to programs. Discussing semantics allows us to describe more formally the relation a program computes. The first chapter informally describes the meaning of a logic program P as the set of ground instances that are deducible from by P via a finite number of applications of the rule of universal modus ponens. This section considers more formal approaches.

The *operational* semantics is a way of describing procedurally the meaning of a program. The operational meaning of a logic program P is the set of ground goals that are instances of queries that are solved by P using the abstract interpreter given in Figure 4.2. This is an alternative formulation of the previous semantics, which defined meaning in terms of logical deduction.

The *declarative* semantics of logic programs is based on the standard model-theoretic semantics of first-order logic. In order to define it, some new terminology is needed.

Let P be a logic program. The *Herbrand universe* of P, denoted $U(P)$, is the set of all ground terms that can be formed from the constants and function symbols appearing in P. For example, consider P to be Program 3.1 defining the natural numbers, repeated below:

```
natural_number(0).
natural_number(s(X)) ← natural_number(X).
```

There is one constant symbol, *0*, and one unary function symbol, *s*. The Herbrand universe of the program, $U(P)$, equals $\{0,s(0),s(s(0)),\ldots\}$. In general the Herbrand universe is infinite unless no function symbols appear in the program. If no constant symbols appear either, one is arbitrarily chosen.

The *Herbrand base*, denoted $B(P)$, is the set of all ground goals that can be formed from the predicates in P and the terms in the Herbrand universe. The Herbrand base is infinite if the Herbrand universe is. For our example program there is one predicate *natural_number*. The Herbrand base, $B(P)$, equals $\{natural\_number(0),natural\_number(s(0)),\ldots\}$.

An *interpretation* for a logic program is a subset of the Herbrand base. An interpretation assigns truth and falsity to the elements of the Herbrand base. A goal in the Herbrand base is *true* with respect to an interpretation if it is a member of it, *false* otherwise.

An *interpretation* I is a *model* for a logic program if for each ground instance of a clause in the program $A \leftarrow B_1,\ldots,B_n$, A is in I if $B_1,\ldots,B_n$ are in I. Intuitively models are interpretations which respect the declarative reading of the clauses of a program.

For our example, *natural_number(0)* must be in every model, and *natural_number(s(X))* is in the model if *natural_number(X)* is. Any model of Program 3.1 thus includes the whole Herbrand base.

It is easy to see that the intersection of two models for a logic program P is again a model. This property allows the definition of the intersection of all models. The model obtained as the intersection of all models is known as the *minimal model* and denoted $M(P)$. The minimal model is the *declarative meaning* of a logic program.

The declarative meaning of the program for *natural_number*, its minimal model, is the complete Herbrand base $\{natural\_number(0),natural\_number(s(0)),$ $natural\_number(s(s(0))),\ldots\}$.

Let us consider the declarative meaning of *append*, defined as Program 3.15 and repeated here:

    append([X|Xs],Ys,[X|Zs]) ← append(Xs,Ys,Zs).
    append([ ],Ys,Ys).

The Herbrand universe is [ ],[[ ]],[[ ],[ ]],..., namely all lists that can be built using the constant []. The Herbrand base is all combinations of lists with the *append* predicate. The declarative meaning is all ground instances of *append([ ],Xs,Xs)*, that is, *append([ ],[ ],[ ])*, *append([ ],[[ ]],[[ ]])*,..., together with goals such as *append([[ ]],[ ],[[ ]])* which are logically implied by application(s) of the rule. This is only a subset of the Herbrand base. For example, *append*([ ],[ ],[[ ]]) is not in the meaning of *append* but is in the Herbrand base.

Denotational semantics assigns meanings to programs based on associating with the program a function over the domain computed by the program. The meaning of the program is defined as the least fixpoint of the function, if it exists. The domain of computations of logic programs is interpretations.

Given a logic program P, there is a natural mapping T_P from interpretations to interpretations, defined as follows:

$$Tp(I) = \{A \ in \ B(P){:}A{\leftarrow}B_1,B_2,\ldots,B_n, \ n \geq 0, \text{ is a ground instance of}$$
$$\text{a clause in } P, \text{ and } B_1,\ldots,B_n \text{ are in } I\}.$$

The mapping is *monotonic* since whenever an interpretation I is contained in an interpretation J, then $Tp(I)$ is contained in $Tp(J)$.

This mapping gives an alternative way of characterizing models. An interpretation I is a model if and only if $Tp(I)$ is contained in I.

Besides being monotonic, the transformation is also *continuous*, a notion that will not be defined here. These two properties ensure that for every logic program P, the transformation T_P has a least fixpoint, which is the meaning assigned to P by its denotational semantics.

Happily, all the different definitions of semantics are actually describing the same object. The operational, denotational, and declarative semantics were demonstrated to be equivalent. This allows us to define the *meaning* of a logic program as its minimal model.

5.2   Program correctness

Every logic program has a well-defined meaning as discussed in Section 5.1. This meaning is neither correct nor incorrect.

The meaning of the program, however, may or may not be what was intended by the programmer. Discussions of correctness must therefore take into consideration the intended meaning of the program. Our previous discussion of proving correctness and completeness similarly was with respect to an intended meaning of a program.

We recall the definitions from Chapter 1. An *intended meaning* of a program P, is a set of ground goals. We use intended meanings to denote the set of goals intended by the programmer for his program to compute. A program P is *correct*

natural_number(X)   X=s(X1)
natural_number(X1)   X1=s(X2)
natural_number(X2)   X2=s(X3)

⋮

Figure 5.1: A nonterminating computation

with respect to an intended meaning M if $M(P)$ is contained in M. A program
P is *complete* with respect to an intended meaning if M is contained in $M(P)$. A
program is thus correct and complete with respect to an intended meaning if the
two meanings coincide exactly.

Another important aspect of a logic program is whether it terminates. A
domain is a set of goals, not necessarily ground, closed under the instance relation.
That is, if A is in D and A' is an instance of A, then A' is in D as well.

A *termination domain* of a program P is a domain D such that every computation of P on every goal in D terminates.

Usually, a useful program should have a termination domain that includes
its intended meaning. However, since the computation model of logic programs is
liberal in the order in which goals in the resolvent can be reduced, most interesting
logic programs will not have interesting termination domains. This situation will
improve when we switch to Prolog. The restrictive model of Prolog allows the
programmer to compose nontrivial programs that terminate over useful domains.

Consider Program 3.1 defining the natural numbers. This program is terminating over its Herbrand base. However the program is nonterminating over the
domain $\{natural\_number(X)\}$. This is caused by the possibility of the nonterminating computation depicted in the trace in Figure 5.1.

For any logic program, it is useful to find domains over which they are terminating. This is usually difficult for recursive logic programs. We need to describe
recursive data types in a way which allows us to discuss termination.

Recall that a type, introduced in Chapter 3, is a set of terms. A type is
complete if the set is closed under the instance relation. With every complete
type T we can associate an *incomplete type* IT, which is the set of terms which
have instances in T and instances not in T.

We illustrate the use of these definitions to find termination domains for the
recursive programs using recursive data types in Chapter 3. Specific instances of
the definitions of complete and incomplete types are given for natural numbers
and lists. A (complete) natural number is either the constant 0, or a term of the
form $s^n(0)$. An incomplete natural number is either a variable, X, or a term of

the form $s^n(X)$ where X is a variable. Program 3.2 for $\leq$ is terminating for the domain consisting of goals where the first and/or second argument is a complete natural number.

A list is *complete* if every instance satisfies Program 3.11. A list is *incomplete* if there are instances which satisfy Program 3.11 and instances which do not. For example, the list $[a,b,c]$ is complete (proved in Figure 3.3), while the variable X is incomplete. Two more interesting examples: $[a,X,c]$ is a complete list, although not ground, whereas $[a,b|Xs]$ is incomplete.

A termination domain for *append* is the set of goals where the first and/or the third argument is a complete list. We discuss domains for other list processing programs in Section 7.2 on termination of Prolog programs.

Exercises for Section 5.2

(i)   Give a domain over which Program 3.3 for *plus* is terminating.

(ii) Particularize the definitions of completeness and incompleteness for binary trees.

5.3   Complexity

We have analyzed informally the complexity of several logic programs, for example, $\leq$ and *plus* (Programs 3.1 and 3.2) in the section on arithmetic, and *append* and the two versions of *reverse* in the section on lists (Programs 3.15, 3.16a, and 3.16b). In this section we briefly describe more formal complexity measures.

The multiple uses of logic programs slightly changes the nature of complexity measures. Instead of looking at a particular use and specifying complexity in terms of the sizes of the inputs, we look at goals in the meaning and see how they were derived. A natural measure of the complexity of a logic program is the length of the proofs it generates for goals in its meaning.

We begin discussion with a new definition, the size of a goal. The *size* of a term is the number of symbols in its textual representation. Constants and variables, consisting of a single symbol, have size one. The size of a compound term is one more than the sum of the sizes of its arguments. For example, the list $[b]$ has size 3, $[a,b]$ has size 5, and the goal $append([a,b],[c,d],Xs)$ has size 12. In general, a list of n elements has size $2 \cdot n + 1$.

Λ program P is of *length complexity* $L(n)$ if for any goal G in the meaning of P of size n there is a proof of G with respect to P of length less than equal to $L(n)$.

Length complexity is related to the usual complexity measures in computer science. For sequential realizations of the computation model, it corresponds to time complexity. Program 3.15 for *append* has linear length complexity. This is demonstrated in exercise (i) at the end of the section.

The applicability of this measure to Prolog programs, as opposed to logic programs, depends on using a unification algorithm without an occurs check. Consider the runtime of the straightforward program for appending two lists. Appending two lists, as shown in Figure 4.3, involves several unifications of *append* goals with the head of the *append* rule $append([X|Xs], Ys, [X|Zs])$. At least three unifications, matching variables against (possibly incomplete) lists, will be necessary. If the occurs check must be performed for each, the argument lists must be searched. This is directly proportional to the size of the input goal. However if the occurs check is omitted, the unification time will be bounded by a constant. The overall complexity of *append* becomes quadratic in the size of the input lists with the occurs check, but only linear without it.

We introduce other useful measures related to proofs. Let R be a proof. We define the *depth* of R to be the deepest invocation of a goal in the associated reduction. The *goal-size* of R is the maximum size of any goal reduced.

A logic program P is of *goal-size complexity* $G(n)$ if for any goal A in the meaning of P of size n, there is a proof of A with respect to P of goal size less than or equal to $G(n)$.

A logic program P is of *depth-complexity* $D(n)$ if for any goal A in the meaning of P of size n, there is a proof of G with respect to P of depth $\leq D(n)$.

Goal-size complexity relates to space. Depth-complexity relates to space of what needs to be remembered for sequential realizations, and to space and time complexity for parallel realizations.

Exercises for Section 5.3

(i) Show that the size of a goal in the meaning of *append* joining a list of length n to one of length m to give a list of length $n+m$ is $4\cdot n + 4\cdot m + 7$. Show that a proof tree has $m+2$ nodes. Hence show that *append* has linear complexity. Would the complexity be altered if the type condition were added?

(ii) Show that Program 3.3 for *plus* has linear complexity.

(iii) Discuss the complexity of other logic programs.

5.4   Search trees

Computations of logic programs given so far resolve the issue of nondeterminism by always making the correct choice. For example, the complexity measures, based on proof trees, assume that the correct clause can be chosen from the program to effect the reduction. Another way of computationally modeling nondeterminism is by developing all possible reductions in parallel. In this section we discuss search trees, a formalism for considering all possible computation paths.

A *search tree* of a goal G with respect to a program P is defined as follows. The root of the tree is G. Nodes of the tree are (possibly conjunctive) goals with one goal selected. There is an edge leading from a node N for each clause in the program whose head unifies with the selected goal. Each branch in the tree from the root is a computation of G by P. Leaves of the tree are *success nodes* where the empty goal has been reached or *failure nodes* where the selected goal at the node cannot be further reduced. Success nodes correspond to solutions of the root of the tree.

There are in general many search trees for a given goal with respect to a program. Figure 5.2 shows two search trees for the query *son(S,haran)?* with respect to Program 1.2. The two possibilities correspond to the two choices of goal to reduce from the resolvent *father(haran,S),male(S)*. The trees are quite distinct, but both have a single success branch corresponding to the solution of the query *S=lot*. The respective success branches are given as traces in Figure 4.4.

We adopt some conventions when drawing search trees. The leftmost goal of a node is always the selected one. This implies that the goals in derived goals may be permuted so that the new goal to be selected for reduction is the first goal. The edges are labeled with substitutions that are applied to the variables in the leftmost goal. These substitutions are computed as part of the unification algorithm.

Search trees correspond closely to traces for deterministic computations. The traces for the *append* query and *hanoi* query given, respectively, in Figures 4.3 and 4.5 can be easily made into search trees. This is exercise (i) at the end of the section.

Search trees contain multiple success nodes if the query has multiple solu-

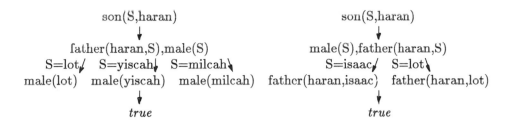

Figure 5.2: Two search trees

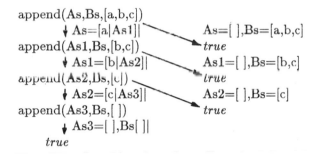

Figure 5.3: Search tree with multiple success nodes

tions. Figure 5.3 contains the search tree for the query *append(As,Bs,[a,b,c])* with respect to Program 3.15 for *append*, asking to split the list [a,b,c] into two. The solutions for *As* and *Bs* are found by collecting the labels of the edges in the branch leading to the success node. For example, in the figure, following the leftmost branch gives the solution {*As=[a,b,c],Bs=[ ]*}.

The number of success nodes is the same for any search tree of a given goal with respect to a program.

Search trees can have infinite branches, which correspond to nonterminating computations. Consider the goal *append(Xs,[c,d],Ys)* with respect to the standard program for *append*. The search tree is given in Figure 5.4. The infinite branch is the nonterminating computation given in Figure 4.6.

Complexity measures can also be defined in terms of search trees. Prolog programs perform a depth-first traversal of the search tree. Therefore measures based on the size of the search tree will be a more realistic measure of the complexity of Prolog programs rather than those based on the complexity of the proof tree. However, the complexity of the search tree is much harder to analyze.

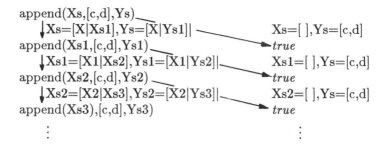

Figure 5.4: Search tree with an infinite branch

There is a deeper point lurking. The relationship between search trees and proof trees is the relationship between deterministic computations and nondeterministic computations. Whether the complexity classes defined via proof trees are equivalent to complexity classes defined via search trees is a reformulation of the classic P=NP question in terms of logic programming.

Exercises for Section 5.3

(i)   Transform the traces of Figure 4.3 and 4.5 into search trees.

(ii) Draw a search tree for the query $sort([2,4,1,5,3],Xs)$ using permutation sort.

5.5   Negation in logic programming

Logic programs are collections of rules and facts describing what is true. Untrue facts are not expressed explicitly; they are omitted. In this section we describe an extension to the logic programming computation model that allows a limited use of negative information in programs.

We define a relation *not G*, and describe its meaning. It is only a partial form of negation from first-order logic. The relation *not* uses the *negation as failure* rule. A goal *not G* will be assumed to be a consequence of a program *P* if *G* is not a consequence of *P*.

We characterize negation by failure in terms of search trees. A search tree of a goal *G* with respect to a program *P* is *finitely failed* if it has no success nodes nor infinite branches. The *finite failure set* of a logic program *P* is the set of goals *G* such that *G* has a finitely failed search tree with respect to *P*.

A goal *not G* is implied by a program *P* by the negation as failure rule if *G*

unmarried_student(X) ← not married(X), student(X).
student(bill).
married(joe).

Program 5.1: A simple program using *not*

is in the finite failure set of *P*.

Let us see a simple example. Consider the program comprised of two facts:

likes(abraham,pomegranates).
likes(isaac,pomegranates).

The goal *not likes(sarah,pomegranates)* follows from the program by negation as failure. The search tree for the goal *likes(sarah,pomegranates)* has a single failure node.

Using negation as failure allows easy definition of many relations. For example, a declarative definition of the relation *disjoint(Xs, Ys)* that two lists, *Xs* and *Ys*, have no elements in common is possible as follows.

disjoint(Xs,Ys) ← not (member(X,Xs), member(X,Ys)).

This reads: *Xs* is disjoint from *Ys* if there is no element *X* which is a member of both *Xs* and *Ys*.

Program 5.1 is another example of a program using negation. It defines a relation *unmarried_student(Person)* indicating that *Person* is an unmarried student. The query *unmarried_student(X)* has the solution *X=bill*.

It is difficult to implement negation as failure both efficiently and correctly. Most Prolog implementations use a version which is correct for simple cases, but leads to logically incorrect conclusions in other circumstances. We will discuss the problems with the Prolog version of Program 5.1 in Section 11.2.

5.6   Background

The classic paper on the semantics of logic programs is of van Emden and Kowalski (1976). Important extensions were given by Apt and van Emden (1981). In particular, they showed that the choice of goal to reduce from the resolvent is arbitrary by showing that the number of success nodes is an invariant for the search trees.

In Shapiro (1984) complexity measures for logic programs are compared with the complexity of computations of alternating Turing machines. It is shown that goal-size is linearly related to alternating space, the product of length and goal-size is linearly related to alternating tree-size, and the product of depth and goal-size is linearly related to alternating time.

The classic name for search trees in the literature is SLD trees. The name SLD was coined by research in automatic theorem proving which preceded the birth of logic programming. SLD resolution is a particular refinement of the resolution principle introduced in Robinson (1965). Computations of logic programs can be interpreted as a series of resolution steps, and in fact SLD resolution steps, and are still commonly described thus in the literature. The acronym SLD stands for Selecting a literal, using a Linear strategy, and searching the space of possible deductions Depth-first.

The first proof of the correctness and completeness of SLD resolution, albeit under the name LUSH-resolution, was given by Hill (1974).

The subject of negation has received a large amount of attention and interest since the inception of logic programming. The fundamental work on the semantics of negation-as-failure is by Clark (1978). Calrk's results were extended by Jaffar et al. (1983) who proved the soundness and completeness of the rule.

The concept of negation as failure is a restricted version of the closed world assumption as discussed in the database world. For more information see Reiter (1978). The exact relationship between different formulations of negation is discussed in Lloyd (1984), which also covers many of the issues raised in this chapter.

Part II
The Prolog Language

In order to implement a practical programming language based on the computational model of logic programming, three issues need attention. The first concerns resolving the choices remaining in the abstract interpreter for logic programs, defined in Chaper 4. The second concerns enhancing the expressiveness of the pure computational model of logic programs by adding meta-logical and extra-logical facilities. Finally, access to some of the capabilities of the underlying computer, such as fast arithmetic and input/output, must be provided. This part discusses how Prolog, the most developed language based on logic programming, handles each of these issues.

Chapter 6
Pure Prolog

A pure Prolog program is a logic program, in which an order is defined for both clauses in the program and goals in the body of the clause. The abstract interpreter for logic programs is specialized to take advantage of this ordering information. This chapter discusses the execution model of Prolog programs as opposed to logic programs, and compares it to more conventional languages.

The relationship between logic programming and Prolog is reminiscent of the relationship between the lambda-calculus and Lisp. Both are concrete realizations of abstract computation models. Logic programs that execute with Prolog's execution mechanism are referred to as *pure Prolog*. Pure Prolog is an approximate realization of the logic programming computation model on a sequential machine. It is certainly not the only possible such realization. However, it is the one with the best practical choices, which balance preserving the properties of the abstract model with catering for efficient implementation.

6.1   The execution model of Prolog

Two major decisions have to be taken to convert the abstract interpreter for logic programs into a form suitable for a concrete programming language. First, the arbitrary choice of which goal in the resolvent to reduce, namely, the scheduling policy, must be specified. Second, the nondeterministic choice of the clause from the program to effect the reduction must be implemented.

Several logic programming languages exist, reflecting different choices. Loosely there are two categories. Prolog and its extensions (Prolog-II, IC-Prolog and MU-Prolog, for example) are based on sequential execution. Other languages, such as PARLOG, Concurrent Prolog and GHC, are based on parallel execution.

The treatment of nondeterminism distinguishes between sequential and parallel languages. The distinction between Prolog and its extensions is in the choice of goal to reduce.

Prolog's execution mechanism is obtained from the abstract interpreter by choosing the leftmost goal instead of an arbitrary one, and replacing the nondeterministic choice of a clause by sequential search for a unifiable clause and backtracking.

In other words, Prolog adopts a stack scheduling policy. It maintains the resolvent as a stack: pops the top goal for reduction, and pushes the derived goals on the resolvent stack.

In addition to the stack policy, Prolog simulates the nondeterministic choice of reducing clause by sequential search and backtracking. When attempting to reduce a goal, the first clause whose head unifies with the goal is chosen. If no unifiable clause is found for the popped goal, the computation is unwound to the last choice mode, and the next unifiable clause is chosen.

A *computation* of a goal G with respect to a Prolog program P is the generation of *all* solutions of G with respect to P. In terms of logic programming concepts, a Prolog computation on a goal G is a complete depth first traversal of the particular search tree of G obtained by always choosing the leftmost goal.

Many different Prolog implementations exist. They differ in syntax, small procedural matters, and the programming facilities. Here we largely follow the conventions of Edinburgh Prolog. All our programs run in a particular implementation, Wisdom Prolog. The syntax is what we have been using for logic programs previously. Indeed many of the logic programs behave correctly as written.

A *trace* of a Prolog computation is an extension of the trace of a computation of a logic program under the abstract interpreter as described in Section 4.2. We revise the computations of Chapters 4 and 5 indicating the similarities and differences. Consider the query $son(X,haran)$? with respect to Program 1.2, the simplified Biblical database, repeated at the top of Figure 6.1. The computation is given in the bulk of Figure 6.1. It corresponds to a depth-first traversal of the first of the search trees in Figure 5.2. It is an extension of the first trace in Figure 4.4, since the whole search tree is searched.

The notation previously used for traces must be extended to handle failure and backtracking. An f after a goal denotes that a goal failed, that is there was no clause in the program whose head unified with the goal. The next goal after a failed goal is where the computation proceeds on backtracking. It already appears as a previous goal in the trace at the same depth of indentation, and can be identified by the variable names. We adopt the Edinburgh Prolog convention

```
father(abraham,isaac).        male(isaac).
father(haran,lot).            male(lot).
father(haran,milcah).         female(yiscah).
father(haran,yiscah).         female(milcah).


son(X,Y) ← father(Y,X), male(X).
daughter(X,Y) ← father(Y,X), female(X).

son(X,haran)?
father(haran,X)                              X=lot
    male(lot)
            true
        Output: X=lot
            ;
father(haran,X)                              X=milcah
    male(milcah)          f
father(haran,X)                              X=yiscah
    male(yiscah)          f
        No (more) choice points
```

Figure 6.1: Tracing a simple Prolog computation

that a ';' typed after a solution denotes a continuation of the computation to search for more solutions. Unifications are indicated as previously.

Trace facilities provided by particular Prolog implementations vary from our description. For example, some Prolog implementations always give all solutions, while others wait for a user response after each solution.

The trace of *append([a,b],[c,d],Ls)?* giving the answer *Ls=[a,b,c,d]* is precisely the trace given in Figure 4.3. Figure 4.5 giving the trace for solving the Towers of Hanoi with 3 discs is also a trace of the *hanoi* program considered as a Prolog program solving the query *hanoi(s(s(s(0)))a,b,c,Moves)?*. The trace of a deterministic computation is the same when considered as a logic program or a Prolog program, provided the order of goals is preserved.

The next example is answering the query *append(Xs,Ys,[a,b,c])?* with respect to Program 3.15 for *append*. There are several solutions of the query. The search tree for this goal was given as Figure 5.3. Figure 6.2 gives the Prolog trace.

Tracing computations is a good way to gain understanding of the execution model of Prolog. We give a slightly larger example, sorting a list with the quick-

append([X|Xs],Ys,[X|Zs]) ← append(Xs,Ys,Zs).
append([ ],Ys,Ys).

append(Xs,Ys,[a,b,c])   Xs=[a|Xs1]
   append(Xs1,Ys,[b,c])   Xs1=[b|Xs2]
      append(Xs2,Ys,[c])   Xs2=[c|Xs3]
         append(Xs3,Ys,[ ])   Xs3=[ ],Ys=[ ]
            true
         Output: (Xs=[a,b,c],Ys=[ ])
            ;
      append(Xs2,Ys,[c])   Xs2=[ ],Ys=[c]
        true
      Output: (Xs=[a,b],Ys=[c])
         ;
   append(Xs1,Ys,[b,c])   Xs1=[ ],Ys=[b,c]
     true
   Output: (Xs=[a],Ys=[b,c])
      ;
append(Xs,Ys,[a,b,c])   Xs=[ ],Ys=[a,b,c]
   true
Output: (Xs=[ ],Ys=[a,b,c])
    ;
      no (more) solutions

Figure 6.2: Multiple solutions for splitting a list

sort program (Program 3.22 reproduced here). Computations using *quicksort* are essentially deterministic, and show algorithmic behavior of a Prolog program. Figure 6.3 gives a trace of the query *quicksort([2,1,3],Xs)?*. Arithmetic comparisons are assumed to be unit operations, and the standard program for *append* is used.

We introduce a distinction between *shallow* and *deep* backtracking. Shallow backtracking occurs when the unification of a goal and a clause fails, and an alternative clause is tried. Deep backtracking occurs when the unification of the last clause of a procedure with a goal fails, and control returns to another goal in the computation tree.

It is sometimes convenient to include, for the purpose of this definition, test predicates that occur first in the body of the clause as part of unification, and to classify the backtracking that occurs as a result of their failure as shallow.

quicksort([X|Xs],Ys) ←
    partition(Xs,X,Littles,Bigs),
    quicksort(Littles,Ls),
    quicksort(Bigs,Bs),
    append(Ls,[X|Bs],Ys).
quicksort([ ],[ ]).
    partition([X|Xs],Y,[X|Ls],Bs) ←
        X ≠ Y, partition(Xs,Y,Ls,Bs).
    partition([X|Xs],Y,Ls,[X|Bs]) ←
        X > Y, partition(Xs,Y,Ls,Bs).
    partition([ ],Y,[ ],[ ]).

quicksort([2,1,3],Qs)
    partition([1,3],2,Ls,Bs)
        1 ≥ 2   Ls=[1|Ls1]
        partition([3],2,Ls1,Bs)
            3 ≥ 2   f   Ls1=[3|Ls2]
        partition([3],2,Ls1,Bs)
            3 > 2   Bs=[3|Bs1]
            partition([ ],2,Ls1,Bs1)   Ls1=[ ]=Bs1
    quicksort([1],Qs1)
        partition([ ],1,Ls2,Bs2)   Ls2=[ ]=Bs2
        quicksort([ ],Qs2)   Qs2=[ ]
        quicksort([ ],Qs3)   Qs3=[ ]
        append([ ],[1],Qs1)   Qs1=[1]
    quicksort([3],Qs4)
        partition([ ],3,Ls3,Bs3)   Ls3=[ ]=Bs3
        quicksort([ ],Qs5)   Qs5=[ ]
        quicksort([ ],Qs6)   Qs6=[ ]
        append([ ],[3],Qs4)   Qs4=[3]
    append([1],[2,3],Qs)   Qs=[1|Ys]
        append([ ],[2,3],Ys)   Ys=[2,3]
                true
        Output: (Qs=[1,2,3])

Figure 6.3: Tracing a *quicksort* computation

An example is Figure 6.3 and the choice of a new clause for the goal *partition([3],2,Ls1,Bs)*.

Exercises for Section 6.1

(i)   Trace the execution of *daughter(X,haran)* with respect to Program 1.2.

(ii) Trace the execution of *sort([3,1,2],Xs)?* with respect to Program 3.21.

(iii) Trace the execution of *sort([3,1,2],Xs)?* with respect to Program 3.20.

6.2   Comparison to conventional programming languages

A programming language is characterized by its control and data manipulation mechanisms. Prolog, as a general purpose programming language, can be discussed in these terms, as are conventional languages. In this section we compare the control flow and data manipulation of Prolog to that of Algol-like languages.

The control in Prolog programs is like in conventional procedural languages, as long as the computation progresses forward. Goal invocation corresponds to procedure invocation, and the ordering of goals in the body of clauses corresponds to sequencing of statements. Specifically, the clause $A \leftarrow B_1,\ldots,B_n$ can be viewed as a definition of a procedure A as follows:

          procedure A
              call B$_1$,
              call B$_2$,
              $\vdots$
              call B$_n$,
          end.

The recursive goal invocation in Prolog is similar in its behavior and its implementation to that of conventional recursive languages. The differences show when backtracking occurs. In a conventional language, if a computation cannot proceed (e.g., all branches of a case statement are false), a runtime error occurs. In Prolog the computation is simply undone to the last choice made, and a different computation path is attempted.

The data structures manipulated by logic programs, terms, correspond to general record structures in conventional programming languages. The handling of data structures is very flexible in Prolog. Like LISP, Prolog is a declaration free, typeless language.

Other differences in the use of data structures in Prolog arise from the nature

of logical variables. Logical variables refer to individuals rather than memory locations. Consequently, having specified a particular individual, the variable cannot
be made to refer to another individual. In other words, logic programming does
not support destructive assignment where the contents of an initialized variable
can change.

Data manipulation in logic programs is achieved entirely via the unification
algorithm. Unification subsumes

- single assignment
- parameter passing
- record allocation
- read/write-once field-access in records

We discuss the trace of the quicksort program in Figure 6.3 pointing out the
various uses of unification. The unification of the initial goal $quicksort([2,1,3],Qs)$
with the head of the procedure definition $quicksort([X|Xs],Ys)$ illustrates several
features. The unification of $[2,1,3]$ with the term $[X|Xs]$ achieves record access to
the list, and also selection of its two fields, the head and tail.

The unification of $[1,3]$ with Xs achieves parameter passing to the *partition*
procedure, due to the sharing of the variables. This gives the first argument of
partition. Similarly, the unification of 2 with X passes the value of the second
parameter to *partition*.

Record creation can be seen with the unification of the goal *parti-
tion*$([1,3],2,Ls,Bs)$ with the head of the partition procedure $partition([X|Ys],Z,$
$[X|Ls1],Bs1)$. As a result Ls is instantiated to $[1|Ls1]$. Specifically, Ls is made
into a list and its head is assigned the value 1, namely record creation and field
assignment via unification.

These analogies may provide hints on how to implement Prolog efficiently
on a von Neumann machine. Indeed, the basic idea of compilation of Prolog
is to translate special cases of unification to conventional memory manipulation
operations, as specified above.

Conventional languages typically incorporate error-handling or exception-
handling mechanisms of various degrees of sophistication. Pure Prolog does not
have an error or exception mechanism built into its definition. The pure Prolog
counterparts of conventional programs which cause an error, e.g., a missing case
in a case statement, or dividing by zero, cause failure in pure Prolog.

Full Prolog, introduced in the following chapters, includes system predicates,
such as arithmetic and I/O, which may cause errors. Current Prolog implementations do not have sophisticated error handling mechanism. Typically, on an error
condition a system predicate prints an error message and either fails or aborts

the computation.

This brief discussion of the different way of manipulating data does not help with the more interesting question: How does programming in Prolog compare with programming in conventional programming languages? That is an implicit topic in the rest of this book.

6.3   Background

The origins of Prolog are shrouded in mystery. All that is known is that the two founders Robert Kowalski, then at Edinburgh, and Alain Colmerauer at Marseille worked on similar ideas during the early 70's, and even worked together during one summer. The results were the formulation of the logic programming philosophy and computation model by Robert Kowalski (1974), and the design and implementation of the first logic programming language, Prolog, by Alain Colmerauer and his colleagues (1973).

A major force behind the realization that logic can be the basis of a practical programming language has been the development of efficient implementation techniques, as pioneered by Warren (1977). Warren's compiler identified special cases of unification and translated them into efficient sequences of conventional memory operations.

Variations of Prolog with extra control features, such as IC-Prolog (Clark and McCabe, 1979), have been developed, but have proved too costly in runtime overhead to be seriously considered as alternatives to Prolog. We will refer to particular interesting variations that have been proposed in the appropriate sections.

Another breed of logic programming languages, which indirectly emerged from IC-Prolog, was concurrent logic languages. The first was the Relational Language (Clark and Gregory, 1981), followed by Concurrent Prolog (Shapiro, 1983b), Parlog (Clark and Gregory, 1984), GHC (Ueda, 1985), and a few other proposals.

References for the variations mentioned in the text are: for Prolog-II (Van Caneghem, 1982), IC-Prolog (Clark et al., 1982) and MU-Prolog (Naish, 1985a).

The syntax of Prolog stems from the clausal form of logic due to Kowalski (1974). The original Marseille interpreter used the terminology of positive and negative literals from resolution theory. The clause $A \leftarrow B_1,...,B_n$ was written $+A-B_1...-B_n$.

Warren et al. adapted Marseille Prolog for the DEC-10, and their decisions have been very influential. Many systems adopted most of the conventions of Prolog-10 (Warren et al., 1979), which has become known more generically as Edinburgh Prolog. Its essential features are described in the widespread primer on Prolog (Clocksin and Mellish, 1984). This book draws mainly on Edinburgh Prolog as described in its manual (Bowen et al., 1981).

A recent paper by Cohen (1986) delves further on the relation between Prolog and conventional languages.

Chapter 7

Programming in Pure Prolog

A major aim of logic programming is to enable the programmer to program at a higher level. Ideally one should write axioms that define the desired relationships, maintaining ignorance of the way they are going to be used by the execution mechanism. Current logic programming languages, Prolog in particular, are still far away from allowing this ideal of declarative programming. The specific, well-defined choices of how their execution mechanisms approximate the abstract interpreter cannot be ignored. Effective logic programming requires knowing and utilizing these choices.

This chapter discusses the consequences of Prolog's execution model for the logic programmer. New aspects of the programming task are introduced. Not only must the programmer come up with a correct and complete axiomatization of a relationship, he must also consider its execution according to the model.

7.1 Rule order

Two syntactic issues, irrelevant for logic programs, are important to consider when composing Prolog programs. The *rule order*, or *clause order*, of clauses in each procedure must be decided. Also the *goal order* of goals in the bodies of each clause must be determined. The consequences of these decisions can be immense. There can be orders of magnitude of difference in efficiency in the performance of Prolog programs. In extreme, though quite common, cases correct logic programs will fail to give solutions due to nontermination.

The rule order determines the order in which solutions are found.

```
parent(terach,abraham).      parent(abraham,isaac).
parent(isaac,jacob).         parent(jacob,benjamin).

ancestor(X,Y) ← parent(X,Y).
ancestor(X,Z) ← parent(X,Y), ancestor(Y,Z).
```

Program 7.1: Yet another family example

Changing the order of rules in a procedure permutes the branches in any search tree for a goal using that procedure. The search tree is traversed depth-first. So permuting the branches causes a different order of traversal of the search tree, and a different order of finding solutions. The effect is clearly seen when using facts to answer an existential query. With our Biblical database and a query such as *father(X,Y)?* changing the order of facts will change the order of solutions found by Prolog. Deciding how to order facts is not very important.

The order of solutions of queries solved by recursive programs is also determined by the clause order. Consider a simple Biblical database together with a program for the relationship *ancestor*, given as Program 7.1.

For the query *ancestor(terach,X)?* with respect to Program 7.1, the solutions will be given in the order, *X=abraham, X=isaac, X=jacob* and *X=benjamin*. If the order of the two rules defining *ancestor* is swapped, the solutions will appear in a different order: namely *X=benjamin, X=jacob, X=isaac* and *X=abraham*.

The different order of *ancestor* clauses changes the order of searching the implicit family tree. In one order, Prolog outputs solutions as it goes along. With the order of the rules swapped, Prolog travels to the end of the family tree and gives solutions on the way back. The desired order of solutions is determined by the application, and the rule order of *ancestor* chosen accordingly.

Changing the order of clauses for the *member* predicate (Program 3.12) also changes the order of search. As written, the program searches the list until the desired element is found. If the order of the clauses is reversed, the program always searches to the end of the list. The order of solutions will also be affected, for example, responding to the query *member(X,[1,2,3])?*. In the standard order, the order of solutions is intuitive; *X=1, X=2, X=3*. With the rules swapped, the order is *X=3, X=2, X=1*. The order of Program 3.12 is more intuitive, and hence preferable.

When the search tree for a given goal has an infinite branch, the order of clauses can determine if any solutions are given at all. Consider the query *append(Xs,[c,d],Zs)?* with respect to *append*. As can be seen from the search tree in Figure 5.4, no solutions would be given. If, however, the *append* fact appeared before the *append* rule, an infinite number of pairs *Xs,Zs* satisfying the query would be given.

There is no consensus as to how to order the clauses of a Prolog procedure. Clearly, the standard dictated in more conventional languages, of testing for the termination condition before proceeding with the iteration or recursion is not mandatory in Prolog. This is demonstrated in Program 3.15 for *append*, as well as in other programs in the book. The reason is that the recursive or iterative clause tests its applicability by unification. This test is done explicitly and independently of the other clauses in the procedure.

Clause order is more important for general Prolog programs, in contrast to pure Prolog programs. Other control features, notably the cut to be discussed in Chapter 11, depend significantly on the clause order. When such constructs are used, clauses lose their independence and modularity, and clause order becomes significant.

In the book we follow the convention that the recursive clauses precede the base clauses.

Exercises for Section 7.1

(i)   Verify the order of solutions for the query *ancestor(abraham,X)* with respect to Program 7.1, and its variant with different rule order for *ancestor*, claimed in the text.

(ii) What is the order of solutions for the query *ancestor(X,benjamin)* with respect to Program 7.1? What if the rule order for *ancestor* is swapped?

7.2   Termination

Prolog's depth-first traversal of search trees has a serious problem. If the search tree of a goal with respect to a program contains an infinite branch, the computation will not terminate. Prolog may fail to find a solution to a goal, even though the goal has a finite computation.

Nontermination arises with recursive rules. Consider adding a relationship *married(Male,Female)* to our database of family relationships. A sample fact from the Biblical situation is *married(abraham,sarah)*. A user querying the *married* relationship should not care whether males or females are first, as the relationship is commutative. The "obvious" way of overcoming the commutativity is adding a recursive rule *married(X,Y) ← married(Y,X)*. If this is added to the program

married(X,Y) ← married(Y,X).
married(abraham,sarah).

married(abraham,sarah)
    married(sarah,abraham)
        married(abraham,sarah)
            married(sarah,abraham)

. . .

Figure 7.1: A nonterminating computation

no computation involving *married* would ever terminate. For example, the trace of the goal *married(abraham,sarah)?* is given in Figure 7.1.

Recursive rules which have the recursive goal as the first goal in the body are known as *left recursive* rules. The problematic *married* axiom is an example. Left recursive rules are inherently troublesome in Prolog. They cause nonterminating computations if called with inappropriate arguments.

The best solution to the problem of left recursion is avoidance. The *married* relationship used a left recursive rule to express commutativity. Commutative relationships are best handled differently, by defining a new predicate that has a clause for each permutation of the arguments of the relationship. For the relationship *married*, a new predicate, *are_married(Person1,Person2)* say, would be defined using two rules:

are_married(X,Y) ← married(X,Y).
are_married(X,Y) ← married(Y,X).

Unfortunately, it is not generally possible to remove all occurrences of left recursion. All the elegant minimal recursive logic programs shown in Chapter 3 are left recursive, and can cause nontermination. However, the appropriate analysis, using the concepts of domains and complete structures introduced in Section 5.2, can determine which queries will terminate with respect to recursive programs.

Let us consider an example, Program 3.15 for appending two lists. The program for *append* is everywhere terminating for the set of goals whose first and/or last argument is a complete list. Any *append* query whose first argument is a complete list will terminate. Similarly all queries where the third argument is a complete list will terminate. The program will also terminate if the first and/or third argument is a ground term that is not a list. The behavior of *append* is best summed up by considering the queries that do not terminate, namely when both the first and third arguments are incomplete lists.

The condition for when a query to Program 3.12 for *member* terminates is also stated in terms of incomplete lists. A query does not terminate if the second argument is an incomplete list. If the second argument of a query to *member* is a complete list the query terminates.

Another guaranteed means of generating nonterminating computations, easy to overlook, is circular definitions. Consider the pair of rules

parent(X,Y) ← child(Y,X).
child(X,Y) ← parent(Y,X).

Any computation involving *parent* or *child*, for example, *parent(haran,lot)?*, will not terminate. The search tree necessarily contains an infinite branch, due to the circularity.

Exercises for Section 7.2

(i)   Discuss the termination behavior of both programs in Program 3.13 determining prefixes and suffixes of lists.

(ii) Discuss the termination of Program 3.14c for *sublist*.

7.3   Goal order

Goal order is more significant than clause order. It is the principal means of specifying sequential flow of control in Prolog programs. The programs for sorting lists, e.g., Program 3.22 for *quicksort*, exploit goal order to indicate the sequence of steps in the sorting algorithms.

We first discuss goal order from the perspective of database programming. The order of goals can affect the order of solutions. Consider the query *daughter(X,haran)?* with respect to a variant of Program 1.2, where the order of the facts *female(milcah)* and *female(yiscah)* is interchanged. The two solutions are given in the order *X=milcah, X=yiscah*. If the goal order of the *daughter* rule were changed to be *daughter(X,Y) ← female(X), father(Y,X)* the order of the solutions to the query, given the same database, would be *X=yiscah, X=milcah*.

The reason why the order of goals in the body of a clause affects the order of solutions to a query is different from why the order of rules in a procedure affects the solution order. Changing rule order does not change the search tree that must be traversed for a given query. The tree is just traversed in a different order. Changing goal order changes the search tree.

Goal order determines the search tree.

Goal order affects the amount of searching the program does in solving a query by determining which search tree is traversed. Consider the two search trees for the query *son(X,haran)?* given in Figure 5.2. They represent two different ways of finding a solution. In the first case, solutions are found by searching for children of *haran* and checking if they are male. The second case corresponds to the rule for *son* being written with the order of the goals in its body swapped, namely as *son(X,Y) ← male(X), parent(Y,X)*. Now the query is solved by searching through all the males in the program and checking if they are children of *haran*. If there were many *male* facts in the program, more search would be involved. For other queries, for example, *son(sarah,X)?* , the reverse order has advantages. Since *sarah* is not male, the query would fail more quickly.

The optimal goal order of Prolog programs varies with different uses. Consider the definition of *grandparent*. There are two possible rules.

grandparent(X,Z) ← parent(X,Y), parent(Y,Z).
grandparent(X,Z) ← parent(Y,Z), parent(X,Y).

If you wish to find someone's grandson with the grandfather relationship with a query such as *grandparent(abraham,X)?*, the first of the rules searches more directly. If looking for someone's grandparent with a query such as *grandparent(X,isaac)?*, the second rule finds the solution more directly. If efficiency is important, then it is advised to have two distinct relationships, grandparent and grandchild, to be used appropriately with the user's discretion.

In contrast to rule order, goal order can determine whether computations terminate. Consider the recursive rule for *ancestor*:

ancestor(X,Y) ← parent(X,Z), ancestor(Z,Y).

If the goals in the body are swapped, the *ancestor* program becomes left recursive, and all Prolog computations with *ancestor* are nonterminating.

The goal order is also important in the recursive clause of the quicksort algorithm in Program 3.22.

sort([X|Xs],Ys) ←
    partition(Xs,X,Ls,Bs),
    sort(Ls,Ls1),
    sort(Bs,Bs1),
    append(Ls1,[X|Bs1],Ys).

The list should be partitioned into its two smaller pieces before recursively sorting the pieces. If, for example, the order of the *partition* goal and recursive sorting goal is swapped, no computations terminate.

We next consider Program 3.16 for reversing a list:

reverse([X|Xs],Zs) ← reverse(Xs,Ys), append(Ys,[X],Zs).
reverse([ ],[ ]).

The goal order is significant. As written, the program terminates with goals where the first argument is a complete list. Goals where the first argument is an incomplete list give nonterminating computations. If the order of the goals in the recursive rule is swapped, the determining factor of the termination of goals is the second argument. Calls to *reverse* with the second argument a complete list terminate. They do not terminate if the second argument is an incomplete list.

A subtler example comes from the definition of the predicate *sublist* in terms of two *append* goals, specifying the sublist as a suffix of a prefix, as given in Program 3.14e. Consider the query *sublist([2,3],[1,2,3,4])?* with respect to the program. The query is reduced to *append(AXs,Bs,[1,2,3,4]),append(As,[2,3],AXs)?*. This has a finite search tree, and the initial query succeeds. If Program 3.15e had its goals reversed, the initial query would be reduced to *append(As,[2,3],AXs),append(AXs,Bs,[1,2,3,4])?* This leads to a nonterminating computation due to the first goal, as illustrated in Figure 5.4.

A useful heuristic for goal order can be given for recursive programs with tests such as arithmetic comparisons, or determining whether two constants are different. The heuristic is to place the tests as early as possible. An example comes in the program for *partition*, which is part of Program 3.22. The first recursive rule is

partition([X|Xs],Y,[X|Ls],Bs) ← X ≤ Y, partition(Xs,Y,Ls,Bs).

The test $X \leq Y$ should go before the recursive call. This leads to a smaller search tree.

In Prolog programming (in contrast, perhaps, to life in general) our goal is fail as quickly as possible. Failing early prunes the search tree, and brings us to the right solution sooner.

Exercises for Section 7.3

(i) Consider the goal order for Program 3.14d defining a sublist of a list as a suffix of a prefix. Why is the order of the *append* goals in Program 3.14d preferable?
(Hint: Consider the query *sublist(Xs,[a,b,c])?*)

(ii) Discuss the clause order, goal order and termination behavior for *substitute*, posed as Exercise 3.3(i).

7.4   Redundant solutions

An important issue when composing Prolog programs, irrelevant for logic programs, is the irredundancy of solutions to queries. The meaning of a logic program is the set of ground goals deducible from it. No distinction was made whether a goal in the meaning could be deduced uniquely from the program, or whether it could be deduced in several distinct ways. The distinction is important for Prolog when considering the efficiency of searching for solutions. Each possible deduction means an extra branch in the search tree. The bigger the search tree, the longer a computation will take. It is desirable in general to keep the size of the search tree as small as possible.

Having redundant programs may cause, in some extreme case, exponential increase in runtime, in the event of backtracking. If a conjunction of n goals is solved, and each goal has one redundant solution, then in the event of backtracking, the conjunction may generate 2^n solutions, thus possibly changing a polynomial-time program (or even a linear one) to be exponential.

One way for redundancy to occur in Prolog programs is by covering the same case with several rules. Consider the following two clauses defining the relation *minimum*.

$$\text{minimum(X,Y,X)} \leftarrow X \leq Y.$$
$$\text{minimum(X,Y,Y)} \leftarrow Y \leq X.$$

The query *minimum(2,2,M)* with respect to these two clauses has a unique solution *M=2* which is given twice: one is redundant.

Careful specification of the cases can avoid the problem. The second clause can be changed to be

$$\text{minimum(X,Y,Y)} \leftarrow Y < X.$$

Now only the first rule covers the case when the two numbers have equal values.

Similar care is necessary with the definition of *partition* as part of Program 3.22 for *quicksort*. The programmer must ensure that only one of the recursive clauses for *partition* covers the case when the number being compared is the same as the number being used to split the list.

Another way redundancy appears in programs is by having too many special cases. Some of these can be motivated by efficiency. An extra fact can be added to Program 3.15 for *append*, namely *append(Xs,[ ],Xs)*, to save recursive computations when the second argument is an empty list. In order to remove redundancy,

$merge(Xs, Ys, Zs) \leftarrow$
    Zs is an ordered list of integers obtained from
    merging the ordered lists of integers Xs and Ys.

merge([X|Xs],[Y|Ys],[X,Zs]) $\leftarrow$
    X < Y, merge(Xs,[Y|Ys],Zs).
merge([X|Xs],[Y|Ys],[X,X|Zs]) $\leftarrow$
    X=Y, merge(Xs,Ys,Zs).
merge([X|Xs],[Y|Ys],[X,Zs]) $\leftarrow$
    X > Y, merge([X|Xs],Ys,Zs).
merge([ ],[X|Xs],[X|Xs]).
merge(Xs,[ ],Xs).

Program 7.2: Merging ordered lists

$member\ check(X, Xs) \leftarrow$
    X is a member of the list Xs.

member_check(X,[X|Xs]).
member_check(X,[Y|Ys]) $\leftarrow$ X $\neq$ Y, member(X,Ys).

Program 7.3: Checking for list membership

each of the other clauses for *append* would have to only cover lists with at least one element as their second argument.

We illustrate these points when composing Program 7.2 for the relation *merge(Xs, Ys, Zs)*, which is true if Xs and Ys are lists of integers sorted in ascending order, and Zs is the ordered list resulting from merging them.

There are three separate recursive clauses. They cover the three possible cases; when the head of the first list is less than, equal to or greater than the head of the second list. We discuss the predicates <, =, and > in Chapter 8. Two cases are needed when the elements in either list have been exhausted. Note that we have been careful that the goal *merge([ ],[ ],[ ])* is only covered by one fact, the bottom one.

Redundant computations occur when using *member* to find whether a particular element occurs in a particular list, and there are multiple occurrences of the particular element being checked for in the list. For example, the search tree for the query *member(a,[a,b,a,c])* would have two success nodes.

The redundancy of previous programs was removed by a careful consideration of the logic. In this case the *member* program is correct. If we want a different

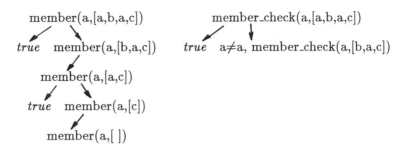

Figure 7.2: Variant search trees

behavior, the solution is indeed to compose a modified version of *member*.

Program 7.3 defines the relationship *member_check(X,Xs)* which checks whether an element *X* is a member of a list *Xs*. The program is a variant of Program 3.12 for *member* which adds a test to the recursive clause. It has the same meaning but behaves differently as a Prolog program. Figure 7.2 contains search trees for the identical query to the two programs that show the difference between them. The left tree is for the goal *member(a,[a,b,a,c])* with respect to Program 3.12. Note there are two success nodes. The right tree is for the goal *member_check(a,[a,b,a,c])* with respect to Program 7.3. It has only one success node.

We restrict use of Program 7.3 to queries where both arguments are ground. This is due to the way ≠ is implemented in Prolog, to be discussed in Section 11.3.

7.5   Recursive programming in pure Prolog

Lists are a very useful data structure for many applications written in Prolog. In this section we revise several logic programs of Sections 3.2 and 3.3 concerned with list processing. The chosen clause and goal orders are explained, and their termination behavior presented. The section also discusses some new examples. Their properties are analyzed, and a reconstruction offered of how they are composed.

Programs 3.12 and 3.15, for *member* and *append* respectively, are correct Prolog programs as written. They are both minimal recursive programs, so there is no issue of goal order. They are in their preferred clause order, the reasons for which have been discussed earlier in the chapter. The termination of the programs

$select\_first(X,Xs,Ys) \leftarrow$
  Ys is the list obtained by removing the
  first occurrence of X from the list Xs.

select_first(X,[X|Xs],Xs).
select_first(X,[Y|Ys],[Y|Zs]) ←
  X ≠ Y, select_first(X,Ys,Zs).

Program 7.4: Selecting the first occurrence of an element from a list

was discussed in Section 7.2.

  Program 3.19 for *select* is analogous to the program for *member*.

select(X,[X|Xs],Xs).
select(X,[Y|Xs],[Y|Ys]) ← select(X,Xs,Ys).

The analysis of *select* is similar to the analysis of *member*. There is no issue of goal order as the program is minimal recursive. The clause order is chosen to reflect the intuitive order of solutions to queries such as $select(X,[a,b,c],Xs)$, namely $\{X=a,Xs=[b,c]\},\{X=b,Xs=[a,c]\},\{X=c,Xs=[a,b]\}$. The first solution is the result of choosing the first element, and so forth. The program terminates unless both the second and third arguments are incomplete lists.

  A variant of *select* is obtained by adding the test $X \neq Y$ in the recursive clause. As before, we assume that $\neq$ is only defined for ground arguments. The variant is given as Program 7.4 defining the relationship *select_first(X,Xs,Ys)*. Program 3.12 and 7.2 defining *member* and *member_check* have the same meaning. Program 7.4, in contrast, has a different meaning from Program 3.19. The goal $select(a,[a,b,a,c],[a,b,c])$ is in the meaning of *select*, whereas $select\_first(a,[a,b,a,c],[a,b,c])$ is not in the meaning of *select_first*.

  The next program considered is Program 3.20 for *permutation*. The order of clauses, analogously to the clause order for *append*, reflects the more likely mode of use:

permutation(Xs,[X|Ys]) ← select(X,Xs,Zs), permutation(Zs,Ys).
permutation([ ],[ ]).

The goal order and the termination behavior of *permutation* are closely related. Computations of *permutation* goals where the first argument is a complete list will terminate. The query calls *select* with its second argument a complete list, which terminates generating a complete list as its third argument. Thus there is a complete list for the recursive *permutation* goal. If the first argument is an

nonmember(*X*,*Xs*) ←
> *X* is not a member of the list *Xs*.

nonmember(X,[Y|Ys]) ← X ≠ Y, nonmember(X,Ys).
nonmember(X,[ ]).

Program 7.5: Non-membership of a list

members(*Xs*, *Ys*) ←
> Each element of the list *Xs* is a member of the list *Ys*.

members([X|Xs],Ys) ← member(X,Ys), members(Xs,Ys).
members([ ],Ys).

Program 7.6: Testing for a subset

incomplete list, the *permutation* query will not terminate, because it calls a *select* goal that will not terminate. If the order of the goals in the recursive rule for *permutation* is swapped, the second argument of a *permutation* query becomes the significant one for determining termination. If it is an incomplete list, the computation will not terminate; otherwise it will.

A useful predicate using ≠ is *non_member*(*X*, *Ys*) which is true if *X* is not a member of a list *Ys*. Declaratively the definition is straightforward: an element is a nonmember of a list if it is not the head and is a nonmember of the tail. The base case is that any element is a nonmember of the empty list. This program is given as Program 7.5.

Because of the use of ≠, *nonmember* is restricted to ground instances. This is sensible intuitively. There are arbitrarily many elements which are not elements of a given list, and also arbitrarily many lists not containing a given element. Thus the behavior of Program 7.5 with respect to these queries is largely irrelevant.

The clause order of *nonmember* follows the convention of the recursive clause preceding the fact. The goal order uses the heuristic of putting the test before the recursive goal.

We reconstruct the composition of two programs concerned with the "subset" relationship. Program 7.6 defines a relationship based on Program 3.12 for *member*, while Program 7.7 defines a relationship based on Program 3.19 for *select*. Both consider the occurrences of the elements of one list in a second list.

Program 7.6 defining *members*(*Xs*, *Ys*) ignores the multiplicity of elements in the lists. For example, *members*([*b*,*b*],[*a*,*b*,*c*]) is in the meaning of the program. There are two occurrences of *b* in the first list, but only one in the second.

selects(Xs, Ys) ←
    The list Xs is a subset of the list Ys.

selects([X|Xs],Ys) ← select(X,Ys,Ys1), selects(Xs,Ys1).
selects([ ],Ys).

select(X,Ys,Zs) ← See Program 3.19.

Program 7.7: Testing for a subset

Program 7.6 is also restrictive with respect to termination. If either the first
or the second argument of a *members* query is an incomplete list the program will
not terminate. The second argument must be a complete list due to the call to
member, while the first argument must also be complete, since that is providing
the recursive control. The query *members*($Xs,[1,2,3]$)? asking for subsets of a
given set does not terminate. Since multiple copies of elements are allowed in
Xs, there are an infinite number of solutions, and hence the query should not
terminate.

Both these limitations are avoided by Program 7.7. The revised relation is
selects(Xs, Ys). Goals in the meaning of Program 7.7 have at most as many copies
of an element in the first list as appear in the second. Related to this property,
Program 7.7 terminates whenever the second argument is a complete list. A query
such as *selects*($Xs,[a,b,c]$) has as solution all the subsets of a given set.

We now consider a different example: translating a list of English words, word
for word, into a list of French words. The relationship is *translate*(*Words,Mots*)
where *Words* is a list of English words, and *Mots* the corresponding list of
French words. Program 7.8 performs the translation. It assumes a dictionary
of pairs of corresponding English and French words, the relation scheme being
dict(*Word,Mot*). The translation is very naive, ignoring issues of number, gender,
subject-verb agreement, and so on. Its range is solving a query such as *translate*([*the,dog,chases,the,cat*]),X)? with solution X=[*le,chien,chasse,le,chat*]. This
program can be used in multiple ways. English sentences can be translated to
French, French ones to English, or two sentences can be checked if they are correct
mutual translations.

Program 7.8 is a typical program performing *mapping*, that is, converting
one list to another by applying some function to each element of the list. The
clause order has the recursive rule(s) first, and the goal order calls *dict* first, so
as not to be left recursive.

We conclude the section with a discussion of the use of data structures in Prolog programs. Data structures are handled somewhat differently in Prolog than

> *translate(Words,Mots)* ←
>   *Mots* is a list of French words which is the
>   translation of the list of English words *Words*.

translate([Word|Words],[Mot|Mots]) ←
    dict(Word,Mot), translate(Words,Mots).
translate([ ],[ ]).

dict(the,le).   dict(dog,chien).
dict(chases,chasse).   dict(cat,chat).

Program 7.8: Translating word for word

in conventional programming languages. Rather than having a global structure, all parts of which are accessible, the programmer specifies logical relationships between various substructures of the data.

Taking a more procedural view, in order to build and modify structures, the Prolog programmer must pass the necessary fields of the structure to sub-procedures. These fields are used and/or acquire values during the computation. Assignment of values to the structures happens via unification.

Let us look more closely at a generic example — producing a single output from some given input. Examples are the standard use of *append*, joining two lists together to get a third, and using Program 7.8 to translate a list of English words into French. The computation proceeds recursively. The initial call instantiates the output to be an incomplete list $[X|Xs]$. The head X is instantiated by the call to the procedure, often in unification with the head of the clause. The tail Xs is progressively instantiated while solving the recursive call. The structure becomes fully instantiated with the solution of the base case and the termination of the computation.

Consider appending the list $[c,d]$ to the list $[a,b]$ as illustrated in Figure 4.3. The output $Ls=[a,b,c,d]$ is constructed in stages, as $Ls=[a|Zs]$, $Zs=[b|Zs1]$, and finally $Zs1=[c,d]$, when the base fact of *append* is used. Each recursive call partially instantiates the originally incomplete list. Note that the recursive calls to *append* do not have access to the list being computed. This is a *top-down* construction of recursive structures, and is typical of programming in Prolog.

The top-down construction of recursive data structures has one limitation. Pieces of the global data structure cannot be referred to deeper in the computation. This is illustrated in a program for the relation *no_doubles(XXs,Xs)* which is true if Xs is a list of all the elements appearing in the list XXs with all duplicates removed.

no_doubles(*Xs, Ys*) ←
    Ys is the list obtained by removing
    duplicate elements from the list *Xs*.

no_doubles([X|Xs],Ys) ←
    member(X,Xs), no_doubles(Xs,Ys).
no_doubles([X|Xs],[X|Ys]) ←
    non_member(X,Xs), no_doubles(Xs,Ys).
no_doubles([ ],[ ]).

nonmember(X,Xs) ← See Program 7.5.

Program 7.9: Removing duplicates from a list

Consider trying to compose *no_doubles* top-down. The head of the recursive clause will be

    no_doubles([X|Xs],···) ←

where we need to fill in the blank. The blank is filled by calling *no_doubles* recursively on *Xs* with output *Ys* and integrating *Ys* with *X*. If *X* has not appeared in the output so far, then it should be added, and the blank will be [X|*Ys*]. If *X* has appeared, then it should not be added and the blank is *Ys*. This cannot be easily said. There is no way of knowing what the output is so far.

The program for *no_doubles* is composed by thinking differently about the problem. Instead of determining whether an element has already appeared in the output, we can determine whether it will appear. Each element *X* is checked to see if it appears again in the tail of the list *Xs*. If *X* appears, then the result is *Ys*, the output of the recursive call to *no_doubles*. If *X* does not appear, then it is added to the recursive result. This version of *no_doubles* is given as Program 7.9. It uses Program 7.5 for *nonmember*.

A problem with Program 7.9 is that the list without duplicates may not have the elements in the desired order. For example, *no_doubles*([a,b,c,b],Xs)? has the solution Xs=[a,c,b], where the solution Xs=[a,b,c] may be preferred. This latter result is possible if the program is rewritten. Each element is deleted from the remainder of the list as it is found. In terms of Program 7.9 this is done by replacing the two recursive calls by a rule

    no_doubles([X|Xs],[X|Ys]) ← delete(X,Xs,Xs1), no_doubles(Xs1,Ys).

The new program builds the output top-down. However it is inefficient for large lists, as will be discussed in Chapter 13. Briefly each call to *delete* rebuilds the whole structure of the list.

$nd\_reverse(Xs, Ys) \leftarrow$
  Ys is the reversal of the list obtained by
  removing duplicate elements from the list Xs.

nd_reverse(Xs,Ys) ← nd_reverse(Xs,[ ],Ys).

nd_reverse([X|Xs],Revs,Ys) ←
    member(X,Revs), nd_reverse(Xs,Revs,Ys).
nd_reverse([X|Xs],Revs,Ys) ←
    non_member(X,Revs), nd_reverse(Xs,[X|Revs],Ys).
nd_reverse([ ],Ys,Ys).

nonmember(X,Xs) ← See Program 7.5.

Program 7.10: Reversing with no duplicates

reverse([a,b,c],Xs)
  reverse([a,b,c],[ ],Xs)
    reverse([b,c],[a],Xs)
      reverse([c],[b,a],Xs)
        reverse([ ],[c,b,a],Xs)   Xs=[c,b,a]
      true

Figure 7.3: Tracing a *reverse* computation

The alternative to building structures top-down is building them *bottom-up*. A simple example of bottom-up construction of data structures is Program 3.16b for reversing a list:

reverse(Xs,Ys) ← reverse(Xs,[ ],Ys).

reverse([X|Xs],Revs,Ys) ← reverse(Xs,[X|Revs],Ys).
reverse([ ],Ys,Ys).

An extra argument is added to *reverse/2* and used to accumulate the values of the reversed list as the computation proceeds. This procedure for *reverse* builds the output list bottom-up rather than top-down. In the trace in Figure 7.3 solving the goal *reverse([a,b,c],Xs)*, the successive values of the middle argument of the calls to *reverse/3* [ ], [a], [b,a], and [c,b,a] represent the structure being built.

A bottom-up construction of structures allows access to the partial results of the structure during the computation. Consider a relation *nd_reverse(Xs, Ys)* combining the effects of *no_doubles* and *reverse*. The meaning of *nd_reverse* is that *Ys* is a list of elements in *Xs* in reverse order and with duplicates removed.

Analogously to *reverse*, *nd_reverse* calls *nd_reverse/3* with an extra argument that builds the result bottom up. This argument is checked to see whether a particular element appears, rather than checking the tail of the list as in Program 7.6 for *no_doubles*. The program is given as Program 7.10.

We emphasize the characteristics of bottom-up construction illustrated here. One argument behaves as an accumulator of the final data structure. It is augmented in the recursive call, so that the more complex version is in the body of the clause rather than in its head. This contrasts with top-down construction, where the more complex version of the data structure being built is in the head of the clause. Another argument is used solely for returning the output, namely the final value of the accumulator. It is instantiated with the satisfaction of the base fact. The argument is explicitly carried unchanged in the recursive call.

The technique of adding an "accumulator" to a program can be generalized. It is used in the next chapter discussing Prolog programs for arithmetic. Accumulators can also be viewed as a special case of incomplete data structures, as will be discussed in Chapter 15.

Exercise for Section 7.5

(i)   Write Program 7.9 for *no_doubles* building the structure bottom-up.

7.6   Background

Prolog was envisaged as a first approximation to logic programming, which would be superseded by further research. Its control has always been acknowledged as limited and naive. An oft-cited slogan due to Kowalski (1979b) is "Algorithm = Logic + Control." The particular control provided in pure Prolog was intended as just one solution on the path to declarative programming and intelligent control. Time has shown otherwise. The control of Prolog has proven adequate for a large range of applications, and the language has not only endured, but has blossomed.

Nonetheless, logic programming researchers have investigated other forms of control. For example, LOGLISP (Robinson and Sibert, 1982) has breadth-first traversal of the search tree, and IC-Prolog (Clark and McCabe, 1978) has co-routining. MU-Prolog (Naish, 1985a) allows suspension to provide a correct implementation of negation, and to prevent the computation from searching infinite branches in certain cases. Wait declarations are generated (Naish, 1985a) which are related to the conditions on termination of Prolog programs given in Section 7.2.

Other research on analyzing the properties of Prolog programs is reported in Mellish (1985).

Chapter 8
Arithmetic

The logic programs for performing arithmetic presented in Section 3.1 are very elegant, but they are not practical. Any reasonable computer provides very efficient arithmetic operations directly in hardware, and practical logic programming languages cannot afford to ignore this feature. Computations such as addition take unit time on most computers independent of the size of the addends (as long as they are smaller than some large constant). The recursive logic program for *plus* (Program 3.3) takes time proportional to the first of the numbers being added. This could be improved by switching to binary or decimal notation, but still won't compete with direct execution by dedicated hardware.

8.1   System predicates for arithmetic

The role of the arithmetic predicates introduced in Prolog is to provide an interface to the underlying arithmetic capablities of the computer in a straightforward way. The price paid for this efficiency is that some of the machine oriented arithmetic operations are not as general as their logical counterparts. The interface provided is an arithmetic evaluator, which uses the arithmetic facilities of the underlying computer. Edinburgh Prolog has a binary operator *is* for arithmetic evaluation. We prefer the more conventional binary operator ':=' for the identical predicate.

Operators are used in order to make programs more readable. People are very flexible and learn to adjust to strange surroundings — they can become accustomed to read Lisp and Fortran programs, for example. We believe nonetheless that syntax is important; the power of a good notation is well known from mathematics. An integral part of a good syntax for Prolog is the ability to specify and use operators.

Operators have been used in earlier chapters, for example, $\neq$ and $<$. We assume Prolog provides several operators, and introduce them as they arise. Most Prologs give the user the ability to define his own binary infix, and unary prefix and postfix operators. Some form of operator declaration is necessary to specify the relative precedence, name, and associative behavior of each operator. The mechanism for specifying this information varies. The form of operator declarations in Edinburgh and Wisdom Prolog is given in Appendix C, together with a list of all operators used in this book and their relative precedences.

The basic query to the evaluator has the form *Value := Expression?*, and is read "Value is Expression." It is interpreted as follows. *Expression* is evaluated as an arithmetic expression. The result of a successful evaluation is unified with *Value*, the goal succeeding or failing accordingly.

Here are some examples of simple addition, illustrating the use and behavior of the evaluator. The goal $(X := 3+5)$? has the solution *X=8*. This is the standard use of the evaluator, instantiating a variable to the value of an arithmetic expression. The goal $(8 := 3+5)$? succeeds. Having both arguments to ":=" instantiated allows checking of the value of an arithmetic expression. $(3+5 := 3+5)$? fails because the left-hand argument, *3+5*, does not unify with *8*, the result of evaluating the expression.

The evaluator allows the standard operators for addition, subtraction, multiplication and division $(+, -, *, /)$, with their precedence from mathematics. We restrict ourselves in this book to integer arithmetic. Thus / denotes integer division, and *mod* denotes integer remainder.

What happens if the term to be evaluated is not a valid arithmetic expression? An expression can be invalid for one of two reasons, which should be treated differently, at least conceptually. A term such as *3+x* for a constant *x* cannot be evaluated. In contrast, a term *3+Y* for a variable *Y* may or may not be evaluable, depending on the value of *Y*.

The semantics of any logic program is completely defined, and, in this sense, logic programs cannot have runtime "errors." For example, the goal $X := 3+Y$ has solutions $\{X=3, Y=0\}$. However, when interfacing logic programs to a computer, the limitations of the machine should be taken into account. A runtime error occurs when the machine cannot determine the result of the computation due to insufficient information, that is, uninstantiated variables. This is distinct from goals that simply fail. Extensions to Prolog and other logic languages handle such "errors" by suspending until the values of the concerned variables are known. The execution model of Prolog as introduced does not permit suspension. Instead of simply failing, we say an error condition occurs.

The goal $(X := 3+x)?$ fails, because the right-hand argument cannot be evaluated as an arithmetic expression. The goal $(X := 3+Y)?$ is an example of a goal which that succeed if Y were instantiated to an arithmetic expression. Here an error condition should be reported.

A common misconception of the Prolog beginner is to regard ":=" as taking the place of assignment that is familiar from conventional languages. It is tempting to write a goal such as $(N := N+1)?$ This is meaningless. The goal fails if N is instantiated, or causes an error if N is a variable.

The ":=" predicate is an example of a *system predicate*. System predicates are provided by the Prolog system for use by the programmer. Another term for a system predicate is an *evaluable predicate*. Appendix B contains a description of the system predicates of Wisdom Prolog used in this book.

Further system predicates for arithmetic are the comparison operators. Instead of the logically defined $<$, $\leq$, $>$, $\geq$, Prolog directly calls the underlying arithmetic. We describe the behavior of $<$; the others are virtually identical. To answer the query $(A < B)?$, A and B are evaluated as arithmetic expressions. The two resultant numbers are compared, and the goal succeeds if the result of evaluating A is less than the result of evaluating B. Again if A or B is not an arithmetic expression the goal will fail, and an error condition should result if A or B are not ground.

Here are some simple examples. The goal $(1 < 2)?$ succeeds, as does the goal $(3-2 < 2*3+1)?$ On the other hand, $(2 < 1)?$ fails, and $(N < 1)?$ generates an error when N is a variable.

Tests for equality and inequality of values of arithmetic expressions are implemented via the system predicates $=:=$ and $=/=$, which evaluate both of their arguments and compare the resulting values.

8.2   Arithmetic logic programs revisited

Performing arithmetic via evaluation rather than logic demands a reconsideration of the logic programs for arithmetic presented in Section 3.1. Calculations can certainly be done more efficiently. For example, finding the minimum of two numbers can use the underlying arithmetic comparison. The program syntactically need not change from Program 3.7. Similarly, the greatest common divisor of two integers can be computed efficiently using the usual Euclidean algorithm, given as Program 8.1. Note that the explicit condition $J > 0$ is necessary to avoid multiple solutions when $J=0$ and errors from calling *mod* with a zero argument.

greatest_common_divisor(X, Y, Z) ←
  Z is the greatest common divisor of the integers X and Y.

greatest_common_divisor(I,0,I).
greatest_common_divisor(I,J,Gcd) ←
  J > 0, R := I mod J, greatest_common_divisor(J,R,Gcd).

Program 8.1: Computing the greatest common divisor of two integers

Two features of logic programs for arithmetic are missing from their Prolog counterparts. First, multiple uses of programs are restricted. Suppose we wanted a predicate *plus*(X, Y, Z) that performed as before, built using ":=." The obvious definition is

plus(X,Y,Z) ← Z := X+Y.

This works correctly if X and Y are instantiated to integers. However, we cannot use the same program for subtraction with a goal such as *plus(3,X,8)?*, which raises an error condition. Meta-logical tests are needed if the same program is to be used for both addition and subtraction. We defer this until meta-logical predicates are introduced in Chapter 10.

Programs effectively become specialized for a single use, and it is tricky to understand what happens when the program is used differently. Program 3.7 for *minimum*, for example, can be used reliably only for finding the minimum of two integers.

The other feature missing from Prolog programs for arithmetic is the recursive structure of numbers. In logic programs, the structure is used to determine which rule applies, and to guarantee termination of computations. Program 8.2 is a Prolog program for computing factorials closely corresponding to Program 3.6. The recursive rule is more clumsy than before. The first argument in the recursive call of *factorial* must be calculated explicitly, rather than emerging as a result of unification. Furthermore, the explicit condition determining the applicability of the recursive rule, $N > 0$, must be given. This is to prevent nonterminating computations with goals such as *factorial(-1,N)?* or even *factorial(3,F)?* Previously, in the logic program, unification with the recursive structure prevented nonterminating computations.

Program 8.2 corresponds to the standard recursive definition of the factorial function. Unlike Program 3.7, the program can be used only to calculate the factorial of a given number. A *factorial* query where the first argument is a variable will cause an error condition.

factorial(*N*,*F*) ←
    F is the integer *N* factorial.

factorial(N,F) ←
    N > 0, N1 := N–1, factorial(N1,F1), F := N∗F1.
factorial(0,1).

Program 8.2: Computing the factorial of a number

We must modify the concept of correctness of a Prolog program to accommodate behavior with respect to arithmetic tests. Other system predicates that generate runtime "errors" are handled similarly. A Prolog program is *totally correct* over a domain *D* of goals if for all goals in *D* the computation terminates, does not produce a runtime error, and has the correct meaning. Program 8.2 is totally correct over the domain of goals where the first argument is an integer.

Exercises for Section 8.2

(i)   The Nth triangular number is the sum of the numbers up to and including *N*. Write a program for the relation *triangle*(*N*, *T*) where *T* is the Nth triangular number.
(Hint: Adapt Program 8.2.)

(ii) Write a Prolog program for *power*(*X*,*N*, *V*), where *V* equals $X {\uparrow} N$. Which way can it be used?
(Hint: Model it on Program 3.5 for *exp*.)

(iii) Write Prolog programs for other logic programs for arithmetic given in the text and exercises in Section 3.1.

8.3   Transforming recursion into iteration

In Prolog there are no iterative constructs as such, and a more general concept, namely recursion, is used to specify both recursive and iterative algorithms. The main advantage of iteration over recursion is in efficiency, mostly space efficiency. In the implementation of recursion, a data structure (called a stack-frame) has to be maintained for every recursive call that has not terminated yet. A recursive computation involving *n* recursive procedure calls would require, therefore, space linear in *n*. On the other hand, an iterative program typically uses only a constant amount of memory, independent of the number of iterations.

```
factorial(N);
    I := 0; T := 1;
    while I < N do
        I := I+1; T := T*I end;
    return T
```

Figure 8.1: Computing factorials iteratively

Nevertheless, there is a restricted class of recursive programs that corresponds quite closely to conventional iterative programs. Under some conditions, to be explained further in Section 11.2 on tail recursion optimization, such Prolog programs can be implemented almost with the same efficiency as iterative programs in conventional languages. For this reason, it is preferable to express a relation using an iterative program, if possible. In this section we show how recursive programs can be made iterative using accumulators.

Recall that a pure Prolog clause is *iterative* if it has one recursive call in the body. We extend this notion to full Prolog, and allow zero or more calls to Prolog system predicates *before* the recursive call. A Prolog procedure is *iterative* if it contains only unit clauses and iterative clauses.

Most simple arithmetic calculations can be implemented by iterative programs.

Factorials can be computed, for example, in a loop where the numbers up to the desired factorial are multiplied together. A procedure in a Pascal-like language using a while loop is given in Figure 8.1. Its iterative behavior can be encoded directly in Prolog with an iterative program.

Prolog does not have storage variables, which can hold intermediate results of the computation and can be modified as the computation progresses. Therefore to implement iterative algorithms, which require the storage of intermediate results, Prolog procedures are augmented with additional arguments, called *accumulators*. Typically, one of the intermediate values constitutes the result of the computation upon termination of the iteration. This value is unified with the result variable using the unit clause of the procedure.

This technique is demonstrated by Program 8.3, which is a Prolog definition of *factorial* that mirrors the behavior of the while loop in Figure 8.1. It uses *factorial*(I,N,T,F) which is true if F is the value of N factorial, and I and T are the values of the corresponding loop variables before the $(I+1)^{th}$ iteration of the loop.

The basic iterative loop is performed by the iterative procedure *factorial/4*.

factorial(N,F) ←
   F is the integer *N* factorial.

factorial(N,F) ← factorial(0,N,1,F).

factorial(I,N,T,F) ←
   I < N, I1 := I+1, T1 := T*I1, factorial(I1,N,T1,F).
factorial(N,N,F,F).

Program 8.3: An iterative *factorial*

factorial(N,F) ←
   F is the integer *N* factorial.

factorial(N,F) ← factorial(N,1,F).

factorial(N,T,F) ‹
   N > 0, T1 :− T*N, N1 :− N 1, factorial(N1,T1,F).
factorial(0,F,F).

Program 8.4: Another iterative *factorial*

Each reduction of a goal using *factorial/4* corresponds to an iteration of the while loop. The call of *factorial/4* by *factorial/2* corresponds to the initialization stage. The first argument of *factorial/4*, the loop counter, is set to *0*.

   The third argument of *factorial/4* is used as an accumulator of the running value of the product. It is initialized to *1* in the call to *factorial/4* by *factorial/2*. The handling of both accumulators in Program 8.3 is a typical programming technique in Prolog. It is closely related to the use of accumulators in Programs 3.16b and 7.10 for collecting elements in a list.

   Accumulators are logical variables, rather than locations in memory. The value is passed between iterations, not an address. Since logical variables are "write-once," the updated value, a new logical variable, is passed each time. Stylistically, we will use variable names with the suffix *1*, for example, *T1* and *I1*, to indicate updated values.

   The computation terminates when the counter *I* equals *N*. The rule for *factorial/4* in Program 8.3 no longer applies, and the fact succeeds. With this successful reduction, the value of the factorial is "returned." This happens as a result of the unification with the accumulator in the base clause. Note that the logical variable representing the solution, the final argument of *factorial/4*, had to be carried throughout the whole computation to be set on the final call of factorial. This passing of values in arguments is characteristic of Prolog programs, and might

$between(I,J,K) \leftarrow$
    K is an integer between the integers I and J, inclusive.

between(I,J,I) ← I ≤ J.
between(I,J,K) ← I < J, I1 := I+1, between(I1,J,K).

Program 8.5: Generating a range of integers

seem strange to the newcomer.

Program 8.3 shows the exact reflection of the while loop for factorial given in Figure 8.1. Another iterative version of *factorial* can be written by counting down from N to 0, rather than up from 0 to N. The basic program structure remains the same, and is given as Program 8.4. There is an initialization call that sets the value of the accumulator, and recursive and base clauses implementing the while loop.

Program 8.4 is marginally more efficient than Program 8.3. In general, the fewer arguments a procedure has, the more readable it becomes, and the faster it runs.

A useful iterative predicate is *between(I,J,K)*, which is true if K is an integer between I and J inclusive. It can be used to generate nondeterministically integer values within a range. This is useful in generate-and-test programs, explained in Section 14.1, and in failure-driven loops, explained in Section 12.5.

Iterative programs can be written for calculations over lists of integers as well. Consider the relation *sumlist(IntegerList,Sum)* where *Sum* is the sum of the integers in the list *IntegerList*. We present two programs for the relation. Program 8.6a is a recursive formulation. To sum a list of integers, sum the tail, and then add the head. Program 8.6b uses an accumulator to compute the progressive sum precisely as Program 8.3 for *factorial* uses an accumulator to compute a progressive product. An auxiliary predicate *sumlist/3* is introduced with an extra argument for the accumulator, whose starting value, 0, is set in the initial call to *sumlist/3*. The sum is passed out in the final call by unification with the base fact. The only difference between Program 8.6b and the iterative versions of *factorial* is that the recursive structure of the list is used to control the iteration rather than a counter.

Let us consider another example. The inner product of two vectors X_i, Y_i is the sum $X_1 \cdot Y_1 + \cdots + X_n \cdot Y_n$. If we represent vectors as lists it is immediate to write a program for the relation *inner_product(Xs,Ys,IP)* where *IP* is the inner product of *Xs* and *Ys*. Programs 8.7a and 8.7b are recursive and iterative versions, respectively. The iterative version of *inner_product* bears the same relation to the

sumlist(Is,Sum) ←
 Sum is the sum of the list of integers *Is*.

sumlist([I|Is],Sum) ← sumlist(Is,IsSum), Sum := I+IsSum.
sumlist([ ],0).

Program 8.6a: Summing a list of integers

sumlist(Is,Sum) ←
 Sum is the sum of the list of integers *Is*.

sumlist(Is,Sum) ← sumlist(Is,0,Sum).

sumlist([I|Is],Temp,Sum) ←
 Temp1 :— Temp+I, sumlist(Is,Temp1,Sum).
sumlist([ ],Sum,Sum).

Program 8.6b: Iterative version of summing a list
    of integers using an accumulator

recursive *inner_product* that Program 8.6b for *sumlist* bears to Program 8.6a.

Both Programs 8.7a and 8.7b are correct for goals *inner_product(Xs, Ys, Zs)* where *Xs* and *Ys* are lists of integers of the same length. There is a built-in check that the vectors are of the same length. The programs fail if *Xs* and *Ys* are of different lengths.

The similarity of the relationship between Programs 8.6a and 8.6b, and between Programs 8.7a and 8.7b suggests that one may be automatically transformed to the other. The transformation of recursive programs to equivalent iterative programs is an interesting research question. Certainly it can be done for the simple examples shown here.

The sophistication of a Prolog program depends on the underlying logical relationship it axiomatizes. Here is a very elegant example of a simple Prolog program solving a complicated problem.

Consider the following problem: Given a closed planar polygon chain $\{P_1,P_2,\ldots,P_n\}$, compute the area of the enclosed polygon, and the orientation of the chain. The area is computed by the line integral

 1/2 ∫xdy−ydx

where the integral is over the polygon chain.

The solution is given in Program 8.8, which defines the relation *area(Chain,*

$inner\_product(Xs, Ys, Value) \leftarrow$
  Value is the inner product of the vectors
  represented by the lists of integers *Xs* and *Ys*.

inner_product([X|Xs],[Y|Ys],IP) ←
  inner_product(Xs,Ys,IP1), IP := X∗Y+IP1.
inner_product([ ],[ ],0).

Program 8.7a: Computing inner products of vectors

$inner\_product(Xs, Ys, Value) \leftarrow$
  Value is the inner product of the vectors
  represented by the lists of integers *Xs* and *Ys*.

inner_product(Xs,Ys,IP) ← inner_product(Xs,Ys,0,IP).

inner_product([X|Xs], [Y|Ys],Temp,IP) ←
  Temp1 := X∗Y+Temp, inner_product(Xs,Ys,Temp1,IP).
inner_product([ ],[ ],IP,IP).

Program 8.7b: Computing inner products of vectors iteratively

$area(Points, Area) \leftarrow$
  Area is the area of the polygon enclosed by the list of points *Points*,
  where the coordinates of each point are represented by a pair (X, Y)
  of integers.

area([Tuple],0).
area([(X1,Y1),(X2,Y2)|XYs],Area) ←
  area([(X2,Y2)|XYs],Area1),
  Area := (X1∗Y2–Y1∗X2)/2 + Area1.

Program 8.8: Computing the area of polygons

Area). *Chain* is given as a list of tuples, for example, $[(4,6),(4,2),(0,8),(4,6)]$. The magnitude of *Area* is the area of the polygon bounded by the chain. The sign of *Area* is positive if the orientation of the polygon is counterclockwise, and negative if it is clockwise. Program 8.8 defines *area*.

The query $area([(4,6),(4,2),(0,8),(4,6)], Area)$? has the solution *Area* = –8. The polygon gains opposite orientation by reversing the order of the tuples. The solution of the query $area([(4,6),(0,8),(4,2),(4,6)], Area)$? is *Area* = 8.

The program shown is not iterative. Converting it to be iterative is the subject of Exercise (v) below.

maximum(*Xs,N*) ←
    N is the maximum of the list of integers *Xs*.

maximum([X|Xs],M) ← maximum(Xs,X,M).

maximum([X|Xs],Y,M) ← X ≤ Y, maximum(Xs,Y,M).
maximum([X|Xs],Y,M) ← X > Y, maximum(Xs,X,M).
maximum([ ],M,M).

Program 8.9: Finding the maximum of a list of integers

length(*Xs,N*) ←
    Xs is a list of length *N*.

length([X|Xs],N) ← N > 0, N1 .= N−1, length(Xs,N1).
length([ ],0).

Program 8.10: Checking the length of a list

length(*Xs,N*) ←
    N is the length of the list *Xs*.

length([X|Xs],N) ← length(Xs,N1), N :− N1+1.
length([ ],0).

Program 8.11: Finding the length of a list

range(*M,N,Ns*) ←
    Ns is the list of integers between *M* and *N* inclusive.

range(M,N,[M|Ns]) ← M < N, M1 :− M+1, range(M1,N,Ns).
range(N,N,[N]).

Program 8.12: Generating a list of integers in a given range

An iterative program can be written to find the maximum of a list of integers. The relation scheme is *maximum*(*Xs,Max*), and the program is given as Program 8.9. An auxiliary predicate *maximum*(*Xs,X,Max*) is used for the relation that *Max* is the maximum of *X* and the elements in the list *Xs*. The second argument of *maximum/3* is initialized to be the first element of the list. Note that the maximum of an empty list is not defined by this program.

The standard recursive program for finding the maximum of a list of integers constitutes a slightly different algorithm. The recursive formulation finds the maximum of the tail of the list, and compares it to the head of the list, to find the maximum element. In contrast, Program 8.9 keeps track of the running maximum as the list is traversed.

Program 3.17 for finding the length of a list is interesting, affording several ways of translating a logic program into Prolog, each of which has its separate features. One possibility is Program 8.10, which is iterative. Queries $length(Xs,N)$? are handled correctly if N is a natural number, either testing if the length of a list is N, generating a list of N uninstantiated elements, or failing. The program is unsuitable, however, for finding the length of a list with a call such as $length([1,2,3],N)$?. This query generates an error.

Finding the length of a list can be done using Program 8.11. This program cannot be used, however, to generate a list of N elements. In contrast to Program 8.10, the computation does not terminate if the first argument is an incomplete list. Different programs for *length* are needed for the different uses.

Similar considerations about the intended use of a program occur when trying to define the relationship $range(M,N,Ns)$, where Ns is the list of integers between M and N inclusive. Program 8.12 has a specific use: generating a list of numbers with the desired range. The program is totally correct over all goals $range(M,N,Ns)$ where M and N are instantiated. The program cannot be used, however, to find the upper and lower limits of a range of integers, due to the test $M < N$. Removing this test would allow the program to answer a query $range(M,N,[1,2,3])$?, but then it would not terminate for the intended use, solving queries such as $range(1,3,Ns)$?.

Exercises for Section 8.3

(i)   Write an iterative version for $triangle(N,T)$ posed as Exercise 8.2(i).

(ii)   Write an iterative version for $power(X,N,V)$ posed as Exercise 8.2(ii).

(iii)   Rewrite Program 8.5 so that the successive integers are generated in descending order.

(iv)   Write an iterative program for the relation $timeslist(IntegerList,Product)$ computing the product of a list of integers, analogous to Program 8.6b for *sumlist*.

(v)   Rewrite Program 8.8 for finding the area enclosed by a polygon so that it is iterative.

(vi)   Write a program to find the minimum of a list of integers.

(vii)   Rewrite Program 8.11 for finding the length of a list so that it is iterative. (Hint: Use a counter as for Program 8.3.)

(viii) Rewrite Program 8.12 so that the range of integers is built bottom-up rather than top-down.

8.4 Background

A program for transforming recursive programs to iterative ones, which handles the examples in the text, is described in Bloch (1984).

Program 8.8, computing the area of a polygon, was shown to us by Martin Nilsson.

Chapter 9
Structure Inspection

All Prolog implementations have a number of system predicates related to the structure of terms. This chapter discusses the predicates to be used in this book.

9.1   Type predicates

Type predicates are unary relations concerning the type of a term. The predicates test whether a given term is a constant or a structure. Further distinctions are made between particular constants, such as integers and atoms. Four type predicates are assumed in this book: *integer/1, atom/1, constant/1* and *compound/1*. These predicates are listed in Figure 9.1, together with their intended meaning.

Each of the type predicates in Figure 9.1 behaves as if it was defined via an infinite table of facts. A table of integers: *integer(0), integer(1), integer(–1),* ... ; a table of the atoms in the program: *atom(foo), atom(bar),* ... ; and a table of the function symbols in the program with variable arguments: *compound(father(X, Y)) , compound(son(X, Y)),* .... The relation *constant* is defined by a table which is the union of the tables of integers and atoms. This is expressed in two rules:

$$\text{constant}(X) \leftarrow \text{integer}(X).$$
$$\text{constant}(X) \leftarrow \text{atom}(X).$$

Although most Prolog implementations handle the predicates differently, we regard the program behavior as if they were defined by a table. However, they can be used by goals that have only a finite number of solutions. If such a predicate

$integer(X) \leftarrow X$ is an integer.
$atom(X) \leftarrow X$ is an atom.
$constant(X) \leftarrow X$ is a constant (integer or atom).
$compound(X) \leftarrow X$ is a compound term.

Figure 9.1: System type predicates

is called with a goal that has an infinity of solutions, an error condition occurs. Consider the goal $integer(X)$?. If X is an integer the call succeeds; if it is an atom or structure the call fails. If X is a variable, an error condition is reported. This is analogous to evaluating arithmetic expressions which contain variables. Note that most Prologs do not follow this convention, and in them $integer(X)$, where X is a variable, simply fails.

It is tempting to use a query such as $atom(X)$? to give all the atoms known in the system on backtracking. This way of using $atom$ is usually not implemented.

The only terms not covered by the predicates in Figure 9.1 are variables. Prolog does provide system predicates relating to variables. The use of such predicates, however, is conceptually very different from the use of structure inspection predicates described in this chapter. Meta-logical predicates (their technical name) are the subject of the next chapter.

We give an example of the use of a type predicate as part of a program for flattening a list of lists. The relation $flatten(Xs, Ys)$ is true if Ys is the list of elements occurring in the list of lists Xs. The elements of Xs can themselves be lists or elements, so elements can be arbitrarily deeply nested. An example of a goal in the meaning of $flatten$ is $flatten([[a],[b,[c,d]],e],[a,b,c,d,e])$.

The simplest program for flattening uses double recursion. To flatten an arbitrary list $[X|Xs]$ where X can itself be a list, flatten the head of the list X, flatten the tail of the list Xs and concatenate the results:

flatten([X|Xs],Ys) ←
    flatten(X,Ys1), flatten(Xs,Ys2), append(Ys1,Ys2,Ys).

What are the base cases? The empty list is flattened to itself. A type predicate is necessary for the remaining case. The result of flattening a constant is a list containing the constant:

flatten(X,[X]) ← constant(X), X≠[ ].

The condition $constant(X)$ is necessary to prevent the rule being used when X is a list. The complete program for $flatten$ is given as Program 9.1a.

$flatten(Xs, Ys) \leftarrow$
    Ys is a list of the elements of Xs.

flatten([X|Xs],Ys) ←
    flatten(X,Ys1), flatten(Xs,Ys2), append(Ys1,Ys2,Ys).
flatten(X,[X]) ←
    constant(X), X≠[ ].
flatten([ ],[ ]).

Program 9.1a: Flattening a list with double recursion

$flatten(Xs, Ys) \leftarrow$
    Ys is a list of the elements of Xs.

flatten(Xs,Ys) ← flatten(Xs,[ ],Ys).

flatten([X|Xs],S,Ys) ←
    list(X), flatten(X,[Xs|S],Ys).
flatten([X|Xs],S,[X|Ys]) ←
    constant(X), X≠[ ], flatten(Xs,S,Ys).
flatten([ ],[X|S],Ys) ←
    flatten(X,S,Ys).
flatten([ ],[ ],[ ]).

list([X|Xs]).

Program 9.1b: Flattening a list using a stack

Program 9.1a, although very clear declaratively, is not the most efficient way of flattening a list. In the worst case, which is a left-linear tree, the program would require a number of reductions whose order is quadratic in the number of elements in the flattened list.

A program for *flatten* which constructs the flattened list top-down is a little more involved than the doubly recursive version. It uses an auxiliary predicate *flatten(Xs,Stack,Ys)* where *Ys* is a flattened list containing the elements in *Xs* and a stack *Stack* to keep track of what needs to be flattened. The stack is represented as a list.

The call of *flatten/3* by *flatten/2* initializes the stack to the empty list. We discuss the cases covered by *flatten/3*. The general case is flattening a list $[X|Xs]$ where X is itself a list. In this case Xs is pushed onto the stack, and X is recursively flattened. The predicate *list(X)* is used to recognize a list. It is defined by the fact *list([X|Xs])*:

flatten($[X|Xs]$,S,Ys) ← list(X), flatten(X,$[Xs|S]$,Ys).

When the head of the list is a constant other then the empty list, it is added to the output, and the tail of the list is flattened recursively:

flatten($[X|Xs]$,S,$[X|Ys]$) ← constant(X),X≠$[\ ]$, flatten(Xs,S,Ys).

When the end of the list is reached, there are two possibilities, depending on the state of the stack. If the stack is nonempty, the top element is popped, and the flattening continues:

flatten($[\ ]$,$[X|S]$,Ys) ← flatten(X,S,Ys).

If the stack is empty, the computation terminates:

flatten($[\ ]$,$[\ ]$,$[\ ]$).

The complete program is given as Program 9.1b.

A general technique of using a stack is demonstrated in Program 9.1b. The stack is managed by unification. Items are pushed onto the stack by recursive calls to a "consed" list. Items are popped by unifying with the head of the list and recursive calls to the tail. Another application of stacks appears in Programs 14.13 and 14.15 simulating pushdown automata.

Note that the stack parameter is an example of an accumulator.

The reader can verify that the revised program requires a number of reductions linear in the size of the flattened list.

Exercise for Section 9.1

(i) Rewrite Program 9.1a for *flatten(Xs, Ys)* to use an accumulator instead of the call to *append*, keeping it doubly recursive.

9.2   Accessing compound terms

Recognizing a term as compound is one aspect of structure inspection. A further aspect is provided by predicates that give access to the functor name, arity and arguments of a compound term. One system predicate for delving into compound terms is *functor(Term,F,Arity)*. This predicate is true if *Term* is a term whose principal functor has name *F* and arity *Arity*. For example, *functor(father(haran,lot),father,2)?* succeeds.

The functor predicate can be defined, analogously to the type predicates, by a table of facts of the form $functor(f(X_1,...,X_N),f,N)$ for each functor f of arity N. For example, $functor(father(X,Y),father,2)$, $functor(son(X,Y),son,2)$, ... Most Prologs consider constants to be functors of arity 0, with the appropriate extension to the functor table.

Calls to *functor* can fail for various reasons. A goal such as $functor(father(X,Y),son,2)$ does not unify with an appropriate fact in the table. Also, there are type restrictions on the arguments of *functor* goals. For example, the third argument of *functor*, the arity of the term, cannot be an atom or a compound term. If these restrictions are violated, the goal fails. A distinction can be made between calls that fail, and calls that should give an error because there are infinitely many solutions, such as $functor(X,Y,2)$?

The predicate *functor* is commonly used in two ways. The first use finds the functor name and arity of a given term. For example, the goal $functor(father(haran,lot),X,Y)$? has the solution $\{X=father, Y=2\}$. The second use builds a term with a particular functor name and arity. A sample query is $functor(T,father,2)$? with solution $T=father(X,Y)$.

The companion system predicate to *functor* is $arg(N,Term,Arg)$ which accesses the arguments of a term rather than the functor name. The goal $arg(N,Term,Arg)$ is true if Arg is the Nth argument of *Term*. For example, $arg(1,father(haran,lot),haran)$ is true.

Like *functor/3*, *arg/3* is commonly used in two ways. One use finds a particular argument of a compound term. A query exemplifying this use is $arg(2,father(haran,lot),X)$? with solution $X=lot$. The other use instantiates a variable argument of a term. For example, the goal $arg(1,father(X,lot),haran)$? succeeds, instantiating X to *haran*.

The predicate *arg* is also defined as if there is an infinite table of facts. A fragment of the table is

> arg(1,father(X,Y),X).   arg(2,father(X,Y),Y).   arg(1,son(X,Y),X).   ....

Calls to *arg* fail if the goal does not unify with the appropriate fact in the table, for example, $arg(1,father(haran,lot),abraham)$. They also fail if the type restrictions are violated, for example, if the first argument is an atom. An error is reported with a goal such as $arg(1,X,Y)$.

Let us consider an example of using *functor* and *arg* to inspect terms. Program 9.2 axiomatizes a relation $subterm(T1,T2)$, which is true if $T1$ is a subterm of $T2$. For reasons that will become apparent later, we restrict $T1$ and $T2$ to be ground.

$subterm(Sub, Term)$ ←
  Sub is a subterm of the ground term $Term$.

subterm(Term,Term).
subterm(Sub,Term) ←
  compound(Term), functor(Term,F,N), subterm(N,Sub,Term).

subterm(N,Sub,Term) ←
  N > 1, N1 := N–1, subterm(N1,Sub,Term).
subterm(N,Sub,Term) ←
  arg(N,Term,Arg), subterm(Sub,Arg).

Program 9.2: Finding subterms of a term

The first clause of Program 9.2 defining *subterm/2* states that any term is a subterm of itself. The second clause states that *Sub* is a subterm of a compound term *Term* if it is a subterm of one of the arguments. The number of arguments, i.e., the arity of the principal functor of the term, is found and used as a loop counter by the auxiliary *subterm/3*, which iteratively tests all the arguments.

The first clause of *subterm/3* decrements the counter and recursively calls *subterm*. The second clause covers the case when *Sub* is a subterm of the *N*th argument of the term.

The *subterm* procedure can be used in two ways: to test whether the first argument is indeed a subterm of the second; and to generate subterms of a given term. Note that the clause order determines the order in which subterms are generated. The order in Program 9.2 gives subterms of the first argument before subterms of the second argument, and so on. Swapping the order of the clauses changes the order of solutions.

Consider the query *subterm(a,f(X, Y))* ?, where the second argument is not ground. Eventually the subgoal *subterm(a,X)* is reached. This succeeds by the first *subterm* rule, instantiating X to a. The subgoal also matches the second *subterm* rule, invoking the goal *compound(X)* which generates an error. This is undesirable behavior.

We defer the issues arising when performing structure inspection on non-ground terms to the next chapter where meta-logical predicates with suitable expressive power are introduced. For the rest of this chapter all programs are assumed to take only ground arguments unless otherwise stated.

Program 9.2 is typical code for programs that perform structure inspection. We look at another example, substituting for a subterm in a term.

substitute(Old,New,OldTerm,NewTerm) ←
  NewTerm is the result of replacing all occurrences of *Old*
  in *OldTerm* by *New*.

substitute(Old,New,Old,New).
substitute(Old,New,Term,Term) ←
    constant(Term), Term ≠ Old.
substitute(Old,New,Term,Term1) ←
    compound(Term),
    functor(Term,F,N),
    functor(Term1,F,N),
    substitute(N,Old,New,Term,Term1).

substitute(N,Old,New,Term,Term1) ←
    N > 0,
    arg(N,Term,Arg),
    substitute(Old,New,Arg,Arg1),
    arg(N,Term1,Arg1),
    N1 := N–1,
    substitute(N1,Old,New,Term,Term1).
substitute(0,Old,New,Term,Term1).

Program 9.3: A program for substituting in a term

The relation scheme for a general program for substituting subterms is *substitute(Old,New,OldTerm,NewTerm)* where *NewTerm* is the result of replacing all occurrences of *Old* in *OldTerm* by *New*. Program 9.3 implementing the relation generalizes substituting for elements in a list, proposed as Exercise 3.3(i) and the logic program (Program 3.26) for substituting for elements in binary trees.

Program 9.3 is a little more complicated than Program 9.2 for *subterm*, but conforms to the same basic pattern. The clauses for *substitute/4* cover three different cases. The last, handling compound terms, calls an auxiliary predicate *substitute/5* which iteratively substitutes in the subterms. The arity of the principal functor of the term is used as the initial value of a loop counter which is successively decremented to control the iteration. We present a particular example to illustrate the interesting points lurking in the code. A trace of the query *substitute(cat,dog,owns(jane,cat),X)?* is given in Figure 9.2.

The query fails to unify with the fact in Program 9.3. The second rule is also not applicable as *owns(jane,cat)* is not a constant.

The third *substitute* rule is applicable to the query. The second call of *functor*

```
substitute(cat,dog,owns(jane,cat),X)                      {X=owns(jane,cat)}
    constant(owns(jane,cat))              f
substitute(cat,dog,owns(jane,cat),X)
    compound(owns(jane,cat)),
    functor(owns(jane,cat),F,N)                           {F=owns,N=2}
    functor(X,owns,2)                                     {X=owns(X1,X2)}
    substitute(2,cat,dog,owns(jane,cat),owns(X1,X2))
        2 > 0
        arg(2,owns(jane,cat),Arg)                         {Arg=cat}
        substitute(cat,dog,cat,Arg1)                      {Arg1=dog}
        arg(2,owns(X1,X2),dog)                            {X2=dog}
        N1 := 2-1                                         {N1=1}
        substitute(1,cat,dog,owns(jane,cat),owns(X1,dog))
            1 > 0
            arg(1,owns(jane,cat),Arg2)                    {Arg2 jane}
            substitute(cat,dog,jane,Arg3)                 {Arg3=jane}
                constant(jane)
                jane ≠ cat
            arg(1,owns(X1,dog),jane)                      {X1=jane}
            N2 := 1-1                                      {N2=0}
            substitute(0,cat,dog,owns(jane,cat),owns(jane,dog))
                0 > 0            f
            substitute(0,cat,dog,owns(jane,cat),owns(jane,dog))
                true
                    Output:  X = owns(jane,dog)
```

Figure 9.2: Tracing the substitute predicate

is interesting. *Name* and *Arity* have been instantiated to *owns* and *2*, respectively, in the previous call of *functor*, so this call builds a term that serves as the answer template to be filled in as the computation progresses. This explicit term building has been achieved by implicit unification in previous Prolog programs. The call to *substitute/5* successively instantiates the arguments of *Term1*. In our example, the second argument of *owns(X1,X2)* is instantiated to *dog*, and then *X1* is instantiated to *jane*.

The two calls to *arg* serve different tasks in *substitute/5*. The first call selects an argument, while the second call of *arg* instantiates an argument.

Substitution in a term is typically done by destructive assignment in conventional languages. Destructive assignment is not possible directly in Prolog. Program 9.3 typifies how Prolog handles changing data structures. The new term

$subterm(Sub, Term) \leftarrow$
　　Sub is a subterm of the ground term $Term$.

subterm(Term,Term).
subterm(Sub,Term) ←
　　compound(Term), Term =.. [F|Args], subterm_list(Sub,Args).

subterm_list(Sub,[Arg|Args]) ←
　　subterm(Sub,Arg).
subterm_list(Sub,[Arg|Args]) ←
　　subterm_list(Sub,Args).

Program 9.4: Subterm defined using =..

is recursively built as the old term is being traversed, by logically relating the corresponding subterms of the terms.

Note that the order of the second *arg* goal and the recursive call to *substitute/5* can be swapped. The modified clause for *substitute/5* is logically equivalent to the previous one, and gives the same result in the context of Program 9.3. Procedurally, however, they are radically different.

Another system predicate for structure inspection is a binary operator =.., called, for historical reasons, *univ*. The goal *Term =.. List* succeeds if *List* is a list whose head is the functor name of the term *Term*, and whose tail is the list of arguments of *Term*. For example, the goal *(father(haran,lot) =.. [father,haran,lot])?* succeeds.

Like *functor* and *arg*, *univ* has two uses. Either it builds a term given a list, for example, *(X =.. [father,haran,lot])?* with solution *X=father(haran,lot)*, or it builds a list given a term, for example, *(father(haran,lot) =.. Xs)?* with solution *Xs=[father,haran,lot]*.

In general, programs written using *functor* and *arg* can also be written with *univ*. Program 9.4 is an alternative definition of *subterm*, equivalent to Program 9.2. As in Program 9.2, an auxiliary predicate investigates the arguments; here it is *subterm_list*. *Univ* is used to access the list of arguments, *Args*, of which subterms are recursively found by *subterm_list*.

Programs using *univ* to inspect structures are usually simpler. However, programs written with *functor* and *arg* are in general more efficient than those using *univ*, since they avoid building intermediate structures.

A neat use of *univ* is formulating the chain rule for symbolic differentiation. The chain rule states that $d/dx\{f(g(x)\} = d/dg(x)\{f(g(x)\} \times d/dx\{g(x)\}$. In

Term =.. List ←
    List is a list containing the functor of *Term* followed
    by the arguments of *Term*.

Term =.. [F|Args] ←
    functor(Term,F,N), args(0,N,Term,Args).

args(I,N,Term,Arg,Args) ←
    I < N, I1 := I+1, arg(I1,Term,Arg), args(I1,N,Term,Args).
args(N,N,Term,[ ]).

Program 9.5a: Constructing the list corresponding to a term

Term =.. List ←
    The functor of *Term* is the first element of the list *List*,
    and its arguments are the rest of *List*'s elements.

Term =.. [F|Args] ←
    length(Args,N), functor(Term,F,N), args(Args,Term,1).

args([Arg|Args],Term,N) ←
    arg(N,Term,Arg), N1 := N+1, args(Args,Term,N1).
args([ ],Term,N).

length(Xs,N) ← See Program 8.11

Program 9.5b: Constructing the term corresponding to a list

Section 3.5 we noted that this rule could not be expressed as a single clause of a logic program as part of Program 3.29. A Prolog rule encapsulating the chain rule is

derivative(F_G_X,X,DF*DG) ←
    F_G_X =.. [F,G_X],
    derivative(F_G_X,G_X,DF),
    derivative(G_X,X,DG).

The function *F_G_X* is split up by *univ* into its function *F* and argument *G_X*, checking that is a function of one argument at the same time. The derivative of *F* with respect to its argument is recursively calculated, as is the derivative of *G_X*. These are combined to give the solution.

Univ can be defined in terms of *functor* and *arg*. Two different definitions are necessary, however, to cover both building lists from terms, and building terms from lists. One definition does not suffice due to errors caused by uninstantiated variables. Other system predicates are similarly precluded from flexible use.

Program 9.5a behaves correctly for building a list from a term. The functor *F* is found by the call to *functor*, and the arguments are recursively found by the predicate *args*. The first argument of *args* is a counter that counts up, so that the arguments will appear in order in the final list. If Program 9.5a is called with *Term* uninstantiated, an error will be generated due to an incorrect call of *functor*.

Program 9.5b behaves correctly for constructing a term from a list. The length of the list is used to determine the number of arguments. The term template is built by the call to *functor*, and a different variant of *args* is used to fill in the arguments. Program 9.5b results in an error if used to build a list, due to the goal *length(Args,N)* being called with uninstantiated arguments.

Exercises for Section 9.2

(i)   Define a predicate *occurrences(Sub, Term,N)* true if *N* is the number of occurrences of subterm *Sub* in *Term*. Assume that *Term* is ground.

(ii) Define a predicate *position(Subterm, Term,Position)* where *Position* is a list of argument positions identifying *Subterm* within *Term*. For example, the position of *X* in *2·sin(X)* is *[2,1]*, since *sin(X)* is the second argument of the binary operator "·", and *X* is the first argument of *sin(X)*.
      (Hint: Add an extra argument for Program 9.2 for *subterm*, and build the position list top-down.)

(iii) Rewrite Program 9.5a so that it counts down.
      (Hint: Use an accumulator.)

(iv) Define *functor* and *arg* in terms of *univ*. How can the programs be used?

(v)   Rewrite Program 9.3 for *substitute* so that it uses *univ*.

9.3   Background

The standard Prolog approach does not distinguish between object- and meta-level type predicates. We have taken a different approach, by defining the type test predicates to work only on instantiated terms, and by treating the meta-logical test predicates (e.g., *var/1* to be discussed in Section 10.1) separately. The predicates for accessing and constructing terms, *functor*, *arg*, and =.., originate from the Edinburgh family. The origin of the =.. is in the old Prolog-10 syntax for lists, which used the operator "..," instead of the current "|" in lists, e.g., $[a,b,c,..Xs]$ instead of $[a,b,c|Xs]$. The ".." on the right-hand side suggested or reminded that the right-hand side of the equality is a list.

Several of the examples in this section were adapted from O'Keefe (1983).

Exercises (i) and (ii) will be used in the equation solver in Chapter 22.

Chapter 10
Meta-Logical Predicates

A useful extension to the expressive power of logic programs is provided by the meta-logical predicates. These predicates are outside the scope of first-order logic, as they query the state of the proof, treat variables (rather than the terms they denote) as objects of the language, and allow the conversion of datastructures to goals.

Meta-logical predicates allow us to overcome two difficulties involving the use of variables encountered in previous chapters. The first difficulty is the behavior of variables in system predicates. For example, evaluating an arithmetic expression with variables gives an error. So does calling type predicates with variable arguments. A consequence of this behavior is to restrict Prolog programs to have a single use in contrast to the multiple uses of the equivalent logic programs.

The second difficulty is the accidental instantiation of variables during structure inspection. Variables need to be considered as specific objects rather than standing for an arbitrary unspecified term. In the previous chapter we handled the difficulty by restricting inspection to ground terms only.

This chapter has four sections, each for a different class of meta-logical predicates. The first section discusses type predicates that determine whether or not a term is a variable. The second section discusses term comparison. The next sections describe predicates enabling variables to be treated as manipulable objects. Finally, a facility is described for converting data into executable goals.

10.1 Meta-logical type predicates

The basic meta-logical type predicate is *var(Term)* which tests whether a given term is at present an uninstantiated variable. Its behavior is similar to the

$plus(X, Y, Z) \leftarrow$
  The sum of the numbers X and Y is Z.

plus(X,Y,Z) ← nonvar(X), nonvar(Y), Z := X+Y.
plus(X,Y,Z) ← nonvar(X), nonvar(Z), Y := Z–X.
plus(X,Y,Z) ← nonvar(Y), nonvar(Z), X := Z–Y.

Program 10.1: Multiple uses for *plus*

type predicates discussed in Section 9.1. The query *var(Term)*? succeeds if *Term* is a variable and fails if *Term* is not a variable. For example, *var(X)*? succeeds, whereas both *var(a)*? and *var([X|Xs])* fail.

The predicate *var* is an extension to pure Prolog programs. A table cannot be used to give all the variable names. A fact *var(X)* means that all instances of X are variables, rather than meaning that the letter "X" denotes a variable. Being able to refer to a variable name is outside the scope of first-order logic in general or pure Prolog in particular.

The predicate *nonvar(Term)* has the opposite behavior to *var*. The query *nonvar(Term)* succeeds if *Term* is not a variable and fails if *Term* is a variable.

The meta-logical type predicates can be used to restore some flexibility to programs using system predicates, and can also be used to control goal order. We demonstrate this by revising some programs from earlier chapters.

Consider the relation $plus(X, Y, Z)$. Program 10.1 is a version of *plus* which can be used for subtraction as well as addition. The idea is to check which arguments are instantiated before calling the arithmetic evaluator. For example, the second rule says that if the first and third arguments, X and Z, are not variables, the second argument, Y, can be determined as their difference. Note that if the arguments are not integers, the evaluation will fail, the desired behavior.

The behavior of Program 10.1 is closer to Program 3.3, the logic program for *plus*. Further, it does not generate any errors. Nonetheless, it does not have the full flexibility of the recursive logic program: it cannot be used to partition a number into two smaller numbers, for example. To partition a number involves generating numbers, for which a different program is needed. It is posed as an exercise at the end of the section.

Meta-logical goals placed initially in the body of a clause to decide which clause in a procedure should be used are called *meta-logical tests*. The *plus* program above is controlled by meta-logical tests. These tests refer to the current state of the computation. Knowledge of the operational semantics of Prolog is

length(Xs,N) ←
    The list *Xs* has length *N*.

length(Xs,N) ← nonvar(Xs), length1(Xs,N).
length(Xs,N) ← var(Xs), nonvar(N), length2(Xs,N).

length1(Xs,N) ← See Program 8.11
length2(Xs,N) ← See Program 8.10

Program 10.2: A multi-purpose *length* program

grandparent(X,Z) ←
    X is the grandparent of *Z*.

grandparent(X,Z) ← nonvar(X), parent(X,Y), parent(Y,Z).
grandparent(X,Z) ← nonvar(Z), parent(Y,Z), parent(X,Y).

Program 10.3: A more efficient version of *grandparent*

required to understand them.

Many Prologs in fact endow the type predicates with a meta-logical ability. For example, in Edinburgh Prolog, the goal *integer(X)* fails if *X* is a variable, rather than giving an error. This enables the rules from Program 10.1 to be written using the system predicate *integer* rather than *nonvar*, for example,

plus(X,Y,Z) ← integer(X), integer(Y), Z := X+Y.

We feel it is preferable to separate type-checking, which is a perfectly legitimate first-order operation, from meta-logical tests, which are a much stronger tool.

Another relation that can have multiple uses restored is *length(Xs,N)* determining the length *N* of a list *Xs*. Separate Prolog programs (8.10 and 8.11) are needed to find the length of a given list and to generate an arbitrary list of a given length, despite the fact that one logic program (3.17) performs both functions. Program 10.2 uses meta-logical tests to define a single *length* relation. The program has an added virtue over Programs 8.10 and 8.11. It avoids the non-terminating behavior present in both, when both arguments are uninstantiated.

Meta-logical tests can also be used to make the best choice of the goal order of clauses in a program. Section 7.3 discusses the definition of *grandparent*:

grandparent(X,Z) ← parent(X,Y), parent(Y,Z).

The optimum goal order changes depending on whether you are searching for the grandchildren of a given grandparent, or the grandparents of a given grandchild.

```
ground(Term) ←
    Term is a ground term.

ground(Term) ←
    nonvar(Term), constant(Term).
ground(Term) ←
    nonvar(Term),
    compound(Term),
    functor(Term,F,N),
    ground(N,Term).

ground(N,Term) ←
    N > 0,
    arg(N,Term,Arg),
    ground(Arg),
    N1 := N–1,
    ground(N1,Term).
ground(0,Term).
```

Program 10.4: Testing if a term is ground

Program 10.3 is a version of *grandparent* that will search more efficiently.

The basic meta-logical type predicates can be used to define more involved meta-logical procedures. Consider a relation *ground(Term)* which is true if *Term* is ground. Program 10.4 gives a definition

The program is in the style of the programs for structure inspection given in Section 9.2, in particular Program 9.3 for *substitute*. The two clauses for *ground/1* are straightforward. In both cases, a meta-logical test is used to ensure that no error is generated. The first clause says that constant terms are ground. The second clause deals with structures. It calls an auxiliary predicate *ground/2* which iteratively checks that all the arguments of the structure are ground.

We look at a more elaborate example of using meta-logical type predicates; writing a unification algorithm. The necessity of Prolog to support unification for matching goals with clause heads, means that explicit unification is readily available. Prolog's underlying unification can be used to give a trivial definition

    unify(X,X).

which is the definition of the system predicate $=/2$, namely $X=X$.

Note that this definition depends on Prolog's underlying mechanism for unification, and hence does not enforce the occurs check.

unify(Term1, Term2) ←
    Term1 and *Term2* are unified, ignoring the occurs check.

unify(X,Y) ←
    var(X), var(Y), X=Y.
unify(X,Y) ←
    var(X), nonvar(Y), X=Y.
unify(X,Y) ←
    var(Y), nonvar(X), Y=X.
unify(X,Y) ←
    nonvar(X), nonvar(Y), constant(X), constant(Y), X=Y.
unify(X,Y) ←
    nonvar(X), nonvar(Y), compound(X), compound(Y), term_unify(X,Y).

term_unify(X,Y) ←
    functor(X,F,N), functor(Y,F,N), unify_args(N,X,Y).

unify_args(N,X,Y) ←
    N > 0, unify_arg(N,X,Y), N1 := N–1, unify_args(N1,X,Y).
unify_args(0,X,Y).

unify_arg(N,X,Y) ←
    arg(N,X,ArgX), arg(N,Y,ArgY), unify(ArgX,ArgY).

Program 10.5: Unification algorithm

A more explicit definition of Prolog's unification is possible using meta-logical type predicates. Although more cumbersome and less efficient, this definition is useful as a basis for more elaborate unification algorithms. One example is unification with occurs check as described in the next section. Another example is unification in other logic programming languages which can be embedded in Prolog, such as read-only unification of Concurrent Prolog.

Program 10.5 is an explicit definition of unification. The relation *unify(Term1, Term2)* is true if *Term1* unifies with *Term2*. The clauses of *unify* outline the possible cases. The first clause of the program says that two variables unify. The next clause is an encapsulation of the rule for unification that if X is a variable then X unifies with Y.

The other case bearing discussion in Program 10.5 is unifying two compound terms, as given in the predicate *term_unify(X, Y)*. This predicate checks that the two terms X and Y have the same principal functor and arity, and then checks that all the arguments unify, using *unify_args*, in a way similar to the structure inspection programs shown before.

Exercises for Section 10.1

(i)   Write a version of *range* Program 8.12 that can be used to in multiple ways.

(ii) Write a version of Program 10.1 for *plus* that partitions a number as well as performing addition and subtraction.
      (Hint: Use *between* to generate numbers.)

10.2   Comparing nonground terms

Consider the problem of extending the explicit unification program, Program 10.5, to handle the occurs check. Recall that the occurs check is part of the formal definition of unification, which requires that a variable not be unified with a term containing this variable. In order to implement it in Prolog, we need to check whether two variables are identical (not just unifiable, as any two variables are). This is a meta-logical test.

Prolog provides a system predicate, $==/2$, for this purpose. The goal $(X == Y)$? succeeds if X and Y are identical constants, identical variables, or both structures whose principal functors have the same name and arity and recursively $(X_i == Y_i)$? succeeds for all corresponding arguments X_i and Y_i of X and Y. The goal fails otherwise. For example, $X == 5$ fails (in contrast to $X = 5$).

There is also a system predicate that has the opposite behavior to $==$. The goal $X \== Y$? succeeds unless X and Y are identical terms.

The predicate $\==$ can be used to define a predicate *not_occurs_in(Sub, Term)* which is true if *Sub* does not occur in *Term*, the relationship that is needed in the unification algorithm with the occurs check. *not_occurs_in(Sub, Term)* is a meta-logical structure inspection predicate. It is used in Program 10.6, a variant of Program 10.5, to implement unification with the occurs check.

Note that the definition of *not_occurs_in* is not restricted to ground terms. Lifting the restriction on Program 9.2 for *subterm* is not as easy. Consider the query *subterm(X, Y)*? This would succeed using Program 9.2, instantiating X to Y.

We define a meta-logical predicate *occurs_in(Sub, Term)* that has the desired behavior.

The predicate $==$ allows a definition of *occurs_in* based on Program 9.2 for *subterm*. All the subterms of the given term are generated on backtracking and

unify(Term1, Term2) ←
  Term1 and *Term2* are unified with the occurs check.

unify(X,Y) ←
  var(X), var(Y), X=Y.
unify(X,Y) ←
  var(X), nonvar(Y), not_occurs_in(X,Y), X=Y.
unify(X,Y) ←
  var(Y), nonvar(X), not_occurs_in(Y,X), Y=X.
unify(X,Y) ←
  nonvar(X), nonvar(Y), constant(X), constant(Y), X=Y.
unify(X,Y) ←
  nonvar(X), nonvar(Y), compound(X), compound(Y), term_unify(X,Y).

not_occurs_in(X,Y) ←
  var(Y), X \== Y.
not_occurs_in(X,Y) ←
  nonvar(Y), constant(Y).
not_occurs_in(X,Y) ←
  nonvar(Y), compound(Y), functor(Y,F,N), not_occurs_in(N,X,Y).

not_occurs_in(N,X,Y) ←
  N>0, arg(N,Y,Arg), not_occurs_in(X,Arg), N1 := N–1,
      not_occurs_in(N1,X,Y).
not_occurs_in(0,X,Y).

term_unify(X,Y) ← See Program 10.5

Program 10.6: Unification with the occurs check

tested to see if they are identical to the variable. The code is given in Program
10.7a.

As defined, *subterm* works properly only for ground terms. However, by
adding meta-logical type tests, as in the definition of *not_occurs_in* in Program
10.6, this problem is easily rectified.

10.3 Variables as objects

The delicate problem associated with explicit manipulation of variables in
defining *occurs_in* in the previous section highlights a deficiency in the expressive
power of Prolog. Variables are not easily handled, and when trying to manipulate

and inspect terms, variables can be unwittingly instantiated.

A similar problem occurs with Program 9.3 for *substitute*. Consider the goal *substitute(a,b,X,Y)*, substituting *a* for *b* in a variable *X* to give *Y*. There are two plausible behaviors for *substitute* in this case. Logically there is a solution when *X* is *a* and *Y* is *b*. This is the solution actually given by Program 9.3, achieved by unification with the base fact *substitute(Old,New,Old,New)*.

In practice another behavior is usually preferred. The two terms *X* and *a* should be considered different, and *Y* should be instantiated to *X*. The other base case from Program 9.3

    substitute(Old,New,Term,Term) ← constant(Term), Term ≠ Old.

covers this behavior. However, the goal would fail because a variable is not a constant.

We can prevent the first (logical) solution by using a meta-logical test to ensure that the term being substituted in is ground. The unification implicit in the head of the clause is then only performed if the test succeeds, and so must be made explicit. The base fact becomes the rule

    substitute(Old,New,Term,New) ← ground(Term), Old = Term.

Treating a variable as different from a constant is handled by a special rule, again relying on a meta-logical test:

    substitute(Old,New,Var,Var) ← var(Var).

Adding the above two clauses to Program 9.3 for *substitute*, and adding other meta-logical tests allows it to handle nonground terms. However, the resultant program is inelegant. It is a mixture of procedural and declarative styles, and demands of the reader an understanding of Prolog's control flow. To make a medical analogy, the symptoms have been treated (undesirable instantiation of variables), but not the disease (inability to refer to variables as objects). Additional meta-logical primitives are necessary to cure the problem.

The difficulty of mixing object and meta-level manipulation of terms stems from a theoretical problem. Strictly speaking meta-level programs should view object-level variables as constants, and be able to refer to them by name.

Prolog can be extended with two system predicates, *freeze(Term,Frozen)* and *melt(Frozen,Thawed)*, to partially solve these problems. Freezing a term *Term* makes a copy of the term, *Frozen*, where all the uninstantiated variables in the term become unique constants. A frozen term looks like, and can be manipulated as, a ground term.

occurs_in(Sub,Term) ←
    Sub is a subterm of the (possibly non-ground term) *Term.*

a: Using ==

occurs_in(X,Term) ←
    subterm(Sub,Term), X == Sub.

b: Using *freeze*

occurs_in(X,Term) ←
    freeze(X,Xf), freeze(Y,Termf), subterm(Xf,Termf).

subterm(X,Term) ← See Program 9.2

Program 10.7: Occurs in

Frozen variables are regarded as ground atoms during unification. Two frozen variables unify if and only if they are identical. Similarly, if a frozen term and an uninstantiated variable are unified, they become an identical frozen term. The behavior of frozen variables in system predicates is the behavior of the constants. For example, arithmetic evaluation involving a frozen variable will fail.

The predicate *freeze* is meta-logical in a similar sense to *var*. It enables the state of a term during the computation to be manipulated directly.

The predicate *freeze* allows an alternative definition of *occurs_in* from the previous section. The idea is to freeze the term so that variables become ground objects. This makes Program 9.2 for *subterm*, which works correctly for ground terms, applicable. The definition is given as Program 10.7b.

Freezing gives the ability to tell whether two terms are identical. Two frozen terms, X and Y, unify if and only if their unfrozen versions are identical, that is, $X == Y$. This property is essential to the correct behavior of Program 10.7b.

The difference between a frozen term and a ground term is that the frozen term can be "melted back" into a nonground term. The companion predicate to *freeze* is *melt(Frozen, Thawed)*. The goal *melt(X, Y)* produces a copy Y of the term X where frozen variables become "regular" Prolog variables. Any instantiations to the variables in X during the time when X has been frozen are taken into account when melting Y.

The combination of *freeze* and *melt* allows us to write a variant of *substitute*, *non_ground_substitute*, where variables are not accidentally instantiated. The procedural view of *non_ground_substitute* is as follows. The term is frozen before substitution; the substitution is performed on the frozen term using the version of *substitute* which works correctly on ground terms; and then the new term is melted:

> non_ground_substitute(X,Y,Old,New) ←
>   freeze(Old,Old1), substitute(X,Y,Old,Old1), melt(Old1,New).

The frozen term can also be used as a template for making copies. The system predicate *melt_new(Frozen, Term)* makes a copy *Term* of the term *Frozen* where frozen variables are replaced by new variables.

One use of *melt_new* is to copy a term. The predicate *copy(Term, Copy)* produces a new copy of a term. It can be defined in a single rule

> copy(Term,Copy) ← freeze(Term,Frozen), melt_new(Frozen,Copy).

The primitives *freeze*, *melt* and *melt_new* are useful in expressing and explaining the behavior of the extra-logical predicates to be introduced in Chapter 12.

10.4 The meta-variable facility

A feature of Prolog is the equivalence of programs and data — both can be represented as logical terms. In order for this to be exploited, programs need to be treated as data, and data must be transformed into programs. In this section we mention a facility which allows a term to be converted into a goal. The predicate *call*(X) calls the goal X for Prolog to solve.

In practice, most Prolog implementations relax the restriction we have imposed on logic programs, that the goals in the body of a clause must be non-variable terms. The *meta-variable facility* allows a variable to appear as a goal in a conjunctive goal or in the body of the clause. During the computation, by the time it is called, the variable must be instantiated to a term. It will then get treated as usual. If the variable is not instantiated when it comes to be called, an error is reported. The meta-variable facility is a syntactic convenience for the system predicate *call*.

The meta-variable facility greatly facilitates meta-programming, in particular the construction of meta-interpreters and shells. Two important examples to be discussed in later chapters are Program 12.6, a simple shell, and Program 19.1, a meta-interpreter. It is also essential for defining negation (Program 11.5) and allowing the definition of higher order predicates to be described in Section 17.3.

$$X \; ; \; Y \leftarrow$$
$$\qquad X \text{ or } Y.$$

X ; Y ← X.
X ; Y ← Y.

Program 10.8: Logical disjunction

We give an example of using the meta-variable facility with a definition of logical disjunction, denoted by the binary infix operator "$;$". The goal $(X;Y)$ is true if X or Y is true. The definition is given as Program 10.8.

10.5 Background

An excellent discussion of meta-logical system predicates in Prolog-10, and how they are used, can be found in O'Keefe (1983b).

The unification procedure for Concurrent Prolog, written in Prolog, is in Shapiro (1983).

The predicates *free*, *melt* and *melt_new* are introduced in Nakashima and Ueda (1984), where an implementation of them in Prolog-10 is discussed.

The name *freeze* has been suggested for other additions to pure Prolog. Most notable is Colmerauer's *geler* (Colmerauer, 1982a), which allows the suspension of a goal and gives the programmer more control over goal order.

Chapter 11

Cuts and Negation

Prolog provides a single system predicate, called *cut*, for affecting the procedural behavior of programs. Its main function is to reduce the search space of Prolog computations by dynamically pruning the search tree. The cut can be used to prevent Prolog from following fruitless computation paths that the programmer knows could not produce solutions.

The cut can also be used, inadvertently or purposefully, to prune computation paths that do contain solutions. By doing so, a weak form of negation can be effected.

The use of cut is controversial. Many of its uses can only be interpreted procedurally, in a contrast to the declarative style of programming we encourage. Used sparingly, however, it can improve the efficiency of programs without compromising their clarity.

11.1 Green cuts: expressing determinism

Consider the program *merge(Xs, Ys, Zs)* (Program 11.1) which merges two sorted lists of numbers *Xs* and *Ys* into the combined sorted list *Zs*.

Merging two lists of sorted numbers is a deterministic operation. Only one of the five *merge* clauses applies for each nontrivial goal in a given computation. Specifically, when comparing two numbers X and Y, only one of the three tests $X<Y$, $X=Y$ and $X>Y$ can be true. Once a test succeeds, there is no possibility that any other test will succeed.

The cut, denoted $!$, can be used to express the mutually exclusive nature of the tests. It is placed after the arithmetic tests. For example, the first *merge* clause is written

$merge(Xs, Ys, Zs) \leftarrow$
    Zs is an ordered list of integers obtained from merging
    the ordered lists of integers Xs and Ys.

merge([X|Xs],[Y|Ys],[X|Zs]) ← X<Y, merge(Xs,[Y|Ys],Zs).
merge([X|Xs],[Y|Ys],[X,Y|Zs]) ← X=Y, merge(Xs,Ys,Zs).

merge([X|Xs],[Y|Ys],[Y|Zs]) ← X>Y, merge([X|Xs],Ys,Zs).
merge(Xs,[ ],Xs).
merge([ ],Ys,Ys).

Program 11.1: Merging ordered lists

merge([X|Xs],[Y|Ys],[X|Zs]) ← X<Y, !, merge(Xs,[Y|Ys],Zs).

Operationally, the cut is handled as follows. *The goal succeeds and commits Prolog to all the choices made since the parent goal was unified with the head of the clause the cut occurs in.*

Although this definition is complete and precise, its ramifications and implications are not always intuitively clear or apparent.

Misunderstandings concerning the effects of a cut are a major source for bugs for experienced and inexperienced Prolog programmers alike. The misunderstandings fall into two categories: assuming that the cut prunes computation paths it does not, and assuming that it does not prune solutions where it actually does.

The following implications may help clarify the cryptic definition above:

- First, a cut prunes all clauses below it. A goal p unified with a clause containing a cut that succeeded would not be able to produce solutions using clauses that occur below that clause.

- Second, a cut prunes all alternative solutions to the conjunction of goals which appear to its left in the clause, that is, a conjunctive goal followed by a cut will produce at most one solution.

- On the other hand, the cut does not affect the goals to its right in the clause. They can produce more than one solution, in the event of backtracking. However, once this conjunction fails, the search proceeds from the last alternative prior to the choice of the clause containing the cut. Let us consider a fragment of the search tree of the query *merge([1,3,5],[2,3], Xs)?* with respect to Program 11.2, a complete version of *merge* with cuts added. The fragment is given as Figure 11.1. The query is first reduced to the conjunctive query *1<2,!,merge([3,5],[2,3],Xs1)?*, the goal *1<2* is

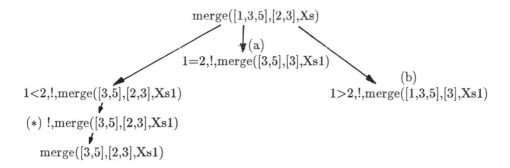

Figure 11.1: The effect of cut

successfully solved, reaching the node marked (∗) in the search tree. The effect of executing the cut is to prune the branches marked (a) and (b).

We return to discussing Program 11.2. The placement of the cuts in the three recursive clauses of *merge* is after the test.[1] The two base cases of *merge* are also deterministic. The correct clause is chosen by unification, and thus a cut is placed as the first goal (and in fact the only goal) in the body of the rule. Note that the cuts eliminates the redundant solution to the goal *merge*([ ],[ ],Xs). Previously, this was accomplished more awkwardly, by specifying that Xs (or Ys) had at least one element.

We restate the effect of a cut in a general clause $C = A \leftarrow B_1, \ldots, B_k, !, B_{k+2}, \ldots, B_n$ in a procedure defining A. If the current goal G unifies with the head of C, and $B_1, \ldots, B_k$ further succeed, the cut has the following effect. The program is committed to the choice of C for reducing G; any alternative clauses for A that might unify with G are ignored. Further should B_i fail for $i > k$, backtracking goes back only as far as the !. Other choices remaining in the computation of B_i, $i \leq k$, are pruned from the search tree. If backtracking actually reaches the cut, then the cut fails, and the search proceeds from the last choice made before G chose C.

The cuts used in the *merge* program express that *merge* is deterministic. That is, for every applicable goal, only one of the clauses can be used successfully for proving it. The cut commits the computation to such a clause, once the computation has progressed enough to determine that this is the only clause to

---

[1] The cut after the third *merge* clause is unnecessary in any practical sense. Procedurally, it will not cause any reduction of search. But it makes the program more symmetric, and like the old joke says about chicken soup, it doesn't hurt.

$merge(Xs, Ys, Zs) \leftarrow$
    Zs is an ordered list of integers obtained from merging
    the ordered lists of integers Xs and Ys.

merge([X|Xs],[Y|Ys],[X|Zs]) ←
    X<Y, !, merge(Xs,[Y|Ys],Zs).
merge([X|Xs],[Y|Ys],[X,Y|Zs]) ←
    X=Y, !, merge(Xs,Ys,Zs).
merge([X|Xs],[Y|Ys],[Y|Zs]) ←
    X>Y, !, merge([X|Xs],Ys,Zs).
merge(Xs,[ ],Xs) ← !.
merge([ ],Ys,Ys) ← !.

Program 11.2: Merging with cuts

$minimum(X, Y, Min) \leftarrow$
    Min is the minimum of the numbers X and Y.

minimum(X,Y,X) ← X≤Y, !.
minimum(X,Y,Y) ← X>Y, !.

Program 11.3: Minimum with cuts

be used.

The information conveyed by the cut prunes the search tree, and hence shortens the path traversed by Prolog, which reduces the computation time. In practice, using cuts in a program is even more important for saving space. Intuitively, knowing that a computation is deterministic means that less information needs to be kept for use in the event of backtracking. This can be exploited by Prolog implementations with tail recursion optimization, discussed below.

Let us consider some other examples. Cuts can be added to the program for computing the minimum of two numbers (Program 3.7) in precisely the same way as to *merge*. Once an arithmetic test succeeds there is no possibility for the other test succeeding. Program 11.3 is the appropriately modified version of *minimum*.

A more substantial example where cuts can be added to indicate that a program is deterministic is provided by Program 3.28. The program defines the relation *polynomial(Term,X)* for recognizing if *Term* is a polynomial in X. A typical rule is

polynomial(Term1+Term2,X)←
    polynomial(Term1,X), polynomial(Term2,X).

polynomial(Term,X) ←
    Term is a polynomial in *X*.

polynomial(X,X) ← !.
polynomial(Term,X) ←
    constant(Term), !.
polynomial(Term1+Term2,X) ←
    !, polynomial(Term1,X), polynomial(Term2,X).
polynomial(Term1–Term2,X) ←
    !, polynomial(Term1,X), polynomial(Term2,X).
polynomial(Term1∗Term2,X) ←
    !, polynomial(Term1,X), polynomial(Term2,X).
polynomial(Term1/Term2,X) ←
    !, polynomial(Term1,X), constant(Term2).
polynomial(Term↑N,X) ←
    !, natural_number(N), polynomial(Term,X).

Program 11.4: Recognizing polynomials

Once the term being tested has been recognized as a sum (by unifying with the head of the rule), it is known that none of the other *polynomial* rules will be applicable. Program 11.4 gives the complete polynomial program with cuts added. The result is a deterministic program, which has a mixture of cuts after conditions and cuts after unification.

When discussing the Prolog programs for arithmetic, which use the underlying arithmetic capabilities of the computer rather than a recursive logic program, we argued that the increased efficiency is often at the price of flexibility. The logic programs lost their multiple uses when expressed as Prolog programs. Prolog programs with cuts also have less flexibility than their "cut-free" equivalents. This is not a problem if the intended use of a program is one-way to begin with, as is often the case.

The examples so far have demonstrated pruning useless alternatives for the parent goal. We give an example where cuts greatly aid efficiency by removing redundant computations of sibling goals. Consider the recursive clause of an interchange sort program,

sort(Xs,Ys) ←
    append(As,[X,Y|Bs],Xs),
    X>Y,
    append(As,[Y,X|Bs],Xs1),
    sort(Xs1,Ys).

$sort(Xs, Ys) \leftarrow$
    Ys is an ordered permutation of the list of integers *Xs*.

sort(Xs,Ys) ←
    append(As,[X,Y|Bs],Xs),
    X>Y,
    !,
    append(As,[Y,X|Bs],Xs1),
    sort(Xs1,Ys).
sort(Xs,Xs) ←
    ordered(Xs),
    !.

ordered(Xs) ← See Program 3.20

Program 11.5: Interchange sort

The program searches for a pair of adjacent elements which are out of order, swaps them, and continues until the list is ordered. The base clause is

sort(Xs,Xs) ← ordered(Xs).

Consider a goal *sort([3,2,1],Xs)?*. This is sorted by swapping *3* and *2*, then *3* and *1*, and finally *2* and *1* to produce the ordered list *[1,2,3]*. It could also be sorted by first swapping *2* and *1*, then swapping *3* and *1*, and finally swapping *3* and *2*, to arrive at the same solution. We know there is only one sorted list. Consequently there is no point in searching for another alternative once an interchange is made. This can be indicated by placing the cut after the test *X>Y*. This is the earliest it is known that an interchange is necessary. The interchange sort program with cut is given as Program 11.5.

The addition of cuts to the programs described in this section does not alter their declarative meaning; all solutions to a given query are found. Conversely, removing the cuts would similarly not affect the meaning of the program. Unfortunately this is not always the case. A distinction has been made in the literature between *green cuts* and *red cuts*. Green cuts have been considered in this section. The addition and removal of green cuts from a program do not affect the program's meaning. Green cuts prune only computation paths that do not lead to new solutions. Cuts that are not green are *red*.

Exercises for Section 11.1

(i)   Add cuts to the partition program from *quicksort*, Program 3.22.

(ii) Add cuts to the differentiation program, Program 3.29.

(iii) Add cuts to the insertion sort program, Program 3.21.

11.2   Tail recursion optimization

As noted before, the main difference from a performance point of view between recursion and iteration is that recursion requires, in general, space linear in the number of recursive calls to execute, whereas iteration can be executed in constant space, independently of the number of iterations performed.

Although recursive programs, defined free of side-effects, might be considered more elegant and pleasing then their iterative counterparts, defined in terms of iteration and local variables, an order of magnitude in space complexity seems an unacceptable price for such pleasures as aesthetics. Fortunately, there is a class of recursive programs, precisely those that can be translated directly into iterative ones, which can be executed in constant space.

The implementation technique which achieves this space saving is called *tail recursion optimization*, or, more precisely, *last call optimization*. Intuitively, the idea of tail recursion optimization is to execute a recursive program as if it were an iterative one.

Consider the reduction of a goal A using the clause

$$A' \leftarrow B_1, B_2, \quad , B_n$$

with most general unifier θ. The optimization is potentially applicable to the last call in the body of a clause, B_n. It re-uses the area allocated for the parent goal A for the new goal B_n.

The key precondition for this optimization to apply is that there are no choice points left from the time the parent goal A reduced to this clause, to the time the last goal B_n is reduced. In other words, that A has no alternative clauses for reduction left, and that no choice points left in the computation of goals to the left of B_n, namely the computation of the conjunctive goal $(B_1, B_2, \ldots, B_{n-1})\theta$, was deterministic.

Most implementations of tail recursion optimization can recognize to a limited extent at runtime whether this condition occurs, by comparing backtracking-related information associated with the goals B_n and A. Another implementation technique, clause indexing, also interacts closely with tail recursion optimization, and enhances the ability of the implementation to detect that this precondition occurs. Indexing performs some analysis of the goal, to detect which clauses are applicable for reduction, before actually attempting to do the unifications. Typically indexing is done on the type and value of the first argument of the goal.

Consider the append program:

append([X|Xs],Ys,[X|Zs]) ← append(Xs,Ys,Zs).
append([ ],Ys,Ys).

If it is used to append two complete lists, then by the time the recursive *append* goal is executed, the preconditions for tail recursion optimization hold. No other clause is applicable to the parent goal (if the first argument unifies with [*X*|*Xs*], it certainly won't unify with [ ], since we assumed that the first argument is a complete list). There are no other goals in the body besides *append*, so that the second precondition holds vacuously.

However, for the implementation to know that the optimization applies, it needs to know that the second clause, although not tried yet, is not applicable. Here indexing comes into play. By analyzing the first argument of *append*, it is possible to know that the second clause would fail even before trying it, and to apply the optimization in the recursive call to *append*.

Not all implementations provide indexing, and not all cases of determinism can be detected by the indexing mechanisms available. Therefore it is in the interest of the programmer to help an implementation, which supports tail recursion optimization, to recognize that the preconditions for applying it hold.

There is a sledgehammer technique for doing so: add a cut before the last goal of a clause, in which tail recursion optimization should always apply, as in

$$A_1 \leftarrow B_1,B_2,\ldots,!,B_n.$$

This cut prunes both alternative clauses left for the parent goal A, and any alternatives left for the computation of $(B_1,B_2,\ldots,B_{n-1})\theta$.

In general, it is not possible to answer if such a cut is green or red, and the programmer's judgment should be applied.

It should be noted that the effect of tail recursion optimization is enhanced greatly when accompanied with a good garbage collector. Stated negatively, the optimization is not very significant without garbage collection. The reason is that most tail recursive programs generate some data structures on each iteration. Most of these structures are temporary, and can be reclaimed (see, e.g., the editor in Program 12.5). Together with a garbage collector, such programs can run, in principle, forever. Without it, although the stack space they consume would remain constant, the space allocated to the uncollected temporary data structures would overflow.

not X ⟨

>   *X* is not provable.

not X ← X, !, fail.
not X.

Program 11.6: Negation as failure

11.3 Negation

The use of green cuts does not change the declarative meaning of Prolog programs. However, by considering the procedural behavior of cut, it can be used to express negative information to a limited extent.

The cut is the basis of implementing a limited form of negation in Prolog called *negation as failure*. Program 11.6 is the standard definition of *not(Goal)*, which is true if *Goal* fails. It uses the meta-variable facility, and a system predicate *fail* that fails (i.e., there are no clauses defined for it). A conjunction of cut and *fail* is referred to as a *cut-fail* combination. We assume that *not* has been defined as a prefix operator.

Let us consider the behavior of Program 11.6 in answering the query *not G?* The first rule applies and *G* is called using the meta-variable facility. If *G* succeeds, the cut is encountered. The computation is then committed to the first rule, and *not G* fails. If the call to *G* fails, then the second rule of Program 11.6 is used, which succeeds. Thus *not G* fails if *G* succeeds and succeeds if *G* fails.

The rule order is essential for Program 11.6 to behave as intended. This introduces a new, not entirely desirable, dimension to Prolog programs. Previously, changing the rule order only changed the order of solutions. Now the meaning of the program can change. Procedures where the rule order is critical in this sense must be considered as a single unit, rather than as a collection of individual clauses.

The termination of a query *not G* depends on the termination of *G*. If *G* terminates then so does *not G*. If *G* does not terminate, then *not G* may or may not terminate depending on whether a success node is found in the search tree before an infinite branch. Consider the nonterminating program:

>   married(abraham,sarah).
>   married(X,Y) ← married(Y,X).

The query *not married(abraham,sarah)?* terminates (with failure) even though *married(abraham,sarah)?* does not terminate.

The meaning of *not* defined by Program 11.6 differs from strict logical negation.[2] Nor is the program a correct or complete implementation of negation by failure as described by the theory of Chapter 5.

The incompleteness of Program 11.6 as an implementation of negation by failure arises from Prolog's incompleteness in realizing the computation model of logic programs. The definition of negation as failure for logic programs is in terms of a finitely failed search tree. A Prolog computation is not guaranteed to find one, even if it exists. There are goals that could fail by negation as failure, that do not terminate under Prolog's computation rule. For example, the query *not* $(p(X),q(X))$*?* does not terminate with respect to the program

$$p(s(X)) \leftarrow p(X).$$
$$q(a).$$

The query would succeed if the $q(X)$ goal were selected first, since that gives a finitely failed search tree.

The inadequacy of Program 11.6 also stems from the order of traversal of the search tree, and arises when *not* is used in conjunction with other goals. Consider using *not* to define a relationship *unmarried_student*(X) for someone who is both not married and a student, as done in Program 5.1:

unmarried_student(X) ← not married(X), student(X).
student(bill).
married(joe).

The query *unmarried_student*(X)*?* fails with respect to the data above, ignoring that $X=bill$ is a solution logically implied by the rule and two facts. The failure occurs in the goal *not married*(X) since there is a solution $X=joe$. The problem can be avoided here by swapping the order of the goals in the body of the rule.

A similar example to the one above is the query *not* $(X=1)$, $X=2$*?* which fails although it is true.

The implementation of negation as failure using the cut-fail combination does not work correctly for nonground goals, as the examples above demonstrate. In most standard implementations of Prolog, it is the responsibility of the programmer to ensure that negated goals are ground before they are solved. This can be done either by a static analysis of the program, or by a runtime check, using the predicate *ground* defined in Program 10.4.

The predicate *not* is very useful. It allows us to define interesting concepts.

---

[2] Prolog-10 in fact calls the predicate \+ instead of *not*, so as not to mislead.

X ≠ Y ←
    X and *Y* are not unifiable.

X ≠ X ← !, fail.
X ≠ Y.

Program 11.7: Implementing ≠

For example, consider a predicate *disjoint*(*Xs, Ys*) true if two lists *Xs* and *Ys* have no elements in common. It can be defined as

disjoint(Xs,Ys) ← not (member(Z,Xs), member(Z,Ys)).

Many other examples of using *not* will appear in the programs throughout the book.

The cut-fail combination used in Program 11.6 is a technique that can be used more generally It allows early failure. A clause with a cut-fail combination says that the search need not (and will not) proceed.

Some cuts in a cut-fail combination are green cuts. That is, the program has the same meaning if the clause containing the cut-fail combination is removed. For example, consider Program 10.4 defining the predicate *ground*. An extra clause can be added, which can reduce the search, without affecting the meaning.

ground(Term) ← var(Term), !, fail.

The use of cut in Program 11.6 implementing *not* is not green, but red. The program does not behave as intended if the cut is removed

The cut-fail combination is used to implement other system predicates involving negation. For example, the predicate ≠ can be simply implemented via unification and cut-fail, rather than via an infinite table, with Program 11.7. This program also works correctly only for ground goals.

With ingenuity, and a good understanding of unification and the execution mechanism of Prolog, interesting definitions can be found for many meta-logical predicates. A sense of the necessary contortions can be found in the program for *same_var*(*X, Y*) which succeeds if *X* and *Y* are the same variable, and otherwise fails:

same_var(foo,Y) ← var(Y), !, fail.
same_var(X,Y) ← var(X), var(Y).

The argument for its correctness follows: "If the arguments to *same_var* are the same variable, binding *X* to *foo* will bind the second argument as well, so the first clause will fail, and the second clause will succeed. If either of the arguments is not a variable, both clauses will fail. If the arguments are different variables, the first clause will fail, but the cut stops the second clause from being considered" (O'Keefe 83).

Exercises for Section 11.3

(i) Define the system predicate \== using == and cut-fail.

(ii) Define *nonvar* using *var* and cut-fail.

11.4 Red cuts: omitting explicit conditions

Prolog's sequential choice of rules and its behavior in executing cut are the key features necessary to compose the program for *not*. The programmer can take into account that Prolog will only execute a part of the procedure if certain conditions hold. This suggests a new, and misguided, style of programming in Prolog, where the explicit conditions governing the use of a rule are omitted.

The prototypical (bad) example in the literature is a modified version of Program 11.3 for *minimum*. The comparison in the second clause of the program can be discarded to give the program

minimum(X,Y,X) ← X≤Y, !.
minimum(X,Y,Y).

The reasoning offered to justify the program is as follows: "If X is less than or equal to Y, then the minimum is X. Otherwise the minimum is Y, and another comparison between X and Y is unnecessary." Such a comparison is performed, however, by Program 11.3.

There is a severe flaw with this reasoning. The modified program has a different meaning from the standard program for *minimum*. It succeeds on the goal *minimum(2,5,5)*. The modified program is a false logic program.

The incorrect *minimum* goal implied by the modified program can be avoided. It is necessary to make explicit the unification between the first and third arguments, which is implicit in the first rule. The modified rule is

minimum(X,Y,Z) ← X≤Y, !, Z=X.

This technique of using the cut to commit to a clause after part of the unification has been done is quite general. But for *minimum* the resultant code is contrived.

It is far better to simply write the correct logic program, adding cuts if efficiency is important, as done in Program 11.3.

Using cut with the operational behavior of Prolog in mind is problematic. It allows the writing of Prolog programs that are false when read as logic programs, that is, have false conclusions, but behave correctly because Prolog is unable to prove the false conclusions. For example, if *minimum* goals are of the form *minimum(X, Y, Z)* where X and Y are instantiated, but Z is not, the modified program behaves correctly.

The only effect of the green cuts presented in Section 11.1 is to prune branches from the search tree, which are known to be useless. Cuts, whose presence in a program changes the meaning of that program, are called *red cuts*. The removal of a red cut from a program changes its meaning, i e , the set of goals it can prove.

A standard Prolog programming technique using red cuts is the omission of explicit conditions. Knowledge of the behavior of Prolog, the order it uses rules in a program, is relied on to omit conditions that could be inferred to be true. This is sometimes essential in practical Prolog programming, since explicit conditions, especially negative ones, are cumbersome to specify, and inefficient to run. But making such omissions is error-prone.

Omitting an explicit condition is possible if the failure of the previous clauses implies the condition. For example, the failure of the comparison, $X \leq Y$ in the *minimum* code implies that X is greater than Y. Thus the test $X > Y$ can be omitted. In general the explicit condition is effectively the negation of the previous conditions. By using red cuts to omit conditions, negation is being expressed implicitly.

Consider Program 11.5 for interchange sort. The first (recursive) rule applies whenever there is an adjacent pair of elements in the list that are out of order. When the second *sort* rule is used, there are no such pairs and the list must be sorted. Thus the condition *ordered(Xs)* can be omitted, leaving the second rule as the fact *sort(Xs,Xs)*. As with *minimum*, this is an incorrect logical statement.

Once the *ordered* condition is removed from the program, the cut changes color from green to red. Removing the cut from the variant without the *ordered* condition leaves a program which gives false solutions.

Let us consider another example of omitting an explicit condition. Consider Program 3.18 for deleting elements in a list. The two recursive clauses cover distinct cases, corresponding to whether or not the head of the list is the element to be deleted. The distinct nature of the cases can be indicated with cuts as given in Program 11.8a.

By reasoning that the failure of the first clause implies that the head of the

$delete(Xs,X,Ys) \leftarrow$
    Ys is the result of deleting all occurrences of X from the list Xs.

delete([X|Ys],X,Zs) ← !, delete(Ys,X,Zs).
delete([Y|Ys],X,[Y|Zs]) ← Y ≠ X, !, delete(Ys,X,Zs).
delete([ ],X,[ ]).

Program 11.8a: Deleting elements from a list

$delete(Xs,X,Ys) \leftarrow$
    Ys is the result of deleting all occurrences of X from the list Xs.

delete([X|Ys],X,Zs) ← !, delete(Ys,X,Zs).
delete([Y|Ys],X,[Y|Zs]) ← !,delete(Ys,X,Zs).
delete([ ],X,[ ]).

Program 11.8b: Deleting elements from a list

$if\_then\_else(P,Q,R) \leftarrow$
    Either P and Q, or not P and R.

if_then_else(P,Q,R) ← P, !, Q.
if_then_else(P,Q,R) ← R.

Program 11.9: If then else statement

list is not the same as the element to be deleted, the explicit inequality test can be omitted from the second clause. The modified program is given as Program 11.8b. The cuts in Program 11.8a are green in comparison to the red cut in the first clause of Program 11.8b.

In general omitting simple tests as in Program 11.8b is inadvisable. The efficiency gain by their omission is minimal compared to the loss of readability and modifiability of the code.

Let us investigate the use of cut to express the if-then-else control structure. Program 11.9 defines the relation $if\_then\_else(P,Q,R)$. Declaratively, the relation is true if P and Q are true, or not P and R are true. Operationally, we prove P and, if successful, prove Q, else prove R.

The utility of a red cut to implement this solution is self-evident. The alternative to using a cut is to make explicit the condition under which R is run. The second clause would read:

if_then_else(P,Q,R) ← not P, R.

This could be expensive computationally. The goal *P* will have to be computed a second time in the determination of *not*.

We have seen so far two kinds of red cuts. One kind is "built-into" the program, as in the definitions of *not* and ≠. A second kind was a green cut that became red when conditions in the programs were removed. However, there is a third kind of red cut. A cut that is introduced into a program as a green cut that just improves efficiency, can turn out to be a red cut that changes the program's meaning.

For example, consider trying to write an efficient version of *member* that does not succeed several times when there are multiple copies of an element in a list. Taking a procedural view, one might use a cut to avoid backtracking once an element is found to be a member of a list. The corresponding code is

member(X,[X|Xs]) ← !.
member(X,[Y|Ys]) ← member(X,Ys).

Adding the cut indeed changes the behavior of the program. However it is now not an efficient variant of *member*, since, for example, on the goal *member(X,[1,2,3])?* it gives only one solution, *X=1*. It is a variant of *member_check*, given as Program 7.3, with the explicit condition $X \neq Y$ omitted, and hence the cut is red.

Exercises for Section 11.4

(i)   Discuss where cuts could be placed in Program 9.3 for *substitute*. Consider whether a cut-fail rule would be useful, and whether explicit conditions can be omitted.

(ii) Analyze the relation between Program 3.19 for *select* and the program obtained by adding a single cut:

select(X,[X|Xs],Xs) ← !.
select(X,[Y|Ys],[Y|Zs]) ← select(X,Ys,Zs).

(Hint: Consider variants of *select*.)

11.5   Default rules

Logic programs with red cuts are essentially comprised of a series of special cases, and a default rule. For example, Program 11.6 for *not* had a special case

pension(Person,Pension) ←
    Pension is the type of pension received by *Person*.

pension(X,invalid_pension) ← invalid(X).
pension(X,old_age_pension) ← over_65(X), paid_up(X).
pension(X,supplementary_benefit) ← over_65(X).

invalid(mc_tavish).

over_65(mc_tavish).   over_65(mc_donald).   over_65(mc_duff).

paid_up(mc_tavish).   paid_up(mc_donald).

Program 11.10a: Determining welfare payments

pension(Person,Pension) ←
    Pension is the type of pension received by *Person*.

pension(X,invalid_pension) ← invalid(X), !.
pension(X,old_age_pension) ← over_65(X), paid_up(X), !.
pension(X,supplem_benefit) ← over_65(X), !.
pension(X,nothing).

Program 11.10b: Determining welfare payments

when the goal G succeeded, and a default fact *not G* used otherwise. The second
rule for *if_then_else* in Program 11.9 is

$$if\_then\_else(P, Q, R) \leftarrow R.$$

It is used by default if P fails.

Using cuts to achieve default behavior is in the logic programming folklore.
We argue, using a simple example, that often it is better to compose an alternative
logical formulation than use cuts for default behavior.

Program 11.10a is a naive program for determining social welfare payments.
The relationship *pension(Person,Pension)* determines which pension, *Pension*, a
person, *Person*, is entitled to. The first *pension* rule says that a person is entitled
to an invalid pension if he is an invalid. The second rule states that people over
the age of 65 are entitled to an old age pension if they have contributed to a
suitable pension scheme for long enough, in short they must be *paid_up*. People
who are not paid up are still entitled to supplementary benefit if they are over 65.

Consider extending Program 11.10a to include the rule that people receive
nothing if they do not qualify for one of the pensions. The procedural "solution"

is to add cuts after each of the three rules, and an extra default fact

$pension(X, nothing)$.

This version is given as Program 11.10b.

Program 11.10b behaves correctly on queries to determine the pension to which people are entitled, for example, $pension(mc\_tavish, X)$? The program is not correct, though. The query $pension(mc\_tavish, nothing)$? succeeds which mc_tavish wouldn't be too happy about, and $pension(X, old\_age\_pension)$? has the erroneous unique answer $X = mc\_tavish$. The cuts prevent alternatives being found. Program 11.10b only works correctly to determine the pension a given person is entitled to.

A better solution is to introduce a new relationship $entitlement(X, Y)$ which is true if X is entitled to Y. It is defined with two rules and uses Program 11.10a for *pension*:

entitlement(X,Y) ← pension(X,Y).
entitlement(X,nothing) ← not pension(X,Y).

This program has all the advantages of Program 11.10b, and neither of the disadvantages mentioned above. It shows that making a person entitled to nothing as the default rule is really a new concept and should be presented as such.

11.6 Background

The cut was introduced already in Marseille Prolog (Colmerauer et al., 1973), and was perhaps one of the most influential design decisions in Prolog. Colmerauer experimented with several other constructs, which corresponded to special cases of the *cut*, before coming up with its full definition.

The terminology of green cuts and red cuts was introduced by van Emden (1982), in order to try and separate between legitimate and illegitimate uses of cuts. Alternative control structures, which are more structured then the cut, are constantly being proposed, but the cut still remains the workhorse of the Prolog programmer. Some of the extensions are *if-then else* constructs (O'Keefe, 1985), and notations for declaring that a relation is functional, or deterministic, as well as, "weak-cuts," "snips," remote-cuts (Chikayama, 1984), and *not* itself, which, as presently implemented, can be viewed as a structured application of the cut.

The cut is also the ancestor of the *commit* operator of concurrent logic languages, which was first introduced by Clark and Gregory (1981) in their Relational

Language. The commit cleans up one of the major drawbacks of the cut, which is destroying the modularity of clauses. The cut is asymmetric, as it eliminates alternative clauses below the clause in which it appears, but not above. Hence a cut in one clause affects the meaning of other clauses. The commit, on the other hand, is symmetric, and therefore cannot implement negation-as-failure, and does not destroy the modularity of clauses.

Attempts have been made to give cut a semantics within Prolog. One treatment can be found in Lloyd (1984).

Tail recursion optimization was first described by Warren (1981) and implemented in Prolog-10. It was implemented concurrently by Bruynooghe (1982) in his Prolog system.

References to negation in logic programming can be found in the background section in Chapter 5. Implementations of a sound negation as failure rule in dialects of Prolog can be found in Prolog-II (van Caneghem, 1982), and MU-Prolog (Naish, 1985a).

The program for *same_var* and its argument for correctness are due to O'Keefe (1983).

Program 11.10a for *pension* is a variant of an example due to Sam Steel for a Prolog course at the University of Edinburgh — hence the Scottish flavor. Needless to say, this is not intended as, nor is it, an accurate expression of the Scottish, or British, social welfare system.

Chapter 12

Extra-Logical Predicates

There is a class of predicates in Prolog that lie outside the logic programming model, and are called *extra-logical* predicates. These predicates achieve a side effect in the course of being satisfied as a logical goal. There are basically three types of extra-logical system predicates: predicates concerned with I/O, predicates for accessing and manipulating the program, and predicates for interfacing with the underlying operating system. Prolog I/O and program manipulation predicates are discussed in this chapter. The interface to the operating system is too system dependent to be discussed in the text. Appendix B lists system predicates for Wisdom Prolog running under Unix.

12.1 Input/Output

A very important class of predicates that produces side effects is that concerned with I/O. Any practical programming language must have a mechanism for both input and output. The execution model of Prolog, however, precludes the expression of I/O within the pure component of the language.

The basic predicate for input is *read(X)*. This goal reads a term from the current input stream, usually from the terminal. The term that has been read is unified with X, and *read* succeeds or fails depending on the result of unification.

The basic predicate for output is *write(X)*. This goal writes the term X on the current output stream, as defined by the underlying operating system, usually to the terminal. Neither *read* nor *write* give alternative solutions on backtracking.

The normal use of *read* is with a variable argument X, which acquires the value of the first term in the current input stream. The instantiation of X to

writeln([X|Xs]) ← write(X), writeln(Xs).
writeln([ ]) ← nl.

Program 12.1: Writing a list of terms

something outside the program lies outside the logical model, since each time the procedure is called, *read(X)* succeeds with a (possibly) different value for *X*.

Read attempts to parse the next term on the input stream. If it fails, it prints an error message on the terminal, and attempts to read the next term.

There is an asymmetry between the extra-logical nature of *read* and *write*. If all calls to *write* were replaced with a goal *true* which always succeeds once, the semantics of the program is unaffected. That is not true for *read*.

Different Prolog systems have different extra utilities that are system dependent.

A useful utility is a predicate *writeln(Xs)*, analogous to the Pascal command. The goal *writeln(Xs)* writes the list of terms *Xs* as a line of output. It is defined in Program 12.1. It uses the system predicate *nl*, which causes the next output to be on a new line.

Character strings are inserted by quoting them. For example, the goal *writeln(['The value of X is ',X])* would produce the output

The value of *X* is *3*

if *X* were instantiated to *3*.

More generally, Prolog supports string manipulation by handling strings as lists of character codes. Assuming ASCII codes, the list [80,114,111,108,111,103] represents "*Prolog.*" The ASCII code for *P* is *80*, for *r 114*, etc. Doubly quoted strings are an alternative notation for lists of ASCII values, for example, "*Prolog.*" Such strings are just syntactic sugar for the list. Manipulating strings can be done via standard list processing techniques.

The system predicate *name(X, Y)* is used to convert names of constants to character strings, and vice versa. The goal *name(X, Y)* succeeds if *X* is an atom, and *Y* is the list of ASCII codes corresponding to the characters in *X*, for example, *name(log,[108,111,103])?* succeeds.

A lower level of I/O than the term level, characterized by *read* and *write*, is the character level. The basic output predicate at the character level is *put(N)*, which places the character corresponding to ASCII code *N* on the current output

```
read_word_list(Ws) ←
    get(C),
    read_word_list(C,Ws).

read_word_list(C,[W|Ws]) ←
    word_char(C),
    read_word(C,W,C1),
    read_word_list(C1,Ws).
read_word_list(C,Ws) ←
    fill_char(C),
    get(C1),
    read_word_list(C1,Ws).
read_word_list(C,[ ]) ←
    end_of_words_char(C).

read_word(C,W,C1) ←
    word_chars(C,Cs,C1),
    name(W,Cs).

word_chars(C,[C|Cs],C0) ←
    word_char(C),
    !,
    get(C1),
    word_chars(C1,Cs,C0).
word_chars(C,[ ],C) ←
    not word_char(C).
```

```
word_char(C) ← 97 ≤ C, C ≤ 122.          % Lower-case letter
word_char(C) ← 65 ≤ C, C ≤ 90.           % Upper-case letter
word_char(95).                           % Underscore

fill_char(32).                           % Blank

end_of_words_char(46).                   % Period
```

Program 12.2: Reading in a list of words

stream. The basic input predicate is *get*(X)[1] which returns in X the ASCII code
of the first character on the input stream.

Program 12.2 is a utility predicate *read_word_list*(*Words*) that reads in a list
of words, *Words*. It is built using *get*. The words can be separated by arbitrarily
many blanks (ASCII code 32), and may contain any mixture of uppercase and

---

[1] This is slightly different from Edinburgh Prolog.

lowercase letters, and underscores. The words are terminated by a full-stop.

The predicate *read_word_list* reads a character, *C*, and calls *read_word_list(C, Words)*. This predicate does one of three actions, depending on what *C* is. If *C* is a word character, then the next word is found, and recursively the rest of the words are found that is an uppercase letter, a lowercase letter or an underscore. The second action is to ignore filling characters, and so the next character is read, and the program continues recursively. Finally, if the character denoting ends of words is reached, the program terminates and returns the list of words.

It is important that the program must always read a character ahead, and then test what it should do. If the character is useful, for example, a word character, it must be passed down to be part of the word. Otherwise characters can get lost on the event of backtracking. Consider the following read and process loop:

$$\text{process}([\ ]) \leftarrow$$
$$\text{get}(C),\ \text{end\_of\_words\_char}(C).$$
$$\text{process}([W|Words]) \leftarrow$$
$$\text{get}(C),\ \text{word\_char}(C),\ \text{get\_word}(C,W),\ \text{process}(Words).$$

If the first character in a word is not an *end_of_words_char*, the first clause will fail, and the second clause will cause the reading of the next character.

Returning to Program 12.2, the predicate *read_word(C,W,C1)* reads a word *W* given the current character *C* and returns the next character after the word, *C1*. The list of characters comprising the word are found by *word_chars/3* (with the same arguments as read_word). The word is created from the list of characters using the system predicate *name*. In *word_chars* there is the same property of looking ahead one character at a time, so that no character is lost.

Predicates such as *fill_char/1* and *word_char/1* exemplify data abstraction in Prolog.

Exercise for Section 12.1

(i)   Extend Program 12.2 so that it handles apostrophes (39) and numbers (48-57) as word characters, and question marks (63) and exclamation marks (33) as terminators. What would be involved in using it to read in sentences, with commas, etc.?

12.2 Program access and manipulation

So far our programs have been assumed to be resident in the computer's memory, without discussion of how they are represented or how they got there. Many applications depend on accessing the clauses in the program. Furthermore, if programs are to be modified at runtime, there must be a way of adding (and deleting) clauses.

The system predicate for accessing the program is *clause(Head,Body)*. The goal *clause(Head,Body)?* must be called with *Head* instantiated. The program is searched for the first clause whose head unifies with *Head*. The head and body of this clause are then unified with *Head* and *Body*. On backtracking, the goal succeeds once for each unifiable clause in the procedure. Note that clauses in the program cannot be accessed via their body.

Facts have the atom *true* as their body. Conjunctive goals are represented using the binary functor ",". The actual representations can be easily abstracted away, however.

Consider Program 3.12 for *member*:

    member(X,[X|Xs]).
    member(X,[Y|Ys]) ← member(X,Ys).

The goal *clause(member(X,Ys),Body)* has two solutions: { $Ys=[X|Xs]$,*Body=true*} and { $Ys=[Y|Ys1]$,*Body=member(X,Ys1)*}. Note that a fresh copy of the variables appearing in the clause is made each time a unification is performed. In terms of the meta-logical primitives *freeze* and *melt*, the clause is stored in frozen form in the program. Each call to *clause* causes a new melt of the frozen clause. This is the logical counterpart of the classic notion of reentrant code.

System predicates are provided both to add clauses to the program, and to remove clauses. The basic predicate for adding clauses is *assert(Clause)*, which adds *Clause* as the last clause of the corresponding procedure. For example, *assert(father(haran,lot))?* adds the *father* fact to the program. When describing rules an extra level of brackets is needed for technical reasons concerning the precedence of terms. For example, *assert((parent(X,Y) ← father(X,Y)))* is the correct syntax.

There is a variant of *assert*, *asserta*, that adds the clause at the beginning of a procedure.

If *Clause* is uninstantiated (or if *Clause* has the form $H←B$ with H uninstantiated), an error condition occurs.

The predicate *retract(C)* removes from the program the first clause in the program unifying with C. Note that to retract a clause such as $a \leftarrow b,c,d$, you need to specify $retract((a \leftarrow C))$. A call to $retract$ may only mark a clause for removal, rather than physically removing it, and the actual removal would occur only when Prolog's top-level query is solved. This is due to implementation reasons, and may lead to anomalous behavior in some Prologs.

Asserting a clause freezes the terms appearing in the clause. Retracting the same clause melts a new copy of the terms. In many Prologs this is exploited to be the easiest way of copying a term. The predicate $copy$ assumed in Chapter 10 can thus be defined as

$$\text{copy}(X,Y) \leftarrow \text{asserta(\$tmp(X)), retract(\$tmp(Y)).}$$

assuming $\$tmp$ is not used elsewhere in the program.

The predicates $assert$ and $retract$ introduce to Prolog the possibility of programming with side effects. Code depending on side effects for its successful execution is hard to read, hard to debug, and hard to reason about formally. Hence these predicates are somewhat controversial, and using them is sometimes a result of intellectual laziness and/or incompetence. When programming, they should be used as little as possible. Many of the programs to be given in this book can be written using $assert$ and $retract$, but the result is less clean and less efficient. Further, as Prolog compiler technology advances, the inefficiency in using $assert$ and $retract$ will become more apparent.

It is possible, however, to give logical justification for some limited uses of $assert$ and $retract$. Asserting a clause is justified, for example, if the clause already logically follows from the program. In such a case adding it will not affect the meaning of the program, since no new consequences can be derived from it, but perhaps only its efficiency, as some consequences could be derived faster. This use is exemplified in the lemma construct, introduced in Section 12.3 below.

Similarly, retracting a clause is justified if the clause is logically redundant. In this case retracting constitutes a kind of logical garbage collection, whose purpose is to reduce the size of the program.

We identify a few other legitimate uses for $assert$ and $retract$. One is setting up and using global switches that affect program execution. This will be discussed in Section 13.2 on programming hacks. Another is for solving problems which by definition require the modification of the program (e.g., $consult$ in Section 12.5, and meta-programs such as editors).

hanoi(N,A,B,C,Moves) ←
>   *Moves* is the sequence of moves required to move *N* discs
>   from peg *A* to peg *B* using peg *C* as an intermediary
>   according to the rules of the Towers of Hanoi puzzle.

hanoi(1,A,B,C,[A to B]).
hanoi(N,A,B,C,Moves) ←
    N > 1,
    N1 := N–1,
    lemma(hanoi(N1,A,C,B,Ms1)),
    hanoi(N1,C,B,A,Ms2),
    append(Ms1,[A to B|Ms2],Moves).

lemma(P) ← P, asserta((P ← !)).

Testing

test_hanoi(N,Pegs,Moves) ←
    hanoi(N,A,B,C,Moves), Pegs = [A,B,C].

Program 12.3: Towers of Hanoi using a memo-function

12.3   Memo-functions

Memo-functions save the results of subcomputations to be used later in a computation. Remembering partial results is impossible within pure Prolog, so memo-functions are implemented using side effects to the program. Programming in this way can be considered bottom-up programming.

The prototypical memo-function is *lemma(Goal)*. Operationally it attempts to prove the goal *Goal*, and, if successful, stores the result of the proof as a lemma. It is implemented as

>   lemma(P) ← P, asserta((P ← !)).

The next time the goal *P* is attempted, the new solution will be used, and there will be no unnecessary recomputation. The cut is present to prevent the more general program being used. Its use is justified only if *P* does not have multiple solutions.

Using lemmas is demonstrated with Program 12.3 for solving the Towers of Hanoi problem. The performance of Program 3.30 in solving the problem is dramatically improved. It is well known that the solution of the Towers of Hanoi with *N* discs requires 2^{N-1} moves. For example, 10 discs require 1023 moves, or

echo ← read(X), echo(X).

echo(X) ← end_of_file(X), !.
echo(X) ← write(X), nl, read(Y), !, echo(Y).

Program 12.4: Basic interactive loop

in terms of Program 3.30, 1023 calls of *hanoi(1,A,B,C,Xs)*. The overall number of general calls of *hanoi/5* is significantly more.

The solution to the Towers of Hanoi repeatedly solves subproblems moving the identical number of discs. A memo-function can be used to recall the moves made in solving each subproblem of moving a smaller number of discs. Later attempts to solve the subproblem can use the computed sequence of moves rather than recomputing them.

The idea is seen with the recursive clause of *hanoi* in Program 12.3. The first call to solve *hanoi* with *N–1* discs is remembered, and can be used by the second call to *hanoi* with *N–1* discs.

The program is tested with the predicate *test_hanoi(N,Pegs,Moves)*. *N* is the number of discs, *Pegs* is a list of the three peg names, and *Moves* is the list of moves that must be made. Note that in order to take advantage of the memo-functions, a general problem is solved first. Only when the solution is complete, and all memo-functions have recorded their results, are the peg names instantiated.

Exercise for Section 12.3

(i)   Two players take turns to say a number between 1 and 3 inclusive. A sum is kept of the numbers, and the player who brings the sum to 20 wins. Write a program to play the game to win, using memo-functions.

12.4 Interactive programs

A common form of a program requiring side effects is an interactive loop. A command is read from the terminal, responded to, and the next command read. Interactive loops are implemented typically by while loops in conventional languages. Program 12.4 gives the basic skeleton of such programs, where a command is read then echoed by being written on the screen.

The read/echo loop is invoked by the goal *echo*. The heart of the program is the relation *echo(X)*, where *X* is the term to be echoed. The program assumes a predicate *end_of_file(X)* which is true if *X* is the end-of-file marker. What is the end-of-life marker is system dependent. If the end-of-file marker is found, the loop terminates; otherwise the term is written and a new term is read.

Note that the testing of the term is separate from its reading. This is necessary to avoid losing a term: terms cannot be reread. The same phenomenon occurred in Program 12.2 for processing characters. The character was read and then separately processed.

Program 12.4 is iterative and deterministic. It can be run efficiently on a system with tail recursion optimization, always using the same small amount of space.

We give two examples of programs using the basic cycle of reading a term then processing it. The first is a line editor. The second interactive program is a shell for Prolog commands, which is essentially a top-level interpreter for Prolog in Prolog.

The first decision in writing a simple line editor in Prolog is how to represent the file. Each line in the file must be accessible, together with the cursor position, that is the current position within the file. We use a structure *file(Before,After)* where *Before* is a list of lines before the cursor, and *After* is a list of lines after the cursor. The cursor position is restricted to be at the end of some line. The lines before the cursor will be in reverse order to give easier access to the lines nearer the cursor. The basic loop accepts a command from the keyboard, and applies it to produce a new version of the file. Program 12.5 is the editor.

An editing session is invoked by *edit*, which initializes the file being processed to the empty file, *file([ ],[ ])*. The interactive loop is controlled by *edit(File)*. It writes a prompt on the screen, using *edit_prompt*, then reads and processes a command. The processing uses the basic predicate *edit(File,Command)* which applies the command to the file. The application is performed by the goal *apply(Command,File,File1)* where *File1* is the new version of the file after the command has been applied. The editing continues by calling *edit/1* on *File1*. The third *edit/2* clause handles the case when no command is applicable, indicated by the failure of *apply*. In this case an appropriate message is printed on the screen and the editing continues. The editing session is terminated by the command *exit*, which is separately tested for by *edit/2*.

Let us look at a couple of *apply* clauses, to give the flavor of how commands are specified. Particularly simple are commands for moving the cursor. The clause

apply(up,file([X|Xs],Ys),file(Xs,[X|Ys])).

edit ← edit(file([ ],[ ])).

edit(File) ←
    write_prompt, read(Command), edit(File,Command).

edit(File,exit) ← !.
edit(File,Command) ←
    apply(Command,File,File1), !, edit(File1).
edit(File,Command) ←
    writeln([Command,' is not applicable']), !, edit(File).

apply(up,file([X|Xs],Ys),file(Xs,[X|Ys])).
apply(up(N),file(Xs,Ys),file(Xs1,Ys1)) ←
    N > 0, up(N,Xs,Ys,Xs1,Ys1).
apply(down,file(Xs,[Y|Ys]),file([Y|Xs],Ys)).
apply(insert(Line),file(Xs,Ys),file(Xs,[Line|Ys])).
apply(delete,file(Xs,[Y|Ys]),file(Xs,Ys)).
apply(print,file([X|Xs],Ys),file([X|Xs],Ys)) ←
    write(X), nl.
apply(print(*),file(Xs,Ys),file(Xs,Ys)) ←
    reverse(Xs,Xs1), write_file(Xs1), write_file(Ys).

up(N,[ ],Ys,[ ],Ys).
up(0,Xs,Ys,Xs,Ys).
up(N,[X|Xs],Ys,Xs1,Ys1) ←
    N > 0, N1 is N−1, up(N1,Xs,[X|Ys],Xs1,Ys1).

write_file([X|Xs]) ←
    write(X), nl, write(Xs).
write_file([ ]).

write_prompt ← write('≫'), nl.

Program 12.5: A line editor

says that we move the cursor up by moving the line immediately above the cursor
to be immediately below the cursor. The command fails if the cursor is at the
top of the file. The command for moving the cursor down is analogous to moving
the cursor up, and is also in Program 12.5.

Moving the cursor up N lines, rather than a single line, involves using an
auxiliary predicate *up/5* to change the cursor position in the file. Issues of ro-
bustness surface in its definition. Note that *apply* tests that the argument to *up*
is sensible, i.e., a positive number of lines, before *up* is invoked. The predicate *up*
itself handles the case when the number of lines to be moved up is greater than

the number of lines in the file. The command succeeds with the cursor placed at the top of the file. Moving a cursor down *N* lines is requested in the exercises.

Other commands given in Program 12.5 insert and delete lines. The command for insert, *insert(Line)*, contains an argument, namely the line to be inserted. The command for delete is straightforward. It fails if the cursor is at the bottom of the screen. Also in the editor are commands for printing the line above the cursor, *print*, and for printing the whole file, *print(∗)*.

The editor commands are mutually exclusive. Only one *apply* clause is applicable for any command. This is indicated by the cut in the second *edit/2* clause. As soon as an *apply* goal succeeds, there are no other possible alternative paths. This method of imposing determinism is a little different than described in Section 11.1 where the cuts would have been applied directly to the *apply* facts themselves. The difference between the two approaches is merely cosmetic.

A possible extension to the editor is to allow each command to handle its own error messages. For example, suppose you wanted a more helpful message than "Command not applicable" when trying to move up when at the top of the file. This would be handled by extending the *apply* clause for moving up in the file.

We shift from editors to shells. A shell accepts commands from a terminal and executes them. We illustrate with an example of a shell for answering Prolog goals. This is presented as Program 12.6.

The shell is invoked by *shell*. The code is similar to the editor. The shell gives a prompt, using *shell_prompt*, then reads a goal and tries to solve it using *shell(Goal)*. A distinction is made between solving ground goals, where a yes/no answer is given, and solving nonground goals where the answer is the appropriately instantiated goal. These two cases are handled by *shell_solve_ground* and *shell_solve* respectively. The shell is terminated by the goal *exit*.

Both *shell_solve_ground* and *shell_solve* use the meta-variable facility to call the goal to be solved. The success or failure of the goal determines the output message. These predicates are the simplest examples of meta-interpreters, a subject discussed in Chapter 19.

The *shell_solve* procedure shows an interesting solve-write-fail combination, which is useful to elicit all solutions to a goal by forced backtracking. Since we do not wish the shell to fail, an alternative clause is provided, which succeeds when all solutions to the goal are exhausted. It is interesting to note that it is not possible to collect all solutions to goals in a straightforward way without using some sort of side effect. This is explained further in Chapter 17 on second-order programming.

```
shell ←
    shell_prompt, read(Goal), shell(Goal).
shell(exit) ← !.
shell(Goal) ←
    ground(Goal), !, shell_solve_ground(Goal), shell.
shell(Goal) ←
    shell_solve(Goal), shell.

shell_solve(Goal) ←
    Goal, write(Goal), nl, fail.
shell_solve(Goal) ←
    write('No (more) solutions'), nl.

shell_solve_ground(Goal) ←
    Goal, !, write('Yes'), nl.
shell_solve_ground(Goal) ←
    write('No'), nl.

shell_prompt ← write('Next command? ').
```

Program 12.6: An interactive shell

The shell can be used as a basis for a logging facility to keep a record of a session with Prolog. Such a facility is given as Program 12.7. This new shell is invoked by *log*, which calls the basic interactive predicate *shell(Flag)* with *Flag* initialized to *log*. The flag takes one of two values, *log* or *nolog*, and indicates whether the output is currently being logged, or not.

The logging facility is an extension of Program 12.6, the major difference being that the principal predicates take an extra argument, indicating the current state of logging. Two extra commands are added, *log* and *nolog*, to turn logging on and off.

The flag is used by the predicates concerned with I/O. Each message written on the screen must also be written in the logging file. Also each goal read is inserted in the log to increase the log's readability. Thus calls to *read* in Program 12.6 are replaced by a call to *shell_read*, and calls to *write* replaced by calls to *shell_write*.

The definition of *shell_write* specifies what must be done.

```
shell_write(X,nolog) ← write(X).
shell_write(X,log) ← write(X), file_write([X],'prolog.log').
```

If the flag is currently *nolog*, the output is written normally to the screen. If

```
log ← shell(log).

shell(Flag) ←
    shell_prompt, shell_read(Goal,Flag), shell(Goal,Flag).

shell(exit,Flag) ←
    !, close_logging_file.
shell(nolog,Flag) ←
    !, shell(nolog).
shell(log,Flag) ←
    !, shell(log).
shell(Goal,Flag) ←
    ground(Goal), !, shell_solve_ground(Goal,Flag), shell(Flag).
shell(Goal,Flag) ←
    shell_solve(Goal,Flag), shell(Flag).

shell_solve(Goal,Flag) ←
    Goal, shell_write(Goal,Flag), nl, fail.
shell_solve(Goal,Flag) ←
    shell_write('No (more) solutions',Flag), nl.

shell_solve_ground(Goal,Flag) ←
    Goal, !, shell_write('Yes',Flag), nl.
shell_solve_ground(Goal,Flag) ←
    shell_write('No',Flag), nl.

shell_prompt ← write('Next command? ').

shell_read(X,log) ← read(X),
    file_write(['Next command? ',X],'prolog.log').
shell_read(X,nolog) ← read(X).

shell_write(X,nolog) ← write(X).
shell_write(X,log) ← write(X), file_write([X],'prolog.log').

file_write(X,File) ← telling(Old), tell(File), writeln(X), tell(Old).

close_logging_file ← tell('prolog.log'), told.
```

Program 12.7: Logging a session

the flag is *log*, an extra copy is written to the file *prolog.log*. The predicate *file_write(X,File)* writes the line *X* to file *File*.

Only two of the predicates in Program 12.7 are system dependent; *file_write* and *close_logging_file*. They depend on additional system predicates for dealing with files. Their definition uses the Edinburgh Prolog primitives *tell*, *told* and *telling* which are discussed in Appendix B. The other assumption built into the code is that the logged output will be recorded in a file *prolog.log*.

Exercises for Section 12.4

(i) Extend Program 12.5, the editor, to handle the following commands
  a. Move the cursor down *N* lines.
  b. Delete *N* lines.
  c. Move to a line containing a given term.
  d. Replace one term by another.
  e. Any command of your choice.

(ii) Modify the logging facility, Program 12.7, so the user can specify the destination file of the logged output.

12.5   Failure-driven loops

The interactive programs in the previous section were all based on tail recursive loops. There is an alternative way of writing loops in Prolog that are analogous to repeat loops in conventional languages. These loops are driven by failure and are called *failure-driven loops*. These loops are useful only when used in conjunction with extra-logical predicates which cause side effects. Their behavior can be understood only from an operational point of view.

A simple example of a failure-driven loop is a query *Goal, write(Goal), nl, fail?* which causes all solutions to a goal to be written on the screen. Such a loop is used in the shells of Programs 12.6 and 12.7.

A failure-driven loop can be used to define the system predicate *tab(N)* for printing *N* blanks on the screen. It uses Program 8.5 for *between*:

  tab(N) ← between(1,N,I), put(32), fail.

Each of the interactive programs in the previous section can be rewritten using a failure-driven loop. The new version of the basic interactive loop is given as Program 12.8. It is based on a nonterminating system predicate *repeat*, which can be defined by the minimal recursive procedure in Program 12.8. Unlike Program 12.4, the goal *echo(X)* fails unless *X* is the end of file marker. The failure causes backtracking to the *repeat* goal, which succeeds and the next term is read and echoed. The cut in the definition of *echo* ensures that the repeat loop is not reentered later.

echo ← repeat, read(X), echo(X), !.

echo(X) ← end_of_file(X), !.
echo(X) ← write(X), nl, fail.

repeat.
repeat ← repeat.

Program 12.8: Basic interactive repeat loop

consult(File) ← see(File), consult_loop, seen.

consult_loop ←
        repeat, read(Clause), process(Clause), !.

process(X) ←
        end_of_file(X), !.
process(Clause) ←
        assert(Clause), fail.

Program 12.9: Consulting a file

Failure-driven loops that use *repeat* are called *repeat loops*, and are the analogue of repeat loops from conventional languages. Repeat loops are useful in
Prolog for interacting with the outside system to repeatedly read and/or write.
Repeat loops require a predicate that is guaranteed to fail (the goal *echo(X)* in
Program 12.8), which causes the iteration to continue. This predicate only succeeds when the loop should be terminated. A useful heuristic for building repeat
loops is that there should be a cut in the body of the clause with the *repeat*
goal, which prevents a non-terminating computation in case the loop is being
backtracked into.

We use a repeat loop to define the system predicate *consult(File)* for reading
in a file of clauses and asserting them. Program 12.9 contains its definition. The
system predicates *see(File)* and *seen* are used for opening and closing a input file,
respectively.

Tail recursive loops are preferable to repeat loops because the latter have
no logical meaning. In practice, repeat loops are often necessary to run large
computations, especially on Prolog implementations without tail recursion optimization and/or without garbage collection. Explicit failure typically initiates
some implementation dependent reclamation of space.

Exercise for Section 12.5

(i)   Define the predicate *abolish*(*F*,*N*) that retracts all the clauses for the procedure *F* of arity *N*.

12.6 Background

Input/output has never really blended well with the rest of the language of Prolog. Its standard implementation, with side effects, relies solely on the procedural semantics of Prolog, and has no connection to the underlying logic programming model. For example, if an output is issued on a failing branch of a computation, it is not undone upon backtracking. If an input term is read, it is lost on backtracking, as the input stream is not backtrackable.

Concurrent logic languages attempt to remedy the problem and to integrate input/output better with the logic programming model, by identifying the input/output streams of devices with the logical streams in the language (Shapiro, 1984). Perpetual recursive processes can produce or consume incrementally those potentially unbounded streams.

Self-modifying programs are a bygone concept in computer science. Modern programming languages preclude this ability, and good assembly-language practice also avoids such programming tricks. It is a historical irony that a programming language which attempts to open a new era in computer programming opens the front door to such archane techniques, using the predicates *assert* and *retract*.

These program manipulation predicates of Prolog were devised initially as a low-level mechanism for loading and reloading programs, implemented in Prolog-10 by the *consult* and *reconsult* predicates. However, like any other feature of a language, they ended up being used for tasks that, we believe, were not intended by their original designers.

Modern implementations of Prolog attempt to remedy some of the damage by introducing alternative constructs, such as *slots* in ESP (Chikayama, 1984), or special declarations for modifiable predicates, as in Quintus Prolog (Quintus, 1985).

Concurrent logic languages can and do eliminate this feature altogether (Silverman et al., 1986), since global, modifiable, data structures can be implemented in them by monitors, which have a pure logical definition as a perpetual recursive process (Shapiro, 1984).

In Edinburgh Prolog there are two system predicates for reading characters, $get0(X)$ and $get(X)$. The distinction between them is that $get0$ returns the next character, while get gets the next printable character, that is one with an ASCII code greater than 32. Only one, the more general, is necessary, which we call get rather than $get0$.

The program for the Towers of Hanoi was shown to us by Shmuel Safra.

The line editor is originally due to Warren (1982b).

Chapter 13

Pragmatics

Programs in the previous chapters on pure Prolog and its extensions emphasized clarity of underlying concepts. In practice, issues of efficiency, constraints of a particular implementation, programming environment, and so forth, also arise. The logic programming folklore has a large body of techniques and tricks that are necessary to construct practical nontrivial Prolog systems. This chapter changes focus to more pragmatic issues in writing Prolog programs.

Software engineering considerations are equally relevant for programming in logic programming languages as in procedural languages. Prolog is no different from any other language in its need for a methodology to build and maintain large programs. A good programming style is important, as is a good program development methodology.

The four sections discuss efficiency, assorted programming tricks, programming style and layout, and program development.

13.1 Efficiency of Prolog programs

Practical Prolog programming requires consideration of efficiency. In order to discuss this issue, we need to set out the criteria for evaluating different programs. The main factor is the number of unifications performed and attempted in the course of a computation. This is related to time. Another criterion is depth of recursion — if the computation exceeds the maximum depth, the computation aborts. In practice this is a major problem. The third issue is the number of data structures generated. Each is discussed in turn.

One should expect that an intelligent translation of a deterministic, sequential algorithm into Prolog would preserve the expected performance of the algorithm.

Typically, the resulting Prolog programs would rely neither on general unification nor on deep backtracking.

A difficulty may arise in the implementation of algorithms that rely heavily on destructive manipulation of data structures, e.g., destructive pointer manipulation and arrays. Such data structures can be simulated directly in Prolog, with a logarithmic overhead, using standard techniques (e.g., simulation by trees). However, in many cases it would be more natural to modify the algorithm itself, to accommodate for the single-assignment nature of the logical variable.

For such algorithms, standard techniques for analyzing the complexity of programs apply. If full unification (the unification of two arbitrary terms in the goal) is not employed, then the reduction of a goal using a clause can be shown to take time bounded by a constant, whose size is program dependent. As a result analyzing the number of reductions a program performs as a function of the size of its input is a good way to determine its time complexity.

When programming in Prolog, its full power might be used. One writes nondeterministic programs, and programs that employ full unification. Analyzing the complexity of such programs is a more difficult task, and requires reasoning about the size of the search space traversed and the size of the input terms being unified.

The first answer to improved performance is better algorithms. Although a declarative language, the notion of an algorithm applies equally well to Prolog as to other languages. Examples of good and bad algorithms for the same problem, together with their Prolog implementations, are shown in previous chapters. Linear reverse using accumulators (Program 3.16b) is clearly more efficient than naive reverse (Program 3.16a). Quicksort (Program 3.22) is better than permutation sort (Program 3.20).

Besides coming up with better algorithms, one can do several other things to influence the performance of one's Prolog programs. One is to choose a better implementation. An efficient implementation is characterized by its raw speed, its indexing capabilities, support for tail recursion optimization, and garbage collection. The speed of logic programming languages is usually measured in LIPS, or *logical inferences per second*. A logical inference corresponds to a reduction in a computation.

Once the implementation is fixed, the programs themselves can be tuned by:

- Good goal ordering, where the rule is: Fail as early as you can.

- Elimination of nondeterminism using explicit conditions and cuts.

- Exploitation of the indexing facility, by ordering arguments appropriately.

Issues in ordering goals are mentioned in Section 7.3. How to use green cuts to express determinism of a program is discussed in Section 11.1.

Indexing is important in conjunction with tail recursion optimization, as discussed in Section 11.2. Even for nontail recursive programs, indexing can improve the performance of programs, by reducing the search for an applicable clause. This is important in programs that represent tables as a set of facts, e.g., a parser and a compiler.

Minimizing the number of data structures being generated is a subject that has not received much attention in the Prolog literature. We give an example analysis to show the reasoning. The predicate $sublist(Xs, Ys)$ for determining whether Xs is a sublist of Ys has several definitions. Let us discuss the relative efficiency of two of them with respect to creating data structures, and with respect to a particular use, testing whether one given list is a sublist of another given list.

The two versions of *sublist* we consider involve Program 3.13 for calculating the prefix and suffix of a list. Clause (i) defines a sublist as a prefix of a suffix, while clause (ii) defines a sublist as a suffix of a prefix:

$$sublist(Xs,AXBs) \leftarrow suffix(XBs,AXBs), prefix(Xs,XBs). \qquad (i)$$
$$sublist(Xs,AXBs) \leftarrow prefix(AXs,AXBs), suffix(Xs,AXs). \qquad (ii)$$

Although logically the same, there is a difference in the performance of the two programs. If the two arguments to *sublist* are complete lists, clause (i) simply goes down the second list, returning a suffix of it, then goes down the first list, checking if the suffix is a prefix of the first list. This execution does not generate any new intermediate data structures. On the other hand, clause (ii) creates a new list, which is a prefix of the second list, then checks if this list is a suffix of the first list. If the check fails, backtracking occurs, and a new prefix of the first list is created.

Even though, on the average, the number of reductions performed by the two clauses is the same, they are different in their efficiency. The first does not generate new structures (does not *cons*, in Lisp jargon). The second one does. When analyzing Lisp programs, it is common to examine the consing performance in great detail, and whether a program conses or not is an important efficiency consideration. We feel that the issue is just as important for Prolog programs, but perhaps the state of the art of studying the performance of large Prolog programs has not matured enough to dictate this as yet.

verify(Goal) ← not not Goal.

Program 13.1: Verifying a goal

```
numbervars('$VAR'(N),N,N1) ←
    N1 := N+1.
numbervars(Term,N1,N2) ←
    nonvar(Term), functor(Term,Name,N),
    numbervars(0,N,Term,N1,N2).

numbervars(N,N,Term,N1,N1).
numbervars(I,N,Term,N1,N3) ←
    I < N,
    I1 := I+1,
    arg(I1,Term,Arg),
    numbervars(Arg,N1,N2),
    numbervars(I1,N,Term,N2,N3).
```

Program 13.2: Numbering the variables in a term

13.2 Programming tricks

Every programming language has its collection of programming tricks, and Prolog is no exception. Here we give a handful of useful Prolog tricks. The tricks in this section are predicates that either manipulate variable instantiations, or show the use of global flags.

An interesting property of *not* is that it never instantiates its arguments. This is due to the explicit failure after the goal succeeds, which undoes any bindings made. This property is exploited to define a procedure *verify(Goal)*, Program 13.1, which determines whether a goal is true without affecting the current state of the variable bindings. Double negation provides the means.

We note, for curiosity only, that negation as implemented in Prolog has a feature in common with negation in natural language. A doubly negated statement is not the same as the equivalent affirmative statement.

A useful system predicate in Edinburgh Prolog is *numbervars(Term,N1,N2)* which successively instantiates the distinct variables in *Term* using the string '$VAR'(N) where N ranges from *N1* to *N2-1*. For example, the goal *numbervars(foo(X,Y),1,N)?* succeeds instantiating X to '$VAR'(1), Y to '$VAR'(2) and N to 3.

It is another example of a predicate performing structure inspection, and is

> variants(Term1,Term2) ←
>   verify((numbervars(Term1,0,N),
>   numbervars(Term2,0,N),
>   Term1=Term2)).

Program 13.3: Variants

given as Program 13.2. The program counts up rather than counts down so that the variables will be numbered in increasing order from left to right. In order not to give an error, calls to *numbervars* must have the second argument instantiated.

Numbervars can be used in a backhanded way to define meta-logical predicates. For example,

> ground(Term) ← numbervars(Term,0,0).

It can also be used to define *freeze*, namely *freeze($X, Term$) ← copy($X, Term$)*, *numbervars($Term,0,N$)*. We defer a definition of *melt* till Chapter 15. Another useful example applies both *verify* and *numbervars*. To motivate the example, we refer back to the discussion of Section 10.2 on meta-logical term comparison.

The predicate $==/2$ defines a notion of equality much stricter than unifiability, i.e., $=/2$. An intermediate notion of equality exists in Prolog, inherited from logic, namely whether two terms are alphabetic variants. Recall that two terms are variants if they are equal up to renaming of variables; that is, they can be made syntactically identical by consistently changing names of variables in one of them. Examples are the pairs $f(X,Y)$ and $f(Y,Z)$, $f(a,X)$ and $f(a,Y)$, and the pair $f(X,X)$ and $f(Y,Y)$.

The predicate *variant($Term1, Term2$)* is true if *Term1* and *Term2* are alphabetic variants. It is defined in Program 13.3. The trick is to instantiate the variables using Program 13.2 for *numbervars*, test whether the terms unify, then undo the instantiation. This can be done with *verify*.

The three forms of comparison, $=/2$, *variant/2* and $==/2$ are progressively stronger, with unifiability being the weakest and most general. Identical terms are alphabetic variants, and variant terms are unifiable. The distinction between the different comparisons vanishes for ground terms; for ground terms all three comparisons return the same result.

Another use of *verify* is to provide prettier appearance of terms containing variables. During a computation the Prolog interpreter assigns its own internal names to variables. These are typically totally unintelligible, making it difficult to read output with variables. Program 13.4 defines *write_vnames(Term)*, a write

```
write_vnames(Term) ⟵  lettervars(Term), write(Term), fail.
write_vnames(Term).
lettervars(Term) ←
     list_of_variables(Term,Vars),
     variable_names(Names),
     unify_variables(Vars,Names).

list_of_variables(V,[V]) ←
     var(V), !.
list_of_variables(V,[ ]) ←
     constant(V), !. list_of_variables(Term,Vs) ←
     functor(Term,F,N),
     list_of_variables(N,Term,Vs1),
     flatten(Vs1,Vs).
list_of_variables(N,Term,[VArgs|Vs]) ←
     N > 0,
     arg(N,Term,Arg),
     list_of_variables(Arg,VArgs),
     N1 := N-1,
     list_of_variables(N1,Term,Vs).
list_of_variables(0,Term,[ ]).

unify_variables([V|Vs],[V|Ns]) ← !, unify_variables(Vs,Ns).
unify_variables([V|Vs],Ns) ← !, unify_variables(Vs,Ns).
unify_variables(Vs,Ns).      % Exhausted variables or names

variable_names(['X','Y','Z','U','V','W','X1','Y1','Z1','U1','V1','W1',
     'X2','Y2','Z2','U2','V2','W2','X3','Y3','Z3','U3','V3','W3']).
```

Program 13.4: Writing out a term with non-numeric variable names

```
set_flag(Name,X) ←
     nonvar(Name),
     retract(flag(Name,Val)), !,
     asserta(flag(Name,X)).
set_flag(Name,X) ←
     nonvar(Name), asserta(flag(Name,X)).
```

Program 13.5: Using global flags

utility that writes variables with names rather than numbers. The predicate
lettervars(X) given in Program 13.4 transforms the variables in X to alphanumeric
strings according to a predefined list of names.

```
gensym(Prefix,V) ←
    var(V),
    atom(Prefix),
    oldvalue(Prefix,N),
    N1 := N+1,
    set_flag(gensym(Prefix),N1),
    string_concatenate(Prefix,N1,V),
    !.

old_value(Prefix,N) ← flag(gensym(Prefix),N)), !.
old_value(Prefix,0).

string_concatenate(X,Y,XY) ←
    name(X,Xs), name(Y,Ys), append(Xs,Ys,XYs), name(XY,XYs).
```

Program 13.6: Generating new symbols

Another programming trick uses simulate *assert* and *retract* to global variables. The predicate *flag(Name, Value)* is used to maintain the current value of the flag, while *set_flag(Name, Value)* sets the value of the flag. The definition of *set_flag* is given as Program 13.5.

One application of the flag procedures is to facilitate the generation of names of constants during a computation. We note, however, that the need for such a function is much smaller than in other languages. Usually such "gensym" functions are used to mimic some subset of the functionality of the logical variables. Having logical variables to begin with decreases most of its utility.

A common choice for implementing a "gensym" function is to have a root prefix, e.g., *x*, and add on suffixes with increasing numeric values, e.g., *x1,x2,...*, etc. The flag is used to keep a counter of the last numeric suffix chosen. The predicate *gensym(Prefix,Constant)*, given as Program 13.6, returns a new constant name *Constant* from the root prefix.

13.3 Programming style and layout

One basic concern in composing the programs in this book has been to make them "as declarative as possible" to increase program clarity and readability. A program must be considered as a whole. Its readability is determined by its physical layout, and by the choice of names appearing in it. This section discusses the guidelines we use when composing programs.

An important influence in making programs easy to read is the naming of the various objects in the program. The choice of all predicate names, variable names, constants and structures appearing in the program affect its clarity. The aim is to emphasize the declarative reading of the program.

We choose predicate names to be a word (or several words) that names relationships between objects in the program, rather than describes what the program is doing. Coining a good declarative name for a procedure does not come easily.

The activity of programming is procedural. It is often easier to name procedurally rather than declaratively (and programs with procedural names usually ran faster). Once the program works, however, we often revise the predicate names to be declarative. Composing a program is a cyclic activity in which names are constantly being reworked to reflect our improved understanding of our creation, and to enhance readability by us and others.

Mnemonic variable names also have an effect on program readability. A name can be a meaningful word (or words), or a standard variable form such as Xs for lists.

Variables that appear only once in a clause can be handled separately. They are in effect *anonymous*, and from an implementation viewpoint need not be named. Several Prologs adopt a special syntactic convention for referring to anonymous variables. Edinburgh Prolog, for example, uses a single underscore. Using this convention, Program 3.12 for *member* would be written

```
member(X,[X|_]).
member(X,[_|Xs]) ← member(X,Xs).
```

The advantage of the convention is to highlight the significant variables for unification. The disadvantage is related; the reading of clauses becomes procedural rather than declarative.

We use different syntactic conventions for separating multiple words in variable names and predicate functors. For variables, composite words are run together, each new word starting with a capital letter. Multiple words in predicate names are linked with underscores. Syntactic conventions are a matter of taste, but it is preferable to have a consistent style.

The layout of individual clauses also has an effect on how easily programs can be understood. We have found the most helpful style to be

$$\begin{aligned}
&\text{foo}(\langle Arguments \rangle) \leftarrow \\
&\quad \text{bar}_1(\langle Arguments_1 \rangle), \\
&\quad \text{bar}_2(\langle Arguments_2 \rangle), \\
&\quad \vdots \\
&\quad \text{bar}_n(\langle Arguments_n \rangle).
\end{aligned}$$

The heads of all clauses are aligned, the goals in the body of a clause are indented and occupy a separate line each. A blank line is inserted between procedures, but there is no space between individual clauses of a procedure.

Layout in a book and the typography used are not entirely consistent with actual programs. If all the goals in the body of a clause are short, then have them on one line. Occasionally we have tables of facts with more than one fact per line.

A program can be self-documenting if sufficient care is taken with these two factors, and the program is sufficiently simple. Given the natural aversion of programmers to comments and documentation, this is very desirable.

In practice, code is rarely self-documenting and comments are needed. One important part of the documentation is the relation scheme, which can be presented before the clauses defining that relation, augmented with further explanations if necessary. The explanations used in the book define the relation a procedure computes. It is not always easy to come up with a precise, declarative, natural-language description of a relation computed by a logic program. However, the inability to do so usually indicates that the programmer does not fully understand his creation, even if his creation actually works. Hence we encourage the use of the declarative documentation conventions adopted in the book. They are a good means of communicating to others what a program defines, as well as a discipline of thought, enabling a programmer to think about and reflect on his own creation.

13.4 Program development

Since programming in (pure) Prolog is as close to writing specifications as any practical programming language has gotten, one might expect pure Prolog programs to be bug free. This, of course, is not the case. Even when axiomatizing one's concepts and algorithms, a wide spectrum of bugs, quite similar to ones found in conventional languages, can be encountered.

Stating it differently, for any formalism there are sufficiently complex problems, for which there are no self-evidently correct formulations of solutions. The difference between low-level and high-level languages, then, is only the threshold after which simple examination of the program is insufficient to determine its correctness.

There are two schools of thought on what to do on such an occasion. The "verification" school suggests that such complex programs be verified, by proving that they behave correctly with respect to an abstract specification. It is not clear how to apply this approach to logic programs, as the distance between the abstract specification and the program is much smaller then in other languages. If the Prolog axiomatization is not self-evident, there is very little hope that the specification, no matter in what language it is written, would be.

One might suggest to use full first-order logic as a specification formalism for Prolog. It is the authors' experience that very rarely a specification in full first-order logic is shorter, simpler, or more readable then the simplest Prolog program defining the relation.

Given this situation, there are weaker alternatives. One is to prove that one Prolog program, perhaps more efficient though more complex, is equivalent to a simpler Prolog program, which, though less efficient, could serve as a specification for the first. Another is to prove that a program satisfies some constraint, such as a "loop invariant," which, though not guaranteeing the program's correctness, increases our confidence in it.

In some sense, Prolog programs are executable specifications. The alternative to staring at them, trying to convince ourselves that they are correct, is to execute them, and see if they behave the way we want them to. This is the standard testing and debugging activity, carried in program development in any other programming language. All the classical methods, approaches, and common wisdom concerning program testing and debugging apply equaly well to Prolog.

What is the difference, then, between program development in conventional, even symbolic languages and Prolog?

One answer is that although Prolog programming is "just" programming, there is a factor of improvement in ease of expression and speed of debugging compared to other lower-level formalisms — we hope the reader has already sensed a glimpse of it.

Another answer is that declarative programming clears your mind. Said less dramatically, programming one's ideas in general, and programming in a declarative and high-level language in particular, clarifies one's thoughts and concepts. For experienced Prolog programmers, Prolog is not just a formalism for "coding" a computer, but also a formalism in which ideas can be expressed and evaluated — a tool for thinking.

A third answer is that the properties of the high-level formalism of logic may eventually lead to a set of practical program development tools that is an order of magnitude more powerful then what is known today. Examples of such tools are automatic program transformers, partial-evaluators, type inference programs, and algorithmic debuggers. The latter are addressed in Section 19.3, where program diagnosis algorithms and their implementation in Prolog are described.

Unfortunately, practical Prolog programming environments incorporating these novel ideas are not yet widely available. In the meantime, a simple tracer, such as explained in Section 19.1, is most of what one can expect. Nevertheless, large and sophisticated Prolog programs can be developed even using the current Prolog environments, perhaps with greater ease than in other available languages.

The current tools and systems do not dictate or support a specific program development methodology. However, as with other symbolic programming languages, rapid prototyping is perhaps the most natural development strategy. In this strategy, one has an evolving, usable prototype of the system in most stages of the development. Development proceeds by either rewriting the prototype program or extending it. Another alternative, or complementary, approach to program development is "think top-down, implement bottom-up." Although the design of a system should be top-down and goal driven, its implementation proceeds best if done bottom up. In bottom-up programming each piece of code written can be debugged immediately. Global decisions, such as representation, can be tested in practice on small sections of the system, and cleaned up and made more robust before most of the programming has been done. Also, experience with one subsystem may lead to changes in design decisions regarding other subsystems.

The size of the chunks of code that should be written and debugged as a whole varys and grows as the experience of the programmer grows. Experienced Prolog programmers can write programs consisting of several pages of code, knowing that what is left after writing is done is mostly simple and mundane debugging. Less experienced programmers might find it hard to grasp the functionality and interaction of more then a few procedures at a time.

We would like to conclude this section with a few moralistic statements. For every programming language, no matter how clean, elegant, and high level, one can find programmers who will use it to write dirty, contorted, and unreadable programs. Prolog is no exception. However, we feel that for most problems that have an elegant solution, there is an elegant expression of their solution in Prolog. It is a goal of the book to convey both this belief and the tools to realize it in concrete cases, by showing that aesthetics and praticality are not necessarily opposing or conflicting goals.

13.5 Background

The practice of analyzing the complexity of Prolog programs is not as developed as for programs in more conventional programming languages. We believe this is due to historical and sociological reasons and does not have much to do with inherent properties of Prolog programs.

There has been little agreement on Prolog benchmarks, other than that LIPS is probably the best measure. One standard is to time Program 3.16a, naive *reverse*, reversing a list. There are 496 reductions for a list with 30 elements.

Several collections of Prolog programming tricks are in the public domain. The main one is the Prolog library on the Arpanet at Stanford, which principally draws on utilities from Edinburgh.

Programming style evolves from experience and interaction with others. A strong influence on the first author was the Prolog programming community at the University of Edinburgh, in particular, the influences of Lawrence Byrd and Richard O'Keefe.

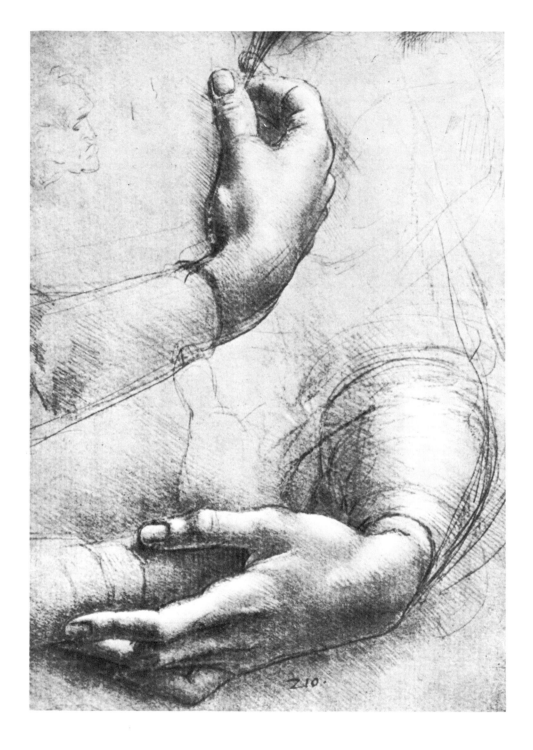

Part III

Advanced Prolog Programming Techniques

The expressive power and high-level nature of logic programming can be exploited to write programs that are not easily expressed in conventional programming languages. Different problem solving paradigms can be supported, and alternative data construction and access mechanisms can be used.

The simple Prolog programs of the previous part are examples of the use of basic programming techniques, reinterpreted in the context of logic programming. This part collects more advanced techniques that have evolved in the logic programming community and exploit the special features of logic programs. We show how they can be used to advantage.

Chapter 14
Nondeterministic Programming

An aspect of the logic programming computation model lacking in conventional programming models is nondeterminism. Nondeterminism is a technical concept used to define, in a concise way, abstract computation models. However, in addition to being a powerful theoretical concept, nondeterminism is also useful for defining and implementing algorithms. This chapter shows how, by thinking nondeterministically, one can construct concise and efficient programs.

Intuitively, a nondeterministic machine is a machine that can choose its next operation correctly, when faced with several alternatives. True nondeterministic machines cannot be realized but can be simulated, or approximated. In particular, the Prolog interpreter approximates the nondeterministic behavior of the abstract logic programs interpreter by sequential search and backtracking, as explained in Chapter 6. However the fact that nondeterminism is only "simulated" without being "really present" can be abstracted away in many cases, in favor of nondeterministic thinking, in much the same way as pointer manipulation details involved in unification can be abstracted away in favor of symbolic thinking.

14.1 Generate-and-test

Generate-and-test is a common technique in algorithm design and programming. In generate-and-test one process, or routine, generates the set of candidate solutions to the problem, and another process, or routine, tests the candidates, trying to find one, or all, of the candidates which actually solve the problem.

Typically, generate-and-test programs are easier to construct then programs that compute the solution directly, but they are also less efficient. A standard technique for optimizing generate and test programs is to try and "push" the tester inside the generator, as "deep" as possible. Ultimately, the tester is completely intertwined with the generator, and only correct solutions are generated to begin with.

It is easy to write logic programs that, under the execution model of Prolog, implement the generate-and-test technique. Such programs typically have a conjunction of two goals, in which one acts as the generator and the other tests whether the solution is acceptable, as in the following clause:

find(X) ← generate(X), test(X).

This Prolog program would actually behave like a conventional, procedural, generate-and-test program. When called with *find(X)?*, *generate(X)* succeeds, returning some *X*, with which *test(X)* is called. If the *test* goal fails, execution backtracks to *generate(X)*, which generates the next element. This continues iteratively until the tester successfully finds a solution with the distinguishing property, or the generator is exhausted of alternative solutions.

The programmer, however, need not be concerned by the generate-and-test cycle, and can view this technique more abstractly, as an instance of nondeterministic programming. In this nondeterministic program the generator guesses correctly an element in the domain of possible solutions, and the tester simply verifies that the guess of the generator is correct.

A program with multiple solutions and commonly used as a generator is Program 3.12 for *member*. The query *member(X,[a,b,c])?* will yield the solutions *X=a*, *X=b*, and *X=c* successively as required. Thus *member* can be used to nondeterministically choose the correct element of a list in a generate-and-test program.

Program 14.1 is a simple example of generate-and-test using *member* as a generator. The program identifies parts of speech of a sentence. We assume that a sentence is represented as a list of words, and there is a database of facts giving the parts of speech of particular words. Each part of speech is a unary predicate whose argument is a word, for example, *noun(man)* indicates that *man* is a noun. The relationship *verb(Sentence,Word)* is true if *Word* is a verb in sentence *Sentence*. The analogous meanings are intended for *noun/2* and *article/2*. The query *verb([a,man,loves,a,woman], V)?* finds the verb *V=loves* in the sentence using generate-and-test. Words in the sentence are generated by *member*, and tested to see if they are a verb.

Another simple example is testing whether two lists have an element in common. Consider the predicate *intersect(Xs, Ys)*, which is true if *Xs* and *Ys* have an

> $verb(Sentence, Verb) \leftarrow$
> $Verb$ is a verb in the list of words $Sentence$.

> verb(Sentence,Word) ← member(Word,Sentence), verb(Word).
> noun(Sentence,Word) ← member(Word,Sentence), noun(Word).
> article(Sentence,Word) ← member(Word,Sentence), article(Word).

Vocabulary

> noun(man).   noun(woman).
> article(a).   verb(loves).

Program 14.1: Finding parts of speech in a sentence

element in common:

> intersect(Xs,Ys) ← member(X,Xs), member(X,Ys).

The first *member* goal in the body of the clause generates members of the first list, which are then tested by the second *member* goal whether they are in the second list. Thinking nondeterministically, the first goal guesses an X in Xs, while the second verifies that the guess is a member of Ys.

Note that when executed as a Prolog program, this clause effectively implements two nested loops. The outer loop iterates over the elements of the first list, and the inner loop checks whether the chosen element is a member of the second list. Hence this nondeterministic logic program achieves, under the execution model of Prolog, a behavior very similar to the standard solution one would compose for this problem in Fortran, Pascal, or Lisp.

The definition of *member* in terms of *append*,

> member(X,Xs) ← append(As,[X|Bs],Xs).

is itself essentially generate-and-test program. The two stages however are amalgamated by the use of unification. The *append* goal generates splits of the list, and immediately a test is made whether the first element of the second list is X.

Let us consider optimizing generate-and-test programs by pushing the tester into the generator. Program 14.2 for permutation sort is another example of a generate and test program. The top level is as follows:

> sort(Xs,Ys) ← permutation(Xs,Ys), ordered(Ys).

Abstractly, this program guesses nondeterministically the correct permutation via *permutation(Xs, Ys)*, and *ordered* checks that it is actually ordered.

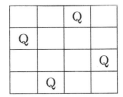

Figure 14.1: A solution to the 4 queens problem

Operationally, the behavior is as follows. A query involving *sort* is reduced to a query involving *permutation* and *ordered*. A failure-driven loop ensues. A permutation of the list is generated by *permutation* and tested by *ordered*. If the permuted list is not ordered, the execution backtracks to the *permutation* goal which generates another permutation to be tested. Eventually an ordered permutation is generated and the computation terminates.

Permutation sort is a highly inefficient sorting algorithm, requiring time exponential in the size of the list to be sorted. Pushing the tester into the generator, however, leads to a reasonable algorithm. The generator for permutation sort, *permutation*, selects an arbitrary element and recursively permutes the rest of the list. The tester, *ordered*, verifies that the first two elements of the permutation are in order, then recursively checks the rest. If we view the combined recursive *permutation* and *ordered* goals as a recursive sorting process, we have the basis for insertion sort, Program 3.21. To sort a list, sort the tail of the list and insert the head of the list into its correct place in the order. The arbitrary selection of an element has been replaced by choosing the first element.

Another example of the advantage of intertwining generating and testing can be seen with programs solving the *N* queens problem.

The *N* queens problem requires the placement of *N* pieces on an *N*-by-*N* rectangular board so that no two pieces are on the same line: horizontal, vertical or diagonal. The original formulation called for 8 queens to be placed on a chessboard, and the criterion of not being on the same line corresponds to two queens not attacking each other under the rules of chess. Hence the problem's name.

The program has been well studied in the recreational mathematics literature. There is no solution for *N=2* and *N=3*, and a unique solution up to reflection for *N=4* shown in Figure 14.1. There are 88 (or 92 depending on strictness with symmetries) solutions for *N=8*.

Program 14.2 is a simplistic program solving the *N* queens problem. The re-

queens(*N, Queens*) ←
    Queens is a placement that solves the *N* queens problem,
    represented as a permutation of the list of numbers [*1,2,...,N*].

queens(N,Qs) ←
    range(1,N,Ns), permutation(Ns,Qs), safe(Qs).

safe(*Qs*) ←
    The placement *Qs* is safe.

safe([Q|Qs]) ← safe(Qs), not attack(Q,Qs).
safe([ ]).

attack(X,Xs) ← attack(X,1,Xs).

attack(X,N,[Y|Ys]) ← X := Y+N ; X := Y–N.
attack(X,N,[Y|Ys]) ← N1 := N+1, attack(X,N1,Ys).

permutation(Xs,Ys) ← See Program 3.20

range(1,N,Ns) ← See Program 8.12

Program 14.2: Naive generate-and-test for the *N* queens problem

lation *queen*(*N, Qs*) is true if *Qs* is a solution to the *N* queens problem. Solutions
are specified as a permutation of the list of the numbers 1 to *N*. The first element
of the list is the row number to place the queen in the first column, the second
element indicates the row number to place the queen in the second column, etc.
Figure 14.1 indicates the solution [2,4,1,3] to the 4 queens problem. This specification of solutions, and the program generating them, has implicitly incorporated
the observation that any solution to the *N* queens problem will have a queen on
each row, and a queen on each column.

    The program behaves as follows. The predicate *range* creates a list *Ns* of the
numbers from *1* to *N*. Then a generate-and-test cycle begins. The *permutation*
predicate generates a permutation *Qs* of *Ns*, which is tested whether it is a solution
to the problem with the predicate *safe*(*Qs*). This predicate is true if *Qs* is a correct
placement of the queens. Since two queens are not placed on the same row or
column, the predicate need only check whether two queens attack each other
along a diagonal. *Safe* is defined recursively. A list of queens is safe if the queens
represented by the tail of the list are safe, and the queen represented by the head
of the list does not attack any of the other queens. The definition of *attack*(*Q,Qs*)
uses a neat encapsulation of the interaction of diagonals. A queen is on the same
diagonal as a second queen *N* columns away if the second queen's row number is
N units greater than, or *N* units less than, the first queen's row number. This

queens(N, Queens) ←
   Queens is a placement that solves the N
   queens problem, represented
   as a permutation of the list of numbers $[1,2,...N]$.

queens(N,Qs) ← range(1,N,Ns), queens(Ns,[ ],Qs).

queens(UnplacedQs,SafeQs,Qs) ←
   select(Q,UnplacedQs,UnplacedQs1),
   not attack(Q,SafeQs),
   queens(UnplacedQs1,[Q|SafeQs],Qs).
queens([ ],Qs,Qs).

select(X,Xs,Ys) ← See Program 3.19.

attack(X,Xs) ← See Program 14.2.

Program 14.3: Placing one queen at a time

is expressed by the first clause of *attack/3* in Program 14.2. The meaning of *attack(Q, Qs)* is that queen Q attacks some queen in Qs. The diagonals are tested iteratively until the end of the board is reached.

Program 14.2 cannot recognize when solutions are symmetric. The program gives two solutions to the query *queens(4, Qs)?*, namely $Qs=[2,4,1,3]$ and $Qs=[3,1,4,2]$.

Although a well written logic program, Program 14.2 behaves inefficiently. Many permutations are generated that have no chance of being solutions. As with permutation sort, we improve the program by pushing the tester, in this case *safe*, into the generator.

Instead of generating the complete permutation, that is, placing all the queens and then testing it, each queen can be checked as it is being placed. Program 14.3 computes solutions to the N queens problem by placing the queens one at a time. It also proceeds by generating and testing, in contrast to insertion sort, which became a deterministic algorithm by the transformation. The generator in the program is *select* and the tester is *attack*, or more precisely its negation.

The positions of the previously placed queens are necessary to test whether a new queen is safe. Therefore the final solution is built upward using an accumulator. This is an application of the basic technique described in Section 7.5. A consequence of using an accumulator is that the queens are placed on the right-hand edge of the board. The two solutions to the query *queens(4, Qs)* are given in the opposite order to Program 14.2.

color_map(Map, Colors) ←
    Map is colored with *Colors*, so that no two neighbors have the same color.
    The map is represented as an adjacency-list of regions
    region(Name, Color, Neighbors), where *Name* is the name of the region,
    Color is its color, and *Neighbors* are the colors of the neighbors.
    The program can be used with all colors initially uninstantiated.

color_map([Region|Regions],Colors) ←
    color_region(Region,Colors),
    color_map(Regions,Colors).
color_map([ ],Colors).

color_region(Region, Colors) ←
    Region and its neighbors are colored using *Colors* so that the
    region's color is different from the color of any of its neighbors.

color_region(region(Name,Color,Neighbors),Colors) ←
    select(Color,Colors,Colors1),
    members(Neighbors,Colors1).

select(X,Xs,Ys) ← See Program 3.19.

members(Xs,Ys) ← See Program 7.6.

Program 14.4: Map coloring

The next problem is to color a planar map so that no two adjoining regions have the same color. A famous conjecture, an open question for a hundred years, was proved in 1976 showing that four colors are sufficient to color any planar map. Figure 14.2 gives a simple map requiring four colors to be colored correctly. This can be proved by enumeration of the possibilities. Hence four colors are both necessary and sufficient.

Program 14.4 which solves the map-coloring problem also uses the generate-and-test programming technique extensively. The program implements the following nondeterministic iterative algorithm.

For each region of the map

    choose a color,
    choose (or verify) colors for the neighboring regions from the
        remaining colors.

A data structure is needed to support the algorithm. The map is represented as a list of regions. Each region has a name, a color, and a list of colors of the

Test data

test_color(Name,Map) ←
    map(Name,Map),
    colors(Name,Colors),
    color_map(Map,Colors).

map(test,[region(a,A,[B,C,D]),region(b,B,[A,C,E]),region(c,C,[A,B,D,E,F]),
    region(d,D,[A,C,F]),region(e,E,[B,C,F]),region(f,F,[C,D,E])]).

map(west_europe,[region(portugal,P,[E]), region(spain,E,[F,P]),
    region(france,F,[E,I,S,B,WG,L]), region(belgium,B,[F,H,L,WG]),
    region(holland,H,[B,WG]), region(west_germany,WG,[F,A,S,H,B,L]),
    region(luxembourg,L,[F,B,WG]), region(italy,I,[F,A,S]),
    region(switzerland,S,[F,I,A,WG]), region(austria,A,[I,S,WG])]).

colors(X,[red,yellow,blue,white]).

Program 14.5: Test data for map coloring

Figure 14.2: A map requiring 4 colours

adjoining regions. The map in Figure 14.2, for example, is represented as

[region(a,A,[B,C,D]),region(b,B,[A,C,E]),region(c,C,[A,B,D,E,F]),
    region(d,D,[A,C,F]),region(e,E,[B,C,F]),region(f,F,[C,D,E])].

The sharing of variables is used to ensure that the same region is not colored with
two different colors by different iterations of the algorithm.

The top-level relation is *color_map(Map,Colors)* where the *Map* is represented as above, and *Colors* is a list of colors used to color the map. Our colors
are *red*, *yellow*, *blue* and *white*. The heart of the algorithm is the definition of
color_region(Region,Colors):

color_region(region(Name,Color,Neighbors),Colors) ←
    select(Color,Colors,Colors1), members(Neighbors,Colors1).

Both the *select* and *members* goals can act as generators or testers depending on

solve_puzzle(Puzzle,Solution) ←
    Solution is a solution of the *Puzzle*,
    where *Puzzle* is *puzzle(Clues,Queries,Solution)*.

solve_puzzle(puzzle(Clues,Queries,Solution),Solution) ←
    solve(Clues),
    solve(Queries).

solve([Clue|Clues]) ←
    Clue, solve(Clues).
solve([ ]).

Program 14.6: A puzzle solver

whether their arguments are instantiated.

Overall the effect of the program is to instantiate a data structure, the map.
The calls to *select* and *members* can be viewed as specifying local constraints.
The predicates either generate, by instantiating arguments in the structure, or
test whether instantiated values satisfy local constraints.

Our final example is solving a logic puzzle. The behavior of the program
is similar to the map-coloring program. The logic puzzle consists of some facts
about some small number of objects that have various attributes. The minimum
number of facts is given about the objects and attributes, to yield a unique way
of assigning attributes to objects.

Here is an example that we will use to describe the technique of solving logic
puzzles.

Three friends came first, second and third in a programming competition.
Each of the three had a different first name, liked a different sport, and had a
different nationality.

Michael likes basketball, and did better than the American. Simon, the
Israeli, did better than the tennis player. The cricket player came first.

Who is the Australian? What sport does Richard play?

Logic puzzles such as the one above are elegantly solved by instantiating the
values of a suitable data structure, and extracting the solution values. Each clue is
translated into a fact about the data structure. This can be done before the exact
form of the data structure is determined using data abstraction. Let us analyze
the first clue: "Michael likes basketball, and did better than the American."
Two distinct people are referred to. One is named Michael and whose sport is
basketball, while the other is American. Further Michael did better than the

American. If we assume the structure to be instantiated is *Friends*, then the clue is expressed as the conjunction of goals

> did_better(Man1,Man2,Friends), name(Man1,michael),
> sport(Man1,basketball), nationality(Man2,american),

Similarly the second clue can be translated to the conditions

> did_better(Man1,Man2,Friends), name(Man1,simon),
> nationality(Man1,israeli), sport(Man2,tennis),

and the third clue to the conditions

> first(Friends,Man), sport(Man,cricket).

A framework for solving puzzles is given as Program 14.6. The relation computed is *solve_puzzle(Puzzle,Solution)*, where *Solution* is the solution to *Puzzle*. The puzzle is represented by the structure *puzzle(Clues,Queries,Solution)*, where the data structure being instantiated is incorporated into the clues and queries, and the values to be extracted are given by *Solution*.

The code for *solve_puzzle* is trivial. All it does is successively solve each clue and query, which are expressed as Prolog goals and are executed with the meta-variable facility.

The clues and queries for our example puzzle are given in Program 14.7. We describe the structure assumed by the clues to solve the puzzle. Each person has three attributes, and can be represented by the structure *friend(Name,Country,Sport)*. There are three friends whose order in the programming competition is significant. This suggests an ordered sequence of three elements as the structure for the problem, i.e. the list

> [friend(N1,C1,S1),friend(N2,C2,S2),friend(N3,C3,S3)].

The programs defining the conditions *did_better*, *name*, *nationality*, *sport*, and *first* are straightforward, and are given in Program 14.7.

The combination of Programs 14.6 and 14.7 works as a giant generate-and-test. Each of the *did_better* and *member* goals access people, and the remaining goals access attributes of the people. Whether they are generators or testers depends on whether the arguments are instantiated or not. The answer to the complete puzzle, for the curious, is that Michael is the Australian, and Richard plays tennis.

Test data

test_puzzle(Name,puzzle(Clues,Queries,Solution)) ←
    structure(Name,Structure),
    clues(Name,Structure,Clues),
    queries(Name,Structure,Queries,Solution).

structure(test,[friend(N1,C1,S1),friend(N2,C2,S2),friend(N3,C3,S3)]).

clues(test,Friends,
    [(did_better(Man1Clue1,Man2Clue1,Friends),   % Clue 1
    name(Man1Clue1,michael), sport(Man1Clue1,basketball),
    nationality(Man2Clue1,american)),
    (did_better(Man1Clue2,Man2Clue2,Friends),   % Clue 2
    name(Man1Clue2,simon), nationality(Man1Clue2,israeli),
    sport(Man2Clue2,tennis)),
    (first(Friends,ManClue3), sport(ManClue3,cricket))   % Clue 3
    ]).

queries(test, Friends,
    [member(Q1,Friends),
        name(Q1,Name),
        nationality(Q1,australian),   % Query 1
        member(Q2,Friends),
        name(Q2,richard),
        sport(Q2,Sport)   % Query 2
    ],
    [['The Australian is ', Name],['Richard plays ', Sport]]
).

did_better(A,B,[A,B,C]).
did_better(A,C,[A,B,C]).
did_better(B,C,[A,B,C]).

name(friend(A,B,C),A).
nationality(friend(A,B,C),B).
sport(friend(A,B,C),C).

first([X|Xs],X).

Program 14.7: A description of a puzzle

Exercises for Section 14.1

(i) Write a program to compute the integer square root of a natural number
     N defined to be the number I such that $I^2 \leq N$, but $(I+1)^2 > N$. Use the
     predicate *between/3*, Program 8.5, to generate successive natural numbers on
     backtracking.

(ii) Write a program to solve the stable marriage problem (Sedgewick, 1983)
      stated as follows:

      Suppose there are N men and N women who want to get married. Each man
      has a list of all the women in his preferred order, and each woman likewise
      has a list of the men in preferred order. The problem is to find a set of
      marriages that is stable.

      A set of marriages is *unstable* if two people who are not married both prefer
      each other to their spouses. For example, suppose there are two men, A and
      B, and two women, X and Y, such that A prefers X to Y, B prefers Y to X,
      X prefers A to B, and Y prefers B to A. The pair of marriages $A-Y$ and $B-X$
      is unstable, since A prefers X to Y, while X prefers A to B.

      Your program should have as input lists of preferences, and produce as output
      a stable set of marriages, i.e., one that is not unstable. It is a theorem from
      graph theory that this is always possible. Test the program on the following
      5 men and 5 women with their associated preferences:

avraham:	chana tamar zvia ruth sarah
binyamin:	zvia chana ruth sarah tamar
chaim:	chana ruth tamar sarah zvia
david:	zvia ruth chana sarah tamar
elazar:	tamar ruth chana zvia sarah
zvia:	elazar avraham david binyamin chaim
chana:	david clazar binyamin avraham chaim
ruth:	avraham david binyamin chaim elazar
sarah:	chaim binyamin david avraham elazar
tamar:	david binyamin chaim elazar avraham

(iii) Use Program 14.4 to color the map of Western Europe. The countries are
      given in Program 14.5.

(iv) Write a program to solve the following logic puzzle. There are five houses,
      each of a different color and inhabited by a man of a different nationality,
      with a different pet, drink and brand of cigarettes.

      1. The Englishman lives in the red house.

2. The Spaniard owns the dog.
3. Coffee is drunk in the green house.
4. The Ukrainian drinks tea.
5. The green house is immediately to the right (your right) of the ivory house.
6. The Winston smoker owns snails.
7. Kools are smoked in the yellow house.
8. Milk is drunk in the middle house.
9. The Norwegian lives in the first house on the left.
10. The man who smokes Chesterfields lives in the house next to the man with the fox.
11. Kools are smoked in the house next to the house where the horse is kept.
12. The Lucky Strike smoker drinks orange juice.
13. The Japanese smokes Parliaments.
14. The Norwegian lives next to the blue house.

Who owns the Zebra? Who drinks water?

(v) Write a program to test whether a graph is planar using the algorithm of Hopcroft and Tarjan (Deo, 1974; Even, 1979).

14.2   Don't-care and don't-know nondeterminism

Two forms of nondeterminism are distinguished in the logic programming literature. They differ in the nature of the choice among alternatives that must be made. For *don't-care nondeterminism*, the choice can be made arbitrarily. In terms of the logic programming computation model, any goal reduction will lead to a solution, and it does not matter which particular solution is found. For *don't-know nondeterminism*, the choice matters but the correct one is not known at the time the choice is made.

Most examples of don't-care nondeterminism are not relevant for the Prolog programmer. A prototypical example is the code for *minimum*. Program 3.7 is the standard, incorporating a limited amount of don't-care nondeterminism, namely when X and Y are the same:

$$minimum(X,Y,X) \leftarrow X \leq Y.$$
$$minimum(X,Y,Y) \leftarrow Y \leq X.$$

In Section 7.4, we termed this redundancy and advised against its use.

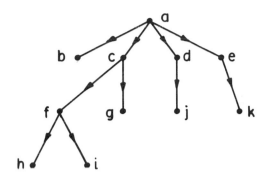
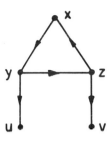

Figure 14.3· Directed graphs

On the other hand, programs exhibiting don't-know nondeterminism are common. Consider the program for testing whether two binary trees are isomorphic (Program 3.25 reproduced below). Each clause is independently correct, but given two isomorphic binary trees, we don't know which of the two recursive clauses should be used to prove the isomorphism. Operationally, only when the computation terminates successfully do we know the correct choice:

> isotree(void,void).
> isotree(tree(X,L1,R1),tree(X,L2,R2)) ← isotree(L1,R1), isotree(L2,R2).
> isotree(tree(X,L1,R1),tree(X,L2,R2)) ← isotree(L1,R2), isotree(L2,R1).

Composing Prolog programs exhibiting either form of nondeterminism can be indistinguishable from composing deterministic programs. Each clause is written independently. Whether inputs match only one clause or several is irrelevant to the programmer. Indeed this is seen from the multiple uses that can be made of Prolog programs. With one form of arguments the program is deterministic, in another nondeterministic, for example, *append*.

The behavior of Prolog programs seemingly having don't-know nondeterminism such as *isotree* is known. A given logic program and a query determine a search tree as discussed in Chapter 5, which is searched depth first by Prolog. Writing a program possessing don't-know nondeterminism is really specifying a depth first search algorithm for solving the problem.

We consider this viewpoint in a little more detail with a particular example: finding whether two nodes in a graph are connected. Figure 14.3 contains two graphs that will be used to test our ideas. The left-hand one is a tree, while the right-hand one is not, containing a cycle. Trees, or more generally directed

connected(*X, Y*) ←
> Node *X* is connected to node *Y*,
> given an *edge/2* relation describing a DAG.

connected(A,A).
connected(A,B) ← edge(A,N), connected(N,B).

Data

edge(a,b).	edge(a,c).	edge(a,d).	edge(a,e).	edge(d,j).
edge(c,f).	edge(c,g).	edge(f,h).	edge(e,k).	edge(f,i).
edge(x,y).	edge(y,z).	edge(z,x).	edge(y,u).	edge(z,v).

Program 14.8: Connectivity in a finite DAG

path(*X, Y, Path*) ←
> *Path* is a path between two nodes *X* and *Y*
> in the DAG defined by the relation *edge/2*.

path(X,X,[X]).
path(X,Y,[X|P]) ← edge(X,N), path(N,Y,P).

Program 14.9: Finding a path by depth-first search

connected(*X, Y*) ←
> Node *X* is connected to node *Y* in the graph defined by *edge/2*.

connected(X,Y) ← connected(X,Y,[X]).

connected(A,A,Visited).
connected(A,B,Visited) ←
> edge(A,N), not member(N,Visited), connected(N,B,[N|Visited]).

Program 14.10: Connectivity in a graph

acyclic graphs (DAGs), behave better than graphs with cycles as we will see in our example programs.

Our first program is a small modification of a logic program of Section 2.3. Program 14.8 defines the relation *connected*(*X, Y*) which is true if two nodes in a graph, *X* and *Y*, are connected. Edges are directed; the fact *edge*(*X, Y*) stating that a directed edge exists from *X* to *Y*. Declaratively the program is a concise, recursive specification of what it means for nodes in a graph to be connected. Interpreted operationally as a Prolog program, it is the implementation of an algorithm to find whether two nodes are connected using depth-first search.

The solutions to the query *connected(a,X)* using the data from the left-hand graph in Figure 14.3 gives the solutions *b, c, f, h, i, g, d, j, e, k.* Their order constitutes a depth-first traversal of the tree.

Program 14.9 is an extension of this simple program that finds a path between two nodes. The predicate *path(X,Y,Path)* is true if *Path* is a path from the node *X* to the node *Y* in a graph. Both endpoints are included in the path. The path is built downward, which fits well with the recursive specification of the *connected* relation. The ease of computing the path is a direct consequence of the depth-first traversal. The equivalent extension of a breadth first traversal is much more difficult, to be discussed in Sections 17.2 and 18.1.

Depth-first search, *dfs*, correctly traverses any finite tree or DAG (directed acyclic graph). There is a problem, however, with traversing a graph with cycles. The computation can become lost in an infinite loop (literally!) around one of the cycles. For example, the query *connected(x,Node)?*, referring to the right-hand graph of Figure 14.3 gives the solution *y, z,* and *x* repeatedly without reaching *u* or *v*.

The problem is overcome by modifying *connected.* An extra argument is added that accumulates the nodes visited so far. A test is made to avoid visiting the same state twice. This is shown in Program 14.10.

Program 14.10 successfully traverses a finite directed graph depth first. The pure Prolog program needed for searching finite DAGs must be extended by negation in order to work correctly. Adding an accumulator of paths visited to avoid entering loops effectively breaks the cycles in the graph by preventing traversal of an edge which would complete a cycle.

The program is not guaranteed to reach every node of an infinite graph. To do so, breadth-first search is necessary. This is discussed further in Section 17.2.

The section is completed with a program for building simple plans in the blocks world. The program is written nondeterministically, essentially performing a depth-first search. It combines the two extensions given above — keeping an accumulator of what has been traversed, and computing a path.

The problem is to form a plan in the blocks world, that is, to specify a sequence of actions for restacking blocks to achieve a particular configuration. Figure 14.4 gives the initial state and the desired final state of a blocks world problem. There are three blocks, *a,b,* and *c,* and three places, *p, q,* and *r.* The actions allowed are moving a block from the top of a block to a place and moving a block from one block to another. For the action to succeed, the top of the moved block must be clear, and also the place or block to which it is being moved.

The top level procedure of Program 14.11, that solves the problem, is *trans-*

transform(State1,State2,Plan) ←
    The *Plan* of actions transforms *State1* into *State2*.

transform(State1,State2,Plan) ←
    transform(State1,State2,[State1],Plan).

transform(State,State,Visited,[ ]).
transform(State1,State2,Visited,[Action|Actions]) ←
    legal_action(Action,State1),
    update(Action,State1,State),
    not member(State,Visited),
    transform(State,State2,[State|Visited],Actions).

legal_action(to_place(Block,Y,Place),State) ←
    on(Block,Y,State), clear(Block,State), place(Place), clear(Place,State).
legal_action(to_block(Block1,Y,Block2),State) ←
    on(Block1,Y,State), clear(Block1,State), block(Block2),
    Block1 B̄lock2, clear(Block2,State).

clear(X,State) ← not member(on(A,X),State).

on(X,Y,State) ← member(on(X,Y),State).

update(to_block(X,Y,Z),State,State1) ←
    substitute(on(X,Y),on(X,Z),State,State1).
update(to_place(X,Y,Z),State,State1) ←
    substitute(on(X,Y),on(X,Z),State,State1).

Program 14.11: A depth-first planner

Testing and data

test_plan(Name,Plan) ←
    initial_state(Name,I), final_state(Name,F), transform(I,F,Plan).

initial_state(test,[on(a,b),on(b,p),on(c,r)]).
final_state(test,[on(a,b),on(b,c),on(c,r)]).

block(a).   block(b).   block(c).
place(p).   place(q).   place(r).

Program 14.12: Testing the depth-first planner

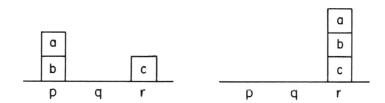

Figure 14.4: Initial and final states of a blocks world problem

form(State1,State2,Plan). A plan of actions, *Plan*, is produced which transforms *State1* into *State2*.

States are represented by a list of relations of the form $on(X,Y)$ where X is a block and Y is a block or place. They represent the facts that are true in the state. For example, the initial and final states in Figure 14.5 are, respectively, $[on(a,b),on(b,p),on(c,r)]$ and $[on(a,b),on(b,c),on(c,r)]$. The *on* relation for a precedes that of b, which precedes the *on* relation for c. The state descriptions allow easy testing whether a block or place X is clear in a given state by checking that there is no relation of the form $on(A,X)$. The predicates *clear/2* and *on/3* in Program 14.11 take advantage of this representation.

The nondeterministic algorithm used by the planner is given by the recursive clause of *transform/4* in the program:

> while the desired state is not reached,
> > find a legal action,
> > update the current state,
> > check that it has not been visited before.

There are two possible actions, moving to a block and moving to a place. For each, the conditions for which it is legal must be specified, and how to update it.

Program 14.11 successfully solves the simple problem given as Program 14.12. The first plan it produces is horrendous, however, being

```
[to_place(a,b,q),to_block(a,q,c),to_place(b,p,q),to_place(a,c,p),
    to_block(a,p,b),to_place(c,r,p),to_place(a,b,r),to_block(a,r,c),
    to_place(b,q,r),to_place(a,c,q),to_block(a,q,b),to_place(c,p,q),
    to_place(a,b,p),to_block(a,p,c),to_place(b,r,p),to_place(a,c,r),
    to_block(b,p,a),to_place(c,q,p),to_block(b,a,c),to_place(a,r,q),
```

to_block(b,c,a),to_place(c,p,r),to_block(b,a,c),to_place(a,q,p),
to_block(a,p,b)].

Block *a* is first moved to *q*, then to *c*. After that block *b* is moved to *q*, block *a* is moved to *p* and *b*, and after 20 more random moves, the final configuration is reached.

It is easy to incorporate a little more intelligence by first trying to achieve one of the goal states. The predicate *legal_action* can be replaced by a predicate *choose_action(Action,State1,State2)* where the action is chosen. A simple definition suffices to produce intelligent behavior in our example problem:

choose_action(Action,State1,State2) ←
    suggest(Action,State2), legal_action(Action,State1).
choose_action(Action,State1,State2) ←
    legal_action(Action,State1).

suggest(to_place(X,Y,Z),State) ←
    member(on(X,Z),State), place(Z).
suggest(to_block(X,Y,Z),State) ←
    member(on(X,Z),State), block(Z).

The first plan now produced is [*to_place(a,b,q),to_block(b,p,c),to_block(a,q,b)*].

14.3 Simulating nondeterministic computation models

In this section we present simple programs simulating some basic computation models. Interpreters for the various classes of automata are very easily written in Prolog.

The simulation programs are a good application of a nondeterministic programming. The operation of a nondeterministic automaton well illustrates don't-know nondeterminism. It is interesting that nondeterministic automata are as easily simulated as deterministic ones due to the nondeterminism of Prolog.

We begin with a (nondeterministic) finite automaton, abbreviated NDFA. An NDFA, is defined as a 5-tuple $\langle Q,S,D,I,F \rangle$ where Q is the set of states, S is the set of symbols, D is a mapping from $Q \times S$ to Q, I is the initial state, and F the set of final states. If the mapping is a function, then the NDFA is deterministic.

In Prolog a finite automaton can be specified by three collections of facts: *initial(Q)*, which is true if Q is the initial state, *final(Q)*, which is true if Q is a final state, and *delta(Q,A,Q1)*, which is true if the NDFA changes from state Q

accept(S) ←
> The string represented by the list *S* is accepted by
> the NDFA defined by *initial/1*, *delta/3*, and *final/1*.

accept(S) ← initial(Q), accept(Q,S).

accept(Q,[X|Xs]) ← delta(Q,X,Q1), accept(Q1,Xs).
accept(Q,[ ]) ← final(Q).

Program 14.13: An interpreter for a nondeterministic finite
automaton

initial(q0).
final(q0).

delta(q0,a,q1).
delta(q1,b,q0).

Program 14.14: An NDFA that accepts the language $(ab)^*$

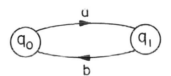

Figure 14.5: A simple automaton

to state *Q1* on receipt of symbol *A*. The set of states and symbols are defined
implicitly as the constants that appear in the predicates.

Program 14.13 is an abstract interpreter for an NDFA. The basic predicate is
accept(S) which is true if the string *S*, represented as a list of symbols, is accepted
by the NDFA.

In order to use the interpreter to simulate the behavior of a particular finite
automaton, the automaton must be specified. That entails defining its initial
state, its final state, and the transition relation *delta*. Program 14.14 gives the
definitions for an NDFA which accepts the language $(ab)^*$. There are two states,
q0 and *q1*. If in state *q0* an *a* is read, the automaton moves to state *q1*, while the
transformation from *q1* to *q0* happens if a *b* is read. The automaton is pictured
in Figure 14.5.

accept(*S*) ←
　　The string represented by the list *S* is accepted by
　　the NPDA defined by *initial/1, delta/5*, and *final/1*.

accept(Xs) ← initial(Q), accept(Q,Xs,[ ]).

accept(Q,[X|Xs],S) ← delta(Q,X,S,Q1,S1), accept(Q1,Xs,S1).
accept(Q,[ ],[ ]) ← final(Q).

Program 14.15: A push-down automaton interpreter

initial(q0).　　　final(q1).

delta(q0,X,S,q0,[X|S]).
delta(q0,X,S,q1,[X|S]).
delta(q0,X,S,q1,S).
delta(q1,X,[X|S],q1,S).

Program 14.16: NPDA for palindromes over a finite alphabet

Another basic computation model is a pushdown automaton, which accepts the class of context-free languages. It extends the model of an NDFA by allowing a single stack for memory in addition to the internal state of the automaton. Formally a (nondeterministic) pushdown automaton, abbreviated NPDA, is a 7-tuple $\langle Q,S,G,D,I,Z,F \rangle$ where Q,S,I,F are as before, G is the list of symbols that can be pushed on the stack, Z is the start symbol on the stack, and D, the delta function, is changed to take account of the stack and current symbol, as well as the internal state.

The operation of an NPDA, defined by the delta function, is determined by the state, the first element in the input string, and the element on the top of the stack. In one operation the NPDA can pop or push one stack element.

An abstract interpreter for an NPDA is very similar to Program 14.13 simulating an NDFA, and is given as Program 14.15. As before, to simulate a particular automaton, the predicates determining the initial and final states of the automaton need be given. The sets of symbols are defined implicitly. Program 14.15 assumes that the stack is initially empty. The change relation *delta*($Q,A,S,Q1,S1$) is slightly different from before. It is true if in state Q on input symbol A and stack state S the NPDA enters state $Q1$ and produces the stack state $S1$.

A particular example of an NPDA is given as Program 14.16. This automaton accepts palindromes over a finite alphabet. A *palindrome* is a string that reads the same forward or backward, for example, *abba* or *abaabaaba*. The automaton has

    palindrome(Xs) ←
       The string represented by the list *Xs* is a palindrome.

    palindrome(Xs) ← palindrome(q0,Xs,[ ]).

    palindrome(q0,[X|Xs],S) ← palindrome(q0,[X|Xs],S]).
    palindrome(q0,Xs,S) ← palindrome(q1,Xs,S).
    palindrome(q0,[X|Xs],S) ← palindrome(q1,Xs,S).
    palindrome(q1,[X|Xs],[X|S]) ← palindrome(q1,Xs,S).
    palindrome(q1,[ ],[ ]).

Program 14.17: A program accepting palindromes

two states: *q0*, when symbols are pushed onto the stack, and *q1*, when symbols
are popped from the stack and compared with the symbols on the input stream.
When to stop pushing and start popping is decided nondeterministically. There
are two *delta* facts that change the state from *q0* to *q1* to allow for palindromes
of both odd and even length.

    The combination of the interpreter plus automaton can be expressed in a
single program. Program 14.17 is an amalgamation of Programs 14.15 and 14.16.
It defines the relation *palindrome(Xs)* which determines whether a string *Xs* is a
palindrome.

    The amalgamation of Programs 14.15 and 14.16 is transformed to Program
14.17 by the technique of *unfolding*. Unfolding is a useful strategy for program
transformation, which is utilized in other places in the book. We digress briefly
to define it.

    Consider a goal A_i in a clause $H ← A_1,\ldots,A_n$ and a clause $C = (A ←
B_1,\ldots B_m)$ where A_i and A unify with mgu θ. *Unfolding* A_i with respect to
its definition C produces the clause $(H ← A_1,\ldots,A_{i-1},B_1,\ldots,B_m,A_{i+1},\ldots,A_n)\theta$.

    This definition is analogous to the definition of unfolding in functional pro-
gramming languages.

    For example, unfolding the *initial(Q)* goal in the clause

      accept(X) ← initial(Q), accept(Q,X,[ ]).

using its definition *initial(q0)* produces the clause

      accept(X) ← accept(q0,X,[ ]).

If the definition of a goal has several clauses, then the unfolding produces several
clauses, one for each in the definition. For example, unfolding the *delta* goal in

the clause

$$accept(Q,[X|Xs],S) \leftarrow delta(Q,X,S,Q1,S1), accept(Q1,Xs,S1).$$

using the definition of *delta* in Program 14.16 produces four clauses.

The derivation of Program 14.17 is now manifest. It results from unfolding the *initial* goal and the *delta* goal in the first two clauses, respectively, of Program 14.15, as described, and unfolding the *final* goal in the remaining clause. Finally, the predicate *accept* has been renamed to *palindrome*.

It is easy to build an interpreter for a Turing machine in a similar style to the interpreters in Programs 14.3 and 14.5. Doing this demonstrates incidentally that Prolog has the power of a Turing machine and hence of all other known computation models.

Exercises for Section 14.3

(i)   Define an NPDA that accepts the language *n* *a*'s followed by *n* *b*'s.

14.4   AI classics: ANALOGY, ELIZA, and McSAM

"The best way to learn a subject is to teach it" is a cliche commonly repeated to new teachers. An appropriate analogue for new programmers is that the best way to understand a program is to rewrite or extend it. In this spirit, we present logical reconstructions of three AI programs. Each is clearly understandable, and easily extended. The exercises at the end of the section encourage the reader to add new facts and rules to the programs.

The three programs chosen are the ANALOGY program of Evans for solving geometric analogy questions from intelligence tests; the ELIZA program of Weizenbaum which simulates or, rather, parodies conversation, and McSAM, a micro-version of SAM, a program for "understanding" stories from the Yale language group. Each of the logical reconstructions are expressed very simply. The nondeterminism of Prolog allows the programmer to ignore the issues of search.

Consider the task of solving the geometric analogy problems typically used in intelligence tests. Several figures are presented in a prototypical problem. Figures *A*, *B* and *C* are singled out from a list of possible answers and the following question is posed: "*A* is to *B* as *C* is to which one of the 'answer' figures?" Figure 14.7 gives a simple problem of this type.

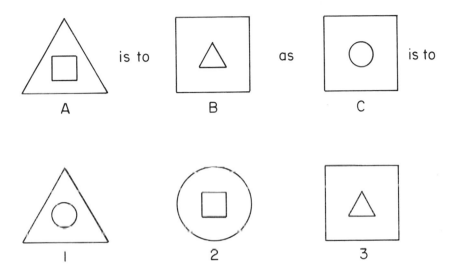

Figure 14.6: A geometric analogy problem

Here is an intuitive algorithm for solving the problem, where terms such as find, apply and rule are left unspecified:

> find a rule that relates A to B,
> apply the rule to C to give a figure X,
> find X, or its nearest equivalent, among the answers.

In the problem in Figure 14.6, the positions of the square and triangle are swapped (with appropriate scaling) between Figures A and B. The "obvious" answer is to swap the square and the circle in Figure C. The resultant figure appears as No. 2 in the possible answers.

Program 14.18 is a simple program for solving analogy problems. The basic relation is *analogy(Pair1,Pair2,Answers)*, where each *Pair* is of the form *X is_to Y*. To parse the program, *is_to* must be declared as an infix operator. The two elements in *Pair1* bear the same relationship as the two elements in *Pair2*, and the second element in *Pair2* appears in *Answers*. The definition of *analogy* implements the intuitive algorithm:

> analogy(A is_to B,C is_to X,Answers) ←
>   match(A,B,Operation), match(C,X,Operation), find(X,Answers).

analogy(Pair1,Pair2,Answers) ←
>   An analogy holds between the two pairs of figures *Pair1* and *Pair2*.
>   The second element of *Pair2* is one of the possible *Answers*.

analogy(A is_to B,C is_to X,Answers) ←
>   match(A,B,Rule),
>   match(C,X,Rule),
>   member(X,Answers).

match(inside(Figure1,Figure2),inside(Figure2,Figure1),invert).
match(above(Figure1,Figure2),above(Figure2,Figure1),invert).

Program 14.18: A program solving geometric analogies

Testing and data

test_analogy(Name,X) ←
>   figures(Name,A,B,C),
>   answers(Name,Answers),
>   analogy(A is_to B,C is_to X,Answers).

figures(test1,inside(square,triangle),inside(triangle,square),
>   inside(circle,square)).
answers(test1,[inside(circle,triangle),inside(square,circle),
>   inside(triangle,square)).

Program 14.19: Analogy test data

A fundamental decision is how the figures in the problem should be represented. The "intelligence" of the program is greatly affected by this decision. In Program 14.18, figures are represented as Prolog terms. Figure A in the diagram in Figure 14.6 is a square inside a triangle, and is represented as the term *inside(square,triangle)*.

The relationship between two figures is found by the predicate *match(A,B, Operation)*. This relation is true if *Operation* matches *A* and *B*. The operation *invert* is used to solve our example problem. The behavior of *invert* is to swap its arguments.

The predicate *match* is used in two distinct ways in this program. The first time it produces an operation matching two given figures. The second time it produces a second figure given an operation and a figure. These details are, however, irrelevant from the nondeterministic viewpoint. Finally, the predicate *find* is implemented simply, checking whether a given figure appears in the list of

I am unhappy.
≫   How long have you been unhappy.
      Six months. Can you help me.
≫   What makes you think I help you.
      You remind me of my father and brother.
≫   Can you tell me more about father.
      I like teasing father.
≫   Does anyone else in your family like teasing father.
      No, only me.
≫   Please go on.

Figure 14.7: Sample conversation with ELIZA

answers.

The next AI classic considered is a simplified version of ELIZA. The program aims to simulate a conversation. A user types in a sentence, and ELIZA responds with an appropriate question or comment. ELIZA does not understand in any real sense, responding to its input by recognizing word patterns and replying by using a corresponding response pattern. To make the patterns of responses more credible, it adopted a psychiatrist setting as its domain. A sample interaction with ELIZA is given in Figure 14.7. Computer responses are preceded by ≫.

The heart of ELIZA is a procedure for matching the input sentence against a pattern. The resulting match is applied to another pattern to determine the program reply. The pair of patterns can be considered as a stimulus/response pair, where the input is matched against the stimulus, and the output generated from the response. A typical stimulus/response pair is

I am ⟨statement⟩   How long have you been ⟨statement⟩?

Using this pair, the response of the program to the input statement "I am unhappy" will be the question "How long have you been unhappy?" The ⟨statement⟩ can be viewed as a slot to be filled.

Program 14.20 is a simple version of ELIZA. It implements the following algorithm:

      read the input.
      while the input is not *bye*,
            choose a stimulus/response pair,
            match the input to the stimulus,
            generate the reply from the response and the above match,
            output the response,
            read the next input.

eliza ←
   Simulates a conversation via side-effects.

eliza ← read_word_list(Input), eliza(Input), !.

eliza([bye]) ←
   writeln(['Goodbye. I hope I have helped you']).

eliza(Input) ←
   pattern(Stimulus,Response),
   match(Stimulus,Dictionary,Input),
   match(Response,Dictionary,Output),
   reply(Output),
   read_word_list(Input1),
   !, eliza(Input1).

match(Pattern,Dictionary, Words) ←
   Pattern matches the list of words *Words*, and matchings are
   recorded in the *Dictionary*.

match([N|Pattern],Dictionary,Target) ←
   integer(N), lookup(N,Dictionary,LeftTarget),
   append(LeftTarget,RightTarget,Target),
   match(Pattern,Dictionary,RightTarget).
match([Word|Pattern],Dictionary,[Word|Target]) ←
   atom(Word), match(Pattern,Dictionary,Target).
match([ ],Dictionary,[ ]).

lookup(Key,Dictionary,Value) ← See Program 15.8

pattern(Stimulus,Response) ←
   Response is an applicable response pattern to the pattern *Stimulus*.

pattern([i,am,1],[how,long,have,you,been,1,?]).
pattern([1,you,2,me],[what,makes,you,think,i,2,you,?]).
pattern([i,like,1],[does,anyone,else,in,your,family,like,1,?]).
pattern([i,feel,1],[do,you,often,feel,that,way,?]).
pattern([1,X,2],[can,you,tell,me,more,about,X]) ← important(X).
pattern([1],[please,go,on]).

important(father).   important(mother).   important(son).
important(sister).   important(brother).   important(daughter).

reply([Head|Tail]) ← write(Head), write(' '), reply(Tail).
reply([ ]) ← nl.

read_word_list(Xs) ← See Program 12.2

Program 14.20: ELIZA

The stimulus/response pairs are represented as facts of the form *pattern(Stimulus,Response)* where both *Stimulus* and *Response* are lists of words and slots. Slots in the patterns are represented by integers. The predicate *match(Pattern,Table,Words)* is used for both the second and third steps of the above algorithm. It expresses a relationship between a pattern *Pattern*, a list of words *Words* and a table *Table* where the table records how the slots in the pattern are filled. A central part of the *match* procedure is played by a nondeterministic use of append to break up a list of words. The table is represented by an *incomplete data structure*, a topic to be discussed in more detail in the next chapter. The missing procedure *lookup/3* will be given in Section 15.3. The reply is generated by *reply(Words)* which is a modified version of *writeln* that leaves spaces between words.

The final program presented in this section is Micro SAM or McSAM. It is a simplified version of the SAM (Script Applier Mechanism) program developed in the natural language group at Yale University. The aim of McSAM is to "understand" stories. Given a story, it finds a relevant script and matches the individual events of the story against the patterns in the script. In the process, events in the script not explicitly mentioned in the story are filled in.

Both the story and the script are represented in terms of Schank's theory of conceptual dependency. For example, consider the input story in Figure 14.8 which is used as an example in our version of McSAM. The English version

"John went to Leones, ate a hamburger and left"

is represented in the program as a list of lists:

```
[  [ptrans, john, john, X1, leones],
   [ingest, X2, hamburger, X3],
   [ptrans, Actor, Actor, X4, X5]  ].
```

The first element in each list, *ptrans* and *ingest*, for example, is a term from conceptual dependency theory. The representation of the story as a list of lists is chosen as a tribute to the original Lisp version.

Programming McSAM in Prolog is a triviality as demonstrated by Program 14.21. The top-level relation is *mcsam(Story,Script)* which expands a *Story* into its "understood" equivalent according to a relevant *Script*. The script is found by the predicate *find(Story,Script,Defaults)*. The story is searched for a non-variable argument that triggers the name of a script. In our example of John visiting Leones, the atom *leones* triggers the *restaurant* script, indicated by the fact *trigger(leones,restaurant)* in Program 14.22.

The matching of the story to the script is done by *match(Script,Story)* which

mcsam(*Story,Script*) ←
    Script describes *Story*.

mcsam(Story,Script) ←
    find(Story,Script,Defaults),
    match(Script,Story),
    name_defaults(Defaults).

find(Story,Script,Defaults) ←
    filler(Slot,Story),
    trigger(Slot,Name),
    script(Name,Script,Defaults).

match(*Script,Story*) ←
    Story is a subsequence of *Script*.

match(Script,[ ]).
match([Line|Script],[Line|Story]) ← match(Script,Story).
match([Line|Script],Story) ← match(Script,Story).

filler(*Slot,Story*) ←
    Slot is a word in the *Story*.

filler(Slot,Story) ←
    member([Action|Args],Story),
    member(Slot,Args).

name_defaults(*Defaults*) ←
    Unifies default pairs in *Defaults*.

name_defaults([ ]).
name_defaults([[N,N]|L]) ← name_defaults(L).
name_defaults([[N1,N2]|L]) ← N1 ≠ N2, name_defaults(L).

Program 14.21: McSAM

associates lines in the story with lines in the script. Remaining slots in the script
are filled in by *name_defaults*(*Defaults*). The "output" is

    [ptrans,john,john,place1,leones]
    [ptrans,john,john,door,seat]
    [mtrans,john,waiter,hamburger]
    [ingest,john,hamburger,[mouth,john]]
    [atrans,john,check,john,waiter]
    [ptrans,john,john,leones,place2].

Testing and data

test_mcsam(Name,UnderstoodStory) ←
    story(Name,Story), mcsam(Story,UnderstoodStory).

story(test,[[ptrans, john, john, X1, leones],
    [ingest, X2, hamburger, X3],
    [ptrans, Actor, Actor, X4, X5]]).

script(restaurant,
    [[ptrans, Actor, Actor, Earlier_place, Restaurant],
      [ptrans, Actor, Actor, Door, Seat],
      [mtrans, Actor, Waiter, Food],
      [ingest, Actor, Food, [mouth, Actor]],
      [atrans, Actor, Money, Actor, Waiter],
      [ptrans, Actor, Actor, Restaurant, Gone]],
    [[Actor, customer], [Earlier_place, place1],
      [Restaurant, restaurant], [Door, door],
      [Seat, seat], [Food, meal], [Waiter, waiter],
      [Money, check], [Gone, place2]]).

trigger(leones, restaurant).
trigger(waiter, restaurant).

Program 14.22: Test data for McSAM

Its translation to English is given in Figure 14.8.

The work done in the original McSAM was all in the searching and pattern matching. This is accomplished in Prolog by nondeterministic programming and unification.

Exercises for Section 14.4

(i) Extend ANALOGY, Program 14.18, to solve the three problems in Figure 14.9.

(ii) Extend ELIZA, Program 14.20, by adding new stimulus/response patterns.

(iii) If the seventh statement in Figure 14.7 is changed to be "I like teasing my father," ELIZA responds with "Does any one else in your family like teasing my father." Modify Program 14.20 to "fix" this behavior, changing references such as I, my, to you, your, etc.

(iv) Rewrite McSAM to use structures.

Input: John went to Leones, ate a hamburger and left.

Output: John went to Leones. He was shown from the door to a seat.
A waiter brought John a hamburger, which John ate by mouth.
The waiter brought John a check, and John left Leones for
another place.

Figure 14.8: A story filled in by McSAM

14.5   Background

Several researchers have discussed the behavior of Prolog in solving the N
queens problem and coloring maps, using generate-and-test programs. They have
used the examples as evidence of Prolog's inadequate control. Suggestions for
improvement include co-routining incorporated in IC-Prolog (Clark and McCabe,
1979) and intelligent backtracking (Bruynooghe and Pereira, 1984). A good discussion of how Prolog handles the N queens problem can be found in Elcock
(1983).

The zebra puzzle, Exercise 14.1(iii), did the rounds on the Prolog Digest in
the early 1980's and was used as an unofficial benchmark to test both the speed
of Prolog implementations and the ability of Prolog programmers to write clear
code.

The definitive discussion of don't-care and don't-know nondeterminism in
logic programming appears in Kowalski (1979).

Program 14.11 for planning is a variant of an example from Kowalski (1979).
The original planning program in Prolog was Warplan (Warren, 1976), reproduced
in Coelho et al. (1980).

Our notation for automata follows Hopcroft and Ullman (1979).

The classic work on unfolding is by Burstall and Darlington (1977).

ANALOGY constituted the Ph.D. thesis of Thomas Evans at MIT in the
mid 1960's. A good description of the program appears in *Semantic Information
Processing* (Minsky, 1968). Evans' program tackled many aspects of the problem
that are made trivial by our choice of representation, for example, identifying that
there are triangles, squares and circles in the figures. Our version, Program 14.17,
emerged from a discussion group of the first author with a group of Epistemics
students at the University of Edinburgh.

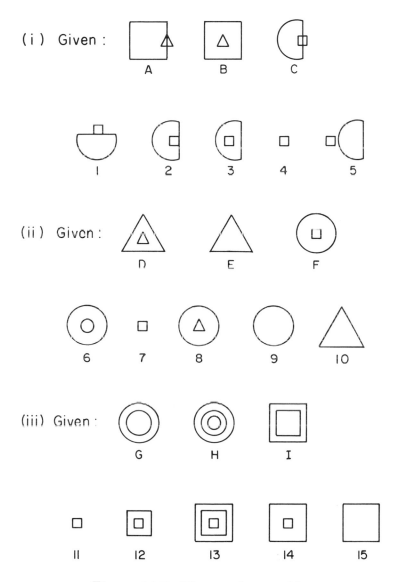

Figure 14.9: Three analogy problems

ELIZA was originally presented in Weizenbaum (1966). Its performance led people to believe that a limited form of the Turing test had been passed. Weizenbaum, its author, was horrified by people's reactions to the program, and to AI more generally, and wrote an impassioned plea against taking the program too seriously (Weizenbaum, 1976). Our version, Program 14.20, is a slight variant of a teaching program attributed to Alan Bundy, Richard O'Keefe and Henry Thompson, which was used for AI courses at the University of Edinburgh.

McSAM is a version of the SAM program, which was tailored for teaching AI programming (Schank and Riesbeck, 1981). Our version, Program 14.21, is due to Ernie Davis and the second author. More information about conceptual dependency can be found in Schank and Abelson (1977).

Chapter 15

Incomplete Data Structures

The programs presented so far have been discussed in terms of relationships between complete data structures. Powerful programming techniques emerge from extending the discussion to incomplete data structures, as demonstrated in this chapter.

The first section discusses difference-lists: an alternative data structure to lists for representing a sequence of elements. They can be used to simplify and increase the efficiency of list-processing programs. Difference-lists generalize the concept of accumulators. Data structures built from the difference of incomplete structures other than lists are discussed in the second section. The third section shows how tables and dictionaries, represented as incomplete structures, can be built incrementally during a computation. The final section discusses queues, an application of difference-lists.

15.1   Difference-lists

Consider the sequence of elements $1,2,3$. It can be represented as the difference between pairs of lists. It is the difference between the lists $[1,2,3,4,5]$ and $[4,5]$, the difference between the lists $[1,2,3,8]$ and $[8]$, and the difference between $[1,2,3]$ and $[\ ]$. Each of these cases is an instance of the difference between two incomplete lists $[1,2,3|Xs]$ and Xs.

We denote the difference between two lists as a structure $As\backslash Bs$, which is called a *difference-list*. As is the *head* of the difference-list and Bs the *tail*. In the above example $[1,2,3|Xs]\backslash Xs$ is the most general difference-list representing the sequence $1,2,3$, where $[1,2,3|Xs]$ is the head of the difference-list and Xs the tail.

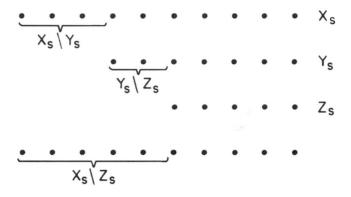

Figure 15.1: Concatenating difference-lists

Logical expressions are unified, not evaluated, so that the name of the binary functor used to denote difference-lists can be arbitrary, as long as it is used consistently. It can even be omitted entirely, the head and tail of the difference-list becoming two separate arguments in a predicate.

Lists and difference-lists are closely related. Both are used to represent sequences of elements. Any list L can be trivially represented as a difference-list $L\backslash[\,]$. The empty list is represented by any difference-list whose head and tail are identical, the most general form being $As\backslash As$.

Difference-lists are an established logic programming technique. The use of difference-lists rather than lists can lead to more concise and efficient programs. The improvement occurs because of the combining property of difference-lists. Two incomplete difference-lists can be concatenated to give a third difference-list in constant time. In contrast, lists are concatenated, using the standard *append* program, in time linear in the length of the first list.

Consider the lists in Figure 15.1. The difference-list $Xs\backslash Zs$ is the result of appending the difference-list $Ys\backslash Zs$ to the difference-list $Xs\backslash Ys$. This can be expressed as a single fact. Program 15.1 defines a predicate *append_dl(As,Bs,Cs)* which is true if the difference-list Cs is the result of appending the difference-list Bs to the difference-list As. We use the suffix *_dl* to denote a variant of a predicate that uses difference-lists.

append_dl(*As*,*Bs*,*Cs*) ←
   The difference-list *Cs* is the result of appending *Bs* to *As*,
   where *As* and *Bs* are compatible difference-lists.

append_dl(Xs\Ys, Ys\Zs, Xs\Zs).

Program 15.1: Concatenating difference-lists

flatten(*Xs*, *Ys*) ←
   Ys is a flattened list containing the elements in *Xs*.

flatten(Xs,Ys) ← flatten_dl(Xs,Ys\[ ]).

flatten_dl([X|Xs],Ys\Zs) ←
   flatten_dl(X,Ys\Ys1), flatten_dl(Xs,Ys1\Zs).
flatten_dl(X,[X|Xs]\Xs) ←
   constant(X), X≠[ ].
flatten_dl([ ],Xs\Xs).

Program 15.2: Flattening a list of lists using difference-lists

A necessary and sufficient condition characterizing when two difference-lists $As\backslash Bs$ and $Xs\backslash Ys$ can be concatenated using Program 15.1 is that *Bs* be unifiable with *Xs*. In that case the two difference-lists are *compatible*. If the tail of a difference-list is uninstantiated, it is compatible with any difference-list. Furthermore, in such a case Program 15.1 would concatenate it in constant time. For example, the result of the query *append_dl*([*a*,*b*,*c*|*Xs*]*Xs*,[*1*,*2*]\[ ], *Ys*)? is (*Xs*=[*1*,*2*], *Ys*=[*a*,*b*,*c*,*1*,*2*]\[ ]).

Difference-lists are the logic programming counterpart of Lisp's *rplacd*, which is also used to concatenate lists in constant time and save "*consing*" (allocating new list-cells). There is a difference between the two: the former are side effect free, and can be discussed in terms of the abstract computation model, whereas *rplacd* is a destructive operation, which can be described only by reference to the machine representation of S-expressions.

A good example of a program which can be improved by using difference-lists is Program 9.1a for flattening a list. It uses double recursion to flatten separately the head and tail of a list of lists, then concatenates the results together. We adapt that program to compute the relation *flatten_dl*(*Ls*,*Xs*), where *Xs* is a difference-list representing the elements which appear in a list of lists *Ls* in correct order. The direct translation of Program 9.1a to use difference-lists appears below.

$$\text{flatten\_dl}([X|Xs],Ys\backslash Zs) \leftarrow$$
$$\text{flatten\_dl}(X,As\backslash Bs), \text{flatten\_dl}(Xs,Cs\backslash Ds),$$
$$\text{append\_dl}(As\backslash Bs,Cs\backslash Ds,Ys\backslash Zs).$$
$$\text{flatten\_dl}(X,[X|Xs]\backslash Xs) \leftarrow$$
$$\text{constant}(X), X{\neq}[\,].$$
$$\text{flatten\_dl}([\,],Xs\backslash Xs).$$

The doubly recursive clause can be simplified by unfolding the *append_dl* goal with respect to its definition in Program 15.1. The result is

$$\text{flatten\_dl}([X|Xs],As\backslash Ds) \leftarrow$$
$$\text{flatten\_dl}(X,As\backslash Bs), \text{flatten\_dl}(Xs,Bs\backslash Ds).$$

The program for *flatten_dl* can be used to implement *flatten* by expressing the connection between the desired flattened list and the difference-list computed by *flatten_dl* as follows:

$$\text{flatten}(Xs,Ys) \leftarrow \text{flatten\_dl}(Xs,Ys\backslash[\,]).$$

Collecting the program and renaming variables yields Program 15.2.

Declaratively Program 15.2 is straightforward. The explicit call to *append* is made unnecessary by flattening the original list of lists into a difference-list rather than a list. The resultant program is more efficient, as the size of its proof tree is linear in the number of elements in the list of lists rather than quadratic.

The operational behavior of programs using difference-lists, such as Program 15.2, is harder to understand. The flattened list seems to be built by magic.

Let us investigate the program in action. Figure 15.2 is a trace of the query *flatten([[a],[b,[c]]],Xs)?* with respect to Program 15.2.

The trace shows that the output, *Xs*, is built top-down (in the terminology of Section 7.5). The tail of the difference-list acts like a pointer to the end of the incomplete structure. The pointer gets set by unification. By using these "pointers" no intermediate structures are built, in contrast to Program 9.1a.

The discrepancy between clear declarative understanding and difficult procedural understanding stems from the power of the logical variable. We can specify logical relationships implicitly, and leave their enforcement to Prolog. Here the concatenation of the difference-lists has been expressed implicitly, and it is mysterious when it happens in the program. Programs using difference-lists are sometimes structurally similar to programs written using accumulators. Exercise 9.1(i) asked for a doubly recursive version of *flatten* which avoided the

flatten([[a],[b,[c]]],Xs)
    flatten_dl([[a],[b,[c]]],Xs\[ ])
        flatten_dl([a],Xs\Xs1)
            flatten_dl(a,Xs\Xs1)   Xs = [a|Xs2]
                constant(a)
                a ≠ [ ]
            flatten_dl([],Xs2\Xs1)   Xs2 = Xs1
        flatten_dl([[b,[c]]],Xs1\[ ])
            flatten_dl([b,[c]],Xs1\Xs3)
                flatten_dl(b,Xs1\Xs4)   Xs1 = [b|Xs4]
                    constant(b)
                    b ≠ [ ]
                flatten_dl([[c]],Xs4\Xs3)
                    flatten_dl([c],Xs4\Xs5)
                        flatten_dl(c,Xs4\Xs6)   Xs4 = [c|Xs6]
                            constant(c)
                            c ≠ [ ]
                        flatten_dl([ ],Xs6\Xs5)   Xs6 = Xs5
                    flatten_dl([ ],Xs5\Xs3)   Xs5 = Xs3
                flatten_dl([ ],Xs3\[ ])   Xs3 = [ ]
        Output: Xs = [a,b,c]

Figure 15.2: Tracing a computation using difference-lists

call to *append* by using accumulators. A solution is the following program:

    flatten(Xs,Ys) ← flatten(Xs,[ ],Ys).

    flatten([X|Xs],Zs,Ys) ←
        flatten(Xs,Zs,Ys1), flatten(X,Ys1,Ys).
    flatten(X,Xs,[X|Xs]) ←
        constant(X), X≠[ ].
    flatten([ ],Xs,Xs).

The similarity of this program to Program 15.2 is striking. There are only two differences between the programs. The first difference is syntactic. The difference-list is represented as two arguments, but in reverse order, the tail preceding the head. The second difference is the goal order in the recursive clause of *flatten*. The net effect is that the flattened list is built bottom-up from its tail, rather than top-down from its head.

$reverse(Xs,Ys) \leftarrow$
  Ys is the reversal of the list Xs.

reverse(Xs,Ys) ← reverse_dl(Xs,Ys\[ ]).

reverse_dl([X|Xs],Ys\Zs) ←
    reverse_dl(Xs,Ys\[X|Zs]).
reverse_dl([ ],Xs\Xs).

Program 15.3: Reverse with difference-lists

$quicksort(List,SortedList) \leftarrow$
  $SortedList$ is an ordered permutation of $List$.

quicksort(Xs,Ys) ← quicksort_dl(Xs,Ys\[ ]).

quicksort_dl([X|Xs],Ys\Zs) ←
    partition(Xs,X,Littles,Bigs),
    quicksort_dl(Littles,Ys\[X|Ys1]),
    quicksort_dl(Bigs,Ys1\Zs).
quicksort_dl([ ],Xs\Xs).

partition(Xs,X,Ls,Bs) ← See Program 3.22.

Program 15.4: Quicksort using difference-lists

We give another example of the similarity between difference-lists and accumulators. Program 15.3 is a translation of "naive" *reverse* (Program 3.16a) where lists have been replaced by difference-lists, and the *append* operation has been unfolded away.

When are difference-lists the appropriate data structure for Prolog programs? Programs with explicit calls to *append* can usually gain in efficiency by using difference-lists rather than lists. A typical example is a doubly recursive program where the final result is obtained by appending the outputs of the two recursive calls. More generally a program that independently builds different sections of a list to be later combined together is a good candidate for using difference-lists.

The logic program for *quicksort*, Program 3.22, is an example of a doubly recursive program where the final result, a sorted list, is obtained from concatenating two sorted sublists. It can be made more efficient by using difference-lists. All the *append* operations involved in combining partial results can be performed implicitly, as shown in Program 15.4.

The call of *quicksort_dl* by *quicksort* is an initializing call as for *flatten* in

Program 15.2. The recursive clause is the quicksort algorithm interpreted for difference-lists where the final result is pieced together implicitly rather than explicitly. The base clause of *quicksort_dl* states that the result of sorting an empty list is the empty difference-list. Note the use of unification to place the partitioning element X after the smaller elements Ys and before the bigger elements $Ys1$ in the call *quicksort_dl*($Littles, Ys\backslash[X|Ys1]$).

Program 15.4 is derived from Program 3.22 in exactly the same way that Program 15.2 is derived from Program 9.1a. Lists are replaced by difference-lists and the *append_dl* goal unfolded away. The initial call of *quicksort_dl* by *quicksort* expresses the relationship between the desired sorted list and the computed sorted difference-list.

An outstanding example of using difference-lists to advantage is a solution to a simplified version of Dijkstra's Dutch flag problem. The problem reads: "Given a list of elements colored *red*, *white*, and *blue*, reorder the list so that all the red elements appear first, then all the white elements, followed by the blue elements. This reordering should preserve the original relative order of elements of the same color." For example, the list $[red(1),white(2),blue(3),red(4),white(5)]$ should be reordered to $[red(1),red(4),white(2),white(5),blue(3)]$.

Program 15.5 is a simple minded solution to the problem which collects the elements in three separate lists, then concatenates the lists. The basic relation is *dutch*(Xs, Ys) where Xs is the original list of colored elements and Ys is the reordered list separated into colors.

The heart of the program is the procedure *distribute* which constructs three lists, one for each color. The lists are built top-down. The two calls to *append* can be removed by having *distribute* build three distinct difference-lists instead of three lists. Program 15.6 is an appropriately modified version of the program.

The implicit concatenation of the difference-lists is done in the initializing call to *distribute_dls* by *dutch*. The complete list is finally "assembled" from its parts with the satisfaction of the base clause of *distribute_dls*.

The Dutch flag example demonstrates a program that builds parts of the solution independently, and pieces them together at the end. It is a more complex use of difference-lists than the earlier examples.

Although easier to read, the use of an explicit constructor for difference-lists incurs noticeable overhead in time and space. Using two separate arguments for that purpose is more efficient. When important, this efficiency can be gained by straightforward manual or automatic transformation.

dutch(Xs,RedsWhitesBlues) ←
> *RedsWhitesBlues* is a list of elements of *Xs* ordered
> by color: red, then white, then blue.

dutch(Xs,RedsWhitesBlues) ←
> distribute(Xs,Reds,Whites,Blues),
> append(Whites,Blues,WhitesBlues),
> append(Reds,WhitesBlues,RedsWhitesBlues).

distribute(Xs,Reds,Whites,Blues) ←
> *Reds*, *Whites*, and *Blues* are the lists of the red, white,
> and blue elements in *Xs*, respectively.

distribute([red(X)|Xs],[red(X)|Reds],Whites,Blues) ←
> distribute(Xs,Reds,Whites,Blues).
distribute([white(X)|Xs],Reds,[white(X)|Whites],Blues) ←
> distribute(Xs,Reds,Whites,Blues).
distribute([blue(X)|Xs],Reds,Whites,[blue(X)|Blues]) ←
> distribute(Xs,Reds,Whites,Blues).
distribute([ ],[ ],[ ],[ ]).

append(Xs,Ys,Zs) ← See Program 3.15

Program 15.5: A solution to the Dutch flag problem

dutch(Xs,RedsWhitesBlues) ←
> *RedsWhitesBlues* is a list of elements of *Xs* ordered
> by color: red, then white, then blue.

dutch(Xs,RedsWhitesBlues) ←
> distribute_dls(Xs,RedsWhitesBlues\WhitesBlues,
>   WhitesBlues\Blues,Blues\[ ]).

distribute_dls(Xs,Reds,Whites,Blues) ←
> *Reds*, *Whites*, and *Blues* are the difference-lists of the
> red, white, and blue elements in *Xs*, respectively.

distribute_dls([red(X)|Xs],[red(X)|Reds]\Reds1,Whites,Blues) ←
> distribute_dls(Xs,Reds\Reds1,Whites,Blues).
distribute_dls([white(X)|Xs],Reds,[white(X)|Whites]\Whites1,Blues) ←
> distribute_dls(Xs,Reds,Whites\Whites1,Blues).
distribute_dls([blue(X)|Xs],Reds,Whites,[blue(X)|Blues]\Blues1) ←
> distribute_dls(Xs,Reds,Whites,Blues\Blues1).
distribute_dls([ ],Reds\Reds,Whites\Whites,Blues\Blues).

Program 15.6: Dutch flag with difference-lists

Exercises for Section 15.1

(i)   Rewrite Program 15.2 so that the final list of elements is in the reverse order
      to how they appear in the list of lists.

(ii) Rewrite Programs 3.27 for *pre_order(Tree,List)*, *in_order(Tree,List)* and
      post_order(Tree,List), which collect the elements occurring as leaves in a bi-
      nary tree, to use difference-lists and avoid an explicit call to append.

(iii) Rewrite Program 12.3 for solving the Towers of Hanoi so that the list of
      moves is created as a difference-list rather than a list.

15.2   Difference-structures

The concept underlying difference-lists is the use of the difference between
incomplete data structures to represent partial results of a computation. This
can be applied to recursive data types other than lists. This section looks at a
specific example, algebraic sums.

Consider the task of normalizing arithmetic expressions, for example sums.
Figure 15.2 contains two sums $(a+b)+(c+d)$ and $(a+(b+(c+d)))$ (Standard Prolog
syntax brackets the term $a+b+c$ as $((a+b)+c)$. We describe a procedure converting a sum into a normalized one that is bracketed to the right. For example the
expression on the left in Figure 15.3 would be converted to the one on the right.
Such a procedure is useful for doing algebraic simplification, facilitating writing
programs to test whether two expressions are equivalent.

We introduce a *difference-sum* as a variant of a difference-list. A difference-
sum is represented as a structure $E1++E2$, where $E1$ and $E2$ are incomplete
normalized sums. It is assumed that $++$ is defined as a binary infix operator. It
is convenient to use U to indicate an empty sum.

Program 15.7 is a program for normalizing sums. The relation scheme is *nor-
malize(Exp,NormExp)* where *NormExp* is an expression equivalent to *Exp* which
is bracketed to the right and preserves the order of the constants appearing in
Exp.

This program is similar in structure to Program 15.2 for flattening lists using
difference-lists. There is an initialization stage where the difference-structure is
set up, typically calling a predicate with the same name but different arity or
different argument pattern. The base case passes out the tail of the incomplete
structure, while the goals in the body of the recursive clause pass the tail of the
first incomplete structure to be the head of the second.

normalize(Sum,NormalizedSum) ←
 NormalizedSum is the result of normalizing the sum expression *Sum*.

normalize(Exp,Norm) ← normalize_ds(Exp,Norm++0).

normalize_ds(A+B,Norm++Space) ←
 normalize_ds(A,Norm++NormB), normalize_ds(B,NormB++Space).
normalize_ds(A,(A+Space)++Space) ←
 constant(A).

Program 15.7: Normalizing plus expressions

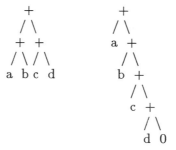

Figure 15.3: Unnormalized and normalized sums

The program builds the normalized sum top-down. By analogy with the programs using difference-lists, the program can be easily modified to build the structure bottom-up, which is an exercise at the end of the section.

The declarative reading of these programs is straightforward. Operationally the programs can be understood in terms of building a structure incrementally, where the "hole" for further results is referred to explicitly. This is entirely analogous to difference-lists.

Exercises for Section 15.2

(i) Define the predicate *normalized_sum(Expression)* which is true if *Expression* is a normalized sum.

(ii) Rewrite Program 15.7 so that
  (a) the normalized sum is built bottom-up,
  (b) the order of the elements is reversed.

(iii) Write a program to normalize products using difference-products, defined analogously to difference-sums.

15.3 Dictionaries

A different use of incomplete data structures enables the implementation of dictionaries. Consider the task of creating, using, and maintaining a set of values indexed under keys. There are two main operations we would like to perform: looking up values stored under a certain key, and entering new keys and their associated values. These operations must ensure consistency — for example the same key should not appear twice with two different values. It is possible to perform both operations, looking up values of keys, and entering new keys, with a single simple procedure, by exploiting incomplete data structures.

Consider a linear sequence of key-value pairs. Let us see the advantages of using an incomplete data structure for its representation. Program 15.8 defines the relation *lookup(Key,Dict,Value)* which is true if the entry under *Key* in the dictionary *Dict* has value *Value*. The dictionary is represented as an incomplete list of pairs of the form *(Key,Value)*.

Let us consider an example where the dictionary is used to remember phone extensions keyed under the names of people. Suppose that *Dict* is initially instantiated to *[(arnold,8881),(barry,4513),(cathy,5950)|Xs]*. The query *lookup(arnold,Dict,N)?* has as answer *N=8881*, and is used for finding Arnold's phone number. The query *lookup(barry,Dict,4513)?* checking Barry's phone number is answered affirmatively.

The entry of new keys and values is demonstrated by the query *lookup(david,Dict,1199)?*. Syntactically this appears to check David's phone number. Its effect is different. The query succeeds, instantiating *Dict* to *[(arnold,8881),(barry,4513),(cathy,5950),(david,1199)|Xs1]*. Thus *lookup* has entered a new value.

What happens if we check Cathy's number with the query *lookup(cathy,Dict, 5951)?* where the number is incorrect? Rather than entering a second entry for Cathy, the query fails due to the test *Key ≠ Key1*.

The *lookup* procedure given in Program 15.8 completes Program 14.20, the simplified ELIZA. Note when the program begins, the dictionary is empty, indicated by being a variable. The dictionary is built up during the matching against the stimulus half of a stimulus-response pair. The constructed dictionary is used to produce the correct response. Note that entries are placed in the dictionary

lookup(Key,Dictionary,Value) ←
  Dictionary contains *Value* indexed under *Key*.
  Dictionary is represented as a list of pairs *(Key,Value)*.

lookup(Key,[(Key,Value)|Dictionary],Value).
lookup(Key,[(Key1,Value1)|Dictionary],Value) ←
  Key ≠ Key1, lookup(Key,Dictionary,Value).

Program 15.8: Dictionary lookup from a list of tuples

lookup(Key,Dictionary,Value) ←
  Dictionary contains *Value* indexed under *Key*.
  Dictionary is represented as an ordered binary tree.

lookup(Key,dict(Key,X,Left,Right),Value) ←
  !, X = Value.
lookup(Key,dict(Key1,X,Left,Right),Value) ←
  Key < Key1, lookup(Key,Left,Value).
lookup(Key,dict(Key1,X,Left,Right),Value) ←
  Key > Key1, lookup(Key,Right,Value).

Program 15.9: Dictionary lookup in a binary tree

without their values being known: a striking example of the power of logical variables. Once an integer is detected, it is put in the dictionary, and its value is determined later.

Searching linear lists is not very efficient for a large number of key-value pairs. Ordered binary trees allow more efficient retrieval of information than linear lists. The insight that an incomplete structure can be used to allow entry of new keys as well as to look up values carries over to binary trees.

The binary trees of Section 3.4 are modified to be a four-place structure *dict(Key,Value,Left,Right)*, where *Left* and *Right* are, respectively, the left and right subdictionaries, and *Key* and *Value* are as before. The functor *dict* is used to suggest a dictionary.

Looking up in the dictionary tree has a very elegant definition, similar in spirit to Program 15.8. It performs recursion on binary trees rather than on lists, and relies on unification to instantiate variables to dictionary structures. Program 15.9 gives the procedure *lookup(Key,Dictionary,Value)*, which as before both looks up the value corresponding to a given key and enters new values.

At each stage the key is compared with the key of the current node. If it

freeze(*A*,*B*) ←
    Freeze term *A* into *B*.

freeze(A,B) ←
    copy(A,B), numbervars(B,0,N).

melt_new(*A*,*B*) ←
    Melt the frozen term *A* into *B*.

melt_new(A,B) ←
    melt(A,B,Dictionary), !.

melt('$VAR'(N),X,Dictionary) ←
    lookup(N,Dictionary,X).
melt(X,X,Dictionary) ←
    constant(X).
melt(X,Y,Dictionary) ←
    compound(X),
    functor(X,F,N),
    functor(Y,F,N),
    melt(N,X,Y,Dictionary).

melt(N,X,Y,Dictionary) ←
    N > 0,
    arg(N,X,ArgX),
    melt(ArgX,ArgY,Dictionary),
    arg(N,Y,ArgY),
    N1 := N 1,
    melt(N1,X,Y,Dictionary).
melt(0,X,Y,Dictionary).

copy(A,B) ← assert('$foo'(A)), retract('$foo'(B)).

numbervars(Term,N1,N2) ← See Program 13.2

lookup(Key,Dictionary,Value) ← See Program 15.9

Program 15.10: Melting a term

is less, the left branch is recursively checked; if it is greater, the right branch is taken. If the key is non-numeric, the predicates < and > must be generalized. The cut is necessary in Program 15.9, in contrast to Program 15.8, due to the nonlogical nature of comparison operators which will give errors if keys are not instantiated.

Given a number of pairs of keys and values, the dictionary they determine is not unique. The shape of the dictionary depends on the order in which queries are posed to the dictionary.

The dictionary can be used to melt a term that has been frozen using Program 13.2 for *numbervars*. The code is given as Program 15.10. Each melted variable is entered into the dictionary, so that the correct shared variables will be assigned.

15.4   Queues

An interesting application of difference-lists is to implement queues. A *queue* is a first-in, first-out store of information. The head of the difference-list represents the beginning of the queue, the tail represents the end of the queue, and the members of the difference-list are the elements in the queue. A queue is empty if the difference-list is empty, that is, its head and tail are identical.

Maintaining a queue is different from the maintenance of a dictionary given above. We consider the relation $queue(S)$ where a queue processes a stream of commands, represented as a list S. There are two basic operations on a queue — enqueueing an element and dequeueing an element — represented, respectively, by the structures $enqueue(X)$ and $dequeue(X)$ where X is the element concerned.

Program 15.11 implements the operations abstractly. The predicate $queue(S)$ calls $queue(S,Q)$ where Q is initialized to an empty queue. $queue/2$ is an interpreter for the stream of enqueue and dequeue commands, responding to each command and updating the state of the queue accordingly. Enqueueing an element exploits the incompleteness of the tail of the queue, instantiating it to a new element and a new tail which is passed as the updated tail of the queue. Clearly, the calls to *enqueue* and *dequeue* can be unfolded, resulting in a more concise and efficient, but perhaps less readable program.

The program terminates when the stream of commands is exhausted. It can be extend to insist that the queue be empty at the end of the commands by changing the base fact to

$$queue([\,],Q) \leftarrow empty(Q).$$

A queue is empty if both its head and tail can be instantiated to the empty list, expressed by the fact $empty([\,]\backslash[\,])$. Logically, the clause $empty(X\backslash X)$ would also be sufficient, however, due to the lack of occurs check in Prolog, discussed in Chapter 4, it may succeed erroneously on a nonempty queue, creating a cyclic data structure.

$queue(S) \leftarrow$
    S is a sequence of enqueue and dequeue operations,
    represented as a list of terms $enqueue(X)$ and $dequeue(X)$.

queue(S) $\leftarrow$ queue(S,Q\Q).

queue([enqueue(X)|Xs],Q) $\leftarrow$
    enqueue(X,Q,Q1), queue(Xs,Q1).
queue([dequeue(X)|Xs],Q) $\leftarrow$
    dequeue(X,Q,Q1), queue(Xs,Q1).
queue([ ],Q).

enqueue(X,Qh\[X|Qt],Qh\Qt)
dequeue(X,[X|Qh]\Qt,Qh\Qt)

Program 15.11: A queue process

We demonstrate the use of queues in Program 15.12 for flattening a list. Although the example is somewhat contrived, it shows clearly how queues can be used.

The basic relation is *flatten_q(Ls,Q,Xs)* where *Ls* is the list of lists to be flattened, *Q* is the queue of lists waiting to be flattened, and *Xs* is the list of elements in *Ls*. The initial clause of *flatten_q/3* by *flatten/2* initializes an empty queue. The basic operation is enqueuing the tail of the list and recursively flattening the head of the list:

flatten_q([X|Xs],Q,Ys) $\leftarrow$
    enqueue(Xs,Q,Q1), flatten_q(X,Q1,Ys).

Unfolding the explicit call to *enqueue* gives

flatten_q([X|Xs],Qh\[Xs|Qt],Ans) $\leftarrow$
    flatten_q(X,Qh\Qt,Ys).

If the element being flattened is a constant, it is added to the output structure being built down, and an element is dequeued (by unifying with the head of the difference list) to be flattened in the recursive call:

flatten_q(X,[Q|Qh]\Qt,[X|Ys]) $\leftarrow$
    constant(X), X$\neq$[ ], flatten_q(Q,Qh\Qt,Ys).

When the empty list is being flattened, either the top element is dequeued

flatten_q([ ],[Q|Qh]\Qt,Ys) $\leftarrow$ flatten_q(Q,Qh\Qt,Ys).

flatten(*Xs*, *Ys*) ←
    Ys is a flattened list containing the elements in *Xs*.

flatten(Xs,Ys) ← flatten_q(Xs,Qs\Qs,Ys).

flatten_q([X|Xs],Ps\[Xs|Qs],Ys) ←
    flatten_q(X,Ps\Qs,Ys).
flatten_q(X,[Q|Ps]\Qs,[X|Ys]) ←
    constant(X), X≠[ ], flatten_q(Q,Ps\Qs,Ys).
flatten_q([ ],[Q|Ps]\Qs,Ys) ←
    flatten_q(Q,Ps\Qs,Ys).
flatten_q([ ],[ ]\[ ],[ ]).

Program 15.12: Flattening a list using a queue

or the queue is empty, and the computation terminates:

flatten_q([ ],[ ]\[ ],[ ]).

Let us reconsider Program 15.11 operationally. Under the expected use of a queue, *enqueue*(X) messages are sent with X determined, and *dequeue*(X) with X undetermined. As long as more elements are enqueued than dequeued, the queue behaves as expected, with the difference between the head of the queue and the tail of the queue being the elements in the queue. However, if the number of dequeue messages received exceeds that of enqueue messages, an interesting thing happens — the content of the queue becomes "negative." The head runs ahead of the tail resulting in the queue containing a negative sequence of undetermined elements, one for each excessive dequeue message.

It is interesting to observe that this behavior is consistent with the associativity of appending of difference-lists. If a queue $Qs\backslash[X1,X2,X3|Qs]$ that contains minus three undetermined elements is appended to the queue $[a,b,c,d,e|Xs]\backslash Xs$ that contains five elements, then the result will be the queue $[d,e|Xs]\backslash Xs$ with two elements, where the "negative" elements $X1,X2,X3$ are unified with a,b,c.

15.5 Background

Difference-lists have been in the logic programming folklore since its inception. The first description of them in the literature is given by Clark and Tarnlund (1977).

The automatic transformation of simple programs without difference-lists to programs with difference-lists, for example, *reverse* and *flatten*, can be found in Bloch (1984).

The elegant *lookup* procedure for ordered binary trees is described by Warren (1980), and is used as a central technique for writing compilers in Prolog, as will be described in Chapter 23.

Maintaining dictionaries and queues can be given a theoretical basis as a perpetual process, as described by van Emden (1984) and Lloyd (1984).

Queues are more important in concurrent logic programming languages, since their input need not be a list of requests but a stream, which is generated incrementally by the processes requesting the services of the queue.

Chapter 16
Parsing with Definite Clause Grammars

A very important application of Prolog and logic programming is parsing. Prolog in fact originated from attempts to use logic to express grammar rules and formalize the parsing process.

The most popular approach to parsing in Prolog is *definite clause grammars* or DCGs. DCGs are a generalization of context-free grammars that are executable, because they are a notational variant of a class of Prolog programs.

Parsing with DCGs is discussed here because of its relevance to the previous two chapters. It is a perfect illustration of Prolog programming using nondeterministic programming and difference-lists.

We begin by discussing context-free grammars. Context-free grammars consist of a set of rules of the form

⟨nonterminal⟩ → ⟨body⟩

where *nonterminal* is a nonterminal symbol and *body* is a sequence of one or more items separated by commas. Each item is either a nonterminal symbol or a sequence of terminal symbols. The meaning of the rule is that *body* is a possible form for a phrase of type *nonterminal*. Nonterminal symbols are written as Prolog atoms, and sequences of terminal symbols as lists of atoms. This is to facilitate the translation of the grammars to Prolog programs.

For each nonterminal symbol, S, a grammar defines a language, which is the set of sequences of terminal symbols, obtained by repeated nondeterministic application of the grammar rules, starting from S.

Consider the simple context-free grammar for a small subset of English given in Figure 16.1. The grammar is self-explanatory, the reading of the first rule being:

Grammar Rules

sentence → noun_phrase, verb_phrase.

noun_phrase → determiner, noun_phrase2.
noun_phrase → noun_phrase2.

noun_phrase2 → adjective, noun_phrase2.
noun_phrase2 → noun.

verb_phrase → verb.
verb_phrase → verb, noun_phrase.

Vocabulary

determiner → [the].   adjective → [decorated]
determiner → [a].

noun → [pieplate].   verb → [surprise].
noun → [surprise].

Figure 16.1: A simple context-free grammar

a sentence consists of a noun phrase followed by a verb phrase. A sample sentence recognized by the grammar is "The decorated pieplate contains a surprise."

The grammar can be immediately written as a Prolog program. Each non-terminal symbol becomes a unary predicate whose argument is the sentence or phrase it identifies. The naive choice for representing the sentence is as a list of words. The various subparts of a sentence will also be lists of words. The first grammar rule becomes

sentence(S) ←
      append(NP,VP,S), noun_phrase(NP), verb_phrase(VP).

The vocabulary rules involving terminal symbols can be expressed as facts, for example,

determiner([the]).   noun([pieplate]).

Completing the grammar of Figure 16.1 as prescribed above leads to a correct program for parsing, but an inefficient one. The calls to *append* suggest that a difference-list might be a more appropriate structure for parsing, which is indeed the case. Program 16.1 is a translation of the grammar of Figure 16.1 to a Prolog program where difference-lists represent the phrases.

The basic relation scheme is *sentence(S)* where *S* is a difference-list of

sentence(S\S0) ←
    noun_phrase(S\S1), verb_phrase(S1\S0).

noun_phrase(S\S0) ←
    determiner(S\S1), noun_phrase2(S1\S0).
noun_phrase(S) ←
    noun_phrase2(S).

noun_phrase2(S\S0) ←
    adjective(S\S1), noun_phrase2(S1\S2).
noun_phrase2(S) ←
    noun(S).

verb_phrase(S) ←
    verb(S).
verb_phrase(S\S0) ←
    verb(S\S1), noun_phrase(S1\S0).

determiner([the|S]\S).   adjective([decorated|S]\S).
determiner([a|S]\S).

noun([pieplate|S]\S).   verb([contains|S]\S).
noun([surprise|S]\S).

Program 16.1: A Prolog program for parsing the language defined
in Figure 16.1

words that forms a sentence according to the rules of the grammar. Similarly *noun_phrase(S)*, *noun_phrase2(S)*, *determiner(S)*, *verb_phrase(S)*, *noun(S)* and *verb(S)* all are true if their argument, a difference-list S of words, is the part of speech their name suggests.

As a parsing program, Program 16.1 is a top-down, left-to-right recursive parser that backtracks when it needs an alternative solution. Although easy to construct, backtracking parsers are in general inefficient. However, the efficiency of the underlying Prolog backtracking mechanism compensates for that, so that DCGs are practical, effective parsers.

The translation of a context-free grammar to an equivalent Prolog program is straightforward. Program 16.2 translates a single grammar rule to its Prolog equivalent. Transforming the entire grammar just involves transforming each individual rule. Grammar rules are assumed to be represented as a term $A \rightarrow B$, where A is a nonterminal symbol and B is a conjunction of nonterminal symbols and lists of terminal symbols. Nonterminal symbols are Prolog atoms, and an

translate(GrammarRule,PrologClause) ←
    PrologClause is the Prolog equivalent of the context free
    grammar rule *GrammarRule.*

translate((Lhs←Rhs),(Head←Body)) ←
    translate(Lhs,Head,Xs\Ys), translate(Rhs,Body,Xs\Ys).

translate((A,B),(A1,B1),Xs\Ys) ←
    translate(A,A1,Xs\Xs1), translate(B,B1,Xs1\Ys).
translate(A,A1,S) ←
    non_terminal(A), functor(A1,A,1), arg(1,A1,S).
translate(Xs,true,S) ←
    terminals(Xs),
    sequence(Xs,S).

non_terminal(A) ← atom(A).

terminals([X|Xs]).

sequence([X|Xs],[X|S]\S0) ← sequence(Xs,S\S0).
sequence([ ],Xs\Xs).

Program 16.2: Translating grammar rules to Prolog clauses

appropriate operator declaration for → is assumed.

The basic relation scheme of Program 16.2 is *translate(GrammarRule,Prolog-Clause).* The procedure for *translate/2* translates the left hand side and right hand side of the grammar rule to the head and body of the equivalent Prolog clause. The basic idea is to add a difference-list to each nonterminal symbol. A new version of *translate, translate(Symbol,Goal,Xs)* is necessary. The relation is true if *Symbol* is translated to *Goal* by adding the difference list *Xs* as an argument. The three clauses for *translate/3* cover the possible terms in a grammar rule. If the term is a conjunction, each conjunct is recursively translated with the appropriate connections between the difference-lists made. Nonterminal symbols are translated into a unary structure, whose functor is the symbol and whose argument is the difference-list. Sequences of terminal symbols are unified into the rule's difference-list using *sequence(Symbol,Xs).* A post-processor can remove the excessive *true* goals, or one can use a difference-structure to prevent their construction in the first place.

The next two programs to be presented augment Program 16.1. The extensions, although simple, typify how DCGs are used to build parsers. They exploit the power of the logical variable.

The first extension is constructing a parse tree for the sentence as it is being parsed. Arguments representing (subparts of) the parse tree must be added to the predicates in Program 16.1. The extension is similar to adding structured arguments to logic programs as discussed in Section 2.2. We modify *sentence/1* to be a binary relation *sentence(Tree, Words)* where *Tree* is the parse tree of *Words* parsed according to the grammar. The other unary predicates representing phrases and parts of speech must similarly be changed to binary predicates. We assume that the parse tree is the first argument.

The first clause of Program 16.1 is extended to be

sentence(sentence(NP,VP),S\S1) ←
    noun_phrase(NP,S\S0), verb_phrase(VP,S0\S1).

The compound term *sentence(NP, VP)* represents the parse tree, with *NP* and *VP* representing the parsed noun phrase and verb phrase.

This extension can also be reflected in augmenting the grammar rules. An extra argument can be added to the nonterminal symbols, so that they become structures. The rule above is represented as

sentence(sentence(NP,VP)) → noun_phrase(NP), verb_phrase(VP).

Adding arguments to nonterminal symbols of context-free grammars increases their utility. The new class of grammars are called definite clause grammars. Definite clause grammars are essentially context-free grammars augmented by the language features of Prolog.

Program 16.2, translating context-free grammars into Prolog programs, can be extended to translate DCGs into Prolog. The extension is posed as Exercise 16(iii). We write DCGs then in grammar rule notation, being aware they are essentially Prolog programs.

The DCGs in Program 16.3 are an extension of Program 16.1 which computes the parse tree at the same time as parsing a sentence. As a logic program, it is similar to Program 2.3 which computed a structure in addition to identifying the circuit components. The program builds the parse tree top-down, exploiting the power of the logical variable.

The next extension concerns subject/object number agreement. Suppose we wanted our grammar also to parse the sentence "The decorated pieplates contain a surprise." A simplistic way of handling plural forms of nouns and verbs, sufficient for the purposes of this book, is to treat different forms as separate words. We augment the vocabulary by adding the facts sentence(sentence(N,V)) → noun_phrase(N), verb_phrase(V).

noun_phrase(np(D,N)) → determiner(D), noun_phrase2(N).
noun_phrase(np(N)) → noun_phrase2(N).

noun_phrase2(np2(A,N)) → adjective(A), noun_phrase2(N).
noun_phrase2(np2(N)) → noun(N).

verb_phrase(vp(V)) → verb(V).
verb_phrase(vp(V,N)) → verb(V), noun_phrase(N).

Vocabulary

determiner(det(the)) → [the].
determiner(det(a)) → [a].

noun(noun(pieplate)) → [pieplate].
noun(noun(surprise)) → [surprise].

adjective(adj(decorated)) → [decorated].
verb(verb(contains)) → [contains].

Program 16.3: A DCG computing a parse tree

noun(noun(pieplates)) → [pieplates].
verb(verb(contain)) → [contain].

The new program would parse "The decorated pieplates contain a surprise," but unfortunately would also parse "The decorated pieplates contains a surprise." There is no insistence that noun and verb must both be singular, or both be plural.

Number agreement can be enforced by adding an argument to the parts of speech that must be the same. The argument indicates whether the part of speech is singular or plural. Consider the grammar rule

sentence(sentence(NP,VP)) →
    noun_phrase(NP,Num), verb_phrase(VP,Num).

The rule insists that both the noun phrase which is the subject of the sentence and the verb phrase which is the object of the sentence have the same number, singular or plural. The agreement is indicated by the sharing of the variable *Num*. Expressing subject/object number agreement is context-dependent information, which is clearly beyond the scope of context-free grammars.

Program 16.4 is an extension of Program 16.3 that handles number agreement

sentence(sentence(N,V)) → noun_phrase(N,Num), verb_phrase(V,Num).

noun_phrase(np(D,N),Num) →
    determiner(D,Num), noun_phrase2(N,Num).
noun_phrase(np(N),Num) → noun_phrase2(N,Num).

noun_phrase2(np2(A,N),Num) → adjective(A), noun_phrase2(N,Num).
noun_phrase2(np2(N),Num) → noun(N,Num).

verb_phrase(vp(V),Num) → verb(V,Num).
verb_phrase(vp(V,N),Num) → verb(V,Num), noun_phrase(N,Num1).

Vocabulary

determiner(det(the),Num) → [the].
determiner(det(a),singular) → [a].

noun(noun(pieplate),singular) → [pieplate].
noun(noun(pieplates),plural) → [pieplates].
noun(noun(surprise),singular) → [surprise].
noun(noun(surprises),plural) → [surprises].

adjective(adj(decorated)) → [decorated].

verb(verb(contains),singular) → [contains].
verb(verb(contain),plural) → [contain].

Program 16.4: A DCG with subject/object agreement

correctly. Noun phrases and verb phrases must have the same number, singular or plural. Similarly the determiners and nouns in a noun phrase must agree in number. The vocabulary is extended to indicate which words are singular and which plural. Where number is unimportant, for example, with adjectives, it can be ignored, and no extra argument is given. The determiner *the* can be either singular or plural. This is handled by leaving the argument indicating number uninstantiated.

The next example of a DCG uses another Prolog feature, the ability to refer to arbitrary Prolog goals in the body of a rule. Program 16.5 is a grammar for recognizing numbers written in English up to one thousand. In doing so, the value of the number recognized is calculated using the arithmetic facilities of Prolog.

The basic relation is *number*(N) where N is the numerical value of the number being recognized. According to the grammar specified by the program, a number is zero or a number N of at most 3 digits, the relationship $xxx(N)$. Similarly $xx(N)$ represents a number N of at most 2 digits, while the predicates *rest_xxx* and *rest_xx*

number(0) → [zero].
number(N) → xxx(N).

xxx(N) → digit(D), [hundred], rest_xxx(N1), {N := D*100+N1}.

rest_xxx(0) → [ ].
rest_xxx(N) → [and], xx(N).

xx(N) → digit(N).
xx(N) → teen(N).
xx(N) → tens(T), rest_xx(N1), {N := T+N1}.

rest_xx(0) → [ ].
rest_xx(N) → digit(N).

digit(1) → [one].   teen(10) → [ten].
digit(2) → [two].   teen(11) → [eleven].
digit(3) → [three].   teen(12) → [twelve].
digit(4) → [four].   teen(13) → [thirteen].
digit(5) → [five].   teen(14) → [fourteen].
digit(6) → [six].   teen(15) → [fifteen].
digit(7) → [seven].   teen(16) → [sixteen].
digit(8) → [eight].   teen(17) → [seventeen].
digit(9) → [nine].   teen(18) → [eighteen].
                           teen(19) → [nineteen].

tens(20) → [twenty].
tens(30) → [thirty].
tens(40) → [forty].
tens(50) → [fifty].
tens(60) → [sixty].
tens(70) → [seventy].
tens(80) → [eighty].
tens(90) → [ninety].

Program 16.5: A DCG for recognizing numbers

denote the rest of a number of 3 and 2 digits, respectively, after the leading digit has been removed. The predicates *digit*, *teen* and *tens* recognize, respectively, single digits, the numbers ten to nineteen inclusive and the multiples of ten from twenty to ninety inclusive.

A new syntactic construct is necessary in the grammar to allow arbitrary Prolog goals. This is done by placing the Prolog goal in curly braces. We illustrate with the rule for determining a three digit number:

$$xxx(N) \rightarrow digit(D), [hundred], rest\_xxx(N1), \{N := D*100+N1\}.$$

This says that a three digit number N must first be a digit with value D followed by the word "hundred" followed by the rest of the number which will have value $N1$. The value for the whole number N is obtained by multiplying D by 100 and adding $N1$.

DCGs inherit another feature from logic programming, the ability to be used backward. Program 16.5 can be used to generate the written representation of a given number up to a thousand. In technical terms, the grammar generates as well as accepts. The behavior in so doing is classic generate-and-test. All the legal numbers of the grammar are generated one by one and tested if they have the correct value, until the actual number posed is reached. This feature is a curiosity rather than an efficient means of writing numbers.

The generative feature of DCGs is not generally useful. Many grammars have recursive rules. For example, the rule in Figure 16.1 defining a *noun_phrase2* as an adjective followed by a *noun_phrase2* is recursive. Using recursively defined grammars for generation results in a nonterminating computation. In the grammar of Program 16.3 noun phrases with arbitrarily many adjectives are produced before the verb phrase is considered.

Exercises for Chapter 16

(i) Write a simple grammar for French that illustrates gender agreement.

(ii) Extend and modify Program 16.5 for parsing numbers so that it covers all numbers less than one million. Don't forget to include things like "thirty five hundred" and not to include "thirty hundred."

(iii) Extend Program 16.2 to translate a DCG grammar rule to a Prolog clause.

16.1 Background

Prolog was connected to parsing right from its very beginning. As mentioned before, the Prolog language grew out of Colmerauer's interest in parsing, and his experience with developing Q-systems (Colmerauer, 1973). The implementors of Prolog-10 were also keen on natural language processing, and wrote one of the more detailed accounts of definite-clause grammars (Pereira and Warren, 1981).

This paper gives a good discussion of the advantages of DCGs as a parsing formalism in comparison with ATNs.

Many Prologs, for example, Wisdom Prolog, provide a hook so that grammar rules are transformed automatically as the file is consulted.

Even though the control structure of Prolog matches directly that of recursive-descent, top-down parsers, other parsing algorithms can also be implemented in it quite easily. For example, Matsumoto et al. (1986) describes a bottom-up parser in Prolog.

The grammar in Program 16.1 is taken from Winograd's book on computational linguistics (Winograd, 1983).

Chapter 17

Second-Order Programming

Chapters 14 and 15 demonstrate Prolog programming techniques based directly on logic programming. This chapter in contrast shows programming techniques that are missing from the basic logic programming model, but can nonetheless be incorporated into Prolog by relying on language features outside of first-order logic. These techniques are called second-order, since they talk about sets and their properties, rather than about individuals.

The first section introduces set-predicates that produce sets as solutions. Computing with set expressions is particularly powerful when combined with programming techniques presented in earlier chapters. The second section gives some applications of set-predicates. The third section looks at lambda expressions and predicate variables, which allow functions and relations to be treated as "first class" data objects.

17.1 Set expressions

Solving a Prolog query with a program entails finding an instance of the query that is implied by the program. What is involved in finding *all* instances of a query that are implied by a program? Declaratively, such a query lies outside the logic programming model presented in the first chapter. It is a second-order question since it asks for the set of elements with a certain property. Operationally, it is also outside the pure Prolog computation model. With pure Prolog all information about a certain branch of the computation is lost on backtracking. This prevents a simple way of using pure Prolog to find the set of all solutions to a query, or even to find how many solutions there are to a given query.

This section discusses predicates that enable the answering of second-order queries. We call such predicates *set-predicates*. They can be regarded as new

father(terach,abraham).   father(haran,lot).
father(terach,nachor).   father(haran,milcah).
father(terach,haran).   father(haran,yiscah).
father(abraham,isaac).

male(abraham).   male(haran).   female(yiscah).
male(isaac).   male(nachor).   female(milcah).
male(lot).

Figure 17.1: Sample data

primitives. However, they are not true extensions to Prolog, since they can be defined in Prolog, using some of its extra-logical features, notably *assert* and *retract*. We present them as a higher-order extension to the language, a quantification over all solutions and show later how they can be implemented. As with the standard implementation of negation, the implementation of set-predicates only approximates their logical specification. But this approximation is very useful for many applications as will be shown in the next section.

We demonstrate the use of set-predicates using part of the Biblical database of Program 1.1 repeated here as Figure 17.1.

Consider the task of finding all the children of a particular father. It is natural to envisage a predicate *children(X,Kids)* where *Kids* is a list of children of X to be extracted from the *father* facts in Figure 17.1. A naive approach is based on using an accumulator as follows:

children(X,Cs) ← children(X,[ ],Cs).

children(X,A,Cs) ←
    father(X,C), not member(C,A), !, children(X,[C|A],Cs).
children(X,Cs,Cs).

The program successfully answers a query such as *children(terach,Xs)?* with answer *Xs=[haran,nachor,abraham]*. The approach of using accumulators has two serious drawbacks, however, that prevent it from being the basis of more general set-predicates. First, each time a solution is added to the accumulator, the whole search tree is traversed afresh. In general the recomputing would be prohibitive. Second, there are problems with generality. A query such as *children(X,Cs)?* gives the answer *X=terach,Cs=[haran,nachor,abraham]* with no alternative on backtracking due to the cut. Once "free" variables are instantiated, no alternative solution is possible. Removing the cut causes incorrect behavior on the query *children(terach,X)*.

The preferred way of implementing set-predicates in Prolog relies on the operational behavior of Prolog, in particular causing side-effects to the program. How this is done is deferred till the end of the section.

The two primitive set-predicates are as follows. The relation *bag_of(Term, Goal,Instances)* is true if *Instances* is the bag (multiset) of all instances of *Term* for which *Goal* is true. Multiple identical solutions are retained. The relation *set_of(Term, Goal,Instances)* is a refinement of *bag_of* where *Instances* is sorted and duplicate elements are removed.

The *children* relation is now easily expressed as

$$\text{children(X,Kids)} \leftarrow \text{set\_of(C,father(X,C),Kids)}.$$

Termination of the set-predicates depends on the termination of the goal whose instances are being collected. The complete search tree for the goal must be traversed. Hence, an infinite branch appearing in the search tree causes non-termination.

Set-predicates can have multiple solutions. Consider the query *set_of(Y, father(X,Y),Kids)?*. There are a number of alternative solutions corresponding to different values of X. For example, $\{X{=}terach,Kids{=}[abraham,nachor,haran]\}$ and $\{X{=}abraham,Kids{=}[isaac]\}$ are equally valid solutions which should be given on backtracking.

There is however another interpretation that can be given to the query *set_of(Y,father(X,Y),Kids)?*. It can be viewed as a request for all the children in the program, irrespective of the father. The logical interpretation is that *Kids* is the set of all values of Y such that there exists some X where *father(X,Y)* is true. For the above data there is a single solution $Kids{=}[abraham,nachor,haran,isaac,lot,milcah,yiscah]$. Extra notation is used to distinguish this "existential" query from the backtrackable query. The accepted form for the second type is is *set_of(Y,X↑(father(X,Y)),Kids)*. In general a query *Y↑Goal* means there exists a Y such that *Goal*.

Set-predicates may be nested. For example, all father-children relations can be computed with the query *set_of(Father–Kids,set_of(X,parent(Father, X),Kids),Ys)?* The solution is $[terach{-}[abraham,nachor,haran],abraham{-}[isaac] ,haran{-}[lot,milcah,yiscah]]$.

There are two possible ways to define the behavior of *set_of(X,Goal,Instances)* when *Goal* fails, i.e., has no true instances. We define *set_of* and *bag_of* to always succeed, returning the empty list as the value of *Instances* when there are no solutions to *Goal*. This definition assumes that the knowledge in the program is all that is true. It is analogous to the approximation of negation by negation as

Set predicates

set_of1(X, Goal, Instances) ← *Instances* is the set of
  instances of *X* for which *Goal* is true, if there are such.

set_of1(X,Goal,Instances) ←
  set_of(X,Goal,Instances), Instances = [I|Is].

bag_of1(X, Goal, Instances) ← *Instances* is the multiset of
  instances of *X* for which *Goal* is true, if there are such.
  The multiplicity of an element is the number of
  different ways *Goal* can be proved with it as an instance of *X*.

bag_of1(X,Goal,Instances) ←
  bag_of(X,Goal,Instances), Instances = [I|Is].

size_of(X, Goal, N) ← *N* is number of distinct
  instances of *X* such that *Goal* is true.

size_of(X,Goal,N) ← set_of(X,Goal,Instances), length(Instances,N).

length(Xs,N) ← See Program 8.11.

Program 17.1: Set predicates

failure.

Versions of *set_of* and *bag_of* can be defined to fail when there are no solutions.
We call the new relations *set_of1* and *bag_of1* and give their definitions in Program
17.1.

Many of the recursive procedures shown before can be rewritten using set-
predicates. For example, Program 7.9 for removing duplicates from a list of
elements can be defined simply in terms of testing for membership:

  no_doubles(Xs,Ys) ← set_of(X,member(X,Xs),Ys).

This definition is significantly less efficient, however, than writing the recursive procedure directly. It is true in general that recursive programs are more
efficient than using set predicates on current Prolog implementations.

Other second-order utility predicates can be defined using these basic set-
predicates. Counting the number of distinct solutions is possible with a program
size_of(X, Goal, N) which determines the number *N* of solutions of *X* to a goal *Goal*.
It is given in Program 17.1. If there are no solutions to *Goal*, *N* is instantiated
to *0*. If the desired behavior of *size_of* was failure on no solutions, *set_of1* can be

for_all(Goal, Condition)
> For all solutions of *Goal, Condition* is true.

for_all(Goal,Condition) ←
> set_of(Condition,Goal,Cases), check(Cases).

check([Case|Cases]) ← Case, check(Cases).
check([ ]).

Program 17.2: Applying set predicates

find_all_dl(X, Goal, Instances) ← *Instances* is the multiset of
> instances of *X* for which *Goal* is true. The multiplicity
> of an element is the number of different ways *Goal* can be
> proved with it as an instance of *X*.

find_all_dl(X,Goal,Xs) ←
> asserta($instance($mark)), Goal, asserta($instance(X)), fail.
find_all_dl(X,Goal,Xs\Ys) ←
> retract($instance(X)), reap(X,Xs\Ys), !.

reap(X,Xs\Ys) ←
> X ≠ $mark, retract($instance(X1)), !, reap(X1,Xs\[X|Ys]).
reap($mark,Xs\Xs).

Program 17.3: Implementing a set predicate using difference-lists,
assert and *retract*

used instead of *set_of*. A version using *bag_of* instead of *set_of* would count the number of solutions with duplicates.

Another set utility predicate checks whether all solutions to a query satisfy a certain condition. Program 17.2 defines a predicate *for_all(Goal, Condition)* succeeding when *Condition* is true for all values of *Goal*. It uses the meta-variable facility.

The query *for_all(father(X,C),male(C))?* checks which fathers have only male children. It produces two answers *X=terach* and *X=abraham*.

A simpler, more efficient but less general version of *for_all* can be written without using set-predicates. A combination of nondeterminism and negation by failure produces a similar effect. The definition is

> for_all(Goal,Condition) ← not (Goal, not Condition).

It successfully answers a query such as *for_all(father(terach,X),male(X))?* but fails to give a solution to the query *for_all(father(X,C),male(C))*?

We conclude this section by showing how to implement a simple variant of *bag_of*. The discussion serves a dual purpose. It illustrates the style of implementation for set-predicates, and gives a utility which will be used in the next section. The predicate *find_all_dl(X,Goal,Instances)* is true if *Instances* is the bag (multiset) of instances of *X*, represented as a difference-list, where *Goal* is true. The procedure differs from *bag_of* by not backtracking to find alternative solutions.

The definition of *find_all_dl* is given as Program 17.3. The program can only be understood operationally. There are two stages to the procedure, as specified by the two clauses for *find_all_dl*. The explicit failure in the first clause guarantees that the second will be executed. The first stage finds all solutions to *Goal* using a failure-driven loop, asserting the associated *X* as it proceeds. The second stage retrieves the solutions.

Asserting "*$mark*" is essential for nested set-expressions to work correctly, lest one set would "steal" solutions produced by the other set-expression.

Exercises for Section 17.1

(i) Define the predicate *intersect(Xs,Ys,Zs)* using a set expression to compute the intersection *Zs* of two lists *Xs* and *Ys*. What should happen if the two lists do not intersect? Compare the code with the recursive definition of *intersect*.

17.2   Applications of set expressions

Set expressions are a significant addition to Prolog. Clean solutions are obtained to many problems by using set expressions, especially when other programming techniques, discussed in previous chapters, are incorporated. This section presents three example programs: traversing a graph breadth first, using the Lee algorithm for finding routes in VLSI circuits, and producing a keyword in context (KWIC) index.

Section 14.2 presents three programs, 14.8, 14.9, and 14.10, for traversing a graph depth first. We discuss here the equivalent programs for traversing a graph breadth first.

The basic relation is *connected(X,Y)* which is true if *X* and *Y* are connected. Program 17.4 defines the relation. Breadth-first search is implemented by keeping a queue of nodes waiting to be expanded. The *connected* clause accordingly calls

(1) Finite trees and DAGs
   Pure Prolog
(2) Finite graphs
   Pure prolog + negation
(3) Infinite graphs
   Pure Prolog + second order + negation

Figure 17.2: Power of Prolog for various searching tasks

connected_bfs(Queue, Y) which is true if *Y* is in the connected component of the graph represented by the nodes in the *Queue*.

Each call to *connected_bfs* removes the current node from the head of the queue, finds the set of edges connected to it, and adds them to the tail of the queue. The queue is represented as a difference-list, and the set predicate used is *findall_dl*. The program fails when the queue is empty. Because difference-lists are an incomplete data structure, the test that the queue is empty must be made explicitly. Otherwise the program would not terminate.

Consider the *edge* clauses in Program 17.4, representing the left-hand graph in Figure 14.3. Using them, the query *connected(a,X)?* gives the solutions *b*, *c*, *d*, *e*, *f*, *g*, *j*, *k*, *h*, *i*, which is a breadth-first traversal of the graph.

Like Program 14.8, Program 17.4 correctly traverses a finite tree or a directed acyclic graph (DAG). If there are cycles in the graph, the program will not terminate. Program 17.5 is an improvement over Program 17.4 where a list of the nodes visited in the graph is kept. Instead of adding all the successor nodes at the end of the queue, each is checked to see if it has been visited before. This is performed by the predicate *filter* in Program 17.5.

Program 17.5 in fact is more powerful than its depth-first equivalent, Program 14.10. Not only will it correctly traverse any finite graph, it will correctly traverse infinite graphs as well. It is useful to summarize what extensions to pure Prolog have been necessary to increase the performance in searching graphs. Pure Prolog correctly searches finite trees, and DAGs, Adding negation allows correct searching of finite graphs with cycles, while set expressions are necessary for infinite graphs. This is shown in Figure 17.2.

Calculating the path between two nodes is a little more awkward than for depth-first search. It is necessary to keep with each node in the queue a list of the nodes linking it to the original node. The technique is demonstrated in the next chapter in Program 18.6.

The next example combines the power of nondeterministic programming with

$connected(X, Y) \leftarrow$
    Node X is connected to node Y in the DAG defined by $edge/2$.

connected(X,Y) ← connected_bfs([X|Xs]\Xs,Y).

connected_bfs([ ]\[ ],Y) ← !,fail.
connected_bfs([X|Xs]\Ys,X).
connected_bfs([X|Xs]\Ys,Y) ←
    find_all_dl(N,edge(X,N),Ys\Zs), connected_bfs(Xs\Zs,Y).

Data

edge(a,b).   edge(a,c).   edge(a,d).   edge(a,e).   edge(f,i).
edge(c,f).   edge(c,g).   edge(f,h).   edge(e,k).   edge(d,j).

edge(x,y)   edge(y,z)   edge(z,x).   edge(y,u).   edge(z,v).

Program 17.4: Testing connectivity breadth-first in a DAG

$connected(X, Y) \leftarrow$
    Node X is connected to node Y in the graph defined by $edge/2$.

connected(X,Y) ← connected([X|Xs]\Xs,Y,[X]).

connected([ ]\[ ],Y,Visited) ← !, fail.
connected([A|Xs]\Ys,A,Visited).
connected([A|Xs]\Ys,B,Visited) ←
    set_of(N,edge(A,N),Ns),
    filter(Ns,Visited,Visited1,Xs\Ys,Xs1),
    connected(Xs1,B,Visited1).

filter([N|Ns],Visited,Visited1,Xs,Xs1) ←
    member(N,Visited), filter(Ns,Visited,Visited1,Xs,Xs1).
filter([N|Ns],Visited,Xs\[N|Ys],Xs\Ys) ←
    not member(N,Visited), filter(Ns,[N|Visited],Visited1,Xs\Ys,Xs1).
filter([ ],V,V,Xs,Xs).

Program 17.5: Testing connectivity breadth first in a graph

the use of second-order programming. It is a program for calculating a minimal cost route between two points in a circuit using the Lee algorithm.

The problem is formulated as follows. Given a grid that may have obstacles, find a shortest path between two specified points. Figure 17.3 shows a grid with obstacles. The heavy solid line represents a shortest path between the two points A and B. The shaded rectangles represent the obstacles.

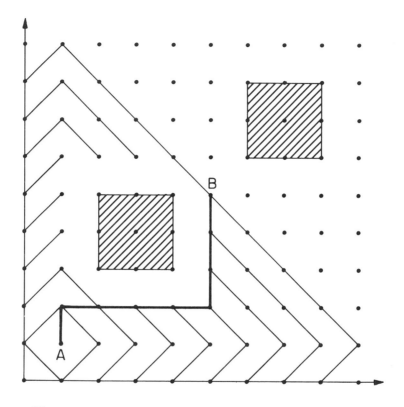

Figure 17.3: The problem of Lee routing for VLSI circuits

We first formulate the problem in a suitable form for programming. The VLSI circuit is modeled by a grid of points, conveniently assumed to be the upper quadrant of the Cartesian plane. A route is a path between two points in the grid, along horizontal and vertical lines only, subject to the constraints of remaining in the grid and not passing through any obstacles.

Points in the plane are represented by their Cartesian coordinates and denoted X–Y. In Figure 17.3, A is *1–1* and B is *5–5*. This representation is chosen for readability, and utilizes the definition of "–" as an infix binary operator. Paths are calculated by the program as a list of points from B to A, including both endpoints. In Figure 17.3 the route calculated is [*5–5,5–4,5–3,5–2,4–2,3–2,2–2,1–2,1–1*], and

lee_route(Source,Destination,Obstacles,Path) ←
    Path is a minimal length path from *Source* to
    Destination which does not cross *Obstacles.*

lee_route(A,B,Obstacles,Path) ←
    waves(B,[[A],[]],Obstacles,Waves),
    path(A,B,Waves,Path).

waves(Destination,WavesSoFar,Obstacles,Waves) ←
    Waves is a list of waves including *WavesSoFar*
    (except, perhaps, its last wave) that leads to *Destination*
    without crossing *Obstacles.*

waves(B,[Wave|Waves],Obstacles,Waves) ← member(B,Wave), !.
waves(B,[Wave,LastWave|LastWaves],Obstacles,Waves) ←
    next_wave(Wave,LastWave,Obstacles,NextWave),
    waves(B,[NextWave,Wave,LastWave|LastWaves],Obstacles,Waves).

next_wave(Wave,LastWave,Obstacles,NextWave) ←
    NextWave is the set of admissible points from *Wave,*
    that is excluding points from *LastWave,*
    Wave and points under *Obstacles.*

next_wave(Wave,LastWave,Obstacles,NextWave) ←
    set_of(X,admissible(X,Wave,LastWave,Obstacles),NextWave).

admissible(X,Wave,LastWave,Obstacles) ←
    adjacent(X,Wave,Obstacles),
    not member(X,LastWave),
    not member(X,Wave).

adjacent(X,Wave,Obstacles) ←
    member(X1,Wave),
    neighbor(X1,X),
    not obstructed(X,Obstacles).

neighbor(X1–Y,X2–Y) ← next_to(X1,X2).
neighbor(X–Y1,X–Y2) ← next_to(Y1,Y2).

next_to(X,X1) ← X1 := X+1.
next_to(X,X1) ← X > 0, X1 := X–1.

obstructed(Point,Obstacles) ←
    member(Obstacle,Obstacles), obstructs(Point,Obstacle).

Program 17.6: Lee routing

obstructs(X–Y,obstacle(X–Y1,X2–Y2)) ← Y1 ≤ Y, Y ≤ Y2.
obstructs(X–Y,obstacle(X1–Y1,X–Y2)) ← Y1 ≤ Y, Y ≤ Y2.
obstructs(X–Y,obstacle(X1–Y,X2–Y2)) ← X1 ≤ X, X ≤ X2.
obstructs(X–Y,obstacle(X1–Y1,X2–Y)) ← X1 ≤ X, X ≤ X2.

path(Source,Destination, Waves,Path) ←
    Path is a path from *Source* to *Destination* going through *Waves*.

path(A,A,Waves,[A]) ← !.
path(A,B,[Wave|Waves],[B|Path]) ←
    member(B1,Wave),
    neighbor(B,B1),
    !, path(A,B1,Waves,Path).

Testing and data

test_lee(Name,Path) ←
    data(Name,A,B,Obstacles), lee_route(A,B,Obstacles,Path).

data(test,1–1,5–5,[obstacle(2–3,4–5),obstacle(6–6,8–8)]).

Program 17.6 (Continued)

is marked by the solid line.

The top level relation computed by the program is *lee_route(A,B,Obstacles, Path)* where *Path* is a route (of minimal distance) from point *A* to point *B* in the circuit. *Obstacles* are the obstacles in the grid. The program has two stages. First, successive *waves* of neighboring grid points are generated, starting from the initial point, until the final point is reached. Second, the path is extracted from the accumulated waves. Let us examine the various components of Program 17.6, the overall program for Lee routing.

Waves are defined inductively. The initial wave is the list [*A*]. Successive waves are sets of points that neighbor a point in the previous wave, and do not already appear in previous waves. They are illustrated by the lighter solid lines in Figure 17.3.

The wave generation is performed by the predicate *waves(B, WavesSoFar, Waves)* which determine the list of *Waves* to reach a destination *B* where *Waves-SoFar* is an accumulator of the waves generated so far in traveling from the source. The predicate terminates when the destination point is in the current wave. The general case calls *next_wave* which uses a set expression to find all the appropriate grid points.

input: programming in prolog
        logic for problem solving
        logic programming
        algorithmic program debugging

output: algorithmic program debugging |,
        debugging | algorithmic program,
        logic for problem solving |,
        logic programming |,
        problem solving | logic for,
        program debugging | algorithmic,
        programming in prolog |,
        programming | logic,
        prolog | programming in,
        solving | logic for problem

Figure 17.4 Input and output for keyword in context problem

Obstacles are assumed to be rectangular blocks. They are represented by the term *obstacle*(*L*,*R*) where *L* is the coordinates of the lower left-hand corner and *R* the coordinates of the upper right-hand corner. An exercise at the end of the section requires modifying the program to handle other obstacles.

The predicate *find_path*(*A*,*B*,*Waves*,*Path*) finds the path *Path* back from *B* to *A* through the *Waves* generated in the process. *Path* is built downward which means the order of the points is from *B* to *A*. This order can be changed by using an accumulator in *find_path*.

Program 17.6 produces no output while computing the Lee route. In practice the user may like to see the computation in progress. This can be easily done by adding appropriate *write* statements to the procedures *next_wave* and *find_path*.

Our final example in this section concerns the keyword in context problem (KWIC). Again a simple Prolog program, combining nondeterministic and second-order programming, suffices to solve a complex task.

Finding keywords in context involves searching text for all occurrences of a set of keywords extracting the contexts in which they appear. We consider here the following variant of the general problem. "Given a list of titles, produce a sorted list of all occurrences of a set of keywords in the titles, together with their context."

Sample input to a program is given in Figure 17.4 together with the expected output. The context is described as a rotation of the title with the end of the title indicated by a "|". In the example the keywords are *algorithmic, debugging, logic, problem, program, programming, prolog* and *solving*, all the 'nontrivial' words.

The relation we want to compute is *kwic(Titles, KwicTitles)* where *Titles* is the list of titles whose keywords are to be extracted, and *KwicTitles* is the sorted list of keywords in their contexts. Both the input and output titles are assumed to be given as lists of words. A more general program, as a preliminary step, would convert freer form input into lists of words, and produce prettier output.

The program is presented in stages. The basis is a nondeterministic specification of a rotation of a list of words. It has an elegant definition in terms of *append*:

$$\text{rotate(Xs,Ys)} \leftarrow \text{append(As,Bs,Xs), append(Bs,As,Ys)}.$$

Declaratively, *Ys* is a rotation of *Xs* if *Xs* is composed of *As* followed by *Bs*, and *Ys* is *Bs* followed by *As*.

The next stage of development involves identifying single words as potential keywords. This is done by isolating the word in the first call to *append*. Note that the new rule is an instance of the previous one:

$$\text{rotate(Xs,Ys)} \leftarrow \text{append(As,[Key|Bs],Xs), append([Key|Bs],As,Ys)}.$$

This definition also improves the previous attempt by removing the duplicate solution when one of the split lists is empty, and the other is the entire list.

The next improvement involves examining a potential keyword more closely. Suppose each keyword *Word* is identified by a fact of the form *keyword(Word)*. The solutions to the *rotate* procedure can be filtered so that only words identified as keywords are accepted. The appropriate version is

$$\begin{aligned}&\text{rotate\_and\_filter(Xs,Ys)} \leftarrow \\&\quad \text{append(As,[Key|Bs],Xs), keyword(Key), append([Key|Bs],As,Ys)}.\end{aligned}$$

Operationally *rotate_and_filter* considers all keys, filtering out the unwanted alternatives. The goal order is important here to maximize the program efficiency.

In Program 17.7, the final version, a complementary view to recognizing keywords is taken. Any word *Word* is a keyword unless otherwise specified by a fact of the form *insignificant(Word)*. Further the procedure is augmented to insert the end of title mark "|", providing the context information. This is done by adding the extra symbol in the second *append* call. Incorporating this discussion yields the clause for *rotate_and_filter* in Program 17.7.

Finally, a set-predicate is used to get all the solutions. Quantification is necessary over all the possible titles. Advantage is derived from the behavior of

kwic(Titles,KWTitles) ←
    KWTitles is a KWIC index of the list of titles *Titles.*

kwic(Titles,KWTitles) ←
    set_of(Ys,Xs↑(member(Xs,Titles),rotate_and_filter(Xs,Ys)),KWTitles).

rotate_and_filter(Xs, Ys) ←
    Ys is a rotation of the list *Xs*, such that
    the first word of *Ys* is significant, and a '|'
    is inserted after the last word of *Xs*.

rotate_and_filter(Xs,Ys) ←
    append(As,[Key|Bs],Xs),
    not insignificant(Key),
    append([Key,'|'|Bs],As,Ys).

Vocabulary of insignificant words

insignificant(a).   insignificant(the).
insignificant(in).   insignificant(for).

Testing and data

test_kwic(Books,Kwic) ←
    titles(Books,Titles), kwic(Titles,Kwic).

titles(lp,[[logic,for,problem,solving],
    [logic,programming],
    [algorithmic,program,debugging],
    [programming,in,prolog]]).

Program 17.7: Producing a KWIC index

set_of in sorting the answers. The complete program is given as Program 17.7, and is an elegant example of the expressive power of Prolog. The test predicate is *test_kwic/2*.

Exercises for Section 17.2

(i)   Modify Program 17.6 to handle obstacles specified differently than as rectangles.

(ii) Adapt Program 17.7 for KWIC so that it extracts keywords from lines of text.

(iii) Write a program to find a minimal spanning tree for a graph.

(iv) Write a program to find the maximum flow in a network design using the Ford-Fulkerson algorithm.

17.3   Other second-order predicates

First-order logic allows quantification over individuals. Second-order logic further allows quantification over predicates. Incorporating this extension in logic programming entails using rules with goals whose predicate names are variables. Predicate names become "first-class" data objects to be manipulated and modified.

A simple example of a second-order relation is the determination of whether all members of a list have a certain property. For simplicity the property is assumed to be described as a unary predicate. Let us define *has_property(Xs,P)* which is true if each element of *Xs* has some property *P*. Extending Prolog syntax to allow variable predicate names enables us to define *has_property* as in Figure 17.5. Because *has_property* allows variable properties, it is a second-order predicate. An example of its use is testing whether a list of people *Xs* is all male with a query *has_property(Xs,male)?*.

Another second-order predicate is *map_list(Xs,P,Ys)*. *Ys* is the map of the list *Xs* under the predicate *P*. That is, for each element *X* of *Xs* there is a corresponding element *Y* of *Ys* such that *P(X,Y)* is true. The order of the elements in *Xs* is preserved in *Ys*. We can use *map_list* to rewrite some of the programs of earlier chapters. For example, Program 7.8 mapping English to French words can be expressed as *map_list(Words,dict,Mots)*. As for *has_property*, *map_list* is easily defined using a variable predicate name. The definition is given in Figure 17.5.

Operationally, allowing variable predicate names implies dynamic construction of goals while answering a query. The relation to be computed is not fixed statically when the query is posed, but is determined dynamically during the computation.

Some Prologs allow the programmer to use variables for predicate names, and allow the syntax of Figure 17.5. It is unnecessary to complicate the syntax however. The tools already exist for implementing second-order predicates. One basic relation is necessary, which we call *apply*; it constructs the goal with a variable functor. The predicate *apply* is defined by a set of clauses, one for each functor name and arity. For example, for functor *foo* of arity n, the clause is

apply(foo,X1,...,Xn) ← foo(X1,...,Xn).

has_property(*Xs,P*) ←
> Each element in the list *Xs* has property *P*.

has_property([X|Xs],P) ←
> apply(P,X), has_property(Xs,P).
has_property([ ],P).

apply(male,X) ← male(X).

maplist(*Xs,P,Ys*) ←
> Each element in the list *Xs* stands in relation
> *P* to its corresponding element in the list *Ys*.

map_list([X|Xs],P,[Y|Ys]) ←
> apply(P,X,Y), maplist(Xs,P,Ys).
map_list([ ],P,[ ]).

apply(dict,X,Y) ← dict(X,Y).

Program 17.8: Second order predicates in Prolog

has_property([X|Xs],P) ← P(X), has_property(Xs,P).
has_property([ ],P).

map_list([X|Xs],P,|Y|Ys]) ← P(X,Y), map_list(Xs,P,Ys).
map_list([ ],P,[ ]).

Figure 17.5: Second-order predicates

The two predicates in Figure 17.5 are transformed into standard Prolog in Program 17.8. Sample definitions of *apply* clauses are given for the examples mentioned in the text.

The predicate *apply* performs structure inspection. The whole collection of *apply* clauses can be generalized by using the structure inspection primitive, *univ*. The general predicate *apply(P,Xs)* applies predicate *P* to a list of arguments *Xs*:

apply(F,Xs) ← Goal =.. [F|Xs], Goal.

We can generalize the function to be applied from a predicate name, i.e., an atom, to a term parameterized by variables. An example is substituting for a value in a list. The relation *substitute/4* from Program 9.3 can be viewed as an instance of *map_list* if a parameterization is allowed. Namely *map_list(Xs,substitute(Old,New),Ys)* has the same effect in substituting the element *New* for the element *Old* in *Xs* to get *Ys* — exactly the relation computed by Program 9.3. In order to handle this correctly the definition of *apply* must be extended a little as below:

apply(P,Xs) ←
    P =.. L1, append(L1,Xs,L2), Goal =.. L2, Goal.

Using *apply* as part of *map_list* leads to inefficient programs. For example, using *substitute* directly rather than through *maplist* results in far less intermediate structures being created, and eases the task of compilation. Hence these second-order predicates are better used in conjunction with a program transformation system that can translate second-order calls to first-order calls at compile-time.

The predicate *apply* can also be used to implement lambda expressions. A lambda expression is one of the form $lambda(X_1,...,X_n).Expression$. If the set of lambda expressions to be used are known in advance, they can be named. For example, the above expression would be replaced by some unique identifier, *foo* say, and defined by an *apply* clause:

apply(foo,X1,...,Xn) ← Expression.

Although possible both theoretically and pragmatically, the use of lambda expressions and second-order constructs such as *has_property* and *maplist* is not widespread as in functional programming languages such as Lisp. We conjecture that this is a combination of cultural bias and the availability of a host of alternative programming techniques. It is possible that the active ongoing work on both extending the logic programming model with higher-order constructs, and integrating it with functional programming, will change the picture.

In the meantime, set expressions seem to be the main and most useful higher-order construct in Prolog.

17.4   Background

An excellent, detailed account of set predicates in Prolog-10 is given by Warren (1982a). He explains their basic logical properties. Our presentation differs from Warren's in the choice of *set_of* as the basic set predicate, rather than *set_of1* (called *setof* in Prolog-10).

Set predicates are a powerful extension to Prolog. They can be used (inefficiently) to implement negation as failure, and meta-logical type predicates (Kahn, 1984). If a goal G has no solutions, which is determined by a predicate such as *set_of*, then *not* G is true. The predicate *var(X)* is implemented by testing whether the goal $X=1;X=2$ has two solutions. Further discussion of such behavior of set-predicates, and a survey of different implementations of set predicates can be found in Naish (1985b).

Further description of the Lee algorithm, and the general routing problem for VLSI circuits can be found in textbooks on VLSI, for example, Breuer and Carter (1983).

KWIC was posed as a benchmark for high-level programming languages by Perlis, and was used to compare several languages. We find the Prolog implementation of it perhaps the most elegant of them all.

Our description of lambda expressions is modeled after Warren (1982a). Predicates such as *apply* and *map_list* were part of the utilities package at the University of Edinburgh. They were fashionable for a while, but fell out of favor because they were not compiled efficiently, and no source-to-source transformation tools were available.

Chapter 18

Search Techniques

In this chapter we show programs encapsulating classic AI search techniques. The first section discusses state-transition frameworks for solving problems formulated in terms of a state-space graph. The second discusses the minimax algorithm with alpha-beta pruning for searching game trees.

18.1 Searching state-space graphs

State-space graphs are used to represent problems. Nodes of the graph are states of the problem. An edge exists between nodes if there is a transition rule, also called a *move*, transforming one state into the next. Solving the problem means finding a path from a given initial state to a desired solution state by applying a sequence of transition rules.

Program 18.1 is a framework for solving problems by searching their state-space graphs, using depth-first search as described in Section 14.2.

No commitment has been made to the representation of states. The moves are specified by a binary predicate *move(State,Move)* where *Move* is a move applicable to *State*. The predicate *update(State,Move,State1)* finds the state *State1* reached by applying the move *Move* to state *State*. It is often easier to combine the *move* and *update* procedures. We keep them separate here to make knowledge more explicit, and retain flexibility and modularity possibly at the expense of performance.

The validity of possible moves is checked by the predicate *legal(State)* which checks if the problem state *State* satisfies the constraints of the problem. The program keeps a history of the states visited to prevent looping. Checking that looping does not occur is done by seeing if the new state appears in the history

solve_dfs(State,History,Moves) ←
    Moves is the sequence of moves to reach a
    desired final state from the current *State*,
    where *History* contains the states visited previously.

solve_dfs(State,History,[ ]) ←
    final_state(State).
solve_dfs(State,History,[Move|Moves]) ←
    move(State,Move),
    update(State,Move,State1),
    legal(State1),
    not member(State1,History),
    solve_dfs(State1,[State1|History],Moves).

Testing the framework

test_dfs(Problem,Moves) ←
    initial_state(Problem,State), solve_dfs(State,[State],Moves).

Program 18.1: A depth-first state-transition framework for
          problem solving

of states. The sequence of moves leading from the initial state to the final state is built incrementally in the third argument of *solve_dfs/3*.

To solve a problem using the framework, the programmer must decide how states are to be represented, and axiomatize the *move*, *update* and *legal* procedures. A suitable representation has profound effect on the success of this framework.

Let us use the framework to solve the wolf, goat and cabbage problem. We state the problem informally. A farmer has a wolf, goat, and cabbage on the left side of a river. The farmer has a boat that can carry at most one of the three, and he must transport this trio to the right bank. The problem is that he dare not leave the wolf with the goat (wolves love to eat goats) or the goat with the cabbage (goats love to eat cabbages). He takes all his jobs very seriously and does not want to disturb the ecological balance by losing a passenger.

States are represented by a triple *wgc(B,L,R)* where B is the position of the boat (left or right), L is the list of occupants of the left bank, and R the occupants of the right bank. The initial and final states are *wgc(left,[wolf,goat,cabbage],[ ])* and *wgc(right,[ ],[wolf,goat,cabbage])*, respectively. In fact, it is not strictly necessary to keep the occupants from both the left and right banks. The occupants from the left bank can be deduced from the occupants of the right bank, and vice versa. Having both makes specifying moves clearer.

States for the wolf, goat and cabbage problem are a structure
wgc(Boat,Left,Right), where *Boat* is the bank where the boat
currently is, *Left* is the list of occupants on the left bank of
the river, and *Right* is the list of occupants of the right bank.

initial_state(wgc,wgc(left,[wolf,goat,cabbage],[ ])).

final_state(wgc(right,[ ],[wolf,goat,cabbage])).

move(wgc(left,L,R),Cargo) ← member(Cargo,L).
move(wgc(right,L,R),Cargo) ← member(Cargo,R).
move(wgc(B,L,R),alone).

update(wgc(B,L,R),Cargo,wgc(B1,L1,R1)) ←
    update_boat(B,B1), update_banks(Cargo,B,L,R,L1,R1).

update_boat(left,right).
update_boat(right,left).

update_banks(alone,B,L,R,L,R).
update_banks(Cargo,left,L,R,L1,R1) ←
    select(Cargo,L,L1), insert(Cargo,R,R1).
update_banks(Cargo,right,L,R,L1,R1) ←
    select(Cargo,R,R1), insert(Cargo,L,L1).

insert(X,[Y|Ys],[X,Y|Ys]) ←
    precedes(X,Y).
insert(X,[Y|Ys],[Y|Zs]) ←
    precedes(Y,X), insert(X,Ys,Zs).
insert(X,[ ],[X]).

precedes(wolf,X).
precedes(X,cabbage).

legal(wgc(left,L,R)) ← not illegal(R).
legal(wgc(right,L,R)) ← not illegal(L).

illegal(L) ← member(wolf,L), member(goat,L).
illegal(L) ← member(goat,L), member(cabbage,L).

Program 18.2: Solving the wolf, goat, and cabbage problem

It is convenient for checking for loops to keep the lists of occupants sorted.
Thus *wolf* will always be listed before *goat*, both of whom will be before *cabbage*
if they are on the same bank.

Moves transport an occupant to the opposite bank, and can thus be specified

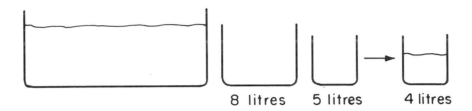

8 litres   5 litres   4 litres

Figure 18.1: The water jugs problem

by the particular occupant who is the *Cargo*. The case when nothing is taken is specified by the cargo *alone*. The nondeterministic behavior of *member* allows a concise description of all the possible moves in three clauses: for moving something from the left bank, from the right bank, or for the farmer rowing in either direction by himself, as shown in Program 18.2.

For each of these moves, the updating procedure must be specified, namely changing the position of the boat (by *update_boat/2*), and updating the banks (by *update_banks*). Using the predicate *select* allows a compact description of the updating process. The *update_banks/3* procedure is necessary to keep the occupant list sorted, facilitating the check if a state has been visited before. It contains all the possible cases of adding an occupant to a bank.

Finally, the test for legality must be specified. The constraints are simple. The wolf and goat cannot be on the same bank without the farmer, nor can the goat and cabbage.

Program 18.2 collects together the facts and rules needed to solve the wolf, goat cabbage problem in addition to Program 18.1. The clarity of the program speaks for itself.

We use the state-transition framework for solving another classic search problem from recreational mathematics — the water jugs problem. There are two jugs of capacity 8 and 5 liters with no markings, and the problem is to measure out exactly 4 liters from a vat containing 20 liters (or some other large number). The possible operations are filling up a jug from the vat, emptying a jug into the vat, and transferring the contents of one jug to another until either the pouring jug is emptied completely, or the other jug is filled to capacity. The problem is depicted in Figure 18.1.

The problem can be generalized to N jugs of capacity $C_1, \ldots, C_N$. The problem is to measure a volume V, different from all the C_i's but less than the largest.

initial_state(jugs,jugs(0,0)).
final_state(jugs(4,V2)).
final_state(jugs(V1,4).

move(jugs(V1,V2),fill(1)).
move(jugs(V1,V2),fill(2)).
move(jugs(V1,V2),empty(1)) ← V1 > 0.
move(jugs(V1,V2),empty(2)) ← V2 > 0.
move(jugs(V1,V2),transfer(2,1)).
move(jugs(V1,V2),transfer(1,2)).

update(jugs(V1,V2),empty(1),jugs(0,V2)).
update(jugs(V1,V2),empty(2),jugs(V1,0)).
update(jugs(V1,V2),fill(1),jugs(C1,V2)) ← capacity(1,C1).
update(jugs(V1,V2),fill(2),jugs(V1,C2)) ← capacity(2,C2).
update(jugs(V1,V2),transfer(2,1),jugs(W1,W2)) ←
    capacity(1,C1),
    Liquid := V1 + V2,
    Excess := Liquid – C1,
    adjust(Liquid,Excess,W1,W2).
update(jugs(V1,V2),transfer(1,2),jugs(W1,W2)) ←
    capacity(2,C2),
    Liquid := V1 + V2,
    Excess := Liquid – C2,
    adjust(Liquid,Excess,W2,W1).

adjust(Liquid, Excess,Liquid,0) ← Excess ≤ 0.
adjust(Liquid,Excess,V,Excess) ← Excess > 0, V := Liquid – Excess.

legal(jugs(V1,V2)).

capacity(1,8).
capacity(2,5).

Program 18.3: Solving the water jugs problem

There is a solution if V is a multiple of the greatest common divisor of the C_i's. Our particular example is solvable because 4 is a multiple of the greatest common divisor of 8 and 5.

The particular problem we solve is for two jugs of arbitrary capacity, but the approach is immediately generalizable to any number of jugs. The program assumes two facts in the database, *capacity(I,CI)*, for I equals *1* and *2*. The natural representation of the state is a structure *jugs(V1,V2)* where *V1* and *V2* represent the volumes of liquid currently in the two jugs. The initial state is *jugs(0,0)* and the desired final state either *jugs(0,X)* or *jugs(X,0)*, where *X* is the desired volume. Assuming that the first jug has larger capacity, only one final state *jugs(X,0)* need be specified, since it is easy to transfer the required amount from the second jug to the first, by emptying the first jug, then transferring to it the contents of the second jug.

The data for solving the jugs problem in conjunction with Program 18.1 are given as Program 18.3. There are six moves: filling each jug, emptying each jug, and transferring the contents of one jug to another. A sample fact for filling the first jug is *move(jugs(V1,V2),fill(1))*. The jugs' state is given explicitly to allow the data to co-exist with other problem solving data such as in Program 18.2. The emptying moves are optimized to prevent emptying an already empty jug. The updating procedure associated with the first four moves is simple, while the transferring operation has two cases. If the total volume in the jugs is less than the capacity of the jug being filled, the pouring jug will be emptied and the other jug will have the entire volume. Otherwise the other jug will be filled to capacity while the difference between the total liquid volume and the capacity of the filled jug will be left in the pouring jug. This is achieved by the predicate *adjust/4*. Note that the test for legality is trivial since all reachable states are legal.

Most interesting problems have too large a search space to be searched exhaustively by a program such as 18.1. One possibility for improvement is to put more knowledge into the moves allowed. Solutions to the jug problem can be found by filling one of the jugs whenever possible, emptying the other whenever possible, and otherwise transferring the contents of the jug being filled to the jug being emptied. Thus instead of six moves only three need be specified, and the search will be more direct, because only one move will be applicable to any given state. This may not give an optimal solution if the wrong jug to be constantly filled is chosen.

Developing this point further, the three moves can be coalesced into a higher-level move, *fill_and_transfer*. This tactic fills one jug and transfers all its contents to the other jug, emptying the other jug as necessary. The code for transferring from the bigger to the smaller jug is

```
move(jugs(V1,V2),fill_and_transfer(1)).

update(jugs(V1,V2),fill_and_transfer(1),jugs(0,V)) ←
        capacity(1,C1),
        capacity(2,C2),
        C1 > C2,
        V := (C1+V2) mod C2.
```

Using this program only three fill and transfer operations from one jug to the other are necessary to solve the problem in Figure 18.1.

Adding such domain knowledge means changing the problem description entirely, and constitutes programming, although at a different level.

Another possibility for improvement of the search performance, investigated by early research in AI, is heuristic guidance. A general framework, based on a more explicit choice of the next state to search in the state space graph, is used. The choice depends on numeric scores assigned to positions. The score, computed by an *evaluation function*, is a measure of the goodness of the position. Depth-first search can be considered as a special case of searching using an evaluation function whose value is the distance of the current state to the initial state, while breadth-first search uses an evaluation function which is the inverse of that distance.

We show two search techniques that use an evaluation function explicitly: hill climbing and best-first search. In the following, the predicate *value(State, Value)* is an evaluation function. The techniques are described abstractly.

Hill climbing is a generalization of depth-first search where the successor position with the highest score is chosen rather than the leftmost one chosen by Prolog. No change is necessary to the top-level framework of Program 18.1. The hill-climbing *move* generates all the states that can be reached from the current one in a single move using *set_of*, and then orders them in decreasing order with respect to the values computed by the evaluation function. The predicate *evaluate_and_order(Moves,State,MVs)* determines the relation that *MVs* is an ordered list of move-value tuples corresponding to the list of moves *Moves* from a state *State*. The overall program is given as Program 18.4.

To demonstrate the behavior of the program we use the example tree of Program 14.8 augmented with a value for each move. This is given as Program 18.5. Program 18.4 combined with Program 18.5, together with the necessary definitions of *update* and *legal* searches the tree in the order *d, j*. The program is easily tested on the wolf, goat, and cabbage problem using as the evaluation function the number of occupants on the right bank.

Program 18.4 contains a repeated computation. The state reached by *Move* is calculated in order to reach a value for the move, and then recalculated by *update*. This recalculation can be avoided by adding an extra argument to *move* and keeping the state along with the move and the value as the moves are ordered. Another possibility if there will be many calculations of the same move is using a memo-function. What is the most efficient method depends on the particular problem. For problems where the *update* procedure is simple, the program as presented will be best.

solve_hill_climb(State,History,Moves) ←
    Moves is the sequence of moves to reach a
    desired final state from the current *State*,
    where *History* are the states visited previously.

solve_hill_climb(State,History,[ ]) ←
    final_state(State).
solve_hill_climb(State,History,[Move|Moves]) ←
    hill_climb(State,Move),
    update(State,Move,State1),
    legal(State1),
    not member(State1,History),
    solve_hill_climb(State1,[State1|History],Moves).

hill_climb(State,Move) ←
    set_of(M,move(State,M),Moves),
    evaluate_and_order(Moves,State,[ ],MVs),
    member((Move,Value),MVs).

evaluate_and_order(Moves,State,SoFar,OrderedMVs) ←
    All the *Moves* from the current *State*
    are evaluated and ordered as *OrderedMoves*.
    SoFar is an accumulator for partial computations.

evaluate_and_order([Move|Moves],State,MVs,OrderedMVs) ←
    update(State,Move,State1),
    value(State1,Value),
    insert((Move,Value),MVs,MVs1),
    evaluate_and_order(Moves,State,MVs1,OrderedMVs).
evaluate_and_order([ ],State,MVs,MVs).

insert(MV,[ ],[MV]).
insert((M,V),[(M1,V1)|MVs],[(M,V),(M1,V1)|MVs]) ←
    V ≥ V1.
insert((M,V),[(M1,V1)|MVs],[(M1,V1)|MVs1]) ←
    V < V1, insert((M,V),MVs,MVs1).

Testing the framework

test_hill_climb(Problem,Moves) ←
    initial_state(Problem,State), solve(State,[State],Moves).

Program 18.4: Hill-climbing problem solving framework

initial_state(tree,a).   value(a,0).   final_state(j).

move(a,b).	value(b,1).	move(c,g).	value(g,6).
move(a,c).	value(c,5).	move(d,j).	value(j,9).
move(a,d).	value(d,7).	move(e,k).	value(k,1).
move(a,e).	value(e,2).	move(f,h).	value(h,3).
move(c,f).	value(f,4).	move(f,i).	value(i,2).

Program 18.5: Test data

Hill climbing is a good technique when there is only one hill and the evaluation function is a good indication of progress. Essentially, it takes a local look at the state space graph, making the decision on where next to search on the basis of the current state alone.

An alternate search method, called *best-first search*, takes a global look at the complete state space. The best state from all those currently unsearched is chosen.

Program 18.6 for best-first search is a generalization of breadth-first search given in Section 17.2. A frontier is kept as for breadth-first search, which is added to as the search progresses. At each stage the next best available move is made. We make the code as similar as possible to Program 18.4 for hill-climbing to allow comparison.

At each stage of the search there is a set of moves to consider rather than a single one. The plural predicate names, for example, *updates* and *legals*, indicate this. Thus *legals(States,States1)* filters a set of successor states checking which ones are allowed by the constraints of the problem. One disadvantage of breadth-first search (and hence best-first search) is that the path to take is not as conveniently calculated. Each state must store explicitly with it the path used to reach it. This is reflected in the code.

Program 18.6 tested on the data of Program 18.5 searches the tree in the same order as for hill climbing.

Program 18.6 makes each step of the process explicit. In practice it may be more efficient to combine some of the steps. When filtering the generated states, for example, it can be tested that a state is new and also legal at the same time. This saves generating intermediate data structures. Program 18.7 illustrates the idea by combining all of the checks into one procedure, *update_frontier*.

solve_best(Frontier,History,Moves) ←
>   *Moves* is the sequence of moves to reach a desired final state from
>   the initial state, where *Frontier* contains the current states under
>   consideration, and *History* contains the states visited previously.

solve_best([state(State,Path,Value)|Frontier],History,Moves) ←
>   final_state(State), reverse(Path,Moves).

solve_best([state(State,Path,Value)|Frontier],History,FinalPath) ←
>   set_of(M,move(State,M),Moves),
>   updates(Moves,Path,State,States),
>   legals(States,States1),
>   news(States1,History,States2),
>   evaluates(States2,Values),
>   inserts(Values,Frontier,Frontier1),
>   solve_best(Frontier1,[State|History],FinalPath).

updates(Moves,Path,State,States) ←
>   *States* is the list of possible states accessible from the
>   current *State*, according to the list of possible *Moves*,
>   where *Path* is a path from the initial node to *State*.

updates([M|Ms],Path,S,[(S1,[M|Path])|Ss]) ←
>   update(S,M,S1), updates(Ms,Path,S,Ss).
updates([ ],Path,State,[ ]).

legals(States,States1) ←
>   *States1* is the subset of the list of *States* that are legal.

legals([(S,P)|States],[(S,P)|States1]) ←
>   legal(S), legals(States,States1).
legals([(S,P)|States],States1) ←
>   not legal(S), legals(States,States1).
legals([ ],[ ]).

news(States,History,States1) ←
>   *States1* is the list of states in *States* but not in *History*.

news([(S,P)|States],History,States1) ←
>   member(S,History), news(States,History,States1).
news([(S,P)|States],History,[(S,P)|States1]) ←
>   not member(S,History), news(States,History,States1).
news([ ],History,[ ]).

Program 18.6: Best-first problem-solving framework

evaluates(States, Values) ←
    Values is the list of tuples of *States* augmented by their value.

evaluates([(S,P)|States],[state(S,P,V)|Values]) ←
    value(S,V), evaluates(States,Values).
evaluates([ ],[ ]).

inserts(States,Frontier,Frontier1) ←
    Frontier1 is the result of inserting *States* into the current *Frontier*.

inserts([Value|Values],Frontier,Frontier1) ←
    insert(Value,Frontier,Frontier0),
    inserts(Values,Frontier0,Frontier1).
inserts([ ],Frontier,Frontier).

insert(State,[ ],[State]).
insert(State,[State1|States],[State,State1|States]) ←
    less_than(State1,State).
insert(State,[State1|States],[State|States]) ←
    equals(State,State1).
insert(State,[State1|States],[State1|States1]) ←
    less_than(State,State1), insert(State,States,States1).

equals(state(S,P,V),state(S,P1,V)).

less_than(state(S1,P1,V1),state(S2,P2,V2)) ← S1 ≠ S2, V1 < V2.

Program 18.6 (Continued)

Exercises for Section 18.2

(i) Redo the water jugs program based on the two fill_and_transfer operations.

(ii) Write a program to solve the missionaries and cannibals problem:

Three missionaries and three cannibals are standing at the left bank of a river. There is a small boat to ferry them across with enough room for only one or two people. They wish to cross the river. If ever there are more missionaries than cannibals on a particular side of the river, the missionaries will convert the cannibals. Find a series of ferryings to transport safely all the missionaries and cannibals across the river without exposing any of the cannibals to conversion.

(iii) Five jealous husbands (Dudeney, 1917):

During a certain flood five married couples found themselves surrounded by

solve_best(Frontier,History,Moves) ←
    Moves is the sequence of moves to reach a desired final state
    from the initial state. *Frontier* contains the current states
    under consideration. *History* contains the states visited previously.

solve_best([state(State,Path,Value)|Frontier],History,Moves) ←
    final_state(State), reverse(Path,[ ],Moves).
solve_best([state(State,Path,Value)|Frontier],History,FinalPath) ←
    set_of(M,move(State,M),Moves),
    update_frontier(Moves,State,Path,History,Frontier,Frontier1),
    solve_best(Frontier1,[State|History],FinalPath).

update_frontier([M|Ms],State,Path,History,F,F1) ←
    update(State,M,State1),
    legal(State1),
    value(State1,Value),
    not member(State1,History),
    insert((State1,[M|Path],Value),F,F0),
    update_frontier(Ms,State,Path,History,F0,F1).
update_frontier([ ],S,P,H,F,F).

insert(State,Frontier,Frontier1) ← See Program 18.6.

Program 18.7: Concise best-first problem solving framework

water, and had to escape from their unpleasant position in a boat that would
only hold three persons at a time. Every husband was so jealous that he
would not allow his wife to be in the boat or on either bank with another
man (or with other men) unless he was himself present. Find a way of getting
these five men and their wives across into safety.

(iv) Compose a general problem solving framework built around breadth first
search analogous to Program 18.1, based on programs in Section 17.2.

(v) Express the eight queens puzzle within the framework. Find an evaluation
function.

18.2 Searching game trees

What happens when we play a game? Starting the game means setting up
the chess pieces, dealing out the cards, or setting out the matches, for example.
Once it is decided who plays first, the players take it in turns to make a move.

After each move the game position is updated accordingly.

We develop the vague specification in the previous paragraph into a simple framework for playing games. The top level statement is

```
play(Game,Result) ←
      initialize(Game,Position,Player),
      display(Position,Player),
      play(Position,Player,Result).
```

The predicate *initialize(Game,Position,Player)* determines the initial game position *Position* for *Game*, and *Player*, the player to start.

A game is a sequence of turns, where each turn consists of a player choosing a move, the move being executed, and the next player being determined. The neatest way of specifying this is as a tail recursive procedure, *play*, with three arguments: a game position, a player to move and the final result. It is convenient to separate the choice of the move by *choose_move/3* from its execution by *move/3*. The remaining predicates in the clause below display the state of the game, and determine the next player:

```
play(Position,Player,Result) ←
      choose_move(Position,Player,Move),
      move(Move,Position,Position1),
      display_game(Position1,Player),
      next_player(Player,Player1),
      !, play(Position1,Player1,Result).
```

Program 18.8 provides a logical framework for game-playing programs. Using it for writing a program for a particular game focuses attention on the important issues for game-playing: what data structures should be used to represent the game position, and how strategies for the game should be expressed. We demonstrate the process in Chapter 20 by writing programs to play Nim and Kalah.

The problem-solving frameworks of the previous section are readily adapted to playing games. Given a particular game state, the problem is to find a path of moves to a winning position.

A game tree is similar to a state-space graph. It is the tree obtained by identifying states with nodes and edges with player's moves. We do not, however, identify nodes on the tree, obtained by different sequence of moves, even if they repeat the same state. In a game tree, each layer is called a *ply*.

Most game trees are far too large to be searched exhaustively. This section discusses the techniques that have been developed to cope with the large search

play(Game) ←
 Play game with name Game.

play(Game) ←
 initialize(Game,Position,Player),
 display_game(Position,Player),
 play(Position,Player,Result).

play(Position,Player,Result) ←
 game_over(Position,Player,Result), !, announce(Result).
play(Position,Player,Result) ←
 choose_move(Position,Player,Move),
 move(Move,Position,Position1),
 display_game(Position1,Player),
 next_player(Player,Player1),
 !, play(Position1,Player1,Result).

Program 18.8: Framework for playing games

evaluate_and_choose(Moves,Position,Record,BestMove) ←
 Chooses the BestMove from the set of Moves from the
 current Position, Record records the current best move.

evaluate_and_choose([Move|Moves],Position,Record,BestMove) ←
 move(Move,Position,Position1),
 value(Position1,Value),
 update(Move,Value,Record,Record1),
 evaluate_and_choose(Moves,Position,Record1,BestMove)
evaluate_and_choose([ ],Position,(Move,Value),Move).

update(Move,Value,(Move1,Value1),(Move1,Value1)) ←
 Value $\leq$ Value1.
update(Move,Value,(Move1,Value1),(Move,Value)) ←
 Value > Value1.

Program 18.9: Choosing the best move

space for two-person games. In particular we concentrate on the minimax algorithm augmented by alpha-beta pruning. This strategy is used as the basis of a
program we present for playing Kalah in Chapter 20.

We describe the basic approach of searching game trees using evaluation functions. Again in this section *value(Position,Value)* denotes an evaluation function
computing the *Value* of *Position*, the current state of the game. Here is a simple

algorithm for choosing the next move:

> Find all possible game states which can be reached in one move.
> Compute the values of the states using the evaluation function.
> Choose the move that leads to the position with the highest score.

This algorithm is encoded as Program 18.9. It assumes a predicate *move(Move,Position,Position1)* that applies a *Move* to the current *Position* to reach *Position1*. The interface to the game framework of Program 18.8 is provided by the clause

> choose_move(Position,computer,Move) ←
>   set_of(M,move(Position,M),Moves),
>   evaluate_and_choose(Moves,Position,(nil,–1000),Move).

The predicate *move(Position,Move)* is true if *Move* is a possible move from the current position.

The basic relation is *evaluate_and_choose(Moves,Position,Record,Move)* which chooses the best move *Move* in the possible *Moves* from a given *Position*. For each of the possible moves, the corresponding position is determined, its value calculated and the move with the highest value chosen. *Record* is a record of the current best move so far. In Program 18.9 it is represented as a tuple *(Move, Value)*. The structure of *Record* has been partially abstracted in the procedure *update/4*. How much data abstraction to use is a matter of style and tradeoff between readability, conciseness, and performance.

Looking ahead one move, the approach of Program 18.9, would be sufficient if the evaluation function were perfect, that is if the score would reflect which positions led to a win and which to a loss. Games become interesting when a perfect evaluation function is not known. Choosing a move on the basis of looking ahead one move is generally not a good strategy. It is better to look several moves ahead, and infer from what is found the best move to make.

The *minimax* algorithm is the standard method for determining the value of a position based on searching the game tree several ply ahead. The idea is as follows.

The algorithm assumes that, when confronted with several choices, the opponent would make the best choice for him, i.e., the worst choice for me. My goal then is to make the move that maximizes for me the value of the position after the opponent will make his best move, i.e., minimizes the value for him. Hence the name minimax. This reasoning proceeds several ply ahead, depending on the resources that can be allocated to the search. At the last ply the evaluation function is used.

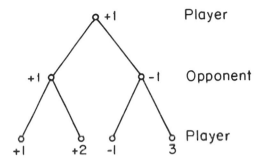

Figure 18.2: A simple game tree

Assuming a reasonable evaluation function, the algorithm will produce better results the more ply are searched. It will produce the best move if the entire tree is searched.

The minimax algorithm is justified by a zero-sum assumption, which says, informally, that what is good for me must be bad for my opponent, and vice versa.

Figure 18.2 depicts a simple game tree of depth 2 ply. The player has two moves in the current position, and the opponent has two replies. The values of the leaf nodes are the values for the player. The opponent wants to minimize the score, so will choose the minimum values, making the positions be worth *+1* and *−1* at one level higher in the tree. The player wants to maximize the value and will choose the node with value *+1*.

Program 18.10 encodes the minimax algorithm. The basic relation is *minimax(D,Position,MaxMin,Move,Value)* which is true if *Move* is the move with the highest *Value* from *Position* obtained by searching *D* ply in the game tree. *MaxMin* is a flag which indicates if we are maximizing or minimizing. It is *1* for maximizing and *−1* for minimizing. A generalization of Program 18.9 is used to choose from the set of moves. Two extra arguments must be added to *evaluate_and_choose*, *D* the number of ply and *MaxMin* the flag. The last argument is generalized to return a record including both a move and a value rather than just a move. The *minimax* procedure does the bookkeeping, changing the number of moves being looked ahead, and also the minimax flag. The initial record is *(nil,−1000)*, where *nil* represents an arbitrary move and *−1000* is a score less than any possible score of the evaluation function.

evaluate_and_choose(Moves,Position,Depth,Flag,Record,BestMove) ←
Choose the *BestMove* from the set of *Moves* from the current
Position using the minimax algorithm searching *Depth* ply ahead.
Flag indicates if we are currently minimizing or maximizing.
Record records the current best move.

evaluate_and_choose([Move|Moves],Position,D,MaxMin,Record,Best) ←
    move(Move,Position,Position1),
    minimax(D,Position1,MaxMin,Move,Value),
    update(Move,Value,Record,Record1),
    evaluate_and_choose(Moves,Position,D,MaxMin,Record1,Best).
evaluate_and_choose([ ],Position,D,MaxMin,Record,Record).

minimax(0,Position,MaxMin,Move,Value) ←
    value(Position,V),
    Value := V∗MaxMin.
minimax(D,Position,MaxMin,Move,Value) ←
    D > 0,
    set_of(M,move(Position,M),Moves),
    D1 := D – 1,
    MinMax := –MaxMin,
    evaluate_and_choose(Moves,Position,D1,MinMax, (nil,–1000),
        (Move,Value)).

update(Move,Value,Record,Record1) ← See Program 18.9

Program 18.10: Choosing the best move with the minimax algorithm

The observation about efficiency that was made about combining the move
generation and update procedures in the context of searching state-space graphs
has an analogue when searching game trees. Whether it is better to compute the
set of positions rather than the set of moves (with the corresponding change in
algorithm) will depend on the particular application.

The minimax algorithm can be improved by keeping track of the results of
the search so far, using a technique known as alpha-beta pruning. The idea is to
keep for each node the estimated minimum value found so far, the alpha value,
along with the estimated maximum value, beta. If, on evaluating a node, beta is
exceeded, no more search on that branch is necessary. In good cases more than
half of the positions in the game tree need not be evaluated.

Program 18.11 is a modified version of Program 18.10 which incorporates
alpha-beta pruning. The new relation scheme is *alpha_beta(Depth,Position,Alpha,*

evaluate_and_choose(*Moves,Position,Depth,Alpha,Beta,Record,BestMove*) ←
    Chooses the *BestMove* from the set of *Moves* from the current
    Position using the minimax algorithm with alpha-beta cutoff searching
    Depth ply ahead. *Alpha* and *Beta* are the parameters of the algorithm.
    Record records the current best move.

evaluate_and_choose([Move|Moves],Position,D,Alpha,Beta,Record,BestMove) ←
    move(Move,Position,Position1),
    alpha_beta(D,Position1,Alpha,Beta,MoveX,Value),
    Value1 := −Value,
    cutoff(Move,Value1,D,Alpha,Beta,Moves,Position,Record,BestMove).
evaluate_and_choose([ ],Position,D,Alpha,Beta,Move,(Move,A)).

alpha_beta(0,Position,Alpha,Beta,Move,Value) ←
    value(Position,Value).
alpha_beta(D,Position,Alpha,Beta,Move,Value) ←
    set_of(M,move(Position,M),Moves),
    Alpha1 := −Beta,
    Beta1 := −Alpha,
    D1 := D−1,
evaluate_and_choose(Moves,Position,D1,Alpha1,Beta1,nil,(Move,Value)).

cutoff(Move,Value,D,Alpha,Beta,Moves,Position,Record,(Move,Value)) ←
    Value ≥ Beta.
cutoff(Move,Value,D,Alpha,Beta,Moves,Position,Record,BestMove) ←
    Alpha < Value, Value < Beta,
    evaluate_and_choose(Moves,Position,D,Value,Beta,Move,BestMove).
cutoff(Move,Value,D,Alpha,Beta,Moves,Position,Record,BestMove) ←
    Value ≤ Alpha,
    evaluate_and_choose(Moves,Position,D,Alpha,Beta,Record,BestMove).

Program 18.11: Choosing a move using minimax with alpha-beta pruning

Beta,Move,Value) which extends minimax by replacing the minimaxing flag with
alpha and beta. The same relationship holds with respect to *evaluate_and_choose*.

Unlike Program 18.10, the version of *evaluate_and_choose* in Program 18.11
does not need to search all possibilities. This is achieved by introducing a predicate *cutoff* which either stops searching the current branch or continues the search,
updating the value of alpha and the current best move as appropriate.

For example, the last node in the game tree in Figure 18.2 does not need to
be searched. Once a move with value *−1* is found, which is less than the value of

+1 the player is guaranteed, no other nodes can contribute to the final score.

The program can be generalized by replacing the base case of *alpha_beta* by a test whether the position is terminal. This is necessary in chess programs, for example, for handling incomplete piece exchanges.

18.3 Background

Search techniques for both planning and game playing are discussed in AI textbooks. For further details of search strategies or the minimax algorithm and its extension to alpha-beta pruning, see, for example, Nilsson (1971) or Winston (1977).

Walter Wilson originally showed us the alpha-beta algorithm in Prolog.

Chapter 19

Meta-Interpreters

Meta-programs treat other programs as data. They analyze, transform, and simulate other programs. The writing of meta-programs, or meta-programming, is particularly easy in Prolog due to the equivalence of programs and data: both being Prolog terms. In fact meta-programming is nothing special in Prolog. Several of the example programs in previous chapters are meta-programs, for example, the editor of Program 12.5, the shell process of Program 12.6, the simulators of automata of Section 14.3, and the translation of grammar rules to Prolog clauses in Program 16.2.

This chapter concentrates on a particular class of meta-programs, meta-interpreters. The first section explains the basics of meta-interpreters. The remaining sections show how meta-interpreters can be enhanced for a wide range of applications. Applications of meta-interpreters to the building of expert system shells are developed in the second section. The third section discusses program debugging algorithms and their implementation.

19.1 Simple meta-interpreters

A *meta-interpreter* for a language is an interpreter for the language written in the language itself. The ability to write a meta-interpreter easily is a very powerful feature a programming language can have. It enables the building of an integrated programming environment and gives access to the computational process of the language. Since a meta-interpreter is a Prolog program, we give a relation scheme. The relation *solve(Goal)* is true if *Goal* is true with respect to the program being interpreted. We use *solve/1* throughout this section to denote a meta-interpreter.

solve(*Goal*) ←
   Goal is deducible from the pure Prolog program
   defined by *clause/2*.

solve(true).
solve((A,B)) ← solve(A), solve(B).
solve(A) ← clause(A,B), solve(B).

Program 19.1: A meta-interpreter for pure Prolog

The simplest meta-interpreter that can be written in Prolog uses the meta-variable facility, namely

   solve(A) ← A.

Its usefulness can be seen in Programs 12.6 and 12.7 where it forms the basis for a shell process and logging facility written in Prolog.

A more interesting meta-interpreter simulates the computational model of logic programs. Goal reduction for pure Prolog programs can be described by the three clauses comprising Program 19.1. This meta-interpreter and its extensions form the basis for this chapter.

Declaratively, the interpreter reads as follows. The constant *true* is true. The conjunction (*A,B*) is true if *A* is true and *B* is true. A goal *A* is true if there is a clause *A* ← *B* in the interpreted program such that *B* is true.

We give also a procedural reading of the three clauses in Program 19.1. The *solve* fact states that the empty goal, represented in Prolog by the atom *true*, is solved. The next clause concerns conjunctive goals. It reads: "To solve a conjunction (*A,B*), solve *A* and solve *B*." The general case of goal reduction is covered by the final clause. To solve a goal, choose a clause from the program whose head unifies with the goal, and recursively solve the body of the clause.

The procedural reading of Prolog clauses is necessary to demonstrate that the meta-interpreter of Program 19.1 indeed reflects Prolog's choices of implementing the abstract computation model of logic programming. The two choices are the selection of the leftmost goal as the goal to reduce, and sequential search and backtracking for the nondeterministic choice of the clause to use to reduce the goal. The goal order of the body of the *solve* clause handling conjunctions guarantees that the leftmost goal in the conjunction is solved first. Sequential search and backtracking comes from Prolog's behavior in satisfying the *clause* goal.

The hard work of the interpreter is borne by the third clause of Program 19.1. The call to *clause* performs the unification with the heads of the clauses

solve(member(X,[a,b,c]))
    clause(member(X,[a,b,c]),B)   {X=a,B=true}
    solve(true)
        true   Output: X=a
               ;

solve(true)
    clause(true,T)   f
    clause(member(X,[a,b,c],B)   {B=member(X,[b,c])}
    solve(member(X,[b,c]))
        clause(member(X,[b,c]),B1)   {X=b,B1=true}
        solve(true)
            true   Output: X=b
               ;

    solve(true)
        clause(true,T)   f
    clause(member(X,[b,c]),B1)   {B1=member(X,[c])}
    solve(member(X,[c]))
        clause(member(X,[c],B2)   {X=c,B2=true}
        solve(true)
        true   Output: X=c
             ;

    solve(true)
        clause(true,T)   f
    clause(member(X,[c],B2))   {B2=member(X,[ ])}
    solve(member(X,[ ]))
        clause(member(X,[ ],B3)   f
    No (more) solutions

Figure 19.1: Tracing the meta-interpreter

appearing in the program. It is also responsible for giving different solutions on backtracking. Backtracking also occurs in the conjunctive rule reverting from *B* to *A*.

Tracing the meta-interpreter of Program 19.1 solving a goal is instructive. The trace of answering the query *solve(member(X,[a,b,c]))* with respect to Program 3.12 for *member* is given in Figure 19.1.

Differences in meta-interpreters can be characterized in terms of their *granularity*, that is the chunks of the computation that are made accessible to the programmer. The granularity of the trivial one clause meta-interpreter is too

> solve(*Goal, Tree*) ←
>> *Tree* is a proof tree for *Goal* given the program defined by *clause/2*.

solve(true,true).
solve((A,B),(ProofA,ProofB)) ←
    solve(A,ProofA), solve(B,ProofB).
solve(A,(A←Proof)) ←
    clause(A,B), solve(B,Proof).

Program 19.2: Building a proof tree

coarse. Consequently there is little scope for applying the meta-interpreter. It is possible, though not as easy, to write a meta-interpreter which models unification and backtracking. The granularity of such a meta-interpreter is very fine. Working at this fine level is usually not worthwhile. The efficiency loss is too much to warrant the extra applications. The meta-interpreter in Program 19.1, at the clause reduction level, has the granularity most suited for the widest range of applications.

A simple application constructs a proof tree as it solves the goal. The technique is similar to constructing a parse tree for a grammar in Program 16.3, and adding structured arguments to logic programs discussed in Section 2.2. The proof tree is useful for explanation facilities for expert systems as is discussed in the next section.

The basic relation is *solve(Goal, Tree)* where *Tree* is a proof tree for solving the goal *Goal*. Proof trees are represented by the structure *Goal←Proof* where *Proof* is a conjunction of the branches proving *Goal*. Program 19.2 implementing *solve/2* is a straightforward extension of Program 19.1. The three clauses correspond exactly to the three clauses of the meta-interpreter for pure Prolog.

The *solve* fact states that the empty goal is true with a trivial proof tree, represented by the atom *true*. The second clause states that the proof tree of a conjunctive goal (*A,B*) is a conjunction of the proof trees for *A* and *B*. The final *solve* clause builds a proof tree *A←Proof* for the goal *A*, where *Proof* is recursively built by solving the body of the clause used to reduce *A*.

We give an example of using Program 19.2 with the pure logic program, Program 1.2. The query *solve(son(lot,haran),Proof)?* has the solution

$$Proof = (son(lot,haran) ←$$
$$((father(haran,lot)←true),$$
$$(male(lot)←true))).$$

system(A := B).   system(A < B).
system(read(X)).   system(write(X)).
system(integer(X)).   system(functor(T,F,N)).
system(clause(A,B)).   system(system(X)).

Figure 19.2: Fragment of a table of system predicates

The query *solve(son(X,haran),Proof)?* has the solution *X=lot* and the same value for *Proof*.

The interpreter of Program 19.1 must be extended to handle language features outside pure Prolog. The various system predicates are not defined by clauses in the program and thus need different treatment. The easiest way to incorporate these system predicates is to call them directly using the meta-variable. A table stating which predicates are system ones is necessary. We assume the table consists of facts of the form *system(Predicate)* for each system predicate. Figure 19.2 gives part of that table. The clause in the meta-interpreter handling system predicates is

solve(A) ← system(A), A.

The extra *solve* clause makes the behavior of the system predicates invisible to the meta-interpreter. This can be extended to non-system predicates whose behavior one wants to be invisible. Conversely, there are some system provided predicates which should be made visible. Examples are predicates for negation and second-order programming. These are best handled by having a special clause for each in the meta-interpreter. Example clauses are

solve(not A) ← not solve(A).
solve(set_of(X,Goal,Xs)) ← set_of(X,solve(Goal),Xs).

Simulating the behavior of the cut correctly is a problem with this meta-interpreter. The naive solution is to consider cut as a system predicate. Effectively this means adding the clause

solve(!) ← !.

This clause does not have the required effect. The cut in the clause guarantees commitment to the current *solve* clause rather than affecting the search tree of which the cut is a part. In other words, the scope of the cut is too local.

A neater solution uses a system predicate known as *ancestor cut*. Ancestor cut is provided in Wisdom Prolog and Waterloo Prolog, but not in Edinburgh Prolog. The general form is !(*Ancestor*), where *Ancestor* refers to an ancestor of

solve(*Goal*) ←
        Goal is deducible from the Prolog program
        defined by *clause/2*.

solve(true).
solve((A,B)) ← solve(A), solve(B).
solve(!) ← !(reduce(A)).
solve(not A) ← not solve(A).
solve(set_of(X,Goal,Xs)) ← set_of(X,solve(Goal),Xs).
solve(A) ← system(A), A.
solve(A) ← reduce(A).

reduce(A) ← clause(A,B), solve(B).

Program 19.3: A meta-interpreter for full Prolog

the current goal. If *Ancestor* is a positive integer, n say, the nth ancestor of the
current goal is considered. Counting is done upward from the current goal, so
the first ancestor is the parent goal, the second ancestor is the grandparent goal,
etc. If *Ancestor* is a noninteger term, the first ancestor unifying with *Ancestor* is
considered. In either case all siblings of the specified ancestor are pruned from
the search tree in the same manner as if a cut had been applied directly to the
ancestor goal.

To handle cut correctly using ancestor cut, a separate predicate from *solve*
is necessary; *reduce*(*Goal*) is used here. The correct scope for cut is obtained by
allowing the meta-interpreter to cut the previous *reduce* goal with the ancestor
cut.

All the observations and improvements of the above discussion are incorporated into a meta-interpreter for Prolog in Program 19.3.

The meta-interpreter in Program 19.3 can be made more efficient by adding
cuts. The choice of the appropriate clause in the collection of *solve* clauses is
deterministic. Once the correct clause has been identified it can be committed to.

Clauses can be added for the extensions to pure Prolog in Program 19.2, the
meta-interpreter building proof trees. System goals are handled with the clause

    solve(A,(A←true))← system(A), A.

The proof tree for a system goal A is $A ← true$.

We give an example of an enhanced meta-interpreter that traces a computation in the style presented in Section 6.1. We present two versions. The first

version, Program 19.4, handles only success branches of the computations in pure Prolog, and does not display failure nodes in the search tree. It is capable of generating the trace in Figure 6.2 of the query *append(Xs, Ys,[a,b,c])*. The second version, Program 19.5, handles system predicates, and more importantly failure nodes in the search tree. It is capable of generating the traces of Figures 6.1 and 6.3 of the queries *son(X,haran)* and *quicksort([2,1,3],Xs)*, respectively.

The basic predicate is *trace(Goal,Depth)* where *Goal* is solved at some *Depth*. The starting depth is assumed to be *0*. The three clauses in Program 19.4 correspond to the three clauses of Program 19.1. The first two clauses state that the empty goal is solved at any depth, and the depth of solving each conjunct in a conjunction is the same. The final clause matches the goal with the head of a program clause, displays the goal, increments the depth and solves the body of the program clause at the new depth.

The predicate *display(Goal,Depth)*, which displays a *Goal* at a given *Depth*, is an interface for printing the traced goal. The depth in the proof tree is indicated by depth of indentation. The definition of *display* uses an indentation which is some multiple of the depth in the tree.

There is some subtlety in the goal order of the clause

        trace(Goal,Depth) ←
            clause(A,B),
            display(A,Depth),
            Depth1 := Depth+1,
            trace(B,Depth1).

The *display* goal is between the *clause* goal and the *trace* goal. This ensures that the goal is displayed each time Prolog backtracks to *clause*. If the order of the *clause* and *display* goals are swapped, only the initial call of the goal *A* is displayed.

Using Program 19.4 for the query *trace(append(Xs, Ys,[a,b,c]))* with Program 3.15 for *append* generates a trace as presented in Section 6.1. The output messages and semicolons for alternative solutions are provided by the underlying Prolog. There is only one difference from the trace in Figure 6.2. The unifications are already performed.

Program 19.4 can be extended in order to trace the failure of goals. In order to print failed goals, we must rely on the operational behavior of Prolog, in particular the use of clause order. Cuts are added to the first two clauses, and an extra clause is added at the end of the program:

trace(Goal) ←
>   *Goal* is deducible from the pure Prolog program defined by
>   *clause/2*. The program traces the proof by side-effects.

```
trace(Goal) ←
    trace(Goal,0).

trace(true,Depth).
trace((A,B),Depth) ←
    trace(A,Depth), trace(B,Depth).
trace(A,Depth) ←
    clause(A,B),
    display(A,Depth),
    Depth1 := Depth+1,
    trace(B,Depth1).

display(A,Depth) ←
    tab(Depth), write(A), nl.
```

Program 19.4: A tracer for pure Prolog

trace(Goal) ←
>   *Goal* is deducible from the Prolog program defined by
>   *clause/2*. The program traces the proof by side effects.

```
trace(Goal) ← trace(Goal,0).
trace(true,Depth) ← !.
trace((A,B),Depth) ←
    !, trace(A,Depth), trace(B,Depth).
trace(A,Depth) ←
    system(A), A, !, display(A,Depth), nl.
trace(A,Depth) ←
    clause(A,B),
    display(A,Depth), nl,
    Depth1 := Depth + 1,
    trace(B,Depth1).
trace(A,Depth) ←
    not clause(A,B), display(A,Depth), tab(8), write(f), nl, fail.

display(A,Depth) ←
    Spacing := 3*Depth, tab(Spacing), write(A).
```

Program 19.5: A tracer for Prolog

trace(A,Depth) ←
   not clause(A,B), display(A,Depth), tab(10), write(f), nl, fail.

Note that *display* is modified not to start on a new line, so that the failure message is consistent with the traces in Chapter 6. An extra new line command is necessary to the clauses that call *display*.

  System goals are handled by the clause

   trace(A,Depth) ← system(A), A, !, display(A,Depth).

The call to *display* is after the goal has succeeded, to correctly use the last rule if the goal should fail. The cut is necessary to distinguish from the last clause. The new program is given as Program 19.5. It can give the trace of Figure 6.3, and also that of Figure 19.1.

Exercises for Section 19.1

(i) Write a meta-interpreter to count the number of procedure calls made by a program.

(ii) Extend Program 19.5 to handle full Prolog analogously to Program 19.3.

(iii) Write an interactive tracer which prompts the user for a response before each goal reduction.

(iv) Extend Program 19.3 to interpret ancestor cut.

19.2 Enhanced meta-interpreters for expert systems

  The typical decomposition of expert systems into a knowledge base and an inference engine is not entirely appropriate for expert systems written in Prolog. Much of an inference engine is provided by Prolog itself. Knowledge bases are executable. However Prolog does not provide important features expected of expert systems usually embedded in the inference engine. Examples are generating explanations and uncertainty reasoning.

  In this section we show a series of enhanced meta-interpreters demonstrating three features of expert systems: interaction between the user and the program, an explanation facility, and an uncertainty reasoning mechanism.

  We demonstrate the explanation facility and interactive shell using the toy expert system in Program 19.6. The program can decide where to place a dish in

place_in_oven(Dish,Rack) ←
    Dish should be placed in the oven at level *Rack* for baking.

place_in_oven(Dish,top) ←
    pastry(Dish), size(Dish,small).
place_in_oven(Dish,middle) ←
    pastry(Dish), size(Dish,big).
place_in_oven(Dish,middle) ←
    main_meal(Dish).
place_in_oven(Dish,low) ←
    slow_cooker(Dish).

pastry(Dish) ← type(Dish,cake).
pastry(Dish) ← type(Dish,bread).

main_meal(Dish) ← type(Dish,meat).

slow_cooker(Dish) ← type(Dish,milk_pudding).

Program 19.6: Oven placement expert system

solve(Goal)
    Goal is deducible from the pure Prolog program defined by
    clause/2. The user is prompted for missing information.

solve(true).
solve((A,B)) ←
    solve(A), solve(B).
solve(A) ←
    clause(A,B), solve(B).
solve(A) ←
    askable(A), not known(A), ask(A,Answer), respond(Answer,A).

ask(A,Answer) ←
    display_query(A), read(Answer).

respond(yes,A) ←
    assert(A).
respond(no,A) ←
    assert(untrue(A)), fail.

known(A) ← A.
known(A) ← untrue(A).

display_query(A) ← write(A), write('? ').

Program 19.7: An interactive shell

the oven for baking. Comments on the suitability of Prolog for building expert systems are made at the background section of this chapter.

Program 19.7 is an interactive shell which can query the user for missing information. It assumes that a procedure *askable/1* is defined, which specifies when goals that the interpreter fails to prove by itself can be delegated to the user. To implement this facility, the following clause is added to the end of the meta-interpreter of Program 19.1:

> solve(A) ←
>   askable(A), not known(A), ask(A,Answer), respond(Answer,A).

The predicate *askable(Goal)* is used to screen which information is suitable for asking from the user. For example, the fact *askable(type(Dish, Type))* indicates we can ask the type of a dish.

To avoid asking the same question repeatedly, the program records the answer to the query. This is handled by the predicate *respond/2*. If the answer to the query *A* is *yes*, a fact *A* is asserted into the program. If the answer is *no*, the fact *untrue(A)* is asserted. This information is used by *known/1* to avoid asking questions whose answers should be known to the program.

An improved version of the shell allows the interaction to go the other way as well. When asked a question, the user can respond with a question of her own. We consider how the shell should respond to the user's question "why."

The obvious reply of the shell is the rule whose conclusion the program is trying to establish.

This can be easily incorporated into the shell by extending all the relationships with an extra argument, the current rule being used. The rule must be explicitly represented in an extra argument as there is no access to the global state of the computation in Prolog programs. The *solve* goal must be extended appropriately as discussed below. The interface to the explanation of "why" queries is then

> respond(why,Goal,Rule) ←
>   display_rule(Rule), ask(Goal,Answer), respond(Answer,Goal,Rule).

This version of *respond* writes out the current parent rule, then prompts the user to answer the query once more. The format in which the rule will appear is determined by *display_rule*, a modular extension of the shell to allow the user to represent rules in her favorite way.

Repeated responses of *why* using the above clause for *respond* result in repeated restatement of the parent rule. A better solution is to give the "grandpar-

solve(place_in_oven(dish1,X))?
type(dish1,cake)? *yes.*
size(dish1,small)? *no.*
type(dish1,bread)? *no.*
size(dish1,big)? *why.*
IF pastry(dish1) AND size(dish1,big)
THEN place_in_oven(dish1,middle)
size(dish1,big)? *yes.*

X = middle

Figure 19.3: A session with the interactive shell

place_in_oven(dish1,top) is proved using the rule
IF pastry(dish1) and size(dish1,small)
THEN place_in_oven(dish1,top)

pastry(dish1) is proved using the rule
IF type(dish1,bread)
THEN pastry(dish1)

type(dish1,bread) is a fact in the database.

size(dish1,small) is a fact in the database.

Figure 19.4: Generating an explanation

ent" rule in response to the second *why*, the "greatgrandparent" rule in response
to the next *why*, and so on all the way up the search tree. To achieve this behavior, the code is modified so that the argument containing the rule contains
instead the list of ancestor rules. The new version of *respond* is

respond(why,Goal,[Rule|Rules]) ←
    write_rule(Rule), ask(Goal,Answer), respond(Answer,Goal,Rules).

Repeated requests of *why* then give the ancestor rules in turn. An extra clause is
needed to cover the case when there are no more rules to explain.

The complete interactive shell incorporating why explanations is given as
Program 19.8. A trace using the program is given in Figure 19.3. User responses
are in italics. We explain the remaining predicates in that program.

The second argument of *solve(Goal,Rules)*, used in Program 19.8, is a list
of the rules used to reduce the ancestor nodes of *Goal* in the current proof tree.
The list of rules is updated by the *solve* clause performing goal reduction. The

```
solve(Goal) ←
    Goal is deducible from the pure Prolog program
    defined by clause/2.
    The user is prompted for missing information,
    and can ask for a "why" explanation.

solve(Goal) ← solve(Goal,[ ]).

solve(true,Rules).
solve((A,B),Rules) ←
    solve(A,Rules), solve(B,Rules).
solve(A,Rules) ←
    clause(A,B), solve(B,[rule(A,B)|Rules]).
solve(A,Rules) ←
    askable(A), not known(A), ask(A,Answer), respond(Answer,A,Rules).

ask(A,Answer) ←
    display_query(A), read(Answer).

respond(yes,A,Rules) ←
    assert(A).
respond(no,A,Rules) ←
    assert(untrue(A)), fail.
respond(why,A,[Rule|Rules]) ←
    display_rule(Rule),
    ask(A,Answer),
    respond(Answer,A,Rules).
respond(why,A,[ ]) ←
    writeln(['No more explanation possible']),
    ask(A,Answer),
    respond(Answer,A,Rules).

known(A) ← A.
known(A) ← untrue(A).

display_query(A) ←
    write(A), write('? ').
display_rule(rule(A,B)) ←
    write('IF '), write_conjunction(B), writeln(['THEN ',A]).

write_conjunction((A,B)) ←
    !, write(A), write(' AND '), write_conjunction(B).
write_conjunction(A) ←
    write(A), nl.
```

Program 19.8: An interactive shell with "why" explanations

how(Goal) ←
    Explains how the goal *Goal* was proved.

how(Goal) ←
    solve(Goal,Proof), interpret(Proof).

solve(Goal,Proof) ← See Program 19.2.

interpret((Proof1,Proof2)) ←
    interpret(Proof1), interpret(Proof2).
interpret(Proof) ←
    fact(Proof,Fact),
    nl, writeln([Fact,' is a fact in the database.']).
interpret(Proof) ←
    rule(Proof,Head,Body,Proof1),
    nl, writeln([Head,' is proved using the rule']),
    display_rule(rule(Head,Body)),
    interpret(Proof1).

fact((Fact←true),Fact).

rule((Goal←Proof),Goal,Body,Proof) ←
    Proof ≠ true, extract_body(Proof,Body).

extract_body((Proof1,Proof2),(Body1,Body2)) ←
    !, extract_body(Proof1,Body1), extract_body(Proof2,Body2).
extract_body((Goal←Proof),Goal).

display_rule(Rule) ← See Program 19.8.

Program 19.9: Explaining a proof

representation chosen for rules is a structure *rule(A,B)*. The only other predicate which is affected by this choice of representation is *display_rule*.

Answering a "why" query is a simple explanation facility where a single, local chain of reasoning is reported. Our next example is a more interesting explanation facility that explains the complete proof of a solved query.

The basic idea is interpreting a proof of a goal, where a proof has been collected in a meta-interpreter as shown in Program 19.2. A query *how(Goal) ?*, asking how a goal is proved, is handled by executing the meta-interpreter on the goal and interpreting the resulting proof. A simple program for "how" explanations is given as Program 19.9.

Figure 19.4 gives a trace of using Program 19.9 to explain the goal

place_in_oven(dish1,middle) is proved using the rule
IF pastry(dish1) and size(dish1,big)
THEN place_in_oven(dish1,middle)

pastry(dish1) can be further explained.

size(dish1,big) is a fact in the database.

Figure 19.5: Explaining one rule at a time

how(place_in_oven(dish1,top))?, using the facts *type(dish1,bread)* and *size(dish1, small)*.

The explanation in Figure 19.4 is very clear, but there are hidden shortcomings. One is the exhaustive nature of the explanation. For any but the smallest knowledge base, too much output is produced. The screenfuls of text produced for an expert system with hundreds of rules are not intelligible. A practical modification to Program 19.9 is to restrict the explanation to one level at a time and allow the user to ask for more if necessary. A modified explanation appears as Figure 19.5.

The explanation given in Figure 19.4 exactly mirrors the Prolog computation. This may not be what is wanted. Using a meta-interpreter allows greater flexibility. Explanations can be given that are different from the logic of the program itself, yet constitute the justification for which the rule was derived. We give a very simple example to illustrate the principle.

Suppose the explanation is geared toward an expert baker who knows the classification of dishes: that is, what is a pastry, etc. Although the program must still do the reasoning establishing that a dish is a pastry by being a cake, etc., it is of no interest or relevance to the baker. This can be handled by a special clause for *interpret*, which assumes a predicate *classification(Goal)* for goals which have to do with classification:

interpret((Goal←Proof)) ←
    classification(Goal),
    writeln([Goal,' is a classification example']).

A *classification* fact is an example of domain-specific meta-knowledge. Using such meta-knowledge allows the expert to build a theory of explanation that complements rather than repeats the proof of the expert system. A disparity between what is said and what is done is often true of human experts.

Filtered explanations are useful in describing system predicates performing arithmetic or I/O, for example. Such Prolog goals have a different status from the

solve(Goal, Certainty) ←
    Certainty is our confidence that *Goal* is true.

solve(true,1).
solve((A,B),C) ←
    solve(A,C1), solve(B,C2), minimum(C1,C2,C).
solve(A,C) ←
    clause_cf(A,B,C1), solve(B,C2), C := C1*C2.

minimum(N1,N2,M) ← See Program 11.3.

Program 19.10: A meta-interpreter for reasoning with uncertainty

solve(Goal, Certainty, Threshold) ←
    Certainty is our confidence that *Goal* is true.
    The certainty is greater than *Threshold*.

solve(true,1,T).
solve((A,B),C,T) ←
    solve(A,C1,T), solve(B,C2,T), minimum(C1,C2,C).
solve(A,C,T) ←
    clause_cf(A,B,C1),
    C1 > T,
    T1 := T/C1,
    solve(B,C2,T1),
    C := C1*C2.

minimum(N1,N2,M) ← See Program 11.3.

Program 19.11: Reasoning with uncertainty with threshold cutoff

viewpiont of the user of the expert system. More generally whole Prolog routines that implement algorithms need not be explained, and a more concise report of what the algorithm does can be offered instead.

The final example of using a meta-interpreter for an expert system is the incorporation of an uncertainty reasoning mechanism. The reason for introducing such a mechanism is the availability of uncertain information — rules and facts. A deduction mechanism operating on uncertain assumptions should produce uncertain conclusions. There are several ways for representing uncertainly in rules and for computing the uncertainty of conclusions. The main requirement is that in the limiting case, when all rules are certain, the behavior of the system will mimic the standard deduction mechanism.

We choose the following. We associate with each rule or fact a *certainty factor, c, $0 < c \leq 1$*. A *logic program with uncertainties* is a set of pairs $\langle Clause, Factor \rangle$ where *Clause* is a clause and *Factor* is a certainty factor. We use the following rule for computing uncertainties:

certainty$((A,B)) = \min\{(\text{certainty}(A), \text{certainty}(B)\}$
certainty$(A) \quad = \max\{\text{certainty}(B) \cdot F \mid \langle A \leftarrow B, F \rangle$ is a pair in the program$\}$.

The simple interpreter in Program 19.10 is a straightforward enhancement of the basic meta-interpreter, given as Program 19.1. The top-level relation is *solve(Goal, Certainty)* which is true when *Goal* is satisfied with certainty *Certainty*.

The meta-interpreter computes the combination of certainty factors in a conjunction as the minimum of the certainty factors of the conjuncts. Other combining strategies could be accommodated just as easily. Program 19.10 assumes that clauses with certainty factors are represented using the predicate *clause_cf(A,B,CF)*.

The meta-interpreter in Program 19.10 can be augmented to prune computation paths that do not meet a desired certainty threshold. An extra argument, the size of the cutoff threshold, needs to be added. The new relation is *solve(Goal, Certainty, Threshold)*, and is given in Program 19.11.

The threshold is used in the third clause of Program 19.11. The certainty of any goal must exceed the current threshold. If it does, the computation continues with the new threshold being the quotient of the previous threshold by the certainty of the clause.

Exercises for Section 21.2

(i) Improve *write_rule* to generate English text, rather than Prolog terms.

(ii) Extend the *known* predicate in Programs 19.7 and 19.8 to handle functional concepts.

(iii) Extend Program 19.8 to handle responses other than *yes, no,* and *why.*

(iv) Modify Program 19.9 so that it produces the trace in Figure 19.5.

(v) Combine the interactive and uncertainty reasoning shells to prompt the user for the uncertainty of facts and rules. Record the values so they can be used again.

19.3   Enhanced meta-interpreters for debugging

Debugging is an essential aspect of programming, even in Prolog. The promise of high-level programming languages is not so much in their prospects for writing bug-free programs, but rather in the power of the computerized tools for supporting the process of program development. For reasons of bootstrapping and elegance, these tools are best implemented in the language itself. Such tools are programs for manipulating, analyzing, and simulating other programs, or, in other words, meta-programs.

This section shows meta-programs for supporting the debugging process of pure Prolog programs. The reason for restricting ourselves to the pure part is obvious: the difficulties in handling the impure parts of the language.

To debug a program, we must assume that the programmer has some intended behavior of the program in mind, and an intended domain of application on which the program should exhibit this behavior. Given those, debugging consists of finding discrepancies between the program's actual behavior and the programmer's intended behavior. Recall the definitions of an intended meaning and a domain from Section 5.2. An intended meaning M of a pure Prolog program is the set of ground goals on which the program should succeed. The *intended domain D* of a program is a domain on which the program should terminate. We require the intended meaning of a program to be a subset of the intended domain.

We say that A_1 is a *solution* to a goal A if the program returns on a goal A its instance A_1. We say that a solution A is *true* in an intended meaning M if every instance of A is in M. Otherwise it is *false* in M.

A pure Prolog program can exhibit only three types of bugs, given an intended meaning and an intended domain. When invoked on a goal A in the intended domain, the program may do one of three things:

      a. Fail to terminate.
      b. Return some false solution $A\theta$.
      c. Fail to return some true solution $A\theta$.

We describe algorithms for supporting the detection and identification of each of these three types of bugs.

In general, it is not possible to detect if a Prolog program is nonterminating: the question is undecidable. Second best is to assign some *a priori* bound on the running time or depth of recursion of the program, and abort the computation if the bound is exceeded. It is desirable to save part of the computation to support the analysis of the reasons for nontermination. The enhanced

solve(A,D,Overflow) ←
> *A* has a proof tree of depth less than *D* and
> *Overflow* equals *no_overflow*, or *A* has a
> branch in the computation tree longer than *D*, and
> *Overflow* contains a list of its first *D* elements.

solve(true,D,no_overflow).
solve(A,0,overflow([ ])).
solve((A,B),D,Overflow) ←
    D > 0,
    solve(A,D,OverflowA),
    solve_conjunction(OverflowA,B,D,Overflow).
solve(A,D,Overflow) ←
    D > 0,
    clause(A,B),
    D1 := D–1,
    solve(B,D1,OverflowB),
    return_overflow(OverflowB,A,Overflow).
solve(A,D,no_overflow) ←
    D > 0,
    system(A), A.

solve_conjunction(overflow(S),B,D,overflow(S)).
solve_conjunction(no_overflow,B,D,Overflow) ←
    solve(B,D,Overflow).

return_overflow(no_overflow,A,no_overflow).
return_overflow(overflow(S),A,overflow([A|S])).

Program 19.12: A meta-interpreter detecting a stack overflow

meta-interpreter shown in Program 19.12 achieves this. It is invoked with a call *solve(Goal,D,Overflow)*, where *Goal* is an initial goal, and *D* an upper bound on the depth of recursion. The call succeeds if a solution is found without exceeding the predefined depth of recursion, with *Overflow* instantiated to *no_overflow*. The call also succeeds if the depth of recursion is exceeded, but in this case *Overflow* contains the stack of goals, i.e., the branch of the computation tree, which exceeded the depth-bound *D*.

Note that as soon as a stack overflow is detected, the computation returns, without completing the proof. This is achieved by *solve_conjunction* and *return_overflow*.

$isort(Xs, Ys) \leftarrow$
    Ys is an ordered permutation of Xs. Nontermination program.

isort([X|Xs],Ys) ← isort(Xs,Zs), insert(X,Zs,Ys).
isort([ ],[ ]).

insert(X,[Y|Ys],[X,Y|Ys]) ←
    X < Y.
insert(X,[Y|Ys],[Y|Zs]) ←
    X ≥ Y, insert(Y,[X|Ys],Zs).
insert(X,[ ],[X]).

Program 19.13: A nonterminating insertion sort

For example, consider Program 19.13 for insertion sort.

When called with the goal $solve(isort([2,2],Xs),6,Overflow)$, the solution returned is

Xs = [2,2,2,2,2,2],
Overflow = overflow([
    isort([2,2],[2,2,2,2,2,2]),
    insert(2,[2],[2,2,2,2,2,2]),
    insert(2,[2],[2,2,2,2,2]),
    insert(2,[2],[2,2,2,2]),
    insert(2,[2],[2,2,2]),
    insert(2,[2],[2,2])])

The overflown stack can be further analyzed, upon return, to diagnose the reason for nontermination. This can be caused, for example, by a loop, i.e., by a sequence of goals $G_1, G_2, \ldots, G_n$, on the stack, where G_1 and G_n are called with the same input, or by a sequence of goals that calls each goal with increasingly large inputs. The first situation occurs in the example above. It is clearly a bug, that should be fixed in the program. The second situation is not necessarily a bug, and knowing whether the program should be fixed, or a larger machine should be bought in order to execute it, requires further program-dependent information.

The second type of bug is returning a false solution. A program can return a false solution only if it has a false clause. A clause C is false with respect to an intended meaning M if it has an instance whose body is true in M and head is false in M. Such an instance is called a *counterexample* to C.

Consider, for example, Program 19.14 for insertion sort.

On the goal $isort([3,2,1],Xs)$ it returns the solution $isort([3,2,1],[3,2,1])$ which

$isort(Xs, Ys) \leftarrow$
    Buggy insertion sort.

isort([X|Xs],Ys) ← isort(Xs,Zs), insert(X,Zs,Ys).
isort([ ],[ ]).
insert(X,[Y|Ys],[X,Y|Ys]) ←
        X ≥ Y.
insert(X,[Y|Ys],[Y|Zs]) ←
        X > Y, insert(X,Ys,Zs).
insert(X,[ ],[X]).

Program 19.14: Incorrect and incomplete insertion sort

is clearly false.

The false clause in the program is

insert(X,[Y|Ys],[X,Y|Ys]) ← X ≥ Y.

and a counterexample to it is:

insert(2,[1],[2,1]) ← 2 ≥ 1.

Given a ground proof tree corresponding to a false solution, one can find a false instance of a clause as follows: traverse the proof tree in post order. Check whether each node in the proof tree is true. If a false node is found, the clause whose head is the false node and whose body is the conjunction of its sons is a counterexample to a clause in the program. That clause is false, and should be removed or modified.

The correctness of this algorithm follows from a simple inductive proof. The algorithm is embedded in an enhanced meta-interpreter, shown as Program 19.15.

The algorithm, and its implementation, assume an *oracle* that can answer queries concerning the intended meaning of the program. The oracle is some entity external to the diagnosis algorithm. It can be the programmer, who can respond to queries concerning the intended meaning of his program, or another program, which has been shown to have the same meaning as the intended meaning of the program under debugging. The second situation may occur in developing a new version of a program, and using the older version as an oracle. It can also occur when developing an efficient program (e.g., quicksort), given an inefficient executable specification of it (i.e., permutation sort), and using the specification as an oracle.

false_solution(A,Clause) ←
    If *A* is a provable false instance, then *Clause* is
    a false clause in the program. Bottom up algorithm.

false_solution(A,Clause) ←
    solve(A,Proof),
    false_clause(Proof,Clause).

false_clause(true,ok).
false_clause((A,B),Clause) ←
    false_clause(A,ClauseA),
    check_conjunction(ClauseA,B,Clause).
false_clause((A←B),Clause) ←
    false_clause(B,ClauseB),
    check_clause(ClauseB,A,B,Clause).

check_conjunction(ok,B,Clause) ←
    false_clause(B,Clause).
check_conjunction((A←B1),B,(A←B1)).

check_clause(ok,A,B,Clause) ←
    query_goal(A,Answer),
    check_answer(Answer,A,B,Clause).
check_clause((A1←B1),A,B,(A1←B1)).

check_answer(true,A,B,ok).
check_answer(false,A,B,(A←B1)) ←
    extract_body(B,B1).

extract_body(true,true).
extract_body((A←B),A).
extract_body(((A←B),Bs),(A,As)) ←
    extract_body(Bs,As).

query_goal(A,true) ←
    system(A).
query_goal(Goal,Answer) ←
    not system(Goal),
    writeln(['Is the goal ',Goal,' true?']),
    read(Answer).

Program 19.15: Bottom-up diagnosis of a false solution

When invoked with the goal *false_solution(isort([3,2,1],X),C)?* the algorithm exhibits the following interactive behavior:

false_solution(isort([3,2,1],X),C)?
Is the goal isort([ ],[ ]) true?
true.
Is the goal insert(1,[ ],[1]) true?
true.
Is the goal isort([1],[1]) true?
true.
Is the goal insert(2,[1],[2,1]) true?
false.

X = [3,2,1],
C = insert(2,[1],[2,1]) ← 2 ≥ 1.

Which returns a counterexample to the false clause.

The proof tree returned by *solve/2* is not guaranteed to be ground, in contrast to the assumption of the algorithm. However, every instance of a proof tree is a proof tree. Hence this problem can be remedied by either instantiating variables left in the proof tree to arbitrary constants, before activating the algorithm, or requesting the oracle to instantiate the queried goal when it contains variables. Different instances might imply different answers. Since the goal of this algorithm is to find a counterexample as soon as possible, the oracle should instantiate the goal to a false instance if it can.

One of the main concerns with diagnosis algorithms is improving their query complexity, i.e. reducing the number of queries they require to diagnose the bug. Given that the human programmer may have to answer the queries, this desire is clearly understandable. The query complexity of the above diagnosis algorithm is linear in the size of the proof tree. There is a better strategy, whose query complexity is linear in the depth of the proof tree, not its size. In contrast to the previous algorithm which is bottom-up, the second algorithm traverses the proof tree top-down. At each node it tries to find a false son. If it fails, then the current node constitutes a counterexample, as the goal at the node is true, and all its sons are false. If it finds such a node, it recurses with it.

The implementation of the algorithm is shown in Program 19.16.

Note the use of cut to implement implicit negation in the first clause of *false_goal/2*, and the use of *query_goal/2* as a test predicate.

Compare the behavior of the bottom-up algorithm with the following trace of the interactive behavior of Program 19.16:

false_solution(A,Clause) ←
    If *A* is a provable false instance, then *Clause*
    is a false clause in the program. Top-down algorithm.

false_solution(A,Clause) ←
    solve(A,Proof),
    false_goal(Proof,Clause).

false_goal((A←B),Clause) ←
    false_conjunction(B,Clause), !.
false_goal((A←B),(A←B1)) ←
    extract_body(B,B1).

false_conjunction(((A←B),Bs),Clause) ←
    query_goal(A,false), !,
    false_goal((A←B),Clause).
false_conjunction((A←B),Clause) ←
    query_goal(A,false), !,
    false_goal((A←B),Clause).
false_conjunction((A,As),Clause) ←
    false_conjunction(As,Clause).

extract_body(Tree,Body) ← See Program 19.15

query_goal(A,Answer) ← See Program 19.15

Program 19.16: Top-down diagnosis of a false solution

false_solution(isort([3,2,1],X),C)?
Is the goal isort([2,1],[2,1]) true?
false.
Is the goal isort([1],[1]) true?
true.
Is the goal insert(2,[1],[2,1]) true?
false.

X = [3,2,1],
C = insert(2,[1],[2,1]) ← 2 ≥ 1

There is a diagnosis algorithm for false solutions with an even better query complexity, called *divide-and-query*. The algorithm progresses by splitting the proof tree into two approximately equal parts, and querying the node at the splitting point. If the node is false, the algorithm is applied recursively to the subtree rooted by this node. If the node is true, its subtree is removed from the

$missing\_solution(A, Goal) \leftarrow$
　　If A is a non-provable true ground goal, then $Goal$ is a
　　true ground goal which is uncovered by the program.

missing_solution((A,B),Goal) ← !,
　　(not A, missing_solution(A,Goal) ;
　　A, missing_solution(B,Goal)).
missing_solution(A,Goal) ←
　　clause(A,B),
　　query_clause((A←B)), !,
　　missing_solution(B,Goal).
missing_solution(A,A) ←
　　not system(A).

query_clause(Clause) ←
　　writeln(['Enter a true ground instance of ',Clause,
　　'if there is such, or "no" otherwise']),
　　read(Answer),
　　!, check_answer(Answer,Clause).

check_answer(noClause) ← !, fail.
check_answer(Clause,Clause) ← !.
check_answer(Answer,Clause) ←
　　write('Illegal answer'),
　　!, query_clause(Clause).

Program 19.17: Diagnosing missing solution

tree and replaced by *true*, and a new middle point is computed. The algorithm can
be shown to require a number of queries logarithmic in the size of the proof tree.
In case of close-to-linear proof trees, this constitutes an exponential improvement
over both the top-down and the bottom-up diagnosis algorithms.

The third possible type of bug is a missing solution. Diagnosing a missing
solution is more difficult then the previous bugs. We say that a clause *covers* a
goal A with respect to an intended interpretation M if it has an instance whose
head is an instance of A and whose body is in M.

For example, consider the goal *insert(2,[1,3],Xs)*. It is covered by the clause

　　insert(X,[Y|Ys],[X,Y|Ys]) ← X ≥ Y.

of Program 19.14 with respect to the intended interpretation M of the program,
since in the following instance of the clause

$$\text{insert}(2,[1,3],[1,2,3]) \leftarrow 2 \geq 1.$$

the head is an instance of A and the body is in M.

It can be shown that if a program P has a missing solution with respect to an intended meaning M, then there is a goal A in M, which is not covered by any clause in P. The proof of this claim is beyond the scope of the book. It is embedded in the diagnosis algorithm below.

Diagnosing a missing solution imposes a heavier burden on the oracle. Not only does it have to know whether a goal has a solution, but it must also provide it, if it exists. Using such an oracle, an uncovered goal can be found as follows.

The algorithm is given a missing solution, i.e., a goal in the intended interpretation M of the program P, for which P fails. The algorithm starts with the initial missing solution. For every clause that unifies with it, it checks, using the oracle, if the body of the clause has an instance in M. If there is no such clause, the goal is uncovered, and the algorithm terminates. Otherwise, the algorithm finds a goal in the body that fails. At least one of them should fail, else the program would have solved the body, and hence the goal, in contrast to our assumption. The algorithm is applied recursively to this goal.

An implementation of this algorithm is shown in Program 19.17. The program attempts to trace the failing path of the computation, and find a true goal which is uncovered. A session with the program is shown below:

missing_solution(isort([2,1,3],[1,2,3]),C)?

Enter a true ground instance of
(isort([2,1,3],[1,2,3]) $\leftarrow$ isort([1,3],Xs),insert(2,Xs,[1,2,3]))
if there is such, or 'no' otherwise

(*isort([2,1,3],[1,2,3]) $\leftarrow$ isort([1,3],[1,3]),insert(2,[1,3],[1,2,3]))*.

Enter a true ground instance of
(isort([1,3],[1,3]) $\leftarrow$ isort([3],Ys),insert(1,Ys,[1,3]))
if there is such, or 'no' otherwise

(*isort([1,3],[1,3]) $\leftarrow$ isort([3],[3]),insert(1,[3],[1,3]))*.

Enter a true ground instance of
(insert(1,[3],[1,3]) $\leftarrow$ 1 $\geq$ 3)
if there is such, or 'false' otherwise

false.

C = insert(1,[3],[1,3])

The reader can verify that the goal *insert(1,[3],[1,3])* is not covered by Program

19.14.

The three algorithms shown can form the basis of a high-quality interactive program development environment for Prolog.

19.4 Background

The concept of a meta-interpreter (or, rather, of meta-circular interpreter) is due to Sussman and Steele (1978), who were the first to propose using the ability of the language to specify itself as a fundamental criteria for language design.

Prolog is a natural language for building expert systems. Although Program 19.6 is very simple, it is suggestive of early backward chaining expert systems. We compare the program with a rule from MYCIN (Shortliffe, 1976), an expert system for diagnosing and treating bacterial infections.

> IF   the gram stain of the organism is gram negative,
>   the morphology of the organism is rod,
>   the aerobicity of the organism is anaerobic
> THEN   there is suggestive evidence (0.5) that the identity
>   of the organism is Bacteroides.

There are two aspects to the above rule. First, the heuristic identification of a bacteria based on its gram stain, morphology, and aerobicity. Second, there is a certainty factor attached to the rule. We argue that these should be separate. The uncertainty is best handled by an enhanced meta-interpreter such as Program 19.10 The heuristic knowledge is expressed int he Prolog rule:

> identity(Organism,bacteroides) ←
>   gram_stain(Organism,gram_negative),
>   morphology(Organism,rod),
>   aerobicity(Organism,anaerobic).

Note that the rule above, and those in Program 19.6, are essentially ground. The only variable appearing in the "contect" of object under study. For MYCIN, the context in the above rule is the organism, for the oven management system it is the dish.

Rules using more of the power of Prolog are just as easy to write. Here is a clause from a toy medical expert system, which gives a flavor of what is possible. The credit evaluation expert system in Chapter 21 provides further examples.

```
prescribe(Patient,Drug) ←
    complaint(Patient,Symptom),
    suppresses(Symptom,Drug),
    suitable(Drug,Patient).
```

The relationships *complaint, suppresses* and *suitable* are themselves described by facts and rules.

The first to argue explicitly for the use of Prolog to build expert systems were Clark and McCabe (1982). That paper discusses how explanation facilities and uncertainty reasoning can be added to simple expert systems such as Program 19.6. The technique proposed is adding extra arguments to the program's predicates. An explanation facility and a query the user facility were incorporated in the APES expert system shell by Hammond and Sergot (Hammond, 1984). Using meta-interpreters as a basis for explanation facilities in expert systems was proposed by Sterling (1984). An explanation shell built using enhanced meta-interpreters is described by Sterling and Lalee (1985). Using enhanced meta-interpreters for handling uncertainties comes from Shapiro (1983c).

Suggesting that enhanced meta-interpreters should be the basis of a programming environment was done by Shapiro (1983a). That book also contains and discusses the debugging algorithms used in Section 19.3.

Takeuchi and Furukawa (1985) have shown that partial evaluation can eliminate the runtime overhead of meta-interpreters. The effect of partial evaluation is to compile an object program and an enhanced meta-interpreter into a new object program that inherits the functionality of the meta-interpreter but not its overhead. Sterling and Beer (1986) particularizes the work for expert systems. Both papers report speedups by a factor of 40.

Meta-interpreters, and more generally meta-programs, have also been composed to affect the control flow of Prolog programs. References are Dincbas and LePape (1984), Gallaire and Lasserre (1980), and Pereira (1982).

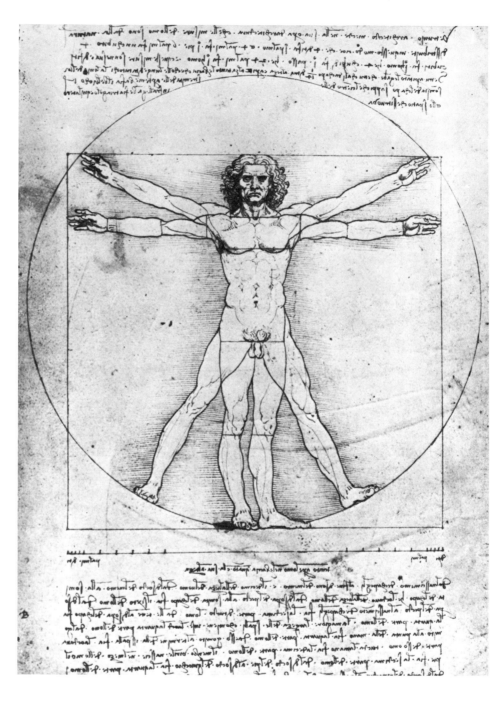

Part IV
Applications

Prolog has been used for a wide range of applications: expert systems, natural language understanding, symbolic algebra, compiler writing, building embedded languages, and architectural design to name a few. In this chapter we give a flavor of writing application programs in Prolog.

The first chapter looks at programs for playing three games: mastermind, Nim, and Kalah. The next chapter presents an expert system for evaluating requests for credit. The third chapter presents a program for solving symbolic equations, while the final chapter looks at a compiler for a Pascal-like language.

The emphasis in presentation in these chapters is on writing clear programs. Knowledge embedded in the programs is made explicit. Minor efficiency gains are ignored if they obscure the declarative reading of the program.

Chapter 20
Game-Playing Programs

Learning how to play a game is fun. As well as understanding the rules of the game, we must constantly learn new strategies and tactics until the game is mastered. Writing a program to play games is also fun, and a good vehicle for showing how to use Prolog for writing nontrivial programs.

20.1 Mastermind

Our first program guesses the secret code in the game of mastermind. It is a good example of what can be programmed in Prolog easily with just a little thought.

The version of mastermind we describe is what we played as kids. It is a variant on the commercial version and needs less hardware (only pencil and paper). Player A chooses a secret code, a list of N distinct decimal digits (usually N equals 4 for beginners, 5 for advanced players). Player B makes guesses, and queries player A for the number of *bulls* (number of digits that appear in identical positions in the guess and in the code) and *cows* (number of digits that appear in both the guess and the code, but in different positions). The code is determined when a guess has N bulls.

There is a very simple algorithm for playing the game: impose some order on the set of legal guesses; then iterate, making the next guess that is consistent with all the information you have so far until you find the secret code.

Rather than defining the notion of consistency formally, we appeal to the reader's intuition: a guess is consistent with a set of answers to queries if the answers to the queries would have remained the same if the guess was the secret code.

The algorithm performs quite well compared with experienced players: an average of 4 to 6 guesses for a code with 4 digits with an observed maximum of 8. However, it is not an easy strategy for humans to apply, because of the amount of bookkeeping needed. On the other hand, the control structure of Prolog — nondeterministic choice, simulated by backtracking — is ideal for implementing the algorithm.

We describe the program top-down. The entire program is given as Program 20.1. The top level procedure for playing the game is

> mastermind(Code) ←
>   cleanup, guess(Code), check(Code), announce.

The heart of the top level is a generate-and-test loop. The guessing procedure *guess(Code)*, which acts as a generator, uses the procedure *selects(Xs, Ys)* (Program 7.7) to select nondeterministically a list *Xs* of elements from a list *Ys*. According to the rules of the game, *Xs* is constrained to be of four distinct elements, while *Ys* is the list of the ten decimal digits:

> guess(Code) ←
>   Code = [X1,X2,X3,X4], selects(Code,[1,2,3,4,5,6,7,8,9,0]).

The procedure *check(Guess)* tests the proposed code *Guess*. It first verifies that *Guess* is consistent with all (i.e., not inconsistent with any) of the answers to queries already made; then it asks the user for the number of bulls and cows in *Guess*. The *ask(Guess)* procedure also controls the generate-and-test loop, succeeding only when the number of bulls is four, indicating the correct code is found:

> check(Guess) ←
>   not inconsistent(Guess), ask(Guess).

Ask stores previous answers to queries in the relation *query(X,B,C)*, where *X* is the guess, *B* is the number of bulls in it, and *C* the number of cows. A guess is inconsistent with a previous query if the number of bulls and cows do not match:

> inconsistent(Guess) ←
>   query(Old,Bulls,Cows),
>   not bulls_and_cows_match(Old,Guess,Bulls,Cows).

The bulls match between a previous guess *OldGuess* and a conjectured guess *Guess* if the number of digits in the same position in the two guesses equals the number of *Bulls* in *OldGuess*. It is computed by the predicate *exact_matches(OldGuess,Guess,Bulls)*. The cows match if the number of common

```
mastermind(Code) ←
    cleanup, guess(Code), check(Code), announce.
guess(Code) ←
    Code = [X1,X2,X3,X4], selects(Code,[1,2,3,4,5,6,7,8,9,0]).
```

Verify the proposed guess

```
check(Guess) ←
    not inconsistent(Guess), ask(Guess).

inconsistent(Guess) ←
    query(OldGuess,Bulls,Cows),
    not bulls_and_cows_match(OldGuess,Guess,Bulls,Cows).

bulls_and_cows_match(OldGuess,Guess,Bulls,Cows) ←
    exact_matches(OldGuess,Guess,N1),
    Bulls =:= N1,                            % Correct number of bulls
    common_members(OldGuess,Guess,N2),
    Cows =:= N2–Bulls.                       % Correct number of cows

exact_matches(X,Y,N) ←
    size_of(A,same_place(A,X,Y),N).
common_members(X,Y,N) ←
    size_of(A,(member(A,X),member(A,Y)),N).

same_place(X,[X|Xs],[X|Ys]).
same_place(A,[X|Xs],[Y|Ys]) ← same_place(A,Xs,Ys).
```

Asking a guess

```
ask(Guess) ←
    repeat,
    writeln(['How many bulls and cows in ',Guess,'?']),
    read((Bulls,Cows)),
    sensible(Bulls,Cows), !,
    assert(query(Guess,Bulls,Cows)),
    Bulls = 4.

sensible(Bulls,Cows) ←
    integer(Bulls), integer(Cows), Bulls+Cows ≤ 4.
```

Bookkeeping

```
cleanup ← abolish(query,3).

announce ←
    size_of(X,A↑(B↑(query(X,A,B))),N),
    writeln(['Found the answer after ',N,' queries']).
```

Program 20.1: Playing Mastermind

size_of(X,G,N) ← See Program 17.1

selects(X,Xs,Ys) ← See Program 7.7

abolish(F,N) ← See Exercise 12.4(i).

Program 20.1 (Continued)

digits without respect to order corresponds to the sum of *Bulls* and *Cows*, and is computed by the procedure *bulls_and_cows_match*. It is easy to count the number of matching digits and common digits in two queries, using the set-predicate *size_of/3*.

The *ask(Guess)* procedure is a memo-function which records the answer to the query. It performs some limited consistency checks on the input with the procedure *sensible(Response)* and succeeds only if the answer is 4 bulls. The expected syntax for the user's reply is a tuple (*Bulls, Cows*).

The remaining (top-level) predicates are for bookkeeping. The first, *cleanup*, removes unwanted information from previous games. The predicate *announce* tells how many guesses were needed using the set-predicate utility *size_of*.

A more efficient implementation of the *exact_matches* and *common_members* procedures can be obtained by writing iterative versions:

exact_matches(Xs,Ys,N) ← exact_matches(Xs,Ys,0,N).

exact_matches([X|Xs],[X|Ys],K,N) ←
    K1 := K+1, exact_matches(Xs,Ys,K1,N).
exact_matches([X|Xs],[Y|Ys],K,N) ←
    X ≠ Y, exact_matches(Xs,Ys,K,N).
exact_matches([ ],[ ],N,N).

common_members(Xs,Ys,N) ← common_members(Xs,Ys,0,N).

common_members([X|Xs],Ys,K,N) ←
    member(X,Ys), K1 := K+1, common_members(Xs,Ys,K1,N).
common_members([X|Xs],Ys,K,N) ←
    common_members(Xs,Ys,K,N).
common_members([ ],Ys,N,N).

Using the more efficient versions of *exact_matches* and *common_members* saves about 10-30% of the execution time.

```
                                     I
                                   I I I
                                 I I I I I
                               I I I I I I I
```

Figure 20.1: A starting position for Nim

20.2 Nim

We turn our attention now from mastermind to Nim, also a game for two players. There are *N* piles of matches, and the players take turns to remove some of the matches (up to all) in a pile. The winner is the player who takes the last match. Figure 20.1 gives a common starting position, with four piles of *1*, *3*, *5* and *7* matches respectively.

To implement the Nim playing program, we use the game-playing framework given as Program 18.8.

The first decision is the representation of the game position and the moves. A natural choice for positions is a list of integers where elements of the list correspond to piles of matches. A move is a tuple (*N,M*) for taking *M* matches from pile *N*. Writing the procedure *move(Move,Position,Position1)*, where *Position* is updated to *Position1* by *Move*, is straightforward. The recursive rule counts down match piles until the desired pile is reached. The remaining piles of matches representing the new game position is computed routinely:

> move((K,M),[N|Ns],[N|Ns1]) ←
>   K > 1, K1 := K–1, move((K1,M),Ns,Ns1).

There are two possibilities for updating the specified pile of matches, the base case of the procedure. If all the matches are taken, the pile is removed from the list. Otherwise the new number of matches in the pile is computed, and checked to be legal:

> move((1,N),[N|Ns],Ns).
> move((1,M),[N|Ns],[N1|Ns]) ← N > M, N1 := N–M.

The mechanics of turns for two person games is specified by two facts.

The initial piles of matches and who moves first must be decided by the two players. Assuming the computer moves second, the game of Figure 20.1 is specified as

> initialize(nim,[1,3,5,7],opponent).

```
        1
       1 1
      1 0 1
      1 1 1
     ───────
      0 0 0
```

Figure 20.2: Computing nim-sums

The game is over when the last match is taken. This corresponds to the game position being the empty list. The person having to move next is the loser, and the output messages of *announce* are formulated accordingly. The details are in Program 20.2.

It remains to specify how to choose the moves. The opponent's moves are accepted from the keyboard; how much flexibility is allowed in input is the responsibility of the programmer. Here, because we concentrate on the logic of the game, we assume the player will enter legal moves:

>   choose_move(Position,opponent,Move) ←
>   writeln(['please make move']), read(Move).

Choosing a move for the computer requires a strategy. A simple strategy to implement is taking all of the first pile of matches. It is recommended only for use against extremely poor players:

>   choose_move([N|Ns],computer,(1,N)).

A winning strategy is known for Nim. It involves dividing game states, or positions, into two classes, safe and unsafe. To determine the category of a position, the binary representation of the number of matches in each pile is computed. The *nim-sum* of these binary numbers is then calculated as follows. Each column is summed independently modulo 2. If the total in each column is zero, the position is *safe*. Otherwise the position is *unsafe*.

Figure 20.2 illustrates the process of the classification for the four piles of matches in Figure 20.1. The binary representations of *1*, *3*, *5* and *7* are *1*, *11*, *101* and *111*. Calculating the nim-sum: there are four *1*'s in the units column, two *1*'s in the *2*'s column and two *1*'s in the *4*'s column; an even number of *1*'s in each. The nim-sum is zero making the position *[1,3,5,7]* safe. On the other hand the position *[2,6]* is unsafe. The binary representations are *10* and *110*. Summing them gives one *1* in the *4*'s column and two *1*'s in the *2*'s column. The single *1* in the *4*'s column makes the position unsafe.

The winning strategy is to always leave the position safe. Any unsafe position can be converted to a safe position (though not all moves do), while any move from

play(Game) ← See Program 18.8

Choosing moves

choose_move(Position,opponent,Move) ←
   writeln(['please make G move']), read(Move).

choose_move(Ns,computer,Move) ←
   unsafe(Ns,Sum), safe_move(Ns,Sum,Move).

choose_move(Ns,computer,(1,1)) ←   % The computer's 'arbitrary move'
   safe(Ns).

move(Move,Position,Position1) ←
   Position1 is the result of executing the move
   Move from the current *Position*.

move((K,M),[N|Ns],[N|Ns1]) ←
   K > 1, K1 := K–1, move((K1,M),Ns,Ns1).

move((1,N),[N|Ns],Ns).

move((1,M),[N|Ns],[N1|Ns]) ←
   N > M, N1 := N–M.

display_game(Position,X) ← write(Position), nl.

next_player(computer,opponent).   next_player(opponent,computer).

game_over([ ],Player,Player).

announce(computer) ← write('You won! Congratulations.'), nl.

announce(opponent) ← write('I won.'), nl.

initialize(nim,[1,3,5,7],opponent).

unsafe(Position,Sum) ←
   Position with nim-sum *Sum* is unsafe.

unsafe(Ns,Sum) ← nim_sum(Ns,[],Sum), not zero(Sum).

safe(Ns) ← not unsafe(Ns,Sum).

nim_sum(Position,SoFar,Sum) ←
   Sum is the nim-sum of the current *Position*,
   and *SoFar* is an accumulated value.

nim_sum([N|Ns],Bs,Sum) ←
   binary(N,Ds), nim_add(Ds,Bs,Bs1), nim_sum(Ns,Bs1,Sum).

nim_sum([ ],Sum,Sum).

nim_add(Bs,[ ],Bs).

nim_add([ ],Bs,Bs).

nim_add([B|Bs],[C|Cs],[D|Ds]) ←
   D := (B+C) mod 2, nim_add(Bs,Cs,Ds).

Program 20.2: A program for playing a winning game of Nim

```
binary(1,[1]).
binary(N,[D|Ds]) ←
    N > 1, D := N mod 2, N1 := N/2, binary(N1,Ds).

decimal(Ds,N) ← decimal(Ds,0,1,N).
decimal([ ],N,T,N).
decimal([D|Ds],A,T,N) ← A1 := A+D*T, T1 := T*2, decimal(Ds,A1,T1,N).

zero([ ]).
zero([0|Zs]) ← zero(Zs).
```

safe_move(Position,NimSum,Move) ←
    Move is a move from the current *Position* with
    the value *NimSum* which leaves a safe position.

```
safe_move(Piles,NimSum,Move) ←
    safe_move(Piles,NimSum,1,Move).

safe_move([Pile|Piles],NimSum,K,(K,M)) ←
    binary(Pile,Bs), can_zero(Bs,NimSum,Ds,0), decimal(Ds,M).
safe_move([Pile|Piles],NimSum,K,Move) ←
    K1 := K+1, safe_move(Piles,NimSum,K1,Move).

can_zero([],NimSum,[ ],0) ←
    zero(NimSum).
can_zero([B|Bs],[0|NimSum],[C|Ds],C) ←
    can_zero(Bs,NimSum,Ds,C).
can_zero([B|Bs],[1|NimSum],[D|Ds],C) ←
    D := 1–B*C, C1 := 1–B, can_zero(Bs,NimSum,Ds,C1).
```

Program 20.2 (Continued)

a safe position creates an unsafe one. The best strategy is to make an arbitrary
move when confronted with a safe position hoping the opponent will blunder, and
convert unsafe positions to safe ones.

To implement this strategy, we need two algorithms. One to compute the
nim-sum of a given position, and the other to determine a move to convert an
unsafe position to a safe one. The move to make is determined by the safety of
the position. If the position is unsafe, use the algorithm to find a move to make
the position safe and win the game. If the position is safe, make an arbitrary
move (one match from the first pile) and hope:

```
choose_move(Ns,computer,Move) ←
     unsafe(Ns,Sum), safe_move(Ns,Sum,Move).
choose_move(Ns,computer,(1,1)) ← % The computer's 'arbitrary move'
     safe(Ns).
```

The predicate *unsafe(Ns,Sum)* succeeds if the position represented by *Ns* is unsafe. It is defined by calculating the nim-sum *Sum* of the piles of matches (by a procedure *nim_sum/3* and testing whether it is zero:

```
unsafe(Ns,Sum) ← nim_sum(Ns,[ ],Sum), not zero(Sum).
```

In a prior version of the program *unsafe* did not return *Sum*. When writing *safe_move* it transpired that the nim-sum was helpful, and it was sensible to pass the already computed value, rather than recomputing it. The predicate *safe* is easily defined in terms of *unsafe*.

The nim-sum is computed by *nim_sum(Ns,SoFar,Sum)*. The relation computed is that *Sum* is the nim-sum of the numbers *Ns* added to what has been accumulated in *SoFar*. To perform the additions, the numbers must first be converted to binary, done by *binary/2*:

```
nim_sum([N|Ns],Bs,Sum) ←
     binary(N,Ds), nim_add(Ds,Bs,Bs1), nim_sum(Ns,Bs1,Sum).
```

The binary form of a number is represented here as a list of digits. To overcome the difficulty of adding lists of unequal length, the least significant digits are earliest in the list. Thus *2* (in binary *10*) is represented as *[0,1]*, while *6* is represented as *[0,1,1]*. The two numbers can then be added from least significant digit to most significant digit, as is usual for addition. This is done by *nim_add/3* and is slightly simpler than regular addition since no carry needs to be propagated. The code for both *binary* and *nim_add* appears in Program 20.2.

The nim-sum *Sum* is used by the predicate *safe_move(Ns,Sum,Move)* to find a winning move *Move* from the position described by *Ns*. The piles of matches are checked in turn by *safe_move/4* to see if there is a number of matches which can be taken from the pile to leave a safe position. The interesting clause is

```
safe_move([Pile|Piles],NimSum,K,(K,M)) ←
     binary(Pile,Bs), can_zero(Bs,NimSum,Ds,0), decimal(Ds,M).
```

The heart of the program is *can_zero(Bs,NimSum,Ds,Carry)*. This relation is true if replacing the binary number *Bs* by the binary number *Ds* would make *NimSum* zero. The number *Ds* is computed digit by digit. Each digit is determined by the corresponding digit of *Bs*, *NimSum* and a carry digit *Carry* initially set to 0. The number is converted to its decimal equivalent by *decimal/2* in order to get the correct move.

Program 20.2 is a complete program for playing Nim interactively incorporating the winning strategy. As well as being a program for playing the game, it is also an axiomatization of what constitutes a winning strategy.

20.3 Kalah

We now present a program for playing the game of Kalah that uses alpha-beta pruning. Kalah is a game which fits well into the paradigm of game trees for two reasons. First, the game has a simple, reasonably reliable evaluation function, and, second, its game tree is tractable, which is not true for games such as chess and go. It has been claimed that Kalah programs that have been written are unbeatable by human players. Certainly, the one presented here beats us.

Kalah is played on a board with two rows of six holes facing each other. Each player owns a row of six holes, plus a kalah to the right of the holes. In the initial state there are six stones in each hole and the two kalahs are empty. This is pictured in the top half of Figure 20.3.

A player begins his move by picking up the stones of one of his holes. Proceeding counterclockwise around the board, he puts one of the picked-up stones in each hole and in his own kalah skipping the opponent's kalah, until no stones remain to be distributed. There are three possible outcomes. If the last stone lands on the kalah, the player has another move. If the last stone lands on an empty hole owned by the player, and the opponent's hole directly across the board contains at least one stone, the player takes all the stones in the hole plus his last landed stone and puts them all in his kalah. Otherwise the player's turn ends, and his opponent moves.

The bottom kalah board in Figure 20.3 represents the following move from the top board by the owner of the top holes. He took the six stones in the rightmost hole and distributed them, the last one ending in the kalah, allowing another move. The stones in the fourth hole from the right were then distributed.

If all of the holes of a player become empty (even if it is not his turn to play), the stones remaining in the holes of the opponent are put in the opponent's kalah and the game ends. The winner of the game is the first player to get more than half of the stones in his kalah.

The difficulty for programming the game in Prolog is in finding an efficient data structure to represent the board, to facilitate the calculation of moves. We

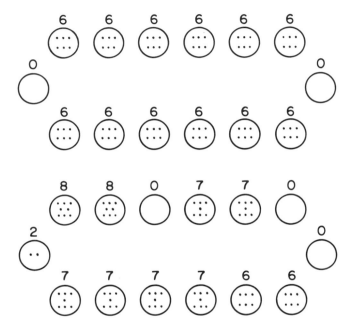

Figure 20.3: Board positions for Kalah

use a 4-argument structure *board(Holes,Kalah,OppHoles,OppKalah)* where *Holes*
is a list of the numbers of stones in your six holes, *Kalah* is the number of stones in
your kalah, while *OppHoles* and *OppKalah* are, respectively, the list of the numbers
of stones in the opponent's holes and the number of stones in his kalah. Lists
were chosen rather than six-place structures to facilitate the writing of recursive
programs for distributing the stones in the holes.

A move consists of choosing a hole and distributing the stones therein. A
move is specified as a list of integers with values between *1* and *6* inclusive, where
the numbers refer to the holes. Hole *1* is farthest from the player's kalah, while
hole *6* is closest. A list is necessary rather than a single integer because a move
may continue. The move depicted in Figure 20.3 is [1, 6].

Play framework

play(Game) ← See Program 18.8.

Choosing a move by minimax with alpha-beta cut-off

choose_move(Position,computer,Move) ←
    lookahead(Depth),
    alpha_beta(Depth,Position,–40,40,Move,Value),
    nl, write(Move), nl.
choose_move(Position,opponent,Move) ←
    nl, writeln(['please make move']), read(Move), legal(Move).

alpha_beta(0,Position,Alpha,Beta,Move,Value) ←
    value(Position,Value).
alpha_beta(D,Position,Alpha,Beta,Move,Value) ←
    D > 0,
    set_of(M,move(Position,M),Moves),
    Alpha1 := Beta,
    Beta1 := –Alpha,
    D1 := D–1,
    evaluate_and_choose(Moves,Position,D1,Alpha1,Beta1,nil,(Move,Value)).

evaluate_and_choose([Move|Moves],Position,D,Alpha,Beta,Record,BestMove) ←
    move(Move,Position,Position1),
    alpha_beta(D,Position1,Alpha,Beta,MoveX,Value),
    Value1 := –Value,
    cutoff(Move,Value1,D,Alpha,Beta,Moves,Position,Record,BestMove), !.
evaluate_and_choose([ ],Position,D,Alpha,Beta,Move,(Move,Alpha)).

cutoff(Move,Value,D,Alpha,Beta,Moves,Position,Record,(Move,Value)) ←
    Value ≥ Beta, !.
cutoff(Move,Value,D,Alpha,Beta,Moves,Position,Record,BestMove) ←
    Alpha < Value, Value < Beta, !,
    evaluate_and_choose(Moves,Position,D,Value,Beta,Move,BestMove).
cutoff(Move,Value,D,Alpha,Beta,Moves,Position,Record,BestMove) ←
    Value ≤ Alpha, !,
    evaluate_and_choose(Moves,Position,D,Alpha,Beta,Record,BestMove).

move(Board,[M|Ms]) ←
    member(M,[1,2,3,4,5,6]),
    stones_in_hole(M,Board,N),
    extend_move(N,M,Board,Ms).
move(board([0,0,0,0,0,0],K,Ys,L),[ ]).

Program 20.3: A complete program for playing Kalah.

stones_in_hole(M,board(Hs,K,Ys,L),Stones) ←
    nth_member(M,Hs,Stones), Stones > 0.

extend_move(Stones,M,Board,[ ]) ←
    Stones =\= (7–M) mod 13, !.
extend_move(Stones,M,Board,Ms) ←
    Stones =:= (7–M) mod 13, !,
    distribute_stones(Stones,M,Board,Board1),
    move(Board1,Ms).

Executing a move

move([N|Ns],Board,FinalBoard) ←
    stones_in_hole(N,Board,Stones),
    distribute_stones(Stones,N,Board,Board1),
    move(Ns,Board1,FinalBoard).
move([ ],Board1,Board2) ←
    swap(Board1,Board2).

distribute_stones(Stones,Hole,Board,Board1) ←
    Board1 is the result of distributing the number of stones,
    Stones, from *Hole* from the current *Board*.
    It consists of two stages: distributing the stones in the player's
    holes, *distribute_my_holes*, and distributing the stones
    in the opponent's holes, *distribute_your_holes*.

distribute_stones(Stones,Hole,Board,FinalBoard) ←
    distribute_my_holes(Stones,Hole,Board,Board1,Stones1),
    distribute_your_holes(Stones1,Board1,FinalBoard).

distribute_my_holes(Stones,N,board(Hs,K,Ys,L),board(Hs1,K1,Ys,L),Stones1) ←
    Stones > 7–N, !,
    pick_up_and_distribute(N,Stones,Hs,Hs1),
    K1 := K+1, Stones1 := Stones+N–7.
distribute_my_holes(Stones,N,board(Hs,K,Ys,L),Board,0) ←
    pick_up_and_distribute(N,Stones,Hs,Hs1),
    check_capture(N,Stones,Hs1,Hs2,Ys,Ys1,Pieces),
    update_kalah(Pieces,N,Stones,K,K1),
    check_if_finished(board(Hs2,K1,Ys1,L),Board).

Program 20.3 (Continued)

```
check_capture(N,Stones,Hs,Hs1,Ys,Ys1,Pieces) ←
    FinishingHole := N+Stones,
    OppositeHole := 7−FinishingHole,
    nth_member(OppositeHole,Ys,Y),
    Y > 0, !,
    n_substitute(OppositeHole,Hs,0,Hs1),
    n_substitute(FinishingHole,Ys,0,Ys1),
    Pieces := Y+1.
check_capture(N,Stones,Hs,Hs,Ys,Ys,0) ← !.

check_if_finished(board(Hs,K,Ys,L),board(Hs,K,Hs,L1)) ←
    zero(Hs), !, sumlist(Ys,YsSum), L1 := L+YsSum.
check_if_finished(board(Hs,K,Ys,L),board(Ys,K1,Ys,L)) ←
    zero(Ys), !, sumlist(Hs,HsSum), K1 := K+HsSum.
check_if_finished(Board,Board) ← !.

update_kalah(0,Stones,N,K,K) ← Stones < 7−N, !.
update_kalah(0,Stones,N,K,K1) ← Stones =:= 7−N, !, K1 := K+1.
update_kalah(Pieces,Stones,N,K,K1) ← Pieces > 0, !, K1 := K+Pieces.

distribute_your_holes(0,Board,Board) ← !.
distribute_your_holes(Stones,board(Hs,K,Ys,L),board(Hs,K,Ys1,L)) ←
    1 ≤ Stones, Stones ≤ 6,
    non_zero(Hs), !,
    distribute(Stones,Ys,Ys1).
distribute_your_holes(Stones,board(Hs,K,Ys,L),board(Hs,K,Ys1,L)) ←
    Stones > 6, !,
    distribute(6,Ys,Ys1),
    Stones1 := Stones−6,
    distribute_stones(Stones1,1,board(Hs,K,Ys1,L),Board).
distribute_your_holes(Stones,board(Hs,K,Ys,L),board(Hs,K,Hs,L1)) ←
    zero(Hs), !, sumlist(Ys,YsSum), L1 := Stones+YsSum+L.
```

Lower level stone distribution

```
pick_up_and_distribute(1,N,[H|Hs],[0|Hs1]) ←
    !, distribute(N,Hs,Hs1).
pick_up_and_distribute(K,N,[H|Hs],[H|Hs1]) ←
    K > 1, !, K1 := K−1, pick_up_and_distribute(K1,N,Hs,Hs1).

distribute(0,Hs,Hs) ← !.
distribute(N,[H|Hs],[H1|Hs1]) ←
    N > 0, !, N1 := N−1, H1 := H+1, distribute(N1,Hs,Hs1).
distribute(N,[ ],[ ]) ← !.
```

Program 20.3 (Continued)

Evaluation function

value(board(H,K,Y,L),Value) ← Value := K–L.

Testing for the end of the game

game_over(board(0,N,0,N),Player,draw) ←
    pieces(K), N =:= 6∗K, !.
game_over(board(H,K,Y,L),Player,Player) ←
    pieces(N), K > 6∗N, !.
game_over(board(H,K,Y,L),Player,Opponent) ←
    pieces(N), L > 6∗N, next_player(Player,Opponent).
announce(opponent) ← writeln(['You won! Congratulations.']).
announce(computer) ← writeln(['I won.']).
announce(draw) ← writeln(['The game is a draw']).

Miscellaneous game utilities

nth_member(N,[H|Hs],K) ←
    N > 1, !, N1 := N–1, nth_member(N1,Hs,K).
nth_member(1,[H|Hs],H).

n_substitute(1,[X|Xs],Y,[Y|Xs]) ← !.
n_substitute(N,[X|Xs],Y,[X|Xs1]) ←
    N > 1, !, N1 := N–1, n_substitute(N1,Xs,Y,Xs1).

next_player(computer,opponent).
next_player(opponent,computer).

legal([N|Ns]) ← 0 < N, N < 7, legal(Ns).
legal([ ]).

swap(board(Hs,K,Ys,L),board(Ys,L,Hs,K)).

display_game(Position,computer) ←
    show(Position).
display_game(Position,opponent) ←
    swap(Position,Position1), show(Position1).

show(board(H,K,Y,L)) ←
    reverse(H,HR), write_stones(HR), write_kalahs(K,L), write_stones(Y).

write_stones(H) ←
    nl, tab(5), display_holes(H).

display_holes([H|Hs]) ←
    write_pile(H), display_holes(Hs).
    display_holes([ ]) ← nl.

Program 20.3 (Continued)

```
write_pile(N) ← N < 10, write(N), tab(4).
write_pile(N) ← N ≥ 10, write(N), tab(3).

write_kalahs(K,L) ←
    write(K), tab(34), write(L), nl.

zero([0,0,0,0,0,0]).
non_zero(Hs) ← Hs ≠ [0,0,0,0,0,0].
```

Initializing

```
lookahead(2).
initialize(kalah,board([N,N,N,N,N,N],0,[N,N,N,N,N,N],0),opponent) ←
    pieces(N).
pieces(6).
```

Program 20.3 (Continued)

The code gives all moves on backtracking. The predicate *stones*(*M*, *Board*, *N*) returns the number of stones *N* in hole *M* of the *Board* if *N* is greater than *0*, failing if there are no stones in the hole. The predicate *extend_move*(*M*,*Board*,*N*,*Ms*) returns the continuation of the move *Ms*. The second clause for *move* handles the special case when all the player's holes become empty during a move.

Testing whether the move continues is nontrivial, since it may involve all the procedures for making a move. If the last stone is not placed in the kalah, which can be determined by simple arithmetic, the move will end, and there is no need to distribute all the stones. Otherwise the stones are distributed, and the move continues recursively.

The basic predicate for making a move is *distribute_stones*(*Stones*,*N*,*Board*, *Board1*) which computes the relation that *Board1* is obtained from *Board* by distributing the number of stones in *Stones* starting from hole number *N*. There are two stages to the distribution, putting the stones in the player's holes, *distribute_my_holes*, and putting the stones in the opponent's holes, *distribute_your_holes*.

The simpler case is distributing the stones in the opponent's holes. The holes are updated by *distribute*, and the distribution of stones continues recursively if there is an excess of stones. A check is made to see if the player's board has become empty during the course of the move, and, if so, the opponent's stones are added to his kalah.

Distributing the player's stones must take into account two possibilities, distributing from any particular hole, and continuing the distribution for a large number of stones. The *pick_up_and_distribute* is the generalization of *distribute* to handle these cases. The predicate *check_capture* checks if a capture has occurred, and updates the holes accordingly, while *update_kalah* updates the number of stones in the player's kalah. Some other necessary utilities such as *n_substitute* are also included in the program.

The evaluation function is the difference between the number of stones in the two kalahs:

$$\text{value(board(H,K,Y,L),Value)} \leftarrow \text{Value} := \text{K–L}.$$

The central predicates have been described. A running program is now obtained by filling in the details for I/O, for initializing and terminating the game, etc. Simple suggestions can be found in the complete program for the game, given as Program 20.3.

In order to optimize the performance of the program, cuts can be added. Another tip is to rewrite the main loop of the program as a failure-driven loop rather than a tail recursive program. This is sometimes necessary in implementations which do not incorporate tail recursion optimization and a good garbage collector.

20.4 Background

The mastermind program, slightly modified, originally appeared in SIGART (Shapiro, 1983d) in response to a program for playing mastermind in Pascal. The SIGART article provoked several reactions, both of theoretical improvements to algorithms for playing mastermind, and practical improvements to the program. Most interesting was an analysis and discussion by Powers (1984) of how a Prolog program could be rewritten to good benefit using the mastermind code as a case study. Eventually speedup by a factor of 50 was achieved.

A proof of the correctness of the algorithm for playing Nim can be found in any textbook discussing games on graphs, for example, Berge (1962).

Kalah was an early AI target for game-playing programs (Slagle & Dixon, 1969).

Chapter 21

A Credit Evaluation
Expert System

At the time of writing this book, there has been a surge of activity in the application of artificial intelligence to industry. Of particular interest are expert systems — programs designed to perform tasks previously allocated to highly paid human experts. One important feature of expert systems is the explicit representation of knowledge.

This entire book is relevant for programming expert systems. The example programs typify code that might be written. For instance, the equation-solving program of the next chapter can be, and has been, viewed as an expert system.

The knowledge of expert systems is usually expressed in a rulelike form. Prolog whose basic statements are rules is thus a natural language for implementing expert systems. We briefly discuss the relationship of Prolog rules to classical expert systems such as MYCIN in the background to Chapter 19.

The chapter presents an account of developing a prototype expert system. The example comes from the world of banking: to evaluate requests for credit from small business ventures.

We give a fictionalized account of the development of a simple expert system for evaluating client requests for credit from a bank. The account is from the point of view of Prolog programmers, or knowledge engineers, commissioned by the bank to write the system. It begins after the most difficult stage of building an expert system, extracting the expert knowledge, has been underway for some time. In accordance with received wisdom, the programmers have been consulting with a single bank expert, Chas E. Manhattan. Chas has told us that three factors are of the utmost importance in considering a request for credit from a "client." Clients refer to small business ventures.

The most important factor is the collateral that can be offered by the client in case the venture folds. The various types of collateral are divided into categories. Currency deposits, whether local or foreign, are *first-class* collateral. Stocks are examples of *second-class* collateral, while the collateral provided by mortgages and the like is regarded as *illiquid.*

Also very important is the client's financial record. Experience in the bank has shown that the two most important factors are the client's net worth per assets, and the current gross profits on sales. The client's short-term debt per annual sales should be considered in evaluating the record, and slightly less significant is last year's sales growth. For knowledge engineers with some understanding of banking no further explanation of such concepts is necessary. In general a knowledge engineer must understand the domain sufficiently to be able to communicate with the domain expert.

The remaining factor to be considered is the expected yield to the bank. This is a problem that the bank has been working on for a while. Programs exist to give the yield of a particular client profile. The knowledge engineer can thus assume that the information will be available in the desired form.

Chas uses qualitative terms in speaking about these three factors: "The client had an excellent financial rating, or a good form of collateral. His venture would provide a reasonable yield, etc." Even concepts that could be determined quantitatively are discussed in qualitative terms. The financial world is too complicated to be expressed only with the numbers and ratios constantly being calculated. In order to make judgments, experts in the financial domain tend to think in qualitative terms with which they are more comfortable. To echo expert reasoning and to be able to interact with Chas further, qualitative reasoning must be modeled.

On talking to Chas, it became clear that a significant amount of the expert knowledge he described could be naturally expressed as a mixture of procedures and rules. On being pressed a little on the second and third interviews Chas gave rules for determining ratings for collateral, and financial rating. These involved considerable calculations, and in fact Chas admitted that to save himself work in the long term, he did a quick initial screen to see if the client was at all suitable.

This information is sufficient to build a prototype. We show how these comments and observations are translated into a system. The top level basic relation is *credit(Client,Answer)* where *Answer* is the reply given to the request by *Client* for credit. The code has three modules — *collateral, financial_rating* and *bank_yield* — corresponding to the three factors the expert said were important. The initial screen that the client is worth considering in the first place is performed by the predicate *ok_profile(Client)*. The answer *Answer* is then determined with the predicate *evaluate(Profile,Answer)* which evaluates the *Profile* built by the three modules.

Being proud knowledge engineers, we stress the features of the top level formulation in *credit/2*. The modularity is apparent. Each of the modules can be developed independently without affecting the rest of the system. Further there is no commitment to any particular data structure, i.e., data abstraction is used. For this example a structure *profile(C,F,Y)* represents the profile of collateral rating *C*, the financial rating *F* and the yield *Y* of a client. However, nothing central depends on this decision and it would be easy to change it. Let us consider some of the modular pieces.

Let us look at the essential features of the collateral evaluation module. The relation *collateral_rating/2* determines a rating for a particular client's collateral. The first step is to determine an appropriate profile. This is done with the predicate *collateral_profile* which classifies the client's collateral as *first_class*, *second_class* or *illiquid*, and gives the percentage each covers of the amount of credit the client requested. The relation uses facts in the database concerning both the bank and the client. In practice there may be separate databases for the bank and the client. Sample facts shown in Program 21.1 indicate, for example, that local currency deposits are a first class collateral.

The profile is evaluated to give a rating by *collateral_evaluation*. It uses "rules of thumb" to give a qualitative rating of the collateral: as excellent, good, etc. The first *collateral_evaluation* rule, for example, reads that: "The rating is *excellent* if the coverage of the requested credit amount by first class collateral is greater than or equal to 100 percent."

Two features of the code bear comment. First, the terminology used in the program is the terminology of Chas. This makes the program (almost) self-documenting to the experts, and means they can modify it with little help from the knowledge engineer. Allowing people to think in domain concepts also facilitates debugging, and assists in using a domain independent explanation facility as discussed in Section 19.2. Second, the apparent naivete of the evaluation rules is deceptive. There is a lot of knowledge and experience hidden behind these simple numbers. Choosing poor values for these numbers may mean suffering severe losses.

The financial evaluation module evaluates the financial stability of the client. It uses items taken mainly from the balance and profit/loss sheets. The financial rating is also qualitative. A weighted sum of financial factors is calculated (by *score*) and used by *calibrate* to determine the qualitative class.

Client data

credit(*Client,Answer*) ←
 Answer is the reply to a request by *Client* for credit.

credit(Client,Answer) ←
 ok_profile(Client),
 collateral_rating(Client,CollateralRating),
 financial_rating(Client,FinancialRating),
 bank_yield(Client,Yield),
 evaluate(profile(CollateralRating,FinancialRating,Yield),Answer).

The collateral rating module

collateral_rating(*Client,Rating*) ←
 Rating is a qualitative description assessing the collateral
 offered by *Client* to cover the request for credit.

collateral_rating(Client,Rating) ←
 collateral_profile(Client,FirstClass,SecondClass,Illiquid),
 collateral_evaluation(FirstClass,SecondClass,Illiquid,Rating).

collateral_profile(Client,FirstClass,SecondClass,Illiquid) ←
 requested_credit(Client,Credit),
 collateral_percent(first_class,Client,Credit,FirstClass),
 collateral_percent(second_class,Client,Credit,SecondClass),
 collateral_percent(illiquid,Client,Credit,Illiquid).

collateral_percent(Type,Client,Total,Value) ←
 set_of(X, Collateral↑(collateral(Collateral,Type),
 amount(Collateral,Client,X)),Xs),
 sumlist(Xs,Sum),
 Value := Sum*100/Total.

Evaluation rules

collateral_evaluation(FirstClass,SecondClass,Illiquid,excellent) ←
 FirstClass $\geq$ 100.
collateral_evaluation(FirstClass,SecondClass,Illiquid,excellent) ←
 FirstClass $>$ 70, FirstClass + SecondClass $\geq$ 100.
collateral_evaluation(FirstClass,SecondClass,Illiquid,good) ←
 FirstClass + SecondClass $>$ 60,
 FirstClass + SecondClass $<$ 70,
 FirstClass + SecondClass + Illiquid $\geq$ 100.

Program 21.1: A credit evaluation system

Bank data – classification of collateral

collateral(local currency_deposits,first_class).
collateral(foreign_currency_deposits,first_class).
collateral(negotiate_instruments,second_class).
collateral(mortgage,illiquid).

Financial rating

financial_rating(Client,Rating) ←
    Rating is a qualitative description assessing the financial
    record offered by *Client* to support the request for credit.

financial_rating(Client,Rating) ←
    financial_factors(Factors),
    score(Factors,Client,0,Score),
    calibrate(Score,Rating).

Financial evaluation rules

calibrate(Score,bad) ← Score ≤ −500.
calibrate(Score,medium) ← −500 < Score, Score < 150.
calibrate(Score,good) ← 150 ≤ Score, Score < 1000.
calibrate(Score,excellent) ← Score ≥ 1000.

Bank data – weighting factors

financial_factors([(net_worth_per_assets,5),
    (last_year_sales_growth,1),
    (gross_profits_on_sales,5),
    (short_term_debt_per_annual_sales,2)]).

score([(Factor,Weight)|Factors],Client,Acc,Score) ←
    value(Factor,Client,Value),
    Acc1 is Acc + Weight*Value,
    score(Factors,Client,Acc1,Score).
    score([ ],Client,Score,Score).

Final evaluation

evaluate(Profile,Outcome) ←
    Outcome is the reply to the client's *Profile*.

evaluate(Profile,Answer) ←
    rule(Conditions,Answer), verify(Conditions,Profile).

Program 21.1 (Continued)

verify([condition(Type,Test,Rating)|Conditions],Profile) ←
    scale(Type,Scale),
    select_value(Type,Profile,Fact),
    compare(Test,Scale,Fact,Rating),
    verify(Conditions,Profile).
verify([ ],Profile).

compare('=',Scale,Rating,Rating).
compare('>',Scale,Rating1,Rating2) ←
    precedes(Scale,Rating1,Rating2).
compare('≥',Scale,Rating1,Rating2) ←
    precedes(Scale,Rating1,Rating2) ; Rating1 = Rating2.
compare('<',Scale,Rating1,Rating2) ←
    precedes(Scale,Rating2,Rating1).
compare('≤',Scale,Rating1,Rating2) ←
    precedes(Scale,Rating2,Rating1) ; Rating1 = Rating2.

precedes([R1|Rs],R1,R2).
precedes([R|Rs],R1,R2) ← R ≠ R2, precedes(Rs,R1,R2).

select_value(collateral,profile(C,F,Y),C).
select_value(finances,profile(C,F,Y),F).
select_value(yield,profile(C,F,Y),Y).

Utilities

sumlist(Xs,Sum) ← See Program 8.6b.

Bank data and rules

rule([condition(collateral,'≥',excellent),condition(finances,'≥',good),
    condition(yield,'≥',reasonable)],give_credit).
rule([condition(collateral,'=',good),condition(finances,'=',good),
    condition(yield,'≥',reasonable)],consult_superior).
rule([condition(collateral,'≤',moderate),condition(finances,'≤',medium)],
    refuse_credit).

scale(collateral,[excellent,good,moderate]).
scale(finances,[excellent,good,medium,bad]).
scale(yield,[excellent,reasonable,poor]).

Program 21.1 (Continued)

Client Data

bank_yield(client1,excellent).
requested_credit(client1,50000).

amount(local_currency_deposits,client1,30000).
amount(foreign_currency_deposits,client1,20000).
amount(bank_guarantees,client1,3000).

amount(negotiate_instruments,client1,5000).
amount(stocks,client1,9000).

amount(mortgage,client1,12000).
amount(documents,client1,14000).

value(net_worth_per assets,client1,40).
value(last_year_sales_growth,client1,20).
value(gross profits_on_sales,client1,45).
value(short_term_debt_per_annual_sales,client1,9).

ok_profile(client1).

Program 21.2: Test data for the credit evaluation system

It should be noted that both the modules giving the collateral rating and the financial rating reflect the point of view and style of a particular expert, Chas Manhattan, rather than the universal truth. Within the bank there is no consensus about the subject. Some people tend to be conservative and some are prepared to take considered risks.

Programming the code for determining the collateral and financial ratings proceeded easily. The knowledge provided by the expert was more-or-less directly translated into the program. The module for the overall evaluation of the client, however, was more challenging.

The major difficulty was formulating the relevant expert knowledge. Our expert was less forthcoming with general rules for overall evaluation than for rating the financial record, for example. He happily discussed the profiles of particular clients, and the outcome of their credit requests and loans, but was reluctant to generalize. He preferred to react to suggestions rather than volunteer rules.

This forced a close re-evaluation of the exact problem we were solving. There were three possible answers the system could give: approve the request for credit, refuse the request, or ask for advice. There were three factors to be considered. Each factor had a qualitative value that was one of a small set of possibilities. For example, the financial rating could be *bad, medium, good* or *excellent*. Further the possible values were ranked on an ordinal scale.

Our system clearly faced an instance of a general problem: find an outcome from some ordinal scale based on the qualitative results of several ordinal scales. Rules to solve the problem were thus to give a conclusion based on the outcome of the factors. We pressed Chas with this formulation and he rewarded us with several rules. Here is a typical one: "If the client's collateral rating is excellent (or better), her financial rating good (or better), and her yield at least reasonable, then grant the credit request."

An immediate translation of the rule is

$$\text{evaluate(profile(excellent,good,reasonable),give\_credit)}.$$

But this misses many cases covered by the rule, for example, when the client's profile is (*excellent,good,excellent*). All the cases for a given rule can be listed. It seemed more sensible, however, to build a more general tool to evaluate rules expressed in terms of qualitative values from ordinal scales.

There is potentially a problem with using ordinal scales due to the large number of individual cases that may need to be specified. If each of the N modules have M possible outcomes, there are N^M cases to be considered. In general, it is infeasible to have a separate rule for each possibility. Not only is space a problem for so many rules, but the search involved in finding the correct rule may be prohibitive. So instead we defined a small *ad hoc* set of rules. We hoped the rules defined, which covered many possibilities at once, would be sufficient to cover the clients the bank usually deal with. We chose the structure *rule(Conditions,Conclusion)* for our rules, where *Conditions* is a list of conditions under which the rule applies and *Conclusion* is the rule's conclusion. A condition has the form *condition(Factor,Relation,Rating)*, insisting that the rating from the factor named by *Factor* bears the relation named by *Relation* to the rating given by *Rating*.

The relation is represented by the standard relational operators: $<, =, >$, etc. The previously mentioned rule is represented as

$$\text{rule([condition(collateral,'}\geq\text{',excellent),condition(finances,'}\geq\text{',good),}$$
$$\text{condition(yield,'}\geq\text{',reasonable)],give\_credit)}.$$

Another rule given by Chas reads: "If both the collateral rating and financial rating are good, and the yield is at least reasonable, then consult your superior." This is translated to

> rule([condition(collateral,'=',good),condition(finances,'=',good),
>   condition(yield,'≥',reasonable)],consult_superior).

Factors can be mentioned twice to indicate they lie in a certain range, or might not be mentioned at all. For example, the rule

> rule([condition(collateral,'≤',moderate),condition(finances,'≤',medium)],
>   refuse_credit).

states that a client should be refused credit if the collateral rating is no better than moderate and the financial rating is at best medium. The yield is not relevant, and so is not mentioned.

The interpreter for the rules is written nondeterministically. The procedure is: "Find a rule and verify that its conditions apply," as defined by *evaluate*. The predicate *verify(Conditions,Profile)* checks that the relation between the corresponding symbols in the rule and the ones that are associated with the *Profile* of the client is as specified by *Conditions*. For each *Type* that can appear, a scale is necessary to give the order of values the scale can take. Examples of scale facts in the bank database are *scale(collateral, [excellent,good,moderate])* and *scale(finances, [excellent,good,medium,bad])*. The predicate *select_value* returns the appropriate symbol of the factor under the ordinality test which is performed by *compare*. It is an access predicate, and consequently the only predicate dependent on the choice of data structure for the profile.

At this stage the prototype program is tested. Some data from real clients is necessary, and the answer the system gives on these individuals is tested against what the corresponding bank official would say. The data for *client1* is given in Program 21.2. The reply to the query *credit(client1,X)* is *give_credit*.

Our prototype expert system is a composite of styles and methods — not just a backward chaining system. Heuristic rules of thumb are used to determine the collateral rating; an algorithm, albeit a simple one, is used to determine the financial rating; and there is a rule language, with an interpreter, for expressing outcomes in terms of values from discrete ordinal scales. The rule interpreter proceeds forwards from conditions to conclusion, rather than backward as in Prolog. Expert systems must become such composites in order to exploit the different forms of knowledge already extant.

The development of the prototype was not the only activity of the knowledge engineers. Various other features of the expert system were developed in parallel. An explanation facility was built as an extension of Program 19.9. A simulator for rules based on ordinal scales was built to settle the argument among the knowledge engineers as to whether a reasonable collection of rules would be sufficient to cover the range of outcomes in the general case.

Finally a consistency checker for the rules was built. The following meta-rule is an obvious consistency principle: "If all of client A's factors are better than or equal to client B's, then the outcome of client A must be better than or equal to that of client B."

21.1 Background

More details on the credit evaluation system can be found in Ben-David and Sterling (1985).

Chapter 22

An Equation Solver

A very natural area for Prolog applications is symbolic manipulation. For example, a Prolog program for symbolic differentiation, a typical symbol manipulation task, is just the rules of differentiation in different syntax, as shown in Program 3.29.

In this chapter we present a program for solving symbolic equations. It is a simplification of PRESS (PRolog Equation Solving System) developed in the mathematical reasoning group of the department of Artificial Intelligence at the University of Edinburgh. PRESS performs at the level of a mathematics student in her final year of high school.

The structure of the chapter is as follows. The first section gives an overview of equation solving with some example solutions. The remaining four sections cover the four major equation solving methods implemented in equation solver.

22.1 An overview of equation solving

The task of equation solving can be described syntactically. Given an equation $Lhs=Rhs$ in an unknown X, transform the equation into an equivalent equation $X=Rhs1$, where $Rhs1$ does not contain X. This final equation is the solution. Two equations are equivalent if one is transformed into the other by a finite number of applications of the axioms and rules of algebra.

Successful mathematics students do not solve equations by blindly applying axioms of algebra. Instead they learn, develop and use various methods and strategies. Our equation solver, modeling this behavior, is accordingly a collection of methods to be applied to an equation to be solved. Each method transforms the equation by applying identities of algebra expressed as rewrite rules. The

(i) $\cos(x) \cdot (1 - 2 \cdot \sin(x)) = 0$

(ii) $x^2 - 3 \cdot x + 2 = 0$

(iii) $2^{2 \cdot x} - 5 \cdot 2^{x+1} + 16 = 0$

Figure 22.1: Test equations

methods can and do take widely different forms. They can be a collection of rules for solving the class of equations to which the method is applicable, or algorithms implementing a decision procedure.

Abstractly a method has two parts: a condition testing whether the method is applicable, and the application of the method itself.

The type of equations our program can handle are indicated by the three examples in Figure 22.1. They consist of *algebraic functions* of the unknown, that is $+$, $-$, $*$, $/$, and exponentiation to an integer power, and also trigonometric and exponential functions. The unknown is x in all three equations.

We briefly show how each equation is solved.

The first step in solving equation (i) in Figure 22.1 is factorization. The problem to be solved is reduced to solving $cos(x) = 0$ and $1-2 \cdot sin(x) = 0$. A solution to either of these equations is a solution to the original equation.

Both the equations $cos(x)=0$ and $1-2 \cdot sin(x)=0$ are solved by making x the subject of the equation. This is possible since x occurs once in each equation.

The solution to $cos(x)=0$ is $x=arccos(0)$. The solution of $1-2 \cdot sin(x)=0$ takes the following steps:

$$1-2 \cdot \sin(x) = 0,$$
$$2 \cdot \sin(x) = 1,$$
$$\sin(x) = 1/2,$$
$$x = \arcsin(1/2).$$

In general, equations with a single occurrence of the unknown can be solved by an algorithmic method, called *isolation*. The method repeatedly applies an appropriate inverse function to both sides of the equation until the single occurrence of the unknown is "isolated" as the left-hand side of the equation. Isolation solves $1-2 \cdot sin(x)=0$ by producing the above sequence of equations.

Equation (ii) in Figure 20.1, $x^2-3 \cdot x+2=0$, is a quadratic equation in x. We all learn in high school a formula for solving quadratic equations. The discriminant, $b^2-4 \cdot a \cdot c$, is calculated, in this case $(-3)^2-4 \cdot 1 \cdot 2$ which equals 1, and two solutions are given: $x=(-(-3)+\sqrt{1})/2$ which equals 2, and $x=(-(-3)-\sqrt{1})/2$ which equals 1.

The key to solving equation (iii) in Figure 22.1 is to realize that the equation is really a quadratic equation in 2^x. The equation $2^{2 \cdot x} - 5 \cdot 2^{x+1} + 16 = 0$ can be rewritten as $(2^x)^2 - 5 \cdot 2 \cdot 2^x + 16 = 0$. This can be solved for 2^x giving two solutions of the form $2^x = Rhs$, where Rhs is free of x. Each of these equations are solved for x to give solutions to equation (iii).

PRESS was tested on equations taken from British A-level examinations in mathematics. It seems that examiners liked posing questions such as equation (iii) which involved the student manipulating logarithmic, exponential or other transcendental functions into forms where they could be solved as polynomials. A method called *homogenization* evolved to solve equations of these type.

The aim of homogenization is to transform the equation into a polynomial in some term containing the unknown. (We simplify the more general homogenization of PRESS for didactic purposes.) The method consists of four steps which we illustrate for equation (iii). The equation is first parsed and all maximal non-polynomial terms containing the unknown are collected with duplicates removed. This set is called the *offenders set*. In the example it is $\{2^{2x}, 2^{x+1}\}$. The second step is finding a term, known as the *reduced term*. The result of homogenization is a polynomial equation in the reduced term. The reduced term in our example is 2^x. The third step of homogenization is finding rewrite rules that express each of the elements of the offenders set as a polynomial in the reduced term. Finding such a set guarantees that homogenization will succeed. In our example the rewrite rules are $2^{2x} = (2^x)^2$ and $2^{(x+1)} = 2 \cdot 2^x$. Finally, the rewrite rules are applied to produce the polynomial equation.

We complete this section with a brief overview of the equation solver. The basic predicate is *solve_equation(Equation,X,Solution)*. The relation is true if *Solution* is a solution to *Equation* in the unknown X. The complete code appears as Program 22.1.

Program 22.1 has four clauses for *solve_equation*, one for each of the four methods needed to solve the equations in Figure 22.1. More generally, there is a clause for each equation solving method. The full PRESS system had several more methods.

Our equation solver ignores several features that might be expected. There is no simplification of expressions, no rational arithmetic, no record of the last equation solved, no help facility, and so forth. PRESS did contain many of these facilities as discussed briefly in the background section at the end of this chapter.

22.2 Factorization

Factorization is the first method attempted by the equation solver. Note that the test whether factorization is applicable is trivial, being unification with the equation $A*B=0$. If the test succeeds, the simpler equations are recursively solved. The top-level clause implementing factorization is

> solve_equation(A*B=0,X,Solution) ←
>   factorize(A*B,X,Factors\[ ]),
>   remove_duplicates(Factors,Factors1),
>   solve_factors(Factors1,X,Solution).

The top-level clause in Program 22.1 has a cut as the first goal in the body. This is a green cut: none of the other methods depend on the success or failure of factorization. In general we omit green cuts from clauses we describe in the text.

22.3 Isolation

A useful concept to locate and manipulate the single occurrence of the unknown is its *position*. The position of a subterm in a term is a list of argument numbers specifying where it appears. Consider the equation $cos(x)=0$. The term $cos(x)$ containing x is the first argument of the equation, and x is the first (and only) argument of $cos(x)$. The position of x in $cos(x)=0$ is therefore $[1,1]$. This is indicated in the diagram in Figure 22.2. The figure also shows the position of x in $1-2 \cdot sin(x)=0$ which is $[1,2,2,1]$.

The clause defining the method of isolation is

> solve_equation(Equation,X,Solution) ←
>   single_occurrence(X,Equation),
>   position(X,Equation,[Side|Position]),
>   maneuver_sides(Side,Equation,Equation1),
>   isolate(Position,Equation1,Solution).

The condition characterizing when isolation is applicable is that there be a single occurrence of the unknown X in the equation, checked by *single_occurrence*. The method calculates the position of X with the predicate *position*. The isolation of X then proceeds in two stages. First, *maneuver_sides* ensures that X appears on the left-hand side of the equation, and second, *isolate* makes it the subject of the formula.

solve_equation(Equation, Unknown, Solution) ←
    Solution is a solution to the equation *Equation* in the unknown *Unknown*

solve_equation(A*B=0,X,Solution) ←
    !,
    factorize(A*B,X,Factors\[ ]),
    remove_duplicates(Factors,Factors1),
    solve_factors(Factors1,X,Solution).

solve_equation(Equation,X,Solution) ←
    single_occurrence(X,Equation),
    !,
    position(X,Equation,[Side|Position]),
    maneuver_sides(Side,Equation,Equation1),
    isolate(Position,Equation1,Solution).

solve_equation(Lhs=Rhs,X,Solution) ←
    polynomial(Lhs,X),
    polynomial(Rhs,X),
    !,
    polynomial_normal_form(Lhs–Rhs,X,PolyForm),
    solve_polynomial_equation(PolyForm,X,Solution).

solve_equation(Equation,X,Solution) ←
    homogenize(Equation,X,Equation1,X1),
    !,
    solve_equation(Equation1,X1,Solution1),
    solve_equation(Solution1,X,Solution).

The factorization method

factorize(Expression,Subterm,Factors) ←
    splits the multiplicative term *Expression* into a
    difference-list of *Factors* containing the *Subterm*.

factorize(A*B,X,Factors\Rest) ←
    !, factorize(A,X,Factors\Factors1), factorize(B,X,Factors1\Rest).
factorize(C,X,[C|Factors]\Factors) ←
    subterm(X,C), !.
factorize(C,X,Factors\Factors).

solve_factors(Factors, Unknown, Solution) ←
    Solution is a solution of the equation *Factor=0* in the
    Unknown for some *Factor* in the list of *Factors*.

Program 22.1: A program for solving equations

solve_factors([Factor|Factors],X,Solution) ←
    solve_equation(Factor=0,X,Solution).
solve_factors([Factor|Factors],X,Solution) ←
    solve_factors(Factors,X,Solution).

The isolation method

single_occurrence(Subterm,Term) ←
    occurrence(Subterm,Term,1).

maneuver_sides(1,Lhs = Rhs,Lhs = Rhs) ← !.
maneuver_sides(2,Lhs = Rhs,Rhs = Lhs) ← !.

isolate([N|Position],Equation,IsolatedEquation) ←
    isolax(N,Equation,Equation1),
    isolate(Position,Equation1,IsolatedEquation).
isolate([ ],Equation,Equation).

Axioms for Isolation

isolax(1,–Lhs = Rhs,Lhs = –Rhs).	% Unary minus
isolax(1,Term1+Term2 = Rhs,Term1 = Rhs–Term2).	% Addition
isolax(2,Term1+Term2 = Rhs,Term2 = Rhs–Term1).	% Addition
isolax(1,Term1–Term2 = Rhs,Term1 = Rhs+Term2).	% Subtraction
isolax(2,Term1–Term2 = Rhs,Term2 = Term1–Rhs).	% Subtraction
isolax(1,Term1*Term2 = Rhs,Term1 = Rhs/Term2) ← Term2 ≠ 0.	% Multiplication
isolax(2,Term1*Term2 = Rhs,Term2 = Rhs/Term1) ← Term1 ≠ 0.	% Multiplication
isolax(1,Term1↑Term2 = Rhs,Term1 = Rhs↑(–Term2)).	% Exponentiation
isolax(2,Term1↑Term2 = Rhs,Term2 = log(base(Term1),Rhs)).	% Exponentiation
isolax(1,sin(U) = V,U = arcsin(V)).	% Sine
isolax(1,sin(U) = V,U = π–arcsin(V)).	% Sine
isolax(1,cos(U) = V,U = arccos(V)).	% Cosine
isolax(1,cos(U) = V,U = –arccos(V)).	% Cosine

The polynomial methods

polynomial(Term,X) ← See Program 11.4

polynomial_normal_form(Expression,Term,PolyNormalForm) ←
    PolyNormalForm is the polynomial normal form of
    Expression, which is a polynomial in *Term*

Program 22.1 (Continued)

polynomial_normal_form(Polynomial,X,NormalForm) ←
    polynomial_form(Polynomial,X,PolyForm),
    remove_zero_terms(PolyForm,NormalForm), !.

polynomial_form(X,X,[(1,1)]).
polynomial_form(X↑N,X,[(1,N)]).
polynomial_form(Term1+Term2,X,PolyForm) ←
    polynomial_form(Term1,X,PolyForm1),
    polynomial_form(Term2,X,PolyForm2),
    add_polynomials(PolyForm1,PolyForm2,PolyForm).
polynomial_form(Term1−Term2,X,PolyForm) ←
    polynomial_form(Term1,X,PolyForm1),
    polynomial_form(Term2,X,PolyForm2),
    subtract_polynomials(PolyForm1,PolyForm2,PolyForm).
polynomial_form(Term1*Term2,X,PolyForm) ←
    polynomial_form(Term1,X,PolyForm1),
    polynomial_form(Term2,X,PolyForm2),
    multiply_polynomials(PolyForm1,PolyForm2,PolyForm).
polynomial_form(Term↑N,X,PolyForm) ← !,
    polynomial_form(Term,X,PolyForm1),
    binomial(PolyForm1,N,PolyForm).
polynomial_form(Term,X,[(Term,0)]) ←
    free_of(X,Term), !.

remove_zero_terms([(0,N)|Poly],Poly1) ←
    !, remove_zero_terms(Poly,Poly1).
remove_zero_terms([(C,N)|Poly],[(C,N)|Poly1]) ←
    C ≠ 0, !, remove_zero_terms(Poly,Poly1).
remove_zero_terms([ ],[ ]).

Polynomial manipulation routines

add_polynomials(Poly1,Poly2,Poly) ←
    Poly is the sum of *Poly1* and *Poly2*, where *Poly1*,
    Poly2 and *Poly* are all in polynomial form

add_polynomials([ ],Poly,Poly) ← !.
add_polynomials(Poly,[ ],Poly) ← !.
add_polynomials([(Ai,Ni)|Poly1],[(Aj,Nj)|Poly2],[(Ai,Ni)|Poly]) ←
    Ni > Nj, !, add_polynomials(Poly1,[(Aj,Nj)|Poly2],Poly).
add_polynomials([(Ai,Ni)|Poly1],[(Aj,Nj)|Poly2],[(A,Ni)|Poly]) ←
    Ni =:= Nj, !, A := Ai+Aj, add_polynomials(Poly1,Poly2,Poly).
add_polynomials([(Ai,Ni)|Poly1],[(Aj,Nj)|Poly2],[(Aj,Nj)|Poly]) ←
    Ni < Nj, !, add_polynomials([(Ai,Ni)|Poly1],Poly2,Poly).

Program 22.1 (Continued)

subtract_polynomials(Poly1,Poly2,Poly) ←
    Poly is the difference of *Poly1* and *Poly2*, where *Poly1*,
    Poly2 and *Poly* are all in polynomial form.

subtract_polynomials(Poly1,Poly2,Poly) ←
    multiply_single(Poly2,(−1,0),Poly3),
    add_polynomials(Poly1,Poly3,Poly), !.

multiply_single(Poly1,Monomial,Poly) ←
    Poly is the product of *Poly1* and Monomial, where *Poly1*,
    and *Poly* are in polynomial form, and Monomial has the
    form *C,N*) denoting the monomial *C*∗*X^N*

multiply_single([(C1,N1)|Poly1],(C,N),[(C2,N2)|Poly]) ←
    C2 := C1∗C, N2 := N1+N, multiply_single(Poly1,(C,N),Poly).
multiply_single([ ],Factor,[ ]).

multiply_polynomials(Poly1,Poly2,Poly) ←
    Poly is the product of *Poly1* and *Poly2*, where *Poly1*,
    Poly2 and Poly are all in polynomial form

multiply_polynomials([(C,N)|Poly1],Poly2,Poly) ←
    multiply_single(Poly2,(C,N),Poly3),
    multiply_polynomials(Poly1,Poly2,Poly4),
    add_polynomials(Poly3,Poly4,Poly).
multiply_polynomials([ ],P,[ ]).

binomial(Poly,1,Poly).

Polynomial equation solver

solve_polynomial_equation(Equation,Unknown,Solution) ←
    Solution is a solution to the
    polynomial *Equation* in the unknown *Unknown*

solve_polynomial_equation(PolyEquation,X,X = −B/A) ←
    linear(PolyEquation), !,
    pad(PolyEquation,[(A,1),(B,0)]).
solve_polynomial_equation(PolyEquation,X,Solution) ←
    quadratic(PolyEquation), !,
    pad(PolyEquation,[(A,2),(B,1),(C,0)]),
    discriminant(A,B,C,Discriminant),
    root(X,A,B,C,Discriminant,Solution).

discriminant(A,B,C,D) ← D := B∗B − 4∗A∗C.

Program 22.1 (Continued)

root(X,A,B,C,0,X= –B/(2∗A)).
root(X,A,B,C,D,X= (–B+sqrt(D))/(2∗A)) ← D > 0.
root(X,A,B,C,D,X= (–B–sqrt(D))/(2∗A)) ← D > 0.

pad([(C,N)|Poly],[(C,N)|Poly1]) ←
    !, pad(Poly,Poly1).
pad(Poly,[(0,N)|Poly1]) ←
    pad(Poly,Poly1).
pad([ ],[ ]).

linear([(Coeff,1)|Poly]).
quadratic([(Coeff,2)|Poly]).

The homogenization method

homogenize(Equation,X,Equation1,X1) ←
    The *Equation* in *X* is transformed to the polynomial
    Equation1 in *X1* where *X1* contains *X*.

homogenize(Equation,X,Equation1,X1) ←
    offenders(Equation,X,Offenders),
    reduced_term(X,Offenders,Type,X1),
    rewrite(Offenders,Type,X1,Substitutions),
    substitute(Equation,Substitutions,Equation1).

offenders(Equation, Unknown, Offenders) ←
    Offenders is the set of offenders of the equation in the *Unknown*

offenders(Equation,X,Offenders) ←
    parse(Equation,X,Offenders1\[ ]),
    remove_duplicates(Offenders1,Offenders).
    multiple(Offenders).

reduced_term(X,Offenders,Type,X1) ←
    classify(Offenders,X,Type),
    candidate(Type,Offenders,X,X1).

Heuristics for exponential equations

classify(Offenders,X,exponential) ←
    exponential_offenders(Offenders,X).

exponential_offenders([A↑B|Offs],X) ←
    free_of(X,A), subterm(X,B), exponential_offenders(Offs,X).
exponential_offenders([ ],X).

candidate(exponential,Offenders,X,A↑X) ←
    base(Offenders,A), polynomial_exponents(Offenders,X).

Program 22.1 (Continued)

base([A↑B|Offs],A) ← base(Offs,A).
base([ ],A).

polynomial_exponents([A↑B|Offs],X) ←
 is_polynomial(B,X), polynomial_exponents(Offs,X).
polynomial_exponents([ ],X).

Parsing the equation and making substitutions

parse(Expression, Term, Offenders) ←
 Expression is traversed to produce the set of Offenders in Term,
 that is, the nonalgebraic subterms of Expression containing Term

parse(A+B,X,L1\L2) ←
 !, parse(A,X,L1\L3), parse(B,X,L3\L2).
parse(A*B,X,L1\L2) ←
 !, parse(A,X,L1\L3), parse(B,X,L3\L2).
parse(A–B,X,L1\L2) ←
 !, parse(A,X,L1\L3), parse(B,X,L3\L2).
parse(A=B,X,L1\L2) ←
 !, parse(A,X,L1\L3), parse(B,X,L3\L2).
parse(A↑B,X,L) ←
 integer(B), !, parse(A,X,L).
parse(A,X,L\L) ←
 free_of(X,A), !.
parse(A,X,[A|L]\L) ←
 subterm(X,A), !.

substitute(Equation,Substitutions,Equation1) ←
 The list of *Substitutions* is applied to *Equation* to produce *Equation1*

substitute(A+B,Subs,NewA+NewB) ←
 !, substitute(A,Subs,NewA), substitute(B,Subs,NewB).
substitute(A*B,Subs,NewA*NewB) ←
 !, substitute(A,Subs,NewA), substitute(B,Subs,NewB).
substitute(A–B,Subs,NewA–NewB) ←
 !, substitute(A,Subs,NewA), substitute(B,Subs,NewB).
substitute(A=B,Subs,NewA=NewB) ←
 !, substitute(A,Subs,NewA), substitute(B,Subs,NewB).
substitute(A↑B,Subs,NewA↑B) ←
 integer(B), !, substitute(A,Subs,NewA).
substitute(A,Subs,B) ←
 member(A=B,Subs), !.
substitute(A,Subs,A).

Program 22.1 (Continued)

Finding homogenization rewrite rules

rewrite([Off|Offs],Type,X1,[Off=Term|Rewrites]) ←
    homog_axiom(Type,Off,X1,Term),
    rewrite(Offs,Type,X1,Rewrites).
rewrite([ ],Type,X,[ ]).

Homogenization axioms

homog_axiom(exponential,A↑(N*X),A↑X,(A↑X)↑N).
homog_axiom(exponential,A↑(−X),A↑X,1/(A↑X)).
homog_axiom(exponential,A↑(X+B),A↑X,A↑B*A↑X).

Utilities

subterm(Sub,Term) ← See Program 9.2.

position(Term,Term,[ ]) ← !.
position(Sub,Term,Path) ←
    compound(Term), functor(Term,F,N), position(N,Sub,Term,Path), !.

position(N,Sub,Term,[N|Path]) ←
    arg(N,Term,Arg), position(Sub,Arg,Path).
position(N,Sub,Term,Path) ←
    N > 1, N1 := N−1, position(N1,Sub,Term,Path).

free_of(Subterm,Term) ←
    occurrence(Subterm,Term,N), !, N=0.

single_occurrence(Subterm,Term) ←
    occurrence(Subterm,Term,N), !, N=1.

occurrence(Term,Term,1) ← !.
occurrence(Sub,Term,N) ←
    compound(Term), !, functor(Term,F,M), occurrence(M,Sub,Term,0,N)
occurrence(Sub,Term,0).

occurrence(M,Sub,Term,N1,N2) ←
    M > 0, !, arg(M,Term,Arg), occurrence(Sub,Arg,N), N3 := N+N1,
    M1 := M−1, occurrence(M1,Sub,Term,N3,N2).
occurrence(0,Sub,Term,N,N).

multiple([X1,X2|Xs]).

Testing and data

test_press(X,Y) ← equation(X,E,U), solve_equation(E,U,Y).

equation(1,cos(x)*(1−2*sin(x))=0,x).

equation(2,x↑2−3*x+2=0,x).

equation(3,2↑(2*x)−5*2↑(x+1)+16=0,x).

Program 22.1 (Continued)

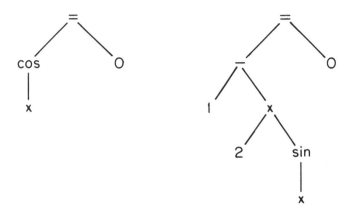

Figure 22.2: Position of subterms in terms

It is useful to define *single_occurrence* in terms of the more general predicate *occurrence(Subterm, Term,N)* which counts the number of times *N* that *Subterm* occurs in the term *Term*. Both *occurrence* and *position* are typical structure inspection predicates. Both are posed as exercises at the end of Section 9.2. Code for them appears in the utilities section of Program 22.1.

The predicate *maneuver_sides(N,Equation,Equation1)* consists of two facts:

```
maneuver_sides(1,Lhs = Rhs,Lhs = Rhs).
maneuver_sides(2,Lhs = Rhs,Rhs = Lhs).
```

Its effect is to ensure that the unknown appears on the left-hand side of *Equation1*. The first argument *N*, the head of the position list, indicates the side of the equation in which the unknown appears. A *1* means the left-hand side, and the equation is left intact. A *2* means the right-hand side, and so the sides of the equation are swapped.

The transformation of the equation is done by *isolate/3*. It repeatedly applies rewrite rules until the position list is exhausted:

```
isolate([N|Position],Equation,IsolatedEquation) ←
    isolax(N,Equation,Equation1),
    isolate(Position,Equation1,IsolatedEquation).
isolate([ ],Equation,Equation).
```

The rewrite rules, or isolation axioms, are specified by the predicate *isolax(N,Equation,Equation1)*. Let us consider an example used in solving *1-2·sin(x)=0*. An equivalence transformation on equations is adding the same quantity to both sides of an equation. We show its translation into an *isolax* axiom for manipulating equations of the form *u−v=w*. Note that rules need only simplify the left-hand side of equations, since the unknown is guaranteed to be on that side.

Two rules are necessary to cover the two cases whether the first or second argument of *u−v* contains the unknown. The term *u−v=w* can be rewritten to either *u−w+v* or *v=u−w*. The first argument of *isolax* specifies which argument of the sum contains the unknown. The Prolog equivalent of the two rewrite rules is then

```
isolax(1,Term1−Term2 = Rhs,Term1 = Rhs+Term2).
isolax(2,Term1−Term2 = Rhs,Term2 = Term1−Rhs).
```

Other isolation axioms are more complicated. Consider simplifying a product on the left-hand side of an equation. One of the expected rules would be

```
isolax(1,Term1*Term2 = Rhs,Term1 = Rhs/Term2).
```

If *Term2* equals zero, however, the rewriting is invalid. A test is therefore added which prevents the axioms for multiplication being applied, if the term by which it divides is *0*. For example,

```
isolax(1,Term1*Term2 = Rhs,Term1 = Rhs/Term2) ← Term2 ≠ 0.
```

Isolation axioms for trigonometric functions illustrate another possibility that must be catered for — multiple solutions. An equation such as *sin(x) = 1/2* that is reached in our example has two solutions between *0* and *2·π*. The alternate solutions are handled by having separate *isolax* axioms:

```
isolax(1,sin(U) = V,U = arcsin(V)).
isolax(1,sin(U) = V,U = π − arcsin(V)).
```

In fact the equation has a more general solution. Integers of the form *2·n·π* can be added to either solution for arbitrary values of *n*. The decision whether a particular or general solution is desired depends on context, and semantic information, independent of the equation solver.

Further examples of isolation axioms are given in the complete equation solver, Program 22.4.

The code described so far is sufficient to solve the first equation in Figure 22.1, $cos(x) \cdot (1-2 \cdot sin(x))=0$. There are four answers; $arccos(0)$, $-arccos(0)$, $arcsin((1-0)/2)$, $\pi-arcsin((1-0)/2)$. Each can be simplified, for example, $arcsin((1-0)/2)$ to $\pi/6$, but will not be unless the expression is explicitly evaluated.

The usefulness of an equation solver depends on how well it can perform such simplification, even though simplification is not strictly part of the equation solving task. Writing an expression simplifier is nontrivial, however. It is undecidable whether two expressions are equivalent in general. Some simple identities of algebra can be easily incorporated, for example, rewriting $0+u$ to u. Choosing between other preferred forms, e.g., $(1+x)^3$ and $1+3 \cdot x+3 \cdot x^2+x^3$, depends on context.

22.4 Polynomial

Polynomial equations are solved by a polynomial equation solver, applying various polynomial methods. Both sides of the equation are checked whether they are polynomials in the unknown. If the checks are successful, the equation is converted to a polynomial normal form by *polynomial_normal_form*, and the polynomial equation solver *solve_polynomial_equation* is invoked:

```
solve_equation(Lhs=Rhs,X,Solution) ←
    polynomial(Lhs,X),
    polynomial(Rhs,X),
    polynomial_normal_form(Lhs-Rhs,X,Poly),
    solve_polynomial_equation(Poly,X,Solution).
```

The polynomial normal form is a list of tuples of the form (A_i, N_i), where A_i is the coefficient of X^{N_i}, which is necessarily nonzero. The tuples are sorted into strictly decreasing order of N_i; for each degree there is at most one tuple. For example, the list $[(1,2),(-3,1),(2,0)]$ is the normal form for $x^2-3 \cdot x+2$. The leading term of the polynomial, is the head of the list. The classical algorithms for handling polynomials are applicable to equations in normal form. Reduction to polynomial normal form occurs in two stages:

```
polynomial_normal_form(Polynomial,X,NormalForm) ←
    polynomial_form(Polynomial,X,PolyForm),
    remove_zero_terms(PolyForm,NormalForm).
```

The predicate *polynomial_form(X,Polynomial,PolyForm)* decomposes the polynomial. *PolyForm* is a sorted list of coefficient-degree tuples, where tuples with zero coefficients may occur.

It is convenient for many of the polynomial methods to assume that all the terms in the polynomial form have nonzero coefficients. Therefore the final step of *polynomial_normal_form* is removing those terms whose coefficients are zero. This is achieved by a simple recursive procedure *remove_zero_terms.*

The code for *polynomial_form* directly echoes the code for *is_polynomial.* For each clause used in the parsing process, there is a corresponding clause giving the resultant polynomial. For example, the polynomial form of a term x^n is $[(1,n)]$ which is expressed in the clause

> polynomial_form(X↑N,X,[(1,N)]).

The recursive clauses for *polynomial_form* manipulate the polynomials in order to preserve the polynomial form. Consider the clause

> polynomial_form(Poly1+Poly2,X,PolyForm) ←
>   polynomial_form(Poly1,X,PolyForm1),
>   polynomial_form(Poly2,X,PolyForm2),
>   add_polynomials(PolyForm1,PolyForm2,PolyForm).

The procedure *add_polynomials* contains an algorithm for adding polynomials in normal form. The code is a straightforward list of the possibilities that can arise.

> add_polynomials([ ],Poly,Poly).
> add_polynomials([P|Poly],[ ],[P|Poly]).
> add_polynomials([(Ai,Ni)|Poly1],[(Aj,Nj)|Poly2],[(Ai,Ni)|Poly]) ←
>   Ni > Nj, add_polynomials(Poly1,[(Aj,Nj)|Poly2],Poly).
> add_polynomials([(Ai,N)|Poly1],[(Aj,N)|Poly2],[(A,N)|Poly]) ←
>   Ni =:= Nj, A := Ai+Aj, add_polynomials(Poly1,Poly2,Poly).
> add_polynomials([(Ai,Ni)|Poly1],[(Aj,Nj)|Poly2],[(Aj,Nj)|Poly]) ←
>   Ni < Nj, add_polynomials([(Ai,Ni)|Poly1],Poly2,Poly).

Similarly, the procedures *subtract_polynomials, multiply_polynomials* and *binomial* are algorithms for subtracting, multiplying and binomially expanding polynomials in normal form to produce results in normal form. The subsidiary predicate *multiply_single(Poly1,Monomial,Poly2)* multiplies a polynomial by a monomial *(C,N)* to produce a new polynomial.

Once the polynomial is in normal form, the polynomial equation solver is invoked. The structure of the polynomial solver is identical to the structure of the overall equation solver. The solver is a collection of methods that are tried in order to see which is applicable and can be used to solve the equation. The predicate *solve_polynomial_equation* is the analogous relation to *solve_equation*.

The second equation in Figure 22.1 is quadratic and can be solved with the standard formula. The equation solver mirrors the human method. The polynomial is identified as being suitable for the quadratic method by checking (with *quadratic*) if the leading term in the polynomial is of second degree. Since zero terms have been removed in putting the polynomial into its normal form, *pad* puts them back if necessary. The next two steps are familiar: calculating the discriminant, and returning the roots according to the value of the discriminant. Again multiple solutions are indicated by having multiple possibilities:

> solve_polynomial_equation(Poly,X,Solution) ←
>   quadratic(Poly),
>   pad(Poly,[(A,2),(B,1),(C,0)]),
>   discriminant(A,B,C,Discriminant),
>   root(X,A,B,C,Discriminant,Solution).

> discriminant(A,B,C,D) ← D := (B∗B − 4∗A∗C).

> root(X,A,B,C,0,X= −B/(2∗A)).
> root(X,A,B,C,D,X= (−B+sqrt(D))/(2∗A)) ← D > 0.
> root(X,A,B,C,D,X= (−B−sqrt(D))/(2∗A)) ← D > 0.

Other clauses for *solve_polynomial_equation* constitute separate methods for solving different polynomial equations. Linear equations are solved with a simple formula. In PRESS, cubic equations are handled by guessing a root and then factoring, reducing the equation to a quadratic. Other tricks recognize obvious factors, or that quartic equations missing a cubic and a linear term are really disguised quadratics.

22.5   Homogenization

The top-level clause for homogenization reflects the transformation of the original equation into a new equation in a new unknown, which is recursively solved, and its solution obtained for the original unknown:

> solve_equation(Equation,X,Solution) ←
>   homogenize(Equation,X,Equation1,X1),
>   solve_equation(Equation1,X1,Solution1),
>   solve_equation(Solution1,X,Solution).

The code for *homogenize/4* implements the four stages of homogenization as described in Section 22.1. The offenders set is calculated by *offenders/3* which checks that there are multiple offenders. If there is only a single offender, homogenization will not be useful:

    homogenize(Equation,X,Equation1,X1) ←
        offenders(Equation,X,Offenders),
        reduced_term(X,Offenders,Type,X1),
        rewrite(Offenders,Type,X1,Substitutions),
        substitute(Substitutions,Equation,Equation1).

The predicate *reduced_term/4* finds a *reduced term*, that is a candidate for the new unknown. In order to structure the search for the reduced term, the equation is classified into a type. This type is used in the next stage to find rewrite rules expressing each element of the offenders set as an appropriate function of the reduced term. The type of the example equation is *exponential*. PRESS encodes a lot of heuristic knowledge about finding a suitable reduced term. The heuristics are dependent on the type of the terms appearing in the offenders set. To aid the structuring (and retrieval) of knowledge, finding a reduced term proceeds in two stages — classifying the type of the offenders set and finding a reduced term of that type:

    reduced_term(X,Offenders,Type,X1) ←
        classify(Offenders,X,Type),
        candidate(Type,Offenders,X,X1).

We look at the set of rules appropriate to our particular equation. The offenders set is of exponential type because all the elements in the offenders set have the form A^B where A does not contain the unknown, but B does. Standard recursive procedures check that this is true.

The heuristic used to select the reduced term in this example is that if all the bases are the same, A, and each exponent is a polynomial in the unknown, X, then a suitable reduced term is A^X:

    candidate(exponential,Offenders,X,A↑X) ←
        base(Offenders,A), polynomial_exponents(Offenders,X).

The straightforward code for *base* and *polynomial_exponents* is in the complete program. The heuristics in PRESS are better developed than the ones shown here. For example, the greatest common divisor of all the leading terms of the polynomials is calculated and used to choose the reduced term.

The next step is checking whether each member of the offenders set can be rewritten in terms of the reduced term candidate. This involves finding an appropriate rule. The collection of clauses for *homogenize_axiom* constitute the possibly applicable rewrite rules. In other words, relevant rules must be specified in advance. The applicable rules in this case are

homogenize_axiom(exponential,A↑(N∗X),A↑X,(A↑X)↑N).
homogenize_axiom(exponential,A↑(X+B),A↑X,A↑B∗A↑X).

Substituting the term in the equation echoes the parsing process used by *offenders* as each part of the equation is checked whether it is the appropriate term to rewrite.

Exercises for Chapter 22

(i)   Add isolation axioms to Program 22.1 to handle quotients on the left-hand side of the equation. Solve the equation $x/2=5$.

(ii) Add to the polynomial equation solver the ability to solve disguised linear and disguised quadratic equations. Solve the equations $2x^3-8=x^3$, and $x^4-5x^2+6=0$.

(iii) The equation $cos(2·x)-sin(x)=0$ can be solved as a quadratic equation in $sin(x)$ by applying the rewrite rule $cos(2·x)=1-2·sin^2(x)$. Add clauses to Program 22.1 to solve this equation. You will need to add rules for identifying terms of type *trigonometric*, heuristics for finding trigonometric reduced terms, and appropriate homogenization axioms.

(iv) Rewrite the predicate *free_of(Term,X)* so that it fails as soon as it finds an occurrence of X in *Term*.

(v)   Modify Program 22.1 so that it solves simple simultaneous equations.

22.6 Background

Symbolic manipulation was an early application area for Prolog. Early examples are programs for symbolic integration (Bergman and Kanoui, 1973) and for proving theorems in geometry (Welham, 1976).

The PRESS program, from which Program 22.1 is adapted, owes a debt to many people. Many of the researchers in the mathematical reasoning group working with Alan Bundy at the University of Edinburgh have tinkered with the code. Published descriptions of the program appear in Bundy and Welham (1981), Sterling et al. (1982) and Silver (1986). The last reference has a detailed discussion of homogenization.

PRESS includes various modules, not discussed in the chapter, that are interesting in their own right: for example, a package for interval arithmetic (Bundy, 1984), an infinite precision rational arithmetic package developed by Richard O'Keefe, and an expression simplifier based on difference-structures as described in Section 15.2, developed by Lawrence Byrd. The successful integration of all these modules is strong evidence for the practicality of Prolog for large programming projects.

The development of PRESS showed up classic points of software engineering. For example, at one stage the program was being tuned prior to publishing some statistics. Profiling was done on the program, which showed that the predicate most commonly called was *free_of*. Rewriting it as suggested in Exercise (iv) above resulted in a speedup of 35 percent in the performance of PRESS.

Program 22.1 is a considerably cleaned-up version of PRESS. Tidying the code enabled further research. Program 22.1 was easily translated to other logic programming languages, Concurrent Prolog and FCP (Sterling and Codish, 1986). Making the conditions when methods were used more explicit, enabled the writing of a program to learn new equation solving methods from examples (Silver, 1986).

Chapter 23

A Compiler

Our final application is a compiler. The program is presented top-down. The first section outlines the scope of the compiler and gives its definition. The next three sections describe the three components: the parser, the code generator and the assembler.

23.1 Overview of the compiler

The source language for the compiler is PL, a simplified version of Pascal designed solely for the purposes of this chapter. It contains an assignment statement, an if-then-else statement, a while statement and simple I/O statements. The language is best illustrated with an example. Figure 23.1 contains a program for computing factorials written in PL. A formal definition of the syntax of the language is implicit in the parser in Program 23.1.

The target language is a machine language typical for a one-accumulator computer. Its instructions are given in Figure 23.2. Each instruction has one (explicit) operand which can be one of four things: an integer constant, the address of a storage location, the address of a program instruction, or a value to be ignored. Most of the instructions also have a second implicit operand which is either the accumulator or its contents. In addition there is a pseudoinstruction *block* that reserves a number of storage locations as specified by its integer operand.

The scope of the compiler is clear from its behavior on our example. Figure 23.3 is the translation of the PL program in Figure 23.1 into machine language. The compiler produces the columns labeled *instruction* and *operand*.

The task of compiling can be broken down into the five stages given in Figure 23.4. The first stage transforms a source text into a list of tokens. The list of

```
program factorial;
    begin
        read value;
        count := 1;
        result := 1;
        while count < value do
            begin
                count := count+1;
                result := result*count
            end ;
        write result
    end
```

Figure 23.1: A PL-program for computing factorials

ARITHMETIC		CONTROL	I/O, etc.
Literals	Memory		
		jumpeq	read
addc	add	jumpne	write
subc	sub	jumplt	halt
mulc	mul	jumpgt	
divc	div	jumple	
loadc	load	jumpge	
store		jump	

Figure 23.2: Target language instructions

tokens is parsed in the second stage, syntax analysis, to give a source structure. The third and fourth stages, respectively, transform the source structure into relocatable code, and assemble this into absolute object code. The final stage outputs the object program.

Our compiler implements the middle three stages. Both the first stage of lexical analysis and the final output stage are relatively uninteresting and are not considered here. The top level of the code handles syntax analysis, code generation and assembly.

The basic predicate *compile(Tokens, ObjectCode)* relates a list of tokens *Tokens* to the *ObjectCode* of the program the tokens represent. The compiler compiles correctly any legal PL program, but does not handle errors; that is outside the scope of this chapter. The list of tokens is assumed to be input from some

symbol	address	instruction	operand	symbol
	1	READ	21	VALUE
	2	LOADC	1	
	3	STORE	19	COUNT
	4	LOADC	20	
	5	STORE	20	RESULT
LABEL1	6	LOAD	19	COUNT
	7	SUB	21	VALUE
	8	JUMPGE	16	LABEL2
	9	LOAD	19	COUNT
	10	ADDC	1	
	11	STORE	19	COUNT
	12	LOAD	20	RESULT
	13	MUL	19	COUNT
	14	STORE	20	RESULT
	15	JUMP	6	LABEL1
LABEL2	6	LOAD	20	RESULT
	17	WRITE	0	
	18	HALT	0	
COUNT	19	BLOCK	3	
RESULT	20			
VALUE	21			

Figure 23.3 Assembly code version of a factorial program

Source Text → Lexical Analysis → Token List → Syntax Analysis → Source Structure

Code Generation → Object Structure (relocatable) → Assembly → Object Structure (absolute) → Output → Object Program

Figure 23.4: The stages of compilation

previous stage of lexical analysis. The parser performing the syntax analysis, implemented by the predicate *parse*, produces from the *Tokens* an internal parse tree *Structure*. The structure is used by the code generator *encode* to produce relocatable code *Code*. A dictionary associating variable locations to memory addresses and keeping track of labels is needed to generate the code. This is the

compile(Tokens, ObjectCode) ←
      ObjectCode is the result of compilation of
      a list of *Tokens* representing a PL program.

compile(Tokens,ObjectCode) ←
      parse(Tokens,Structure),
      encode(Structure,Dictionary,Code),
      assemble(Code,Dictionary,ObjectCode).

The parser

parse(Tokens,Structure) ←
      Structure represents the successfully parsed list of *Tokens*.

parse(Source,Structure) ←
      pl_program(Structure,Source\[ ]).

pl_program(S) → [program], identifier(X), [';'], statement(S).

statement((S;Ss)) →
      [begin], statement(S), rest_statements(Ss).
statement(assign(X,V)) →
      identifier(X), [':−'], expression(V).
statement(if(T,S1,S2)) →
      [if], test(T), [then], statement(S1), [else], statement(S2).
statement(while(T,S)) →
      [while], test(T), [do], statement(S).
statement(read(X)) →
      [read], identifier(X).
statement(write(X)) →
      [write], expression(X).

rest_statements((S;Ss)) → [';'], statement(S), rest_statements(Ss).
rest_statements(void) → [end].

expression(X) → pl_constant(X).
expression(expr(Op,X,Y)) → pl_constant(X), arithmetic_op(Op), expression(Y).

arithmetic_op('+') → ['+'].
arithmetic_op('−') → ['−'].
arithmetic_op('*') → ['*'].
arithmetic_op('/') → ['/'].

pl_constant(name(X)) → identifier(X).
pl_constant(number(X)) → pl_integer(X).

Program 23.1: A compiler from PL to machine language

identifier(X) → [X], {atom(X)}.
pl_integer(X) → [X], {integer(X)}.

test(compare(Op,X,Y)) → expression(X), comparison_op(Op), expression(Y).

comparison_op('=') → ['='].
comparison_op('≠') → ['≠'].
comparison_op('>') → ['>'].
comparison_op('<') → ['<'].
comparison_op('≥') → ['≥'].
comparison_op('≤') → ['≤'].

The code generator

encode(Structure,Dictionary,RelocatableCode) ←
    RelocatableCode is generated from the parsed *Structure*
    building a *Dictionary* associating variables with addresses.

encode((X;Xs),D,(Y;Ys)) ←
    encode(X,D,Y), encode(Xs,D,Ys).
encode(void,D,no_op).
encode(assign(Name,E),D,(Code; instr(store,Address))) ←
    lookup(Name,D,Address), encode_expression(E,D,Code).
encode(if(Test,Then,Else),D,
    (TestCode; ThenCode; instr(jump,L2); label(L1); ElseCode; label(L2))) ←
        encode_test(Test,L1,D,TestCode),
        encode(Then,D,ThenCode),
        encode(Else,D,ElseCode).
encode(while(Test,Do),D,
    (label(L1); TestCode; DoCode; instr(jump,L1); label(L2))) ←
        encode_test(Test,L2,D,TestCode), encode(Do,D,DoCode).
encode(read(X),D,instr(read,Address)) ←
    lookup(X,D,Address).
encode(write(E),D,(Code; instr(write,0))) ←
    encode_expression(E,D,Code).

encode_expression(Expression,Dictionary,Code) ←
    Code corresponds to an arithmetic *Expression*.

encode_expression(number(C),D,instr(loadc,C)).
encode_expression(name(X),D,instr(load,Address)) ←
    lookup(X,D,Address).
encode_expression(expr(Op,E1,E2),D,(Load;Instruction)) ←
    single_instruction(Op,E2,D,Instruction),
    encode_expression(E1,D,Load).

Program 23.1 (Continued)

encode_expression(expr(Op,E1,E2),D,Code) ←
    not single_instruction(Op,E2,D,Instruction),
    single_operation(Op,E1,D,E2Code,Code),
    encode_expression(E2,D,E2Code).

single_instruction(Op,number(C),D,instr(OpCode,C)) ←
    literal_operation(Op,OpCode).
single_instruction(Op,name(X),D,instr(OpCode,A)) ←
    memory_operation(Op,OpCode), lookup(X,D,A).

single_operation(Op,E,D,Code,(Code;Instruction)) ←
    commutative(Op), single_instruction(Op,E,D,Instruction).
single_operation(Op,E,D,Code,
    (Code;instr(store,Address);Load;instr(OpCode,Address))) ←
        not commutative(Op),
        lookup('temp',D,Address),
        encode_expression(E,D,Load),
        op_code(Op,E,OpCode)

op_code(Op,number(C),OpCode) ← literal_operation(Op,OpCode).
op_code(Op,name(X),OpCode) ← memory_operation(Op,OpCode).

literal_operation('+',addc).   memory_operation('+',add).
literal_operation('−',subc).   memory_operation('−',sub).
literal_operation('*',mulc).   memory_operation('*',mul).
literal_operation('/',divc).   memory_operation('/',div).

commutative('+').   commutative('*').

encode_test(compare(Op,E1,E2),Label,D,(Code; instr(OpCode,Label))) ←
    comparison_opcode(Op,OpCode),
    encode_expression(expr('−',E1,E2),D,Code).

comparison_opcode('=',jumpne).   comparison_opcode('≠',jumpeq).
comparison_opcode('>',jumple).   comparison_opcode('≥',jumplt).
comparison_opcode('<',jumpge).   comparison_opcode('≤',jumpgt).

lookup(Name,Dictionary,Address) ← See Program 15.7

The assembler

assemble(Code,Dictionary, TidyCode) ←
    TidyCode is the result of assembling *Code* removing
    no_ops and *labels*, and filling in the *Dictionary*.

Program 23.1 (Continued)

```
assemble(Code,Dictionary,TidyCode) ←
    tidy_and_count(Code,1,N,TidyCode\(instr(halt,0);block(L))),
    N1 := N+1,
    allocate(Dictionary,N1,N2),
    L := N2–N1, !.

tidy_and_count((Code1;Code2),M,N,TCode1\TCode2) ←
    tidy_and_count(Code1,M,M1,TCode1\Rest),
    tidy_and_count(Code2,M1,N,Rest\TCode2).
tidy_and_count(instr(X,Y),N,N1,(instr(X,Y);Code)\Code) ←
    N1 := N+1.
tidy_and_count(label(N),N,N,Code\Code).
tidy_and_count(no_op,N,N,Code\Code).

allocate(void,N,N).
allocate(dic(Name,N1,Before,After),N0,N) ←
    allocate(Before,N0,N1),
    N2 := N1+1,
    allocate(After,N2,N).
```

Program 23.1 (Continued)

second argument of *encode*. Finally, the relocatable code is assembled into object code by *assemble* with the aid of the constructed *Dictionary*.

The testing data and instructions for the program are given as Program 23.2. The program *factorial* is the PL program of Figure 23.1 translated into a list of tokens. The two small programs consist of a single statement each, and test features of the language not covered by the factorial example. The program *test1* tests compilation of a nontrivial arithmetic expression, while *test2* checks the if-then-else statement.

23.2 The parser

The parser proper is written as a definite clause grammar, as described in Chapter 16. The predicate *parse* as given in Program 23.1 is just an interface to the DCG, whose top-level predicate is *pl_program*. The DCG has a single argument, the structure corresponding to the statements, as will be described. A variant of Program 16.2 is assumed to translate the DCG into Prolog clauses. The convention of that program is that the last argument of the predicates defined by the DCG is a difference-list:

test_compiler(X,Y) ←
    program(X,P), compile(P,Y).

program(test1,[program,test1,';',   begin,write,x,'+',y,'−',z,'/',2,end]).
program(test2,[program,test2,';',
    begin,if,a,'>',b,then,max,':=',a,else,max,':=',b,end]).

program(factorial,
    [program,factorial,';'
    ,begin
        ,read,value,';'
        ,count,':=',1,';'
        ,result,':=',1,';'
        ,while,count,'<',value,do
            ,begin
                ,count,':=',count,'+',1,';'
                ,result,':=',result,'*',count
            ,end,','
        ,write,result
    ,end]).

Program 23.2: Testing and data

parse(Source,Structure) ←
    pl_program(Structure,Source\[ ]).

The first statement of any PL program must be a program statement. A program statement consists of the word *program* followed by the name of the program. We call words that must appear for rules of the grammar to apply *standard identifiers*, the word *program* being an example. The name of the program is an identifier in the language. What constitutes identifiers, and more generally constants, will be discussed in the context of arithmetic expressions. The program name is followed by a semicolon, another standard identifier, and then the program proper begins. The body of a PL program consists of statements, or more precisely a single statement that may itself consist of several statements. All this is summed up in the top level grammar rule:

pl_program(S) → [program], identifier(X), [';'], statement(S).

The structure returned as the output of the parsing is the statement constituting the body of the program. For the purpose of code generation the top level program statement has no significance, and is ignored in the structure built.

The first statement we describe is a *compound statement*. Its syntax is the standard identifier *begin* followed by the first statement, S say, in the *compound* statement, and then the remaining statements *Ss*. The structure returned for a compound statement is (S;Ss) where ; is used as a two-place infix functor. Since S, Ss or both may be compound statements or contain them, the structure is returned recursive. The semicolon is chosen as functor to echo its use in PL for denoting sequencing of statements:

statement((S;Ss)) → [begin], statement(S), rest_statements(Ss).

Statements in PL are delimited by semicolons. The rest of the statements is accordingly defined as a semicolon followed by a nonempty statement, and recursively the remaining statements:

rest_statements((S;Ss)) → [';'], statement(S), rest_statements(Ss).

The end of a sequence of statements is indicated by the standard identifier *end*. The atom *void* is used to mark the end of a statement in the internal structure. The base case of *rest_statements* is therefore

rest_statements(void) → [end].

The above definition of statements precludes the possibility of empty statements. Programs and compound statements in PL cannot be empty.

The next statement to discuss is the assignment statement. It has a simple syntactic definition — a left-hand side, followed by the standard identifier :=, followed by the right-hand side. The left-hand side is restricted to being a PL identifier while the right-hand side is any arithmetic expression, whose definition is to be given:

statement(assign(X,E)) → identifier(X), [':='], expression(E).

The structure returned by the successful recognition of an assignment statement has the form *assign(X,E)*. The (Prolog) variable E represents the structure of the arithmetic expression, while X is the name of the (PL) variable to be assigned the value of the expression. It is implicitly assumed that X will be a PL identifier.

For simplicity, we restrict ourselves to a subclass of arithmetic expressions. Two rules define the subclass. An expression is either a constant, or a constant followed by an arithmetic operator and recursively an arithmetic expression. Examples of expressions in the subclass are *x*, *3*, *2·t* and *x+y−z/2*, the expression in the test case *test1* in Program 23.2:

$$\text{expression(X)} \rightarrow \text{pl\_constant(X)}.$$
$$\text{expression(expr(Op,X,Y))} \leftarrow$$
$$\text{pl\_constant(X), arithmetic\_op(Op), expression(Y)}.$$

This subclass of expressions does not respect the standard precedence of arithmetic operators. The expression $x\cdot 2+y$ is parsed as $x\cdot(2+y)$. On the other hand, the expression $x+y-z/2$ is interpreted unambiguously as $x+(y-(z/2))$. We restrict ourselves to the subclass to simplify both the code and its explanation in this chapter.

For this example, we restrict ourselves to two types of constants in PL: identifiers and integers. The specification of *pl_constant* duly consists of two rules. Which of the two is found is reflected in the structure returned. For identifiers X, the structure *name(X)* is returned, while *number(X)* is returned for the integer X:

$$\text{pl\_constant(name(X))} \rightarrow \text{identifier(X)}.$$
$$\text{pl\_constant(number(X))} \rightarrow \text{pl\_integer(X)}.$$

For simplicity we assume that PL integers and PL identifiers are Prolog integers and atoms, respectively. This allows the use of Prolog system predicates to identify the PL identifiers and integers. Recall that the curly braces notation of DCGs is used to specify Prolog goals:

$$\text{identifier(X)} \rightarrow \text{[X], \{atom(X)\}}.$$
$$\text{pl\_integer(X)} \rightarrow \text{[X], \{integer(X)\}}.$$

In fact all grammar rules that use PL identifiers and constants could be modified to call the Prolog predicates directly if greater efficiency is needed.

A list of arithmetic operators is necessary to complete the definition of arithmetic expressions. The form of the statement for addition, represented by "+", is given below. The grammar rules for subtraction, multiplication and division are analogous, and appear in the full parser in Program 23.2:

$$\text{arithmetic\_op('+')} \rightarrow \text{['+']}.$$

The next statement to be discussed is the conditional statement, or if-then-else. The syntax for conditionals is the standard identifier *if* followed by a test (to be defined). After the test, the standard identifier *then* is necessary, followed by a statement constituting the then part, the standard identifier *else* and a statement constituting the else part, in that order. The structure built by the parser is *if(T,S1,S2)* where T is the test, *S1* is the *then* part and *S2* is the *else* part:

statement(if(T,S1,S2)) →
    [if], test(T), [then], statement(S1), [else], statement(S2).

Tests are defined to be an expression followed by a comparison operator and another expression. The structure returned has the form $compare(Op,X,Y)$, where Op is the comparison operator, and X and Y are the left-hand and right-hand expressions in the test, respectively:

test(compare(Op,X,Y)) →
    expression(X), comparison_op(Op), expression(Y).

The definition of comparison operators using the predicate *comparison_op* is analogous to the use of *arithmetic_op* to define arithmetic operators. Program 23.1 contains definitions for $=$, $\neq$, $>$, $<$, $\geq$, and $\leq$.

While statements consist of a test and the action to take if the test is true. The structure returned is $while(T,S)$ where T is the test and S is the action. The syntax is defined by the following rule:

statement(while(T,S)) → [while], test(T), [do], statement(S).

I/O is handled in PL with a simple read statement and a simple write statement. The input statement consists of the standard identifier *read* followed by a PL identifier, and returns the structure $read(X)$, where X is the identifier. Write statements are similar:

statement(read(X)) → [read], identifier(X).
statement(write(X)) → [write], expression(X).

Collecting together the various pieces of the DCG described above gives a parser for the language. Note that ignoring the arguments in the DCG gives a formal BNF grammar for PL.

Let us consider the behavior of the parser on the test data in Program 23.2. The parsed structures produced for the two single statement programs have the form $\langle structure \rangle;void$ where $\langle structure \rangle$ represents the parsed statement. The *write* statement is translated to

$$write(\,expr(\,+,name(x),expr(-,name(y),expr(/,name(z),number(2))))),$$

while the if_then_else statement is translated to

$$if(\,compare(>,name(a),name(b)),assign(max,name(a)),assign(max,name(b))).$$

The *factorial* program is parsed into a sequence of five statements followed by *void*. The output after parsing for all three test programs is given in Figure 23.5. This is the input for the second stage of compilation, code generation.

Program test1:

write(expr(+,name(x),expr(−,name(y),expr(/,name(z),number(2))))));void

Program test2:

if(compare(>,name(a),name(b)),assign(max,name(a)),assign(max,name(b))
    );void

Program test3:

read(value);assign(count,number(1));assign(result,number(1));
    while(compare(<,name(count),name(value)),
    (assign(count,expr(+,name(count),number(1)));
    assign(result,expr(*,name(result),name(count)));void));
    write(name(result));void

Figure 23.5: Output from parsing

23.3 The code generator

The basic relation of the code generator is *encode(Structure,Dictionary,Code)*, which generates *Code* from the *Structure* produced by the parser. This section echoes the previous one. The generated code is described for each of the structures produced by the parser representing the various PL statements.

Dictionary relates PL variables to memory locations, and labels to instruction addresses. The dictionary is used by the assembler to resolve locations of labels and identifiers. Throughout this section *D* refers to this dictionary. An incomplete ordered binary tree is used to implement it as described in Section 3 of Chapter 15. The predicate *lookup(Name,D,Value)* (Program 15.7) is used for accessing the incomplete binary tree.

The structure corresponding to a compound statement is a sequence of its constituent structures. This is translated into a sequence of blocks of code, recursively defined by *encode*. The functor ";" is used to denote sequencing. The empty statement denoted by *void* is translated into a null operation, denoted *no_op*. When the relocatable code is traversed during assembly this "pseudoinstruction" is removed.

The structure produced by the parser for the general PL assignment statement has the form *assign(Name,Expression)* where *Expression* is the expression to be evaluated and assigned to the PL variable *Name*. The corresponding compiled form calculates the expression followed by a *store* instruction whose argument is the address corresponding to *Name*. The representation of individual instructions in the compiled code is the structure *instr(X, Y)* where *X* is the instruction and *Y* is the operand. The appropriate translation of the *assign* structure is therefore (*Code; instr(store,Address)*), where *Code* is the compiled form of the expression, which, after execution, leaves the value of the expression in the accumulator. It is generated by the predicate *encode_expression(Expression,D,ExpressionCode)*. Encoding the assignment statement is performed by the clause

> encode(assign(Name,Expression),D,(Code;instr(store,Address))) ←
>   lookup(Name,D,Address), encode_expression(Expression,D,Code).

This clause is a good example of Prolog code which is easily understood declaratively but hides complicated procedural bookkeeping. Logically, relationships have been specified between *Name* and *Address*, and between *Expression* and *Code*. From the programmer's point of view it is irrelevant when the final structure is constructed, and in fact the order of the two goals in the body of this clause can be swapped without changing the behavior of the overall program. Furthermore, the *lookup* goal, in relating *Name* with *Address*, could be making a new entry, or retrieving a previous one, where the final instantiation of the address happens in the assembly stage. None of this bookkeeping needs explicit mention by the programmer. It goes on correctly in the background.

There are several cases to be considered for compiling the expression. Constants are loaded directly; the appropriate machine instruction is *loadc C* where *C* is the constant. Similarly identifiers are compiled into the instruction *load A* where *A* is the address of the identifier. The two corresponding clauses of *encode_expression* are

> encode_expression(number(C),D,instr(loadc,C)).
> encode_expression(name(X),D,instr(load,Address)) ←
>   lookup(X,D,Address).

The general expression is the structure *expr(Op,E1,E2)* where *Op* is the operator, *E1* is a PL constant and *E2* is an expression. The form of the compiled code depends on *E2*. If it is a PL constant, then the final code consists of two statements: an appropriate *load* instruction determined recursively by *encode_expression* and the single instruction corresponding to *Op*. Again it does not matter in which order the two instructions are determined. The clause of *encode_expression* is

> encode_expression(expr(Op,E1,E2),D,(Load;Instruction)) ←
>   single_instruction(Op,E2,D,Instruction),
>   encode_expression(E1,D,Load).

The nature of the single instruction depends on the operator and whether the PL constant is a number or an identifier. Numbers refer to literal operations while identifiers refer to memory operations:

single_instruction(Op,number(C),D,instr(Opcode,C)) ←
    literal_operation(Op,Opcode).
single_instruction(Op,name(X),D,instr(Opcode,A)) ←
    memory_operation(Op,Opcode), lookup(X,D,A).

A separate table of facts is needed for each sort of operation. The respective form of the facts is illustrated for "+".

literal_operation(+,addc).   memory_operation(+,add).

A separate calculation is necessary when the second expression is not a constant and cannot be encoded in a single instruction. The form of the compiled code will be determined from the compiled code for calculating *E2*, and the single operation determined by *Op* and *E1*:

encode_expression(expr(Op,E1,E2),D,Code) ←
    not single_instruction(Op,E2,D,Instruction),
    single_operation(Op,E1,D,E2Code,Code),
    encode_expression(E2,D,E2Code).

In general, the result of calculating *E2* must be stored in some temporary location, called "*$temp*" in the code below. The sequence of instructions is then the code for *E2*, a *store* instruction, a *load* instruction for *E1* and the appropriate memory operation addressing the stored contents. The predicates shown previously are used to construct the final form of the code:

single_operation(Op,E,D,Code,
    (Code;
    instr(store,Address);
    Load;
    instr(OpCode,Address))
) ←
        not commutative(Op),
        lookup('$temp',D,Address),
        encode_expression(E,D,Load),
        op_code(Op,E,OpCode).

An optimization is possible if the operation is commutative, e.g., addition or multiplication, which circumvents the need for a temporary variable. In this case the memory or literal operation can be performed on *E1*, assuming that the result of computing *E2* is in the accumulator:

single_operation(Op,E,D,Code,(Code;Instruction)) ←
    commutative(Op), single_instruction(Op,E,D,Instruction).

The next statement is the conditional if-then-else parsed into the structure *if(Test, Then, Else)*. To compile the structure, we have to introduce labels where instructions can jump to. For the conditional we need two labels marking the beginning and end of the else part respectively. The labels have the form *label*(*N*), where *N* is the address of the instruction. The value of *N* is filled in during the assembling stage, when the label statement itself is removed. The schematic of the code is given by the third argument of the following *encode* clause:

encode(if(Test,Then,Else),D,
    (TestCode;
    ThenCode;
    instr(jump,L2);
    label(L1);
    ElseCode;
    label(L2))
)←
            encode_test(Test,L1,D,TestCode),
            encode(Then,D,ThenCode),
            encode(Else,D,ElseCode).

In order to compare two arithmetic expressions, we subtract the second from the first and make the jump operation appropriate to the particular comparison operator. For example, if the test is whether two expressions are equal, we circumvent the code if the result of subtracting the two is not equal to zero. Thus *comparison_opcode('=',jumpne)* is a fact. Note that the label which is the second argument of *encode_test* is the address of the code following the test.

encode_test(test(Op,E1,E2),Label,D,(Code; instr(OpCode,Label))) ←
    comparison_opcode(Op,OpCode),
    encode_expression(expr('−',E1,E2),D,Code).

The next statement to consider is the while statement. The statement is parsed into the structure *while(Test, Statements)*. A label is necessary before the test, then the test code is given as for the if-then-else statement, then the body of code corresponding to *Statements* and a jump to re-perform the test. A label is necessary after the *jump* instruction for when the test fails.

Program test1:

((((instr(load,Z);instr(div,2));instr(store,Temp);instr(load,Y);
instr(sub,Temp));instr(add,X));instr(write,0));no_op

Program test2:

(((instr(load,A);instr(sub,B));instr(jumple,L1));(instr(load,A);
instr(store,Max));instr(jump,L2);label(L1); (instr(load,B);instr(store,Max));
label(L2));no_op

Program factorial:

instr(read,Value);(instr(loadc,1);instr(store,Count));(instr(loadc,1);
instr(store,Result));(label(L1);((instr(load,Count);instr(sub,Value));
instr(jumpge,L2));(((instr(load,Count);instr(addc,1));instr(store,Count));
((instr(load,Result);instr(mul,Count));instr(store,Result));no_op);
instr(jump,L1);label(L2));(instr(load,Result);instr(write,0));no_op

Figure 23.6: The generated code

```
encode(while(Test,Do),D,
      (label(L1);
      TestCode;
      DoCode;
      instr(jump,L1);
      label(L2))
) ←
            encode_test(Test,L2,D,TestCode),
            encode(Do,D,DoCode).
```

The I/O statements are straightforward. The parsed structure for input, *read*(X), is compiled into a single *read* instruction where the table is used to get the correct address:

```
encode(read(X),D,instr(read,Address)) ←
      lookup(X,D,Address).
```

The output statement is translated into encoding an expression, and then a *write* instruction:

```
encode(write(E),D,(Code; instr(write,0))) ←
      encode_expression(E,D,Code).
```

Figure 23.6 contains the relocatable code after code generation and before assembly for each of the three examples of Program 23.2. Mnemonic variable names have been used for easy reading.

23.4   The assembler

The final stage performed by the compiler is assembling the relocatable code into absolute object code. The predicate *assemble(Code,Dictionary,ObjectCode)* takes the *Code* and *Dictionary* generated in the previous stage, and produces the object code. There are two stages in the assembly. During the first stage, the instructions in the code are counted, at the same time computing the addresses of any labels created during code generation and removing unnecessary null operations. This tidied code is further augmented by a halt instruction, denoted by *instr(halt,0)*, and a block of L memory locations for the L PL variables and temporary locations in the code. The space for memory locations is denoted by *block(L)*. In the second stage addresses are created for the PL and temporary variables used in the program:

assemble(Code,Dictionary,TidyCode) ←
    tidy_and_count(Code,1,N,TidyCode\(instr(halt,0);block(L))),
    N1 := N+1,
    allocate(Dictionary,N1,N2),
    L := N2–N1.

The predicate *tidy_and_count(Code,M,N,TidyCode)* tidies the *Code* into *Tidy-Code* where the correct addresses of labels have been filled in, and the null operations have been removed. Procedurally, executing *tidy_and_count* constitutes a second pass over the code. M is the address of the beginning of the code, while N is one more than the address of the end of the original code. Thus the number of actual instructions in *Code* is $N+1-M$. *TidyCode* is represented as a difference-structure based on ";".

The recursive clause of *tidy_and_count* demonstrates both standard difference-structure technique, and updating of numeric values:

      tidy_and_count((Code1;Code2),M,N,TCode1\TCode2) ←
        tidy_and_count(Code1,M,M1,TCode1\Rest),
        tidy_and_count(Code2,M1,N,Rest\TCode2).

Three types of primitives occur in the code: instructions, labels and no_ops.

Program test1:

instr(load,11);instr(divc,2),instr(store,12);instr(load,10);
instr(sub,12);instr(add,9);instr(write,0);instr(halt,0);block(4)

Program test2:

instr(load,10);instr(sub,11);instr(jumple,7);instr(load,10);
instr(store,12);instr(jump,9);instr(load,11);instr(store,12);
instr(halt,0);block(3)

Program factorial:

instr(read,21);instr(loadc,1);instr(store,19);instr(loadc,1);
instr(store,20);instr(load,19);instr(sub,21);
instr(jumpge,16);instr(load,19);instr(addc,1);instr(store,19);
instr(load,20);instr(mul,19);instr(store,20);
instr(jump,6);instr(load,20);instr(write,0);instr(halt,0);block(3)

Figure 23.7: The compiled object code

Instructions are handled routinely. The address counter is incremented by one, and the instruction is inserted in a difference-structure:

tidy_and_count(instr(X,Y),N,N1,(instr(X,Y);Code)\Code) ←
    N1 := N+1.

Both labels and no_ops are removed without updating the current address or adding an instruction to the tidied code:

tidy_and_count(label(N),N,N,Code\Code).
tidy_and_count(no_op,N,N,Code\Code).

Declaratively the clauses are identical. Procedurally, the unification of the label number with the current address causes a major effect in the program. Every reference to the label address is filled in. This program is another illustration of the power of the logical variable.

The predicate *allocate(Dictionary,M,N)* has primarily a procedural interpretation. During the code generation as the dictionary is constructed, storage locations are associated with each of the PL variables in the program, plus any temporary variables needed for computing expressions. The effect of *allocate* is to assign actual memory locations for the variables, and fill in the references to them in the program.

The variables are found by traversing the *Dictionary*. M is the address of the memory location for the first variable, while N is one more than the address of the last. The order of variables is alphabetic corresponding to their order in the dictionary. The code also completes the dictionary as a data structure.

```
allocate(void,N,N).
allocate(dic(Name,N1,Before,After),N0,N) ←
    allocate(Before,N0,N1),
    N2 := N1+1,
    allocate(After,N2,N).
```

The compiled test programs of Program 23.2 appear in Figure 23.7.

Exercises for Chapter 23

(i)   Extend the compiler so that it handles repeat loops. The syntax is repeat ⟨*statement*⟩ until ⟨*test*⟩. Extensions to both the parser and the compiler need to be made. Test the program on

```
program repeat;
    begin
        i := 1;
        repeat
            begin
                write(i);
                i := i+1
            end
        until i := 11
    end.
```

(ii)   Extend the definition of arithmetic expressions to allow arbitrary ones. In the encoder, you will have to cater for the possibility of needing several temporary variables.

23.5   Background

The compiler described is based on a delightful paper by Warren (1980).

Appendix

A. Working with Prolog

Prolog implementations vary in the details of how the user interacts with the Prolog system, and how it develops Prolog programs. Here we give a general overview of how one might interact with a standard Prolog system.

Prolog systems are usually file-oriented. That is, the source of the program under development resides in one or more files. The standard cycle of program development is:

> While the program is not complete do
> > Compose (part of) the program using a text editor,
> > > and place it in a file;
> > Enter Prolog, and *consult* the file;
> > Run the program, usually under the Prolog debugger.

Consult is the standard Edinburgh Prolog system predicate for loading a set of procedures residing in some file. In an operating system which can keep suspended processes, usually the Prolog system and the text editor processes are both kept simultaneously. If so, only the file that has been changed need to be consulted. Otherwise, the entire program need to be consulted afresh every time. Alternatively, in a Prolog system that can save its state on a file, used under an operating system which cannot keep processes, it may be advised to checkpoint portions of a program which have been debugged into a saved Prolog state, and start Prolog with that saved state.

Some Prolog systems, e.g. Quintus Prolog, allow an even better interaction between Prolog and the text editor.

Considering debugging, each Prolog system has its own conventions. However, most modern debuggers are based on Byrd's box model of debugging (Warren, 1981). In this model, one can inspect a goal when it is called, when it

succeeds, when it fails, and when it is retried. Such a debugger was shown in Chapter 19, and is incorporated in Wisdom Prolog.

B. System Predicates

This section describes all the evaluable system predicates available in Wisdom Prolog. These predicates are provided in advance by the system and they cannot be redefined by the user. Any attempt to add clauses or delete clauses to an evaluable predicate will fail with an error message, and leave the evaluable predicate unchanged. Evaluable predicates are available for the following tasks:

> Input/Output
>> Reading-in programs
>> Opening and closing files
>> Reading and writing Prolog terms
>> Getting and putting characters
> Arithmetic
> Affecting the flow of the execution
> Classifying and operating on Prolog terms
>> (meta-logical facilities)
> Term Comparison
> Debugging facilities
> Environment facilities

NAME	MEANING

Types:

atom(Atom)	Atom is an atom.
integer(I)	I is an integer.
atomic(A)	A is an atom or an integer.
constant(X)	Same as atomic.
functor(St,F,A)	F is the principal functor of St and A is its arity.
arg(N,S,Sn)	Sn is the Nth argument of S.
var(V)	V is a variable
nonvar(C)	C is not a variable.

Program manipulation:

assert(Clause)	Assert a clause at the end of the program.
asserta(Clause)	Assert a clause at the beginning of the program.

assertz(Clause)	Same as assert.
retract(Clause)	Retract a clause unified with Clause.
abolish(F,A)	Retract (erase) all the clauses, with functor F and arity A.
consult(File)	Read-in the program which is in the file File. When a directive is read it is executed. When a clause is read it is put after any clause already read for that procedure.
reconsult(File)	Same as consult but old clauses of procedures defined in File are retracted from the program.
clause(G,B)	B is a body of a clause whose head unifies with G.
listing	List the current program.
listing(Name)	List the predicates named Name in the program.

I/O:

read(T)	T is the next term, delimited by a "fullstop" (a '.' followed by <CR> or a space), on the current input file. Fails if the next element on the current output stream does not unify with T or if passed EOF.
sread(T,Vs)	Read the term T and Vs is a list of pairs; the variable name and the variable itself.
write(T)	Write T on the current output file.
writeq(T)	Write T, with quotes if needed.
display(T)	Display T on the terminal.
displayq(T)	Display T on the terminal with quotes if needed.
displayl(L)	Display a list of objects.
print(T)	Has a hook for pretty printing; write your own "portray(T)".
see(File)	File is the new current input file.
seeing(File)	File is unified with the name of the current input file.
seen	Closes the current input stream.
tell(File)	Let File be the current output stream.
telling(File)	File is unified with the name of the current output file.
told	Close the current output stream.
flush	Flush the current output file (the system uses buffer I/O).
get(C)	Get a printable character from the current Input file.

get0(C)	Get a character from the current input file.
put(C)	Put the character C on the current output file.
tab(N)	Prints N blanks on the current output file.
nl	Print a newline character on the current output file.
skip(C)	Skip characters till C, on the current input stream.
ttyget(C)	Get C from the terminal.
ttyput(C)	Echo an ascii character to the terminal.
ttynl	Echo a newline character to the terminal.
ttyskip(C)	Skip till C from the terminal.
ttytab(N)	Print N blanks on the terminal.
op(P,Type,Op)	Define operator Op with the priority P and type Type.
	Op can also be a list of names.
save(File)	Save the current state on file File.
log	List the data base on file 'log'.

Debugging:

trace	Prompt for a goal to trace.
trace(G)	Trace the goal G.

General:

true	Always succeeds.
fail	Always fails.
!	Cut
exit	End Prolog session.
abort	Abort the execution.
call(G)	Call G.
not(G)	If G succeeds not(G) fails.
name(A,L)	L is the list of the characters in A.
repeat	Succeed any number of times.
,	conjunction.
;	disjunction.
=..	univ.
X = Y	X unifies with Y.
\=	Negation of = .
T1 == T2	T1 and T2 are identical.
T1 \== T2	Negation of == .
system(Comm)	Executes Comm in the operating system.

systemp(F,A)	F is the functor and A is the arity of a system predicate.
save_term(T)	push to stack.
unsave_term(T)	pop out of the stack.
member(X,Xs)	X is a member of Xs.
append(Xs,Ys,Zs)	Zs are the Ys appended to Xs.

Special:

iterate(G)	Do G until it fails (efficiently).
fork_exec(file,Comm)	C-like command.
ancestor(G,N)	The goal G is the Nth ancestor of the current goal (used by the debugger).
cutg(G)	ancestor cut.
retry(G)	Retry goal G.

Arithmetics:

– Arithmetic system calls:

T1 < T2	The value of the arithmetic expression T1 is less than the arithmetic expression T2.
T1 =\= T2	Not equal.
T1 > T2	Greater than.
T1 ≥ T2	Greater than or equal.
T1 ≤ T2	Less than or equal.
T1 =:= T2	Not equal.
R := Exp	R is the result of the arithmetic expression Exp.
R is Exp	Same as := .

– Arithmetic operations:

X + Y	Addition.
X − Y	Substruction.
X * Y	Multiplication.
X / Y	Division.
X mod Y	X modulo Y.
−X	Unary minus.
+X	Unary plus.

Consulting and reconsulting:

reconsulting is called by

[file1, file2, ..., ...].
    or – reconsult(file1), reconsult(file2), ...

whereas consulting is performed by

[+file, +file2, ..., ...].
    or − consult(file1), consult(file2), ...

Note that this can be done only at the top level.

To assert procedures from the terminal you should use the user file:

[user] or [+user]

and then type its clauses.

Hooks:

The user can define his own shell by defining the shell/0 predicate.
The system shell ($shell) by default is defined as:

    $shell :− shell, abort.
    $shell :−

        ttynl, display('| ?−'), sread(Goalb, Vs),
        s_expand_goal(Goalb,Goal),
        user_call(Goal,Vs),abort.

expand_goal:

Is called by the shell converting the top level goal.
Using this predicate the user can define his own conversions
to the top level goal.

expand_clause:

Same as expand_goal but for the consulted clauses.

Shell:

s_expand_goal	System expand goal.
user_call	Execute the call of the user.
display_result(Vs)	Display the value of the variables.
get_reply	Get the user reply from the terminal.
cons_list	For consulting a number of files using lists.

C. Predefined Operators

For I/O of compound terms it is more convenient to use operators, unary or binary. The unary ones may be *prefix*, which means they precede the argument; *postfix* which means they follow the argument; or *infix* — those that come in between two arguments.

To prevent ambiguity, each operator gets a precedence and an association, to distinguish between two operators with the same precedence. The type of association and number of arguments are described by the following conventions:

For prefix:

fx means that the precedence of the argument must be lower than the precedence of the operator.
fy means that the precedence of the argument may be equal to the precedence of the operator.

For postfix:

xf and *yf* – analogously the same conventions of the prefix.

For infix:

xfx xfy yfx – mean that both subexpressions which are the arguments of the operator must be of lower precedence than the operator itself;
only the left-hand argument should be of lower precedence;
only the right-hand argument should be of lower precedence; respectively.

To define an operator type:

| ?– op(Precedence, Type, Op).

Where *Precedence* is from 1 to 1200, *Type* is one of the mentioned above, *Op* is the operator's name or a list of names.

Remember that the precedence of the arguments must be lower then 1000 which is the precedence of the ',' . Thus you should write

assert((A:–B))

and not

assert(A:–B)

Operator definition:

```
:-(op(1200,fx,[ :- , ?- ])).
:-op(1200,xfx,[ (:-) , <-, → ]).
:-op(1100,xfy,';').
:-op(1000,xfy,',').
:-op(900,fx,[not]).
:-op(700,xfx,[ = , \= , is, :=, =.. , ==, \==, =:=, =\=, <, > , ≤, ≥ ]).
:-op(500,yfx,[+,-]).
:-op(500,fx,[(+),(-)]).
:-op(400,yfx,[*,/,//]).
:-op(300,xfx,[mod]).
```

References

Apt, K.R. and van Emden, M.H., Contributions to the Theory of Logic Programming, *J. ACM* **29**, pp. 841–862, 1982.

Ben-David, A. and Sterling, L., A Prototype Expert System for Credit Evaluation, *Proc. International Workshop on Artificial Intelligence in Economics and Management*, Zurich, Switzerland, 1985.

Berge, C., *The Theory of Graphs and its Applications*, Methuen & Co., London, 1962.

Bergman, M. and Kanoui, H., Application of Mechanical Theorem Proving to Symbolic Calculus, *Proc. Third International Symposium on Advanced Computing Methods in Theoretical Physics*, CNRS, Marseille, 1973.

Bloch, C., Source-to-Source Transformations Of Logic Programs, Tech. Report CS 84 22, Department of Applied Mathematics, Weizmann Institute Of Science, Rehovot, Israel, 1984.

Bowen, K. and Kowalski, R., Amalgamating Language and Meta-Language, in (Clark and Tarnlund, 1982), pp. 153–172.

Boyer, R.S. and Moore, J.S., *A Computational Logic*, Academic Press, ACM Monograph Series, 1979.

Bowen, D.L., Byrd, L., Pereira, L.M., Pereira, F.C.N. and Warren, D.H.D., Prolog on the DECSystem-10 user's manual, University of Edinburgh, 1981.

Breuer, G. and Carter, H.W., *VLSI Routing in Hardware and Software Concepts in VLSI*, G. Rabbat (ed.), Van Nostrand Reinhold, 1983.

Bruynooghe, M., The Memory Management of Prolog Implementation, in (Tarnlund, 1980).

Bruynooghe, M. and Pereira, L.M., Deductive Revision by Intelligent Backtracking, in (Campbell, 1984).

Bundy, A., *A Computer Model Of Mathematical Reasoning*, Academic Press, 1983.

Bundy, A., A Generalized Interval Package and its Use for Semantic Checking, *ACM Transactions on Mathematical Software* **10**, pp. 392–407, 1984.

Bundy, A. and Welham, R., Using Meta-level Inference for Selective Application of Multiple Rewrite Rules in Algebraic Manipulation, *Artificial Intelligence* **16**, pp. 189–212, 1981.

Burstall, R.M. and Darlington, J., A Transformation System for Developing Recursive Programs, *J. ACM* **24**, pp. 46–67, 1977.

Byrd, L., Understanding the Control Flow of Prolog programs, in (Tarnlund, 1980).

Campbell, J.A. (ed.), *Implementations Of Prolog*, Ellis Horwood Publication, Distributed By John-Wiley & Sons, New York, 1984.

van Caneghem, M. (ed.), *Prolog-II user's Manual*, 1982.

van Caneghem, M. and Warren, D.H.D. (eds.), *Logic Programming and its Applications*, Ablex Publishing Co., 1986.

Chikayama, T., Unique Features of ESP, *Proc. International Conference on Fifth Generation Computer Systems*, pp. 292–298, Tokyo, Japan, 1984.

Clark, K.L., Negation as Failure, in (Gallaire and Minker, 1978).

Clark, K.L. and Gregory, S., A Relational Language for Parallel Programming, *Proc. ACM Conference on Functional Languages and Computer Architecture*, 1981.

Clark, K.L. and Gregory, S., PARLOG: Parallel Programming in Logic, Research Report 84/4, Department of Computing, Imperial College of Science and Technology, England, 1984.

Clark, K.L. and McCabe, F.G., The Control Facilities of IC-Prolog in *Expert Systems in the Microelectronic Age*, D. Michie (ed.), pp. 153–167, University of Edinburgh, Scotland, 1979.

Clark, K.L. and McCabe, F.G., PROLOG: A Language for Implementing Expert Systems, in *Machine Intelligence 10*, Hayes, Michie and Pao (eds.), pp. 455–470, Ellis Horwood, 1982.

Clark, K.L. and Tarnlund, S.-A., A First Order Theory of Data and Programs, *Information Processing 77*, pp. 939–944, North Holland, 1977.

Clark, K.L. and Tarnlund, S.-A. (eds.), *Logic Programming*, Academic Press, London, 1982.

Clark, K.L, McCabe, F.G. and Gregory, S., IC-Prolog Language Features, in (Clark and Tarnlund, 1982).

Clocksin, W.F. and Mellish, C.S., *Programming in Prolog*, 2nd Edition, Springer-Verlag, New York, 1984.

Coelho, H., Cotta, J.C. and Pereira, L.M., *How to Solve it in Prolog*, 2nd Edition, Laboratorio Nacional de Engenharia Civil, Lisbon, Portugal, 1980.

Cohen, J., Describing Prolog by Its Interpretation and Compilation, *J. ACM* **28**, pp. 1311-1324, 1985.

Colmerauer, A., Les systemes-*Q* ou un Formalisme pour Analyser et Synthesizer des Phrases sur Ordinatuer, Publication Interne No. 43, Dept. d'Informatique, Universite de Montreal, Canada, 1973.

Colmerauer, A., Kanoui, H., Pasero, R. and Roussel, P., Un Systeme de Communication Homme-machine en Francais, Research Report, Groupe Intelligence Artificielle, Universite Aix-Marseille II, France, 1973.

Colmerauer, A., Prolog-II, Manuel de reference et modele theorique, Groupe d'Intelligence Artificielle Universite d'Aix-Marseille II, 1982.

Colmerauer, A., Prolog And Infinite Trees, in (Clark and Tarnlund, 1982).

Deo, N., *Graph Theory with Applications to Engineering and Computer Science*, Pretice-Hall, 1974.

Dincbas,M. and Le Pape,J.P., Metacontrol of Logic Programs in METALOG, *International Conference on Fifth Generation Computer Systems*, November 1984.

Dudeney, H.E., *Amusements in Mathematics*, Thomas Nelson and Sons, London, 1917.

Dwork, C., Kanellakis, P.C. and Mitchell, J.C., On the Sequential Nature of Unification, *J. Logic Programming* **1**, pp. 35 50, 1984.

Eggert, P.R. and Chow, K.P., Logic Programming Graphics with Infinite Terms, Tech. Report University of California, Santa Barbara 83-02, 1983.

Elcock, E.W., The Pragmatics of Prolog: Some Comments, *Proc. Logic programming Workshop '83*, pp. 94–106, Algarve, Portugal, 1983.

van Emden, M., Warren's Doctrine on the Slash, *Logic Programming Newsletter*, December, 1982.

van Emden, M. and Kowalski, R., The Semantics Of Predicate Logic as a Programming Language, *J. ACM* **23**, pp. 733–742, 1976.

Even, S., *Graph Algorithms*, Computer Science Press, 1979.

Gallaire, H. and Lasserre, C., A Control Metalanguage for Logic Programming, in (Clark and Tarnlund, 1982).

Gallaire, H. and Minker, J., *Logic And Databases*, Plenum Publishing Co., New York, 1978.

Gallaire, H., Minker, J. and Nicolas, J.M., Logic and Databases: A Deductive Approach, *Computing Surveys* **16**, pp. 153–185, 1984.

Hammond,P., Micro-Prolog for Expert Systems, Chapter 11 in *Micro-Prolog: Programming in Logic*, Clark and McCabe (eds.), Prentice Hall 1984.

Hill, R., LUSH-Resolution and its Completeness, DCL Memo 78, Department of Artificial Intelligence, University of Edinburgh, 1974.

Hopcroft, J.E. and Ullman, J.D., *Introduction To Automata Theory, Languages, Computation*, Addison-Wesley, Reading, Massachussets, 1979.

Jaffar, J., Lassez, J.L. and Lloyd, J.W., Completeness of the Negation as Failure Rule, *Proc. of the International Joint Conference on Artificial Intelligence*, pp. 500–506, Karlsruhe, Germany, 1983.

Kahn, K.M., A Primitive for the Control of Logic Programs, *Proc. International IEEE Symposium on Logic programming*, Atlantic City, 1984.

Knuth, D., *The Art Of Computer Programming*, Volume 1, Fundamental Algorithms, Addison-Wesley, Reading, Massachussets, 1968.

Knuth, D., *The Art Of Computer Programming*, Volume 3, Sorting and Searching, Addison-Wesley, Reading, Massachussets, 1973.

Kowalski, R., Predicate Logic as a Programming Language, *Proc. IFIP Congress*, North-Holland, Stockholm 1974.

Kowalski, R., *Logic For Problem Solving*, North-Holland, 1979.

Kowalski, R., Algorithm = Logic + Control, *Communications of the ACM* **22**, pp. 424–436, 1979.

Li, D., *A Prolog Database System*, Research Studies Press, Ltd., England, 1984.

Lloyd, J.W., *Foundations Of Logic Programming*, Springer Verlag, 1984.

Martelli, A. and Montanari, U., An Efficient Unification Algorithm, *ACM Transactions on Programming Languages and Systems* **4(1)**, 1982.

Matsumoto, Y., Tanaka, H. and Kiyono, M., BUP: A Bottom-Up Parsing System for Natural Languages, in (van Caneghem and Warren, 1986).

Mellish, C.S., Some Global Optimizations for a Prolog Compiler, *J. Logic Programming* **2**, pp. 13–66, 1985.

Minsky, M., *Semantic Information Processing*, MIT Press, Cambridge, Massachusetts, 1968.

Naish, L., Negation and Control in Prolog, Tech. Report 85/12, University of Melbourne, Australia, 1985.

Naish, L., All Solutions Predicate in PROLOG, *Proc. of IEEE Symposium on Logic Programming*, Boston, 1985.

Naish, L., Automating Control For Logic Programs, *J. Logic Programming* **2**, pp. 167–184, 1985.

Nakashima, H., Tomura S. and Ueda, K., What is a Variable in Prolog? *Proc. of the International Conference on Fifth Generation Computer Systems*, pp. 327–332, ICOT, Tokyo, 1984.

Nilsson, N.J., *Problem Solving Methods In Artificial Intelligence*, Mcgraw-Hill Publications, New York, 1971

Nilsson, N.J., *Principles Of Artificial Intelligence*, Tioga Publishing Co., Palo Alto, California, 1981.

O'Keefe, R.A., Programming Meta Logical Operations in Prolog, DAI Working Paper No. 142, University of Edinburgh, 1983.

O'Keefe, R.A., On the Treatment of Cuts in Prolog Source-Level Tools, *Proc. 1985 Symposium on Logic Programming*, IEEE Computer Society Press, Boston, 1985.

Paterson, M.S. and Wegman, M.N., Linear Unification, *J. Computer and Systems Sciences* **16**, pp. 158–167, 1978.

Pereira, L.M., Logic Control with Logic, *Proc. First International Logic Programming Conference*, pp. 9–18, Marseille, 1982.

Pereira, F.C.N. and Warren, D.H.D., Definite Clause Grammars for Language Analysis – A Survey of the Formalism and a Comparison with Augmented Transition Networks, *Artificial Intelligence* **13**, pp. 231–278, 1980.

Peter, R., *Recursive Functions*, Academic Press, New York, 1967.

Plaisted, D.A., The Occur-Check Problem in Prolog, *New Generation Computing* **2**, pp. 309–322, 1984.

Powers, D., Playing Mastermind More Logically, *SIGART Newsletter* **89**, pp. 28–32, 1984.

Quintus Prolog Reference Manual, Quintus Computer Systems Ltd., 1985.

Reiter, R., On Closed World Databases, in *Logic and Databases*, Gallaire, H. and Minker, J. (eds.), Plenum Press, 1978, pp. 55–76. Also in *Readings in Artificial Intelligence*, webber and Nilsson (eds.), Published by Tioga, 1981.

Robinson, J.A., A Machine-Oriented Logic Based On the Resolution Principle, *J. ACM* **12**, pp. 23–41, January 1965.

Robinson, J.A. and Sibert, E.E., LOGLISP: Motivation, Design and Implementation, in (Clark and Tarnlund, 1982).

Schank, R.C. and Riesbeck, C., *Inside Computer Understanding: Five Programs Plus Miniatures*, Lawrence Erlbaum, Hillsdale, N.J., 1981.

Schank, R.C. and Abelson,R.P., *Scripts, Plans, Goals, and Understanding*, Lawrence Erlbaum, Hillsdale, N.J., 1977.

Sedgewick, R., *Algorithms*, Addison-Wesley, 1983.

Shapiro, E., *Algorithmic Program Debugging*, MIT Press, Cambridge, Massachussets, 1983.

Shapiro, E., A Subset of Concurrent Prolog and its Interpreter, Tech. Report TR-003, ICOT-Institute for New Generation Computer Technology, Tokyo, Japan, January 1983.

Shapiro, E., Logic Programs with Uncertainties: A Tool for Implementing Rule-Based Systems, *Proc. 8th International Joint Conference on Artificial Intelligence*, pp. 529–532, Karlsruhe, Germany, 1983.

Shapiro, E., Playing Mastermind Logically, *SIGART Newsletter* **85**, pp. 28–29, 1983.

Shapiro, E., Alternation and the Computational Complexity of Logic Programs, *J. Logic Programming* **1**, pp. 19–33, 1984.

Shapiro, E., Systems Programming in Concurrent Prolog, in (van Caneghem and Warren, 1986).

Shapiro, E. and Takeuchi, A., Object Oriented Programming in Concurrent Prolog, *New Generation Computing* **1**, 1983.

Shortliffe, E.H., *Computer Based Medical Consultation, MYCIN*, North-Holland, New York, 1976.

Silver, B., *Meta-level Inference*, Elsevier Science, Amsterdam, Netherlands, 1986.

Silverman, W., Hirsch, M., Houri, A. and Shapiro, E., The Logix System User Manual, Weizmann Institute of Science, Rehovot, Israel, 1986.

Slagle, J. and Dixon, J., Experiments with Some Programs that Search Game Trees, *J. ACM* **16**, pp. 189–207, 1969.

Steele, G.L., Jr. and Sussman, G.J., The Art of the Interpreter or, the Modularity, Complex, Technical memorandum AIM-453, MIT AI-Lab, May 1978.

Sterling, L., Expert System = Knowledge + Meta-Interpreter, Tech. Report CS84-17, Weizmann Institute Of Science, Rehovot, Israel, 1984.

Sterling, L. and Codish, M., PRESSing for Parallelism: A Prolog Program Made Concurrent, *J. Logic Programming*, 1986.

Sterling, L. and Bundy, A., Meta-Level Inference and Program Verification, *Proc. of the Sixth Conference on Automated Deduction*, pp. 144–150, Springer Verlag LNCS 138, 1982.

Sterling, L. and Lalee, M., An Explanation Shell for Expert Systems, Tech. Report TR-125-85, Center for Automation and Intelligent Systems Research, CWRU, Cleveland, USA, 1985.

Sterling, L., Bundy, A., Byrd, L., O'Keefe, R. and Silver, B., Solving symbolic equations with PRESS, in *Computer Algebra*, pp. 109–116, Springer-Verlag LNCS 144,

Takeuchi, A. and Furukawa, K., Partial Evaluation of Prolog Programs and its Application to Meta Programming, Tech. Report, ICOT, Tokyo, Japan, 1985.

Tarnlund, S.-A. (ed.), *Proc. of the Logic Programming Workshop*, Debrecen, Hungary, 1980.

Ueda, K., Guarded Horn Clauses, ICOT Tech. Report 103, ICOT, Tokyo, Japan, 1985.

Ullman, J.D., *Principles Of Database Systems*, 2nd edition, Computer Science Press, MD, 1982.

Warren, D.H.D., Generating Conditional Plans and Programs, *Proc. AISB Summer Conference*, pp. 344–354, Edinburgh, 1976.

Warren, D.H.D., Implementing Prolog – Compiling Logic Programs 1 and 2, DAI Research Reports 39 and 40, University of Edinburgh, 1977.

Warren, D.H.D., Logic Programming and Compiler Writing, *Software-Practice and Experience* **10**, Number II, 1980.

Warren, D.H.D., Higher-Order Extensions to Prolog: Are They Needed?, *Machine Intelligence* **10**, pp. 441–454, Hayes, Michie and Pao (eds.), Ellis Horwood, 1982.

Warren, D.H.D., Perpetual Processes – An Unexploited Prolog Technique, *Proc. Prolog programming environments workshop*, Sweden, 1982.

Warren, D.H.D., Optimizing Tail Recursion in Prolog, in (van Caneghem and Warren, 1986).

Warren, D.H.D., Pereira, F. and Pereira L.M., User's Guide to DECsystem-10 Prolog, Occasional Paper 15, Department of Artificial Intelligence, University of Edinburgh, 1979.

Weizenbaum, J., ELIZA – A Computer Program For The Study Of Natural Language Communication Between Man And Machine, *CACM* **9**, pp. 36–45, 1966.

Weizenbaum, J., *Computer Power and Human Reason*, W.H. Freeman & Co., 1976.

Welham, R., Geometry Problem Solving, Research Report 14, Department of Artificial Intelligence, University of Edinburgh, UK, 1976.

Winograd, T., *Language as a Cognitive Process*, Volume I, Syntax, Addison-Wesley, Reading, Massachusetts, 1983.

Winston, P.H., *Artificial Intelligence*, Addison-Wesley, Reading, Massachusetts, 1977.

Index

Order Form for Programming Examples to accompany
The Art of Prolog:
Advanced Programming Techniques
by Leon Sterling and Ehud Shapiro

Tear out or photocopy this page and send to

The MIT Press
College Department
28 Carleton Street
Cambridge, MA 02142
617/253-2884

Note: The programming examples are written in Wisdom Prolog. You may
have to adapt them to other varieties of Prolog.

Please send the following:

Quantity	Version	Code	Unit price	Total
	IBM®	STEPDI	$15.95	
	Macintosh™	STEPDM	$15.95	
	Amiga™	STEPDA	$15.95	
	Postage outside North America, add $2.00			
	Grand total			

All prices in U.S. dollars. Checks must be drawn on U.S. Banks.
__ Check Enclosed payable to The MIT Press
Bill my   __ MasterCard   __ Visa
Credit Card Number _____ exp. date _____
Signature _____
Ship to: Name _____
          Address _____
          City/State/Zip _____
Special Instruction _____
_____

Order form for
WISDOM Prolog
developed by Shmuel Safra
at the Weizmann Institute of Science

A new Prolog interpreter with these special features:
• user definable shell and environment (UNIX™ like)
• 100 system predicates
• 320K RAM used by user-data (PC only); up to 80Mb on UNIX™/VMS
  machines
• powerful debugger
• MS-DOS/UNIX™/VMS™ compatibility
• screen management
• exit to your O.S. w/o leaving the interpreter—so you can use your favorite
  text-editor, invoke a system command (e.g., list the directory), or even
  mount a new shell-interpreter atop the Prolog interpreter

For more information contact Motti Goldberg at: max@wisdom (CSNET or
BITNET)

The MIT Press
College Department
28 Carleton Street
Cambridge, MA 02142
617/253-2884

Please send the following:

Quantity	Version	Code	Unit price	Total
_____	IBM®	SAFWI	$95.00	_____
_____	Macintosh™	SAFWM	$95.00	_____
_____	Amiga™	SAFWA	$95.00	_____
	Postage outside North America, add $2.00			_____
	Grand total			_____

All prices in U.S. dollars. Checks must be drawn on U.S. Banks.
__ Check Enclosed payable to The MIT Press
Bill my ___ MasterCard ___ Visa
Credit Card Number _____ exp. date _____
Signature _____
Ship to: Name _____
         Address _____
         City/State/Zip _____
Special Instruction _____

_____

T